MAKE
THE
KAISER
DANCE

MAKE THE KAISER DANCE

Living Memories of the Doughboy

HENRY BERRY

PRIAM
BOOKS

ARBOR HOUSE   **NEW YORK**

This book is dedicated to Edwin F. Berry (1894–1976), late of the AEF. This grand fellow was captain of the Hartford Public High School baseball nine in 1913. In 1975 he became the first person in the history of the Hartford Golf Club to shoot his age at that challenging links. In between those two milestones in his life he made a tremendous amount of friends.

Library of Congress Cataloging in Publication Data

Berry, Henry.
    Make the Kaiser dance.

    Originally published: 1st ed. Garden City, N.Y. : Doubleday, 1978.
    Includes index.
    1. World War, 1914–1918—Personal narratives, American.
2. World War, 1914–1918—Campaigns—France. 3. France—History—German occupation, 1914–1918. I. Title.
[D570.9.B42   1984]   940.4'81'73   84-14674
ISBN 0-87795-656-1 (pbk.)

Manufactured in the United States of America

10 9 8 7 6 5 4 3 2 1

This book is printed on acid-free paper. The paper in this book meets the guidelines for permanence and durability of the Committee on Production Guidelines for Book Longevity of the Council on Library Resources.

CONTENTS

MAKE
THE
KAISER
DANCE

PREFACE

Jimmy thought that he would take a chance,
See if he could make the Kaiser dance.
Strutting to a tune, all about the silvery moon,
This is what they hear in far-off France.

(From the introduction to the song K-k-k-aty)

They used to have a ritual in New York City that occurred each November 11. At 11:00 A.M. on that date policemen all over the city would blow their whistles, and all traffic would stop for one minute. It was in honor of New York's sons who had fought in France during the Great War.

New York had so many to honor: their 69th Irish of the Rainbow; the kid-glove men of the 7th, buttressed by the so-called roughnecks from Brooklyn and Flushing; the 308th National Army regiment, where it was said you could find practically any ethnic background available; and the 15th New York Colored, which, as the 369th Infantry, showed Europe that America's fighting black man did not have to take a back seat to anyone.

They had similar ceremonies all over America, but they do not have them any longer. What is left of those two million Americans who went "over there" are fast approaching their own personal Armageddon. But there was a time when they were young. It was then that they went to France. And they did indeed "make the Kaiser dance"!

"I Didn't Think Your Country Was in World War I"

"That Rick, he seems to be just another blundering American to me."

"I wouldn't underestimate the blundering of the Americans, Major. I was with them when they blundered all the way to the Rhine in 1918."

—CONVERSATION BETWEEN AN ARROGANT GERMAN MAJOR AND THE FRENCH POLICE CHIEF[1] IN THE FILM *Casablanca*.

Americans? The Rhine? 1918? I saw a rerun of the great film classic *Casablanca* in the spring of 1975. The above dialogue made me give some thought to the American Expeditionary Forces of 1918, those Doughboys who were so prevalent in the 1930s, when I was growing up. I hadn't done that in a long time, and, I suspect, neither had many other people. Three additional American wars and scores of technological advances, such as putting human beings on the moon, have pushed those veterans of 1918 into the musty archives of history before their time. Surely a war where Americans went overseas in puttees and those crazy campaign hats, where they went over the top, had their artillery drawn into battle by horses, and fought against a man called the Kaiser—surely such a war belongs to an antiquated age.

[1] Played so brilliantly by Claude Rains.

Shortly after viewing that film, I had an occasion to take a trip to London. Here I visited with a fellow named Keith Mantle. He is in his early thirties, well educated, and what you would call in England "a top-drawer chap." He asked me what book I was currently working on.

"None," I answered, "but I'm thinking of doing one on the American participation in World War I."

"But Henry," he replied, "I didn't think your country was in World War I."

That did it, or to use a World War I expression, that "cut it." There was no question about it: I would have to show Mr. Mantle that the United States was indeed in World War I, and the best way to do this would be to devote my next book to the forgotten soldier, the 1918 Doughboy.

After committing myself to such a book, I began a crash research program on the AEF; it proved very enlightening. While I have always been extremely interested in American history, I soon found that my knowledge of America's first European venture was not one of my strong points. There were just too many areas where my knowledge was either incomplete or erroneous.

One case in point was America's largest battle of the war. I had always called it the Argonne or the Argonne Forest. In reality, most of the vicious combat that occurred in this fight was not in that wooded area. While the forest itself did experience some very fierce combat, there were over one million Americans involved here, and most of them fought in other parts of the region officially called the Meuse-Argonne.

Then there was the equipment problem. I had always believed that America, the industrial giant of the world, had been the arsenal of the Allied cause, yet she sent her sons naked to the foe. Here I refer not to clothing but to weapons. Tanks, machine guns, automatic rifles, and artillery were initially almost all supplied by Britain and France. When the war started, the U. S. Army had in the Springfield rifle probably the best such weapon in the world. But we never had nearly enough to go around. The majority of the rifles carried by the Doughboys were either the British Enfield or an American version of the same. The airplane situation was even sparser. No American-made pursuit plane flew in France during the war. The DH-4, with its Liberty motor, did begin to arrive in

Europe in August of 1918, but this was for observing. The Ricken-backers of World War I flew first French Nieuports and then Spads. What America did supply for the cause of the Allies was men—over two million of them.

My research quickly began proving fascinating, but it still was not turning up what I really was searching for, namely, a new literary approach to the war. Then I thought of a baseball book I had recently been involved with for which I had interviewed many old-time ballplayers or managers: Ernie Shore, George "High Pockets" Kelly, Burleigh Grimes, Joe McCarthy—they were all of World War I vintage. The remarkable thing about these men had been the keenness of their memories concerning things that had happened when they were young.

This thought gave me my approach: I would seek out Americans who had actually been in France during the Great War and ask them if they would be kind enough to share with me their memories of this service. I had no idea what my reception would be, nor did I know how many veterans I could turn up. In both cases, I was to be elated. I set a goal of one hundred men, and while it took me two years, I was able, either by telephone or in person, to accomplish this.

After I'd decided to start my interviewing, I surmised it would be prudent to have my first meeting with an old Doughboy with whom I had a personal connection. My uncle had been in France with the 304th Infantry of the 76th Division, but I felt that was too close a relationship to be truly productive at the onset. So I turned to my father for his help in recommending, from among his acquaintances, one of those AEFers who was still hale and hearty. He soon thought of Phil Hammerslough, an old high school chum of both his and my uncle's. Phil had gone over early with the 101st Machine Gun Battalion of the 26th (Yankee) Division and had served right through to the Armistice. I decided to put the entire meeting on tape. This would give me the best chance of retaining everything that would be said.

A luncheon meeting was arranged, which included Phil, my father, my uncle, and me. It lasted three hours, and I gladly would have continued it for three hours more. Phil's memory turned out to be excellent, not only on such major happenings as Château-Thierry and Saint Mihiel, but also on the day-to-day details of his life on the front lines that made up the human side of the Dough-boy. This was what I was after.

A pattern began to develop then that was to be repeated in almost all my interviews. First, the halfhearted laughter that normally greeted me when I would say what I was doing.

"If you want to interview one hundred of us from the AEF," Phil said, "you'd better hurry." Almost every man I visited thereafter made a similar allusion to the fact that they were on borrowed time. Not a one of them, however, was ready for the inevitable.

Phil, in this first memorable interview, followed this by stating that the war had happened sixty years ago, and while he would do the best he could to remember, it would be difficult. Again, just about every man I interviewed told me this, but then, almost immediately, they'd start a detailed description of having a boil lanced while in the trenches, or they would recount in minute detail a conversation they'd had while under shellfire. The old adage about the experiences of one's youth becoming crystal clear when one is elderly is indeed an accurate one.

An added plus to this first interview was listening to what it was like to grow up in Hartford, Connecticut, during the first decade of the twentieth century. Such things as going down to Banegan's tobacco shop and asking the adults to give you the baseball card that was frequently enclosed in a pack of Sweet Caporals or Fatimas, watching a Buffalo Bill or a Pawnee Bill's Wild West show come to town, and hanging around the fire house hoping for an alarm, were all part of growing up in the early 1900s.

"That's one thing you kids missed," said my uncle, "watching those snorting horses come tearing out of the station when there was a fire."

Then there were the vaudeville shows. In Hartford this frequently meant Parsons' Theater.

"Oh Parsons," remembered Phil, "you know, I saw Elsie Janis in France. She put on a great show, but it made me tremendously homesick. I'd seen Elsie at Parsons shortly before I went over. God, she made me miss Hartford!"

"Well, at least you saw Elsie," added Uncle Ed. "When I was at Neufchâteau, they told us we were to get a chance to see her. But instead we ended up with that schoolteacher, old-maid daughter of Woodrow Wilson. Jeez, she had a dress on down to her ankles. She ends up singing some song about trees. Oh how the boys wanted to give her the raspberries! The only thing she'd make you homesick for was a sanitorium!"

Still another plus of this meeting for me was their conversation concerning other World War I veterans, most of whom had "gone West," the AEF phrase for dying.

"You remember Harold Benedict, don't you?" said my father. "He left Colgate to join the Marines right after war was declared. He was shot in the leg at Belleau Wood."

"That's right," Uncle Ed chipped in, "you know they were supposed to ask your permission before they'd take a limb off. But Harold always insisted they just told him they were going to *operate* on his leg, and when he woke up, the whole damn leg was gone."[2]

"And what a shame," added my father, "he was a great football player. I was covering sports for the *Owl* [Hartford Public High School's paper] when he scored two touchdowns against New Britain in 1915. The team scored three, but I didn't like the guy who made the other one, so I put in the paper that Harold scored all three. Christ, I thought the other guy was going to kill me!"

This old memory caused some laughter. Then Phil started in on the license plates.

"You know, most of the men from this area who went in early were in either the 101st Machine Gun Battalion or the 102nd Infantry. They were both part of the 26th Division, which was called the Yankee Division, because all its units were from New England.

"Well, it must have been about 1935 or so when Mike Connor was motor vehicle commissioner of the state. Mike had been a captain in the 102nd. He fixed it up so that anyone who had been over with the 26th could have YD on his license plate. Then he ordered YD 102 for himself and YD 26 for his good friend, Tom Brown. I still have mine, but most of the ones you see now belong to children or grandchildren of the men who were in the AEF."

"Oh Brownie," sighed my uncle, "what a great guy he was! Do you remember those wonderful stories he had about the Mexican border?"

[2] As of a few years ago Harold was alive and well, living on St. Croix in the Virgin Islands. I played golf with him. He learned to do wonders on one leg.

"Yes," answered Phil, "and he had some great ones about France also. I remember one about how Butch Lockhart got in Dutch. It was when the 102nd was on the Chemin des Dames. It was colder than a well digger's ass in Alaska. Butch was a second lieutenant then. There wasn't much going on, so he decided it would be a good thing to get some cognac up to his men who were in the trenches."

"Yeah, that's the kind of a guy Butch was," my uncle agreed.

"Well, he got the cognac through to his men and was standing there in the trenches drinking some of it when out of nowhere these two other officers appeared. One of them was Peter Traub,[3] the general in charge of the brigade. Butch couldn't believe his eyes.

"'What the hell are you doing up here?' he yelled. Oh, the minute he did that he knew he was in real trouble.

"'Never mind that,' Traub roared. 'What are *you* doing? Drinking in the trenches, and with the men!' Then he really read Butch the riot act. Of course he put Lockhart under arrest. Poor Butch, he thought they would throw away the key. Then the war saved him. Shortly afterward we were moved into the area near Seicheprey. Lockhart's platoon was one of the ones hit so badly there. He came out of it all right though, and he never heard another word about the cognac."[4]

Then my father joined in. "My favorite story about Brownie happened a few years after World War II ended. He and his pal Joe Murtaugh . . ."

"Oh Joe," contributed Uncle Ed, "he's gone too, used to love to recite from those old dime novels, *Ned in the Blockhouse* and *Deerfoot.*"

"That's right," continued my father. "Well, the two of them decided to go to a YD reunion; I guess it was about 1950. By this time the World War II boys were running the show. Brownie—you remember how much weight he'd put on by then—couldn't really find many people he knew. Finally he cornered a couple of the young veterans, and remember, everyone had knocked down a few drinks by then.

[3] A West Pointer, Traub later was the major general in command of the 35th Division.

[4] Lockhart received the DSC for his actions at Seicheprey.

"'Say,' Tom said to the youngsters, 'did you ever hear what happened to us down on the Mexican border?'

"'Who the hell are you?' one of the ex-GIs said, 'Santa Claus?'

"'Is that so,' roared Tom. 'Well, you don't get one of these driving reindeers'—and he pointed to that little Purple Heart ribbon he used to wear in his lapel. [Tom had been gassed at Seicheprey.]

"This type of thing went on for several minutes. The young veterans were just baiting Brownie, but he was really boiling by now.

"'Oh yeah,' he finally snorted, 'well, you kids never smelled black powder.' Then he and Murtaugh turned around and walked out. They never went back to another reunion."

Well, this banter went on and on. Perhaps he didn't realize it, but Phil was telling me a great deal about the 101st, and all three were adding material about other AEF veterans.

There was Jerry Pierce, who would never play golf on Memorial Day. "We should spend that day thinking about our buddies who didn't come back," he would say.

And Harry Bissell, who became quartermaster general of the state of Connecticut after the war, who had achieved a great record with the 102nd Infantry in France. While serving as the quartermaster general he got himself in a dreadful mess, even though all the 102nd men said it wasn't his fault. Then Howard Johnson stepped in. Johnson had also been in the YD, in a Boston outfit.[5] Later he gave Bissell a chance with one of his chain of restaurants in New Jersey, where Bissell was immensely successful. If there was one thing that came through from all the men I interviewed, it was the tremendous loyalty for the unit they served in.

After the luncheon was over, I returned home and played my tape. Along with all the talk about Hartford, and the World War I men who had passed on, Phil had given me some great information about his days in France. As my interviews grew in number I found that this was almost always the case. When the men talked about their war experiences, the major thrust would be about their buddies, most of whom had passed on. They talked about their personal combat experiences, all right, and the horrors that went with them, but they'd constantly get around to mentioning their friends.

[5] Howard Johnson had been a driver in the 102nd Machine Gun Battalion. Walter Guild told me that Johnson was the best poker player in the battalion.

On countless occasions I heard, "Oh we had this great guy in our outfit," and I heard it from Maine to California and back again.

There was one other thing I learned from my first interview, and it was probably the most important thing to come out of the meeting. You can read diaries that tell of great events, pore over old letters and read autobiographies, but there is nothing else that can provide the impact of a relaxed, lengthy personal conversation.

My next step was to send feelers out to people I knew throughout the country asking them if they were aware of any World War I veterans who would be available for an interview. My first efforts were at best skimpy. Most of the people to whom I talked were actually astonished.

"Hell, Henry, I thought those people were all dead!" was told me on several occasions. Another answer was, "Oh what a shame, my Uncle George would have been great, but he died a few years ago."

Then came the explosion. Many of the people who at first had felt they couldn't possibly know of anyone would call me with the name of a prospect. In short, I could soon clearly say, "My cup runneth over." While I did get some help from veterans' organizations, my best sources ended up being my friends and the veterans themselves. I was indeed on my way.

Over the next two years I traveled throughout the country visiting men who had been born in twenty-two of America's states and seven foreign countries. I talked to men who had served with almost all of the divisions that went overseas, and to those who had fought in each of the AEF's major actions and most of the minor ones.

There were disappointments in my quest, the most heart-breaking involving illness or actual death. One of these concerned a man who had been with the 11th Engineers in November of 1917. They had been caught up in a fight while serving with the British long before any of the American divisions were in active sectors. I called to set up an appointment.

"Sure I was there in '17," he said to me on the phone, "and no one was more surprised than we were when we ended up with rifles in our hands. Hell, we were there to help with the railroads." On the Saturday I was supposed to visit him he was rushed to the hospital and never came out. Similar misfortunes happened on several other occasions. I would gain some valuable information from a phone conversation, but when the time came for our personal meeting, the veteran would not be physically able to meet with me. Eighteen of my interviews ended up being conducted by telephone, while eighty-two were face to face.

I feel I was very fortunate concerning the length of the World War I involvement of most of the men with whom I met. Thirteen of my veterans actually served in France with the British or French before the United States entered the war. Twelve of this group transferred to the American services after President Wilson called for Congress to declare war against Germany in April of 1917, while the thirteenth stayed with the French until the Armistice.

Another successful facet of my interviews was the type of men I was able to contact. Ten of these men received the Distinguished Service Cross. There were only six thousand of these medals given out during World War I, and to visit with ten of these heroes at this late date was indeed a stroke of luck. One of my interviewees was awarded the Congressional Medal of Honor. Only one out of every twenty thousand members of the AEF received this award.

My biggest surprise was the fliers. When I started my project I felt I would be lucky to reach one or two Americans who flew in France during World War I. I ended up talking to twelve such men.

Fifty-four of these men were either infantrymen or machine gunners, eighteen were in the artillery, and eight were ambulance drivers, only one of whom spent the entire war in this capacity; the other seven drivers switched to the Air Service or artillery. Other men I talked to were engineers, laborers, quartermasters, and Signal Corps men, or members of divisional or corps headquarters units. I also visited with a cook, a medic, a tanker, a Stokes mortar-man, and a balloonist. Five of my men were artillery observers, which in World War I was considered intelligence. Many of these men served in more than one of these capacities. Four of these old-timers were in the naval services—three Marines and a member of the Naval Air Corps.

I talked with nineteen men from the first four divisions to go into the lines—the 1st, 2nd, 26th, and 42nd—and a man from the 8th Division who was in the process of landing in France when it all ended. Eighty-four of these men saw combat in various degrees.

Thirty-six were wounded or gassed, and two were captured. Ten of the twelve pilots were either shot down or made crash landings.

Many of the leads I was given turned out to be men who were waiting to leave America for France when it all ended. While I would sometimes have lengthy phone conversations with these veterans, they are not included in my one hundred AEFers. Most of them went into detail about the frustrations they suffered while trying to get overseas.

"Goddamn it," recalled one of them, "I left college right after war was declared and went to Plattsburg for officers' training. I got my commission in August of 1917. I was then sent over to New Jersey to help form the 78th Division. Before the war was over I'd help train two other outfits that went to France, but I was always pulled out before my group went over; Christ, was I mad!

"And I'll tell you something else," he added, "even after it was over, and many of my buddies came back and told me what a mess it had been, I was still furious that I didn't go. I'm eighty-one now and just about at the end of the line. Don't ask me why; I can't give you any reasonable answer, but I can still get worked up about it."

I'm sure this gentleman was telling the truth. The desire to go overseas was extremely strong among the soldiers serving within the United States. There were only five thousand or so men who actually went AWOL from the embarkation ports.

One of the most pleasant aspects of my interviews was the cordial reception I received from almost every old Doughboy. One of them did tell me to go to hell, but this was an exception. And I don't mean that this old tiger told me this in so many words—I mean, plain and simple, he said, "Go to hell." I didn't interview him, which was a shame. He'd been a mule skinner. It probably would have been a good session. Another gentleman told me during a phone conversation that he just didn't have the time.

"I've been twice as busy since I retired from the Senate," he told me, "than I ever was in Washington. I just don't have the time for interviewing." In all probability only a handful of the millions of Americans who watched Sam Ervin conducting the Watergate hearings realized that Senator Sam had been wounded at Soissons in July of 1918. He will probably be the last of the Doughboys to reach national prominence. I wanted very badly to see him, but while he wished me well on my project, it just didn't work out. By and large, though, I was successful in arranging interviews the great majority of the time.

The oldest man I visited was ninety-three-year-old Leighton Frook, who had been a major in the AEF. He had run away from home to join the Army during the Spanish-American War. Another who saw me was General James Van Fleet. He went on special assignment to Vietnam under President Eisenhower. So you could say that men I interviewed covered the U.S. military from the war with Spain up to, and including, the holocaust in Southeast Asia.

The interviews greatly changed my thinking on senility. I had originally thought that this form of mental instability was quite prevalent among those in their eighties (the average age of those I visited with was eighty-two), but I did not find this to be so. I talked to perhaps five men who were over the hill mentally, and another five who were close to it. While it was quite sad to see these veterans try so hard to handle a conversation, they represented a mere 10 per cent of my interviews. Hell, I've been in the magazine business for almost twenty years, and I've seen that high a percentage of fifty-year-old executives who are balmy.

Actually, the excellence of my veterans' memories and coherence presented a problem, for I had much more material than I could use. I had decided to turn twenty-four of my interviews into main sections where I would go into detail on the war memories these men had shared with me. In some cases I had to flip a coin to decide which of these visits I would highlight. Those selected reveal the very human story of the AEF. Hopefully, these personal, living memories will indeed show Mr. Keith Mantle that little-remembered places like Belleau Wood, Soissons, Château-Thierry, the Ourcq River, and the Meuse-Argonne prove without a shadow of a doubt that the United States was indeed in World War I. And it is a good thing for Mr. Mantle's grandfather that it was.

The First Three Years

"And everybody praised the Duke
"Who this great fight did win.
"But what good came of it at last,"
  Quoth little Peterkin,
"Why that I cannot tell," said he,
"But 'twas a famous victory."

—*The Battle of Blenheim*
BY ROBERT SOUTHEY

It was the war that Imperial Germany couldn't lose. The Kaiser's Cousin Georgie, Great Britain's King George V, may have had a larger navy than the Germans, but Wilhelm knew that he had the strongest army in the world. He would crush France so quickly that Britain's mighty fleet really wouldn't matter. Then he could make peace with Great Britain, destroy the primitive Russian Army of Cousin Nickie (Czar Nicholas II), and Germany would have control of Europe—not total control, the way Hitler wanted it a few decades later, but control in a nineteenth-century way, where Berlin would be both the political and economic center of the Continent. Germany would also pick up some colonies—it was then the thing to do—and end up with the largest navy afloat. When the Kaiser would bring his yacht to Cowes, it would get top billing. It was all to be a great adventure, with Germany ending up on the top of the heap.

That is what the Kaiser thought when his invincible army

marched down Unter den Linden in August of 1914. There was thunderous cheering as radiant young *Frauleins* garlanded the proud Aryan knights with roses. It was the last war that people greeted with glee. In spite of the bombastic rhetoric of *der Fuehrer,* the streets of Berlin were deserted when the German people realized in 1939 that their sons were actually fighting in Poland. The Germans would fight extremely well in World War II (they always do) but the glee was gone. It had died on the fields of France along with the previous generation.

But it was still there in 1914 when the Schlieffen plan brought the German Army to Belgium. The plan called for a quick thrust to the Channel ports, pushing all resistance before them. This was to be followed by a massive assault through France, with the extreme right flank of the German Army touching the sea. The plan had been studied and refined for years—it would work. Then everything seemed to fall short of the Teutonic precision that had been the plan's buttress.

First there were the Belgians. They weren't supposed to fight. Protest, yes, and perhaps a token resistance—but defend their land with everything they had? Why, they would be crazy to do this. But it's exactly what the Belgians did do. It shocked the German Army.

Next came the British soldiers, or, as the Germans called them, "that contemptible little army." It was not a certainty that the United Kingdom would even enter the war. However, Berlin did correctly assume that once the first German Uhlan crossed the Belgian frontier, Great Britain would be forced to react. Nevertheless, the Germans thought, it would all be over before the British could send their troops to the Continent. Much to the surprise of the Germans, the British quickly moved over one hundred thousand men across the Channel. This was not a mighty host in World War I terms, but these Tommies were the best that Britain had—the cream of the crop. Their presence, especially the noncoms, would be sorely missed when the United Kingdom started to build a large national Army to supply its war needs, but they were desperately needed on the Continent that late summer of 1914.

Then there were the French, the main Allied actors in the incredible drama that was unfolding in Belgium and France. They were a different breed from Napoleon III's Army, which had been pulverized by Wilhelm's grandfather in 1870. Ever since the humiliating defeat at Sedan (where Napoleon III surrendered), the French Army officers had been living for one thing—the day that they could avenge their mortification. Germany had ended up obtaining Alsace-Lorraine after their victory, and France wanted it back. *"Tout le battle"* became their cry. They died in huge numbers, but this time they fought.

The final unexpected setback for the Germans came from the east —from Russia. One of the major premises of the Schlieffen plan called for a delaying action against the Czar's Army until France had been conquered. Then Germany could rout the archaic Russian forces at their leisure. It was a game Russia refused to play. They had one trump card—men—and they immediately employed them by hurling a huge mass at Germany shortly after the war broke out. Ironically, the only Allied army to fight extensively on German soil belonged to the Czar. Russia's pulling out of the war in 1917 would come perilously close to giving the Germans a victory, but the troops that Berlin had to divert from the Western Front to win the Battle of Tannenburg on August 21, 1914, were sorely missed in France. This above all upset Germany's plans for victory.

Toward the end of August, the first month of battle, the German General Von Moltke[1] ordered a major change in the Schlieffen plan. He terminated the western drive to the sea and called for a more direct route to Paris. The result was the crucial confrontation around the Marne River starting on September 6; here, the opposing armies clashed for five brutal days. The French, aided by what was left of the British, knew that this was the moment of truth. If Paris fell, it would be 1870 all over again. They pulled out all the stops, including the dispatching of some six thousand troops, who were transported to the battlefield by the taxicabs of Paris. The French Commander, Marshal Joffre, issued one of those stand-or-die orders. "Soldiers of France, we are attacking. Advance as long as you can. When you can no longer advance, hold your position. When you can no longer hold it, die." If France lost, there was to be no tomorrow, and Joffre wanted to be sure every soldier knew it.

When the battle was over, the Allies had not only held, but had actually thrown the Germans back to what was to become the Sois-

[1] A nephew of the Von Moltke who had defeated the French in 1870.

sons-Rheims line. France was saved. The exhausted opposing armies sat back and licked their wounds. No one was quite sure what was going to develop, and if they had been told what actually was going to happen, they probably wouldn't have believed it anyway. It was to be a phenomenon, a one-time shot—the world had never seen anything like it before, and never will again.

A battle line, over four hundred miles long, replete with a complicated network of trenches, started out at the North Sea with that small part of Belgium that Germany had not been able to conquer, and moved in a somewhat southwestern manner to the French-Swiss border. It was a line of death that was to see very little major change from the fall of 1914 until the spring of 1918. The opposing forces would succeed in killing each other in droves, but they could not really significantly alter the stalemate. Other battles would wage throughout Europe, and in the Near East and even Africa. But it was there in France, along the battle line from Belgium to Switzerland, where the main event was to be staged. The side that could permanently break the deadlock would undoubtedly win the war.

Of course, the line wasn't as neat and tidy as the words might indicate. Salients stuck out all over the place. Some areas would be a constant bloodbath, while in others it would be difficult to know there was a real war going on. But there it was, two lines of trenches separated by what they soon started to call "no-man's-land." Sometimes these lines would be as much as a mile apart, while in other areas a mere fifty yards would separate the combatants. Behind these front lines a regular system of defense was built up. This would start with the support trenches and usually be followed by a reserve line. In order to launch a successful assault on the system, the attackers would have to count on taking at least the first two lines and, above all, be ready to repulse a counterattack.

For the men who would go in and out of the lines it became a game of Russian roulette. No matter how lucky a soldier would be, if he served enough tours of duty in the trenches, he was almost sure to get hit, one way or another. This fact produced one of the toughest questions that confronted the generals on both sides of the line: How long could you keep a soldier in the trenches at one stretch without having him blow his mind? This was never fully resolved, but maximum efforts were made to rotate the men on a regular basis. A foot soldier with scrambled brains was worthless.

One of the men I visited with, Thomas Crane, joined the Canadian Army in 1915. Now a retired New York City Police lieutenant, Tom spent three years in and out of the trenches. I asked him which was the best of the four seasons to be on the front line.

"None," he answered. Then he told me about one period when he was only about fifty yards from the Germans.

"We used to defecate on the shovels and try and sling it over at the Boche. I don't think we ever reached them, but we had fun trying." He also told me of the rats ("Some of them were as big as small dogs"), the lice, the filth, the fears, and the boredom. Then he spoke of the weather.

"There were very few days that we didn't suffer from it. We'd freeze in the winter, but we knew the summer would bring those goddamn flies. It was never a picnic."

Naturally, these living conditions would vary from sector to sector. In the quiet sectors life could be quite tolerable, but in the active areas it was subhuman. Standing in the mud in the pouring rain, wondering if the enemy would pick that evening to rake the lines with a killing artillery barrage, must have produced stark terror. And would it be HE (high explosives) or gas? If it rained, one could expect HE, but if the weather was good, gas shells were bound to be included in the barrage. This meant the added discomfort of the gas masks and the possibility of severe burns if mustard gas was part of the incoming barrage.

One of the few breaks in the routine was what had been called in previous wars "the charges." In World War I they were known as "offensives." Take the case of any twenty-year-old British Tommy in 1916. He's to "go over" at 4:30 A.M. It's probably been raining which means he'll have to attack through huge areas of mud[2] to face the deadly German machine guns. His lieutenant is about the same age and just as frightened as the "ranker" but is trying not to show it. The realistic British have given each man a good belt of rum. It will help.

Then it's time, H hour, and over they go. Half of them are casualties in ten minutes. Perhaps they reach their objective, perhaps they don't. If they have succeeded, it really won't matter. The Germans will probably retake the area in a day or two. As for the young sol-

[2] In reviewing the mud-dominated field of Paschendale after the battle, a British general exclaimed, "Good God, did we actually send men to fight in this?"

dier, he might be in one piece, but he'll probably catch one in the next attack. The chances are not that good for his officer—he has already been hit.

On and on it went. Little battles and big ones. And it was the same for the French and the Germans. The only difference between the major offensives and the minor ones was the amount of casualties. The British suffered some fifty-five thousand of these during the first two hours of the massive 1916 assault on the Somme. The combined French and German casualties during the six months' fighting around Verdun climbed to over a million. When frontal attacks were employed, based on the Napoleonic tactics (where a single-shot musket was accurate up to fifty yards), against rapid-fire artillery, machine guns, and automatic rifles, brave soldiers were to suffer horribly.

In retrospect, the whole scene seems like something out of a nightmare. The Germans said that the British fought like lions, but that their generals were donkeys. Maybe so, but were the Prussian Junkers any less stupid—or the French generals? Their tactics were the same. In reality, it was a colossal melting of two ages, the collision between a previous flag-waving and story-book version of war, and modern military technology. Tanks, airplanes, Zeppelins, poison gas, rapid-firing machine guns, flame throwers, and shells that could destroy a whole village in a matter of minutes obliterated any false illusions the soldiers may have had. France's lovely Madelon was soon in mourning for a father, brother, or lover, or maybe all three, while England's famous Roses of Picardy were growing on a Tommy's hastily dug, shallow grave.

This animal-like existence of the men in the trenches was bound to warp personalities, and it did. Soldiers of all classes (and all sections of Europe in 1915 had rigid class lines) whose varying exposure to the media of the day had been based on what is referred to as Victorian mores, soon lost most of their Puritanic values. You can call it Protestant ethics, Catholic dogma, or even a plain nineteenth-century belief in Horatio Alger. Whatever it was, and this was also an age of great chauvinistic beliefs, it all soon went out the window. The only value that rivaled out-and-out survival was the comradeship that developed among the men who were sharing this living hell.

One place where this change in thinking could be seen was in the music. The rousing patriotic tunes of the civilians soon became songs that either ridiculed the soldiers' dreary lot or reached the depth of despair, or the height of obscenity. The French had one that told of a faithless wife who had resorted to the farm animals for her satisfaction. After the Americans had been there for a while, they fell right into step. One of their "Hinky, Dinky" versions stated: "The *mademoiselle* is on the Marne, *parlez-vous,* the *mademoiselle* is on the Marne, *parlez-vous,* etc. F— horses in the barn. Hinky, Dinky, *parlez-vous.*"

Another song depicted in glowing terms the Malacca walking canes of the officers. It ended up saying that the only canes the privates had came from the handle of the outhouse broom.

The British popularized a little ditty that ended up:

> Take me over the sea
> Where Allemand can't get at me.
> Oh my, I don't want to die;
> I want to go home.

Their jokes were similar in tone. An AEFer whose division was quartered with the British told me one about two Tommies who had been exposed to extensive shellfire. Finally an HE came over and blew the right hand off one of the soldiers. He started to cry and moan. The other tried to comfort his wounded chum.

" 'Ey, 'ey, matie, don't carry on like that. You've got a blighty. You're 'eading 'ome. At least you won't get killed. You've only lost a 'and."

"I know, I know," moaned the casualty, "but I 'ad me pecker in it."

This then was the world the Doughboy was to enter after America's commitment of 1917, a meat grinder of unrelenting savagery that no one seemed to know how to stop. If the one hundred men I talked to are any indication, the Yanks didn't have the foggiest notion what they were walking into.

"Hell," said one of them, "we all thought the British and the French had the thing won." This wasn't to be the case.

The AEF and the Great War

In October of 1918, General Pershing had his hands full on the southern end of the Allied battle line that cut across France. Officially, the campaign he was conducting was known as the Meuse-Argonne, but to the Doughboys it was simply "Up in the Argonne." Nevertheless, in response to an urgent plea from the French, he dispatched two divisions, the 37th (Buckeye) and the 91st (Wild West), to lend a hand in Belgium. Here they did yeoman service, suffering over twenty-six hundred casualties the last two weeks of the war. Joel Ashcraft, now living outside of Cleveland, Ohio, recalled those days in Belgium.

"God, we lost a great many men, but the toughest part was losing two buddies the afternoon of November 11. We didn't know it was all over, and neither did the Germans." Mr. Ashcraft remembers well. There are several recorded cases of firefights in this area as late as November 12.

When the fighting was finally all over, Albert, the wartime King of the Belgians, summed up the part played by the 37th and the 91st tersely but correctly when he said, "You came when you were needed." It is a statement that can sum up the service of the entire AEF in 1918: They came when they were needed.

To fully understand the part played by the Americans during the last year of the war calls for some knowledge of the previous year, for 1917 was just about the bottom of the barrel for the Allies. The British in Flanders and the French on the Chemin des Dames had both launched gigantic offensives that ended up looking like charnel houses. Haig's British and Empire troops were exhausted, and the French Poilu were equally weary. Many of France's troops went into open revolt. The British victories in Palestine had offered a small piece of sunshine, but it had been more than offset by the crushing defeat of their Italian allies by a German-Austrian army at a place called Caporetto. While the British naval blockade of Germany was hurting the Kaiser's home front, the submarine menace was equally devastating to Britain. While it is an uncommonly large island, Britain is still an island, and it does count on large imports of such essentials as food for survival.

To further complicate the war effort, there were Lenin and his Bolsheviks. They pulled Russia out of the war. Like so many other World War I statistics, it seems impossible to find agreement on just how many German soldiers were now available to move from the Eastern Front to the Western Front, but it must have been at least sixty divisions. One thing is a certainty: There would be enough to break the three-year stalemate on the Western Front and win the war.

There was, however, a problem involved. During 1917 the Germans had pulled one of the most colossal boners in history: They had inadvertently forced the United States into the war. This statement is of course an opinion, but anyone who doesn't realize that half of history is shaded by opinion has not read much of it. Many historians feel that Franklin D. Roosevelt did want to get the United States into World War II, but very few feel that way about Woodrow Wilson and World War I. On April 2, 1917, the college professor-President asked Congress to declare war on Germany; four days later they did just that. In response to his move, Wilson was cheered everywhere he went. This puzzled the President greatly.

"My God," he said, "they're cheering me and I've just sentenced thousands of their sons to their deaths."

Immediately after the declaration of war the beleaguered British and French began sending political and military leaders over to America. Their chore was to present the true picture of the war and to tell the United States what they could do to help win the victory. One of the first requests was for some troops. America should "show the flag" in France. This would be bound to do wonders for the sagging morale of both the British and the French. So on May 28 Major General John J. Pershing and 190 other American soldiers left New York aboard the USS *Baltic*. They were headed first for

Britain and then France. The move was supposed to be cloaked in the utmost secrecy. Pershing boarded the ship in civilian clothing, sporting a nifty camel-hair cap, but the charade was a flop. Several medical officers, trying to look like soldiers, boarded in complete military getup. For several days crates had been stored on the pier clearly marked, "Major General John J. Pershing, American Expeditionary Force." The final *faux pas* was a twenty-one-gun salute from Governors Island. The Yanks were coming, and the whole world soon knew it.

The group that reached France on June 13 was loaded with names that were to play an immensely important part in the AEF. James Harbord's service was to include the command of the 4th (Marine) Brigade at Belleau Wood and the 2nd Division at Soissons. He would end up in charge of the huge Service of Supply Department—an extremely key position, especially during the Meuse-Argonne battle.

Other officers aboard who would also shine in France were John Hines, Fox Conner, Hugh Drum, Benjamin Alvord, and Dennis Nolan. There were also two young men on the *Baltic* who would end up with more military fame than any other men on that ship save Pershing. They were First Lieutenant George S. Patton, Jr., and Sergeant Edward Rickenbacker. Patton was to fight hard in 1918, but his real fame would come smoking across Europe a quarter of a century later during World War II.

Rickenbacker, one of the most famous racing drivers of his day, originally went over as Pershing's chauffeur. He would soon transfer over to the Aviation Section of the Signal Corps and end up America's leading ace of World War I.

But you don't win wars with generals and pilots—you win them with what the grandchildren of these AEF veterans call "grunts," a World War I translation of which means Doughboys. The first contingency of these foot soldiers landed at Saint Nazaire, France, on June 26, 1917. There were about fifteen thousand in this group, including four thousand Marines. If you were among this first bunch, you never forgot it.

"That's right, I was in that first convoy," a man named George Krahnert told me. "Hell, we expected to move right in against those Germans the minute we arrived. I'm damn proud to have been with that first group."

George and most of the other soldiers who landed with him were destined to form the bulk of the 1st Division, U. S. Army Regulars. The Marines were slated for the 4th Marine Brigade of the 2nd Division. These two divisions, the 1st and the 2nd, were to vie for top honors in just about every combat category of the AEF.

By the end of October 1917, the first of the National Guard units had arrived in France. This was the 26th (Yankee) Division, and it wasn't supposed to be the first Guard unit to land in France at all. The premier spot had been allotted to the 42nd (Rainbow) because of its national flavor. It contained a special unit from the National Guards of twenty-six separate states—thus, a rainbow across the land.

The one section not represented in the Rainbow was New England. They had put together a division consisting of Guard units from all six of their states and had somehow managed to reach France a week before the 42nd.

These four divisions—the 1st, 26th, 42nd, and most of the 2nd—still claim the right to be called "The First Hundred Thousand." They are also the ones who suffered throughout the entire severe French winter of 1917–18; it was one of the worst on record. Lem Shepherd, later a Marine commandant during another war, was a second lieutenant in 1917. He called the winter suffering of his 5th Regiment in France just about as bad as anything in Marine Corps history. "Only the Chosin Reservoir in Korea was worse," remembered Shepherd.

By February 20, 1918, two more National Guard divisions had reached France—the 32nd (Michigan and Wisconsin) and the 41st (Far West). Both were slated to become depot divisions. In this capacity they would serve as replacement camps for the other divisions. The 32nd escaped this fate by the skin of their teeth and became one of the truly great fighting divisions of the AEF. Not the 41st; it was doomed. Thousands of its men immediately went into the 1st and 2nd divisions. Major General Liggett, who had trained the 41st and brought it to France, eventually became a lieutenant general in charge of the First Army. For all intents and purposes, the 41st ceased to exist. The same fate that destroyed the 41st awaited six other National Guard divisions. By the time the war ended, every AEF division contained some Guardsmen. As these men were in addition to the eleven National Guard outfits that did

fight as divisions, the huge part played in the war by these citizen-
soldiers is obvious.

The routine for the early-arriving divisions, both regular and National Guard, was a set pattern. First they'd train with the French
(for several divisions arriving in the spring of 1918 it would be the
British), then they'd move into a so-called quiet sector. These areas
were truly a phenomenon of World War I. It was almost as if both
sides had said to each other, "Look, let's use certain sectors for
practice—you know, a place where we can place worn-out and inex-
perienced troops."

That's how it worked out anyway. There'd be enough shelling by
both sides to keep each other honest, but no full-scale fighting. The
1st Division went into one of these quiet sectors in October 1917
and was soon followed by the 26th, 42nd, and 2nd. It was not until
April 1918, however, that the real fighting started for the Americans.

While these combat troops were landing and going through their
training and quiet-sector indoctrination, the backup soldiers were
also arriving by the thousands. It was a war the likes of which the
U. S. Army had never seen.

To an old Indian fighter like Robert Bullard (he'd end up as
commanding officer of the Second Army), the new elements of a
1917 military unit were countless.

"Why," wrote Bullard in his memoirs,[3] "the amount of special
troops needed was extraordinary. Such men as pigeon keepers, dog
trainers, wireless telegraphers, railroad engineers, miners, and wire
stretchers were now a part of the army."

War in France was to be light-years away from subduing the
Moros in the Philippines or chasing Latin American bandits. As one
high-ranking officer commented after being wounded, "I had no
reason to be that close to the front in a first-class war." And a first-
class war it was, which meant that the U. S. Army had to change in
numerous ways if it was to affect the outcome.

Probably the largest innovation needed if the American military
was to come into the twentieth century concerned the air service.
Here the United States started from scratch. Many of the airmen
who landed in France in 1917 had never even been in a plane. The
Aviation Section of the Signal Corps quickly went to work on build-

[3] Lieutenant General Robert Bullard, *Personalities and Reminiscences
of the War* (Garden City, N.Y.: Doubleday, Page & Company, 1925).

ing a base in France at a place called Issoudun. Using as a nucleus
many of the Americans who had been flying for the French and
English, they started to forge an air force. In April of 1918 the
United States' 94th Aero Squadron flew the first real air combat
ever experienced by an American squadron. From then on the
United States' participation in the air war continued to climb.
While almost all the planes they flew in were made in either France
or Britain, American fliers in France by the Armistice numbered in
the thousands. If the war had lasted into the spring of 1919, they
would have dominated the skies.

Along with the historical first combat flight of an American aero
squadron, April of 1918 witnessed two other major events in the
AEF: the arrival of the 77th Division, and the 26th Division's fight
at Seicheprey.

The 77th was something new. It was the first of the national
Army divisions to reach Europe. These were the pure World War I
outfits. Almost all of its enlisted personnel were Selective Service.[4]
It was an ideal choice to be the first one of its type to land in
France because of the tremendous diversity of its personnel, particularly its 308th Infantry Regiment. This was New York City all the
way. While its officers represented the old-school Ivy League types,
the men in the ranks had roots in just about every country of the
world. It has been alleged that forty-two different languages were
spoken within its ranks. But what is definite is that the 308th, and
the other three infantry regiments of this division, saw far more
fighting in the actual Argonne Forest than any other division. The
heroic Lost Battalion was composed of men from the 307th and
308th Infantry regiments.

The 77th was the first of sixteen such divisions that was to join
the AEF. Eight of these organizations suffered over five thousand
casualties, with the 77th leading the list with over ten thousand.

The third major event in the month of April was the massive
trench raid the Germans launched against the 26th Division near
Seicheprey in the Toul Sector. It was the first Doughboy[5] fight
where the casualties showed that America was in the war. It has

[4] By the end of the war all the U.S. divisions were loaded with
draftees.
[5] When the Americans first came to France, they were called Sammies,
after Uncle Sam. This never made it with the Americans and was soon
changed to the old Army term Doughboys, or simply Yanks.

never been firmly established if the Germans were simply after a large group of prisoners, which they did get, or if it was a bona fide offensive. They did enter the village of Seicheprey, but were there for only an hour. Reports of the casualties in this fight vary all over the lot, but the combined German and American total undoubtedly runs into four figures. It was the beginning of what was to come.

In the month before Seicheprey the Germans had launched their great spring offensive against the British. It was an open-and-shut case. Berlin by then knew that if they were going to win the war, they would have to do it before the AEF became a factor—and they knew they'd have to work fast.[6] Bolstered by troops from the Eastern Front, the Boche military wizard, Eric Ludendorff, struck at the British Fifth Army on March 21. He was enormously successful. Not only did the Germans almost completely eliminate Haig's Fifth Army, but they also devastated the British Third Army. The attack gained roughly forty miles. All this placed Pershing in an awkward position. His aim, and also the goal of Woodrow Wilson, was to put together an American Army as soon as possible. Pershing had been standing firm against the tremendous pressures from both Paris and London to do just the opposite—namely, send the Americans into the Allied forces in units that ran the gauntlet from squads to battalions.

Pershing knew he'd have to bend, so in a magnificent gesture, he offered everything he had to Ferdinand Foch,[7] who had been made supreme Allied commander due to the emergency. The French media played Pershing's gesture up tremendously, even attributing a flowering speech to John J. that he undoubtedly didn't make. The phrase that General Tasker Bliss, the U.S. representative on the Supreme War Council, is alleged to have said, probably is accurate.

"Well," said Bliss, "we came over here to get killed; where do you want us?"

Foch wanted them all right, and as quickly as possible. He asked Pershing to send a division into the lines in Picardy near a village

---

[6] German intelligence undoubtedly knew that the United States was working at full tilt to get men to France. Along with the 77th, the 3rd Division also landed in April. The 4th, 5th, 27th, 28th, 30th, 33rd, 35th, 80th, and the 82nd arrived in May.

[7] But at divisional strength—that is, the American divisions could enter British and French armies and fight, but as American divisions.

called Cantigny. They would occupy the town of Villers Tournelles, which is fifty miles northwest of Paris. It is just about as far as the German drive had reached.

It was now up to Pershing to pick the division, and he unquestionably never hesitated. It was to be the 1st. There was always a soft spot in the AEF's commander's heart for the Big Red One, a sentiment that did not always sit too well with the other divisions. The truth of the matter is that the 1st was certainly the most advanced unit he had at the time, and he did make the logical choice. The 1st moved in, and there they sat for six weeks.

While the AEF's overall experience in France was more a war of movement than of the trench stalemate, the six weeks the 1st spent around Cantigny was what the British, French, and Germans had been doing since the autumn of 1914. This was no quiet sector. There were no massive attacks during these six weeks, just a steady, day-to-day holding of a position under a barrage of thousands and thousands of shells. The horrible experience of an American seeing a buddy go completely senseless under the pressure of the shelling became a fact of life for the Americans.

Then, on the morning of May 28, the Americans attacked Cantigny. The actual assault was made by the 28th Infantry of the 1st Division, who had been behind the lines rehearsing it for weeks. It was somewhat of a foregone conclusion that the attack would succeed. What remained to be seen was whether the 1st could hold against the German counterattacks. They did. It must have been a crushing psychological blow to the Germans to realize that these Doughboys, who were now landing in the tens of thousands, could not only capture ground from them, but also hold it.

At the same time that the 1st Division was attacking at Cantigny, the front had exploded about forty miles to the southwest, on the Chemin des Dames.[8] A German offensive had achieved another Western Front rarity—a breakthrough. As in 1914, they were heading for the Marne and the Château-Thierry–Paris road.[9] There

[8] So named because Louis XIV had kept his paramours there.

[9] Once again, a World War I controversy: Did the Germans originally intend to go to Paris at this time, or were they surprised at the success of their initial attack and then decide to go for the French capital? There are two schools of thought here.

was no taxicab army to rush out from Paris this time, but there were twenty-five thousand members of the Americans' 2nd Division.

The original plan had been for the 2nd to relieve the 1st Division in Picardy. But as it always will in war, necessity ruled. The 2nd was piled aboard camions and rushed toward the front. It was like the cavalry riding to a last-minute rescue in a John Ford movie. The men of the 2nd didn't know where they were going, but they knew that if they kept heading eastward, they were bound to meet the Germans eventually. It turned out to be near an old hunting preserve that dated back to the days of the Bourbon kings. It was called Belleau Wood.

The two American infantry brigades were lined up on either side of the road. While the 2nd's 3rd Infantry Brigade (9th and 23rd U.S. regulars) would shine later on, the brunt of the attack fell on the 4th Brigade. This was the Marine Brigade (5th and 6th Marines), and with all the Corps' singing about the halls of Montezuma and the shores of Tripoli, it was here at Belleau Wood where they first played a major role in a full-scale American military operation. They stopped the Germans cold and soon went over to the counterattack. In doing so they suffered more casualties than the Marine Corps had experienced in all its actions put together up until this time, and they created legends that are still part of their lore sixty years later.

One of these concerns a crusty old regular named Dan Daley. This sergeant is said to have yelled:

"Come on, you sons-of-bitches, do you want to live forever?"

It is rumored that a young freckle-faced private from West Virginia answered with the perfect stopper:

"Is seventeen being greedy?" replied the lad, or so the story goes.

When they were originally moving in, they had been confronted with a mass of retreating Frenchmen who were calling on the Marines to turn back.

"Retreat, hell," answered a Marine officer, "we just got here!"

And from the ranks came the inevitable, "Oh, for Christ's sake, some idiots never get the word!"

While statements like this constantly pop up in all wars, their credibility is always in doubt. What is not in question is that starting with the 2nd Division at Belleau Wood,[10] the Americans were in constant action around the Marne, and moving north toward the Vesle River, for three months. Although the Germans had been stunned at Belleau Wood, their offensive was a long way from over. The German advance was to be dealt a death blow between July 15 and 22, and the Americans would play a major role. They would be fighting in French armies, but as an American division was equal in size to 2½ French divisions, the Americans' presence was always felt.

Two of these oversized divisions of Uncle Sam, the 3rd and the 42nd, took a tremendous pasting on July 15, the last major day of the German offensive. One of the 3rd's regiments, the 38th Infantry, was standing on the banks of the Marne on the morning of July 15 when their colonel, Ulysses Grant McAlexander, gave them an order: "Hold." They did and gained for their regiment the sobriquet, "Rock of the Marne." Reginald Sinclair, an aviator with the Lafayette Flying Group, told me that when flying over the river that day, he could see a mass of German uniforms floating on the Marne.

Then, on July 18, the Allied counterattack began. The French XX Corps, containing the 1st and 2nd U.S. divisions, attacked the enemy's line south of Soissons. The Germans here were Bavarians, Saxons, and the Prussian Guards. They were the cream of the Kaiser's Army—the very troops who had confidently expected to capture Paris that same July of 1918. Flanking a French colonial division on both sides, the 1st and the 2nd stepped out at 4:30 A.M. on July 18. No one knew it at the time, but it was the beginning of the end for Imperial Germany.

Over the next five days one of the most important battles of World War I raged with unrelenting fury. The 2nd, still smarting from its fighting in June, was pulled off the lines on July 20. The 1st lasted until July 23 and was literally shot full of holes. A good indication of what a butchery it was is the casualty list among the commissioned officers of the 1st. A total of 232 of what the enlisted men called the "Sam Brownes" were killed or wounded. Between the 1st and the 2nd almost 13,000 men of all ranks were hit. As al-

[10] Actually it started with two companies of the 7th Machine Gun Battalion of the Third Division. They were positioned at bridges crossing the Marne at Château-Thierry and fought there for four days.

ways, the wounded outnumbered the dead by roughly three to one, and many of those wounded would return to their outfits to fight another day. Those 13,000 casualties exceed the number suffered by the United States on June 6, 1944, at Normandy and also those suffered by the United States at Arnhem in September of the same year.

In examining the field after the battle, French observers were appalled at the dead who lay in windrows.

"The Americans were too reckless," they said, "too rash. They didn't need to charge the machine guns like that." Perhaps they had forgotten their own countless casualties in hundreds of such actions over the past four years. The difference here was that while the price was dreadful, gains were made that were to be held. It wasn't the eight bloody miles that were captured during those five days that was vital. It was the turn-around. Germany's soldiers, who had fully expected to win the war that summer, were on the defensive. Tenacious as the Boche were, they had not only been stopped but had also lost the initiative. They would never regain it during the war.

At the same time that the 1st and 2nd were attacking around Soissons, the New Englanders of the 26th Division were striking around Château-Thierry. The story was pretty much the same: over five thousand casualties in three days from the German artillery and machine guns. Four of the men from the 26th with whom I chatted all told me the same thing: "Château-Thierry was our roughest fight." But the pressure was being exercised. There was just no other way to win the war.

The 3rd Division crossed the Marne and joined the attack. The 32nd moved into its first real fight, as did the 28th. This latter group was from the Pennsylvania National Guard and carried in its ranks a young second lieutenant named Hervey Allen. This postwar author of the very successful novel *Anthony Adverse* also penned a magnificent story of the July fighting called *Toward the Flame*. This is a shockingly vivid recounting of the fighting around the Vesle River town of Fismes.

Another division to join the melee toward the end of July was the 4th. While it was regular Army in organization, its ranks were loaded with wartime enlistees and many draftees. Of all the American outfits that went into the lines at this time, it was probably the least trained. Some of its new arrivals barely knew how to put the clips in their rifles, yet they advanced and they held.

Then there was the 42nd—the rainbow across the land. With its infantry regiments from Alabama, Iowa, Ohio, and New York, it moved into a very heavily defended area around the Ourcq River. They eventually crossed the Ourcq, which seemed more like a large stream to the Doughboys. It was here that its 165th Infantry (the old 69th New York Irishers) buried their soldier-poet, Joyce Kilmer. He had refused to join the staff of *The Stars and Stripes*, the Dough-boys' newspaper, because of an intense loyalty to the regiment. Once you were in the 69th, you stayed.

The fighting in this area between the Marne and the Vesle was just as brutal as it had been a week or so before near Soissons. Bill Cronin, a lieutenant in Reilly's famous 149th Field Artillery of the Rainbow (this was the Chicago unit of the division), can attest to its ferociousness.

"It was a little north of the Ourcq," Cronin told me when I visited him in Detroit, "some hill near one of those small towns. We had just moved the horses under fire, a neat trick in itself, I can tell you that, when I came to a mound that gave me a clear view of our infantry attacking. I can't tell you how many times our men went up and down that lousy hill before taking it, but we sure lost a lot of men there."

What Mr. Cronin saw was the leapfrog technique that had de-veloped—the throwing of one line of men after another into the at-tack. It was brutal against machine guns.

The 77th Division joined the push on August 14. When they had first landed, they had been brigaded with the English, but in July Pershing had moved them down to the southern part of the line in anticipation of developing his own army. It was during their Au-gust fighting that Major General Robert Alexander, one of the many leading AEF generals who had worked his way up from the ranks, took command of the 77th. He then led it until the end of the war, including the hellish struggle in the middle of the Argonne Forest.

The entrance of the 77th brought to nine the number of U.S. di-visions actively engaged in this crucial summer fighting. There was another U.S. regiment, the 369th (Colored), very much engaged at this time. Officially it was part of the 93rd Division, but as one of its officers, Hamilton Fish, told me, "We were never really part of a division, just an infantry regiment fighting with the French." All told, over a quarter of a million Americans participated. This does not include the various noncombat troops all over France who were trying to supply them, nor the growing list of fliers. Ted Curtis of the United States' 95th Aero Squadron is one pilot who lasted all the way with his squadron.

"There is no question," Ted told me, "but that combat around the Marne in July was the toughest I saw. Thank God we had Spads by then!"

During this entire period the American divisions were always fighting under French command. Hundreds of thousands of Poilu were also struggling in the area. But it does not in any way detract from the French soldier to surmise that if the Americans had not arrived in force, Paris well might have been captured, and it is unthinkable to imagine the launching of the counterattack without the American divisions.

In the meantime, Pershing was finally winning his battle to create his own army. He was getting ready to take over the southern end of the line by calling in all the American divisions, no matter where they were. Such divisions as the 35th, 78th, and 82nd left their British mentors and came down to the American end of the line. But Marshal Haig kept two superb National Guard outfits, the 27th (New York) and the 30th (the Carolinas and Tennessee). As these two divisions spent their entire war with the British, their magnificently heroic efforts at the Hindenburg Line never received its due recognition back home.

The thought of there being an independent American Army fighting on the southern end of the lines must have haunted the German leaders. Their intelligence was good. Surely they had a pretty good fix on the fact that by September 1 there were a million and a half United States soldiers in France—and more landing every day.

Sid Boyden was one of the Doughboys who landed in September. He wasn't typical because he was a volunteer, not a draftee. But the rapidity with which he reached France was typical of the late summer and early fall of 1918.

"I graduated from high school in June of 1918," reminisced Mr.

Boyden, "and I enlisted in the Army in July. Before the end of August I was on my way to France."

Sid's division, the 86th, was mainly used for replacements. He never got to the actual front. However, Mr. Boyden, and thousands of others like him, were all set to join the American drive set for mid-November. The combination of this ever-increasing army and the knowledge gained in June, July, and August that they would fight, and fight well, had to dictate German policy. Perhaps the Americans were overly eager. But that just meant that the Germans could kill many of them. It certainly didn't mean they could stop them.

By September 12 Pershing had all his ducks in a row. His target was the Saint Mihiel salient, a nasty piece of real estate south of Verdun. It had been a thorn in the side of the French for over three years. The Americans were to reduce it, as a 1918 saying would put it, as fast as you could say "Jack Robinson." As a matter of fact, they probably won the battle with a massive four-hour bombardment that started at 1:10 A.M. on September 12.

"Jeez," one old Doughboy told me, "it sounded as if every cannon on the Western Front was firing at them Heinies."

Thirty-eight of the men I talked to fought at Saint Mihiel. To most of them, particularly if they'd fought around the Marne, Saint Mihiel was a piece of cake. But it wasn't that way for Lester Atwood, one of the early tankers.

"Our tanks were really pretty primitive," recalled Mr. Atwood. "It seems to me that they could only go about five miles an hour. Oh, they were soft pickings for the German artillery. The first day at Saint Mihiel I acted as a runner, going back and forth between the tanks delivering messages. On September 13 it was my turn to go inside. One of the Germans' shells that were landing all around us hit the side of our tank. It was the end of Saint Mihiel and the war for me. By the time I got out of the hospital it was all over."

The Germans claimed that their troops at Saint Mihiel were second-raters (there were a good many Austrians and Hungarians there), and that they'd intended to pull out of the salient anyway. Maybe so, but they didn't get out in time. It ended up a tremendous victory for the Americans, the only question was: Could it even have been greater?

"The door was wide open to Metz and southern Germany,"

wrote the thirty-eight-year-old commander of the 84th Infantry Brigade of the Rainbow Division. "We should have kept going in that direction. We could have gone right into Germany and perhaps ended the war then and there." The brigadier general who said this was Douglas MacArthur, and his views were shared by many of the best military minds in the AEF.

Right or wrong, this was not to be the case. The Saint Mihiel attack was a preliminary for the main bout coming up. It was to be the gigantic Meuse-Argonne drive, the American part of the overall Allied strategy that was set to drive the Germans out of France.

The Doughboys' job was to move northwest of Saint Mihiel and start an attack on both flanks of the Argonne Forest. The plans also called for the Yanks to smash right through the middle of that ten-mile wooded area. It started on September 26 with the Americans going north and leaning northeast on a twenty-four-mile front. When it finally ended on November 11, they had pushed to the Meuse River and were attacking on an eighty-mile front.

It was the biggest campaign in American history up until that time, and if you want to call it all one battle, it is still the largest the United States has fought.

During this six-week period, over one million Americans fought, suffering over 125,000 casualties, of which some 30,000 were dead. Twenty-six divisions were actively engaged at one time or another, including the 93rd (not a complete division), and the 36th, which was under the French at Blanc Mont. As these were the "square divisions," their table of organization called for 28,000 men. By the middle of October most of them would be closer to 20,000, due to casualties and sickness.

Then there were the fliers. From August 10, 1918, until the end of the war, 199 American manned planes were either shot down or forced to crash-land. During the same period the Americans rendered the same fate to 456 German machines. The Americans were also constantly flying bombing and observation flights. And there were thousands more in training.

Shortly before the jumping-off date of September 26, the Allies first began to realistically feel that they could end the war in 1918. The Germans also knew this. The main objective was to try to keep the Allies out of Germany at least until the spring. This way they could try to negotiate the best possible peace.

But there was no way to stop the Allies now. In order to try to contain the Americans in the area sometimes called "The Hinge,"[11] the Germans were forced to keep between four hundred thousand and five hundred thousand troops on their lines. While the deep woods, ravines, and gullies offered ideal defensive positions, the constant pounding by the Americans could not be refuted. However, there is a general opinion that the Americans went into the Argonne and ended the war. This is simply not true. From September 26 until November 1, the AEF had a very rough time. The real breakthrough did not come until five or six very rugged weeks had gone by. However, the Germans, being pinned down by the Americans, could not be sent elsewhere. The presence of the Americans made it very difficult for the Germans to send reinforcements to other sectors. This had never happened before on the Western Front.

One of the Americans who fought in the Argonne is John Gilbertie of Westport, Connecticut, a DSC winner of the 326th Infantry, 82nd Division. His memory is not too keen on recent events, but he is superb concerning 1918.

"You know," mused this ex-sergeant, "there are times when I can't recall what I had for lunch yesterday, but I can even remember the *taste* of some cold steaks that our cook risked his life to get to us up in the Argonne. We hadn't had any real food for five days. The mess sergeant brought us rations for a whole platoon. Unfortunately, there were only about half of us left, so there was plenty to go around."

The same difficulties the men found getting food held true for all supplies. Attacks would be held up while the men waited for deliveries. Sometimes they'd even attack without the needed equipment. What many of the men called "the Kaiser's quick step" ran rampant. As a change of clothing was practically unheard-of, the living conditions became intolerable. It was a tough way to go after an enemy who'd had four years to prepare his defenses.

The Germans were also short of many things, but not artillery and machine guns. One American unit's history tells of knocking out eight Maxims in one day and "suffering harsh casualties from each one."

[11] As this southern end of the line moved, it would have to pull the rest.

It was a nightmarish six weeks that produced a Sergeant York, the Lost Battalion, and any number of brutal firefights that were just as heroic but are long forgotten. Names like the Hagen Stellung, the Volker Stellung, and the Kriemhilde Stellung mean nothing now, but in 1918 they meant thousands of American casualties. For years afterward parlors all over America would contain photographs of a young man with the high collar of the AEF blouse trying to look older than he was. His parents would spend the rest of their days wondering what kind of a life their son would have had if he hadn't been lost in the Argonne. Just about every one of those I interviewed who fought in the Meuse-Argonne, and there were forty-two of them, talked of a buddy who was killed there.

To each of these veterans the battle always had one thing in common: confusion. One of them was a very dignified gentleman of eighty-two years. His recall was perfect, and the interview excellent. I did notice that he hadn't used one word of profanity or vulgarity during the entire visit. Then I asked him about the Argonne.

"Now," he said, "do you want my frank opinion?"

"Absolutely."

"Well, I think it was a fucked-up mess."

Like his phrase or not, it was the general opinion of all the men I saw.

"Attack, attack, that's all we did for weeks," another told me, "then when we started to really push them, the sons-of-bitches quit. Don't get me wrong," he quickly added, "I was glad they threw in the towel; I'd had enough of those machine guns and 77's."

The day they did quit, of course, was November 11, 1918. The whole world gave a huge sigh of relief. According to those I saw who were on the lines at the time, there was very little jubilation. And on that date there were more Americans facing the Germans than there were British.

According to a book called *The History of the World War*, one of these Americans was a Texas lieutenant, probably from the 36th or 90th Division. The book, published in 1919, shows this young Texan to be as accurate a prophet as Macbeth's witches. Watching all the cheering that was coming from the German lines, he sadly shook his head.

"I wonder if we whipped 'em enough?" he muttered. Perhaps

this sage ended up with a son fighting on the Rapido River in Italy twenty-five years later.

To the AEF veteran of today, November 11, 1918, is one date they all remember.

"No, I can't say it is a memory of great glee," said Charlie Bloch, "more a thought of hope. I was at a place called the Heights of the Meuse, and that is just where my mind was, at its height. I was going to be able to go home instead of staying forever in France, like so many of my buddies."

Then I asked the old-timer if he would do it all over again if he had a chance.

"Hell no," he answered, "not for a million dollars." Then he laughed and added, "But I won't take a million dollars for having done it!"

I feel that the most memorable mention of the Armistice came from Devereux Josephs, a former first lieutenant of artillery, who later rose just about as high as you can in business, becoming president of the giant New York Life Insurance Company.

When I visited this gentleman at his apartment in New York City at East Seventy-fifth Street and First Avenue, we sat out on a very pleasant terrace, which was high enough up to offer a commanding view of the city. While he had not been well, Mr. Josephs had spruced up for the occasion and looked great. His mind was particularly sharp as he described his days in the Army. He'd been one of those artillery officers who had their trip overseas postponed due to the spring offensive by the Germans in 1918.

One of the bargains that Pershing had to make with the British was that they'd furnish the Americans with the shipping if the United States would send nothing but infantry and machine gunners over for sixty days. This delayed the transporting of many artillerymen, including First Lieutenant Josephs. He finally got over in time to catch the end of the Argonne campaign. He was there on November 11, 1918.

"We had taken over this chateau the Germans had been using for three years," Mr. Josephs told me, "and it was well stocked with wine. On the evening of November 10 we'd sampled that supply very liberally, and on the morning of the eleventh most of us were a little the worse for wear. There was an old rickety piano in the corner that had been given a real going-over the night before, but none of us felt like hearing it that morning. We were slightly out of the range of normal shelling, but we could hear intensive firing from the front. We were supposed to move back in that evening.

"Then," continued Mr. Josephs, "a sidecar came roaring down the road driven by a messenger. He came in and gave us a snappy salute. 'It is ten-thirty, gentlemen. In thirty minutes it will all be over; the Germans have surrendered.'

"Now, in the meantime we could hear this tremendous shelling.

"'How in the hell can it be over,' one of us asked, 'with all that going on?'

"'I guess the Germans just want to get rid of all their shells,' the messenger replied, 'and our men are answering them. This is official though: It's over at eleven.' Then he drove off.

"I can't remember if it was exactly at eleven when it happened, but if not, it was damn close—that is, the ceasing of the guns. It was weird, a sudden quiet everywhere. The man who had been playing that out-of-tune piano the night before sat down and started to play again. This time it was 'The Star-Spangled Banner.' We all started to sing it. There was no bravado or flag-waving involved—most of us were actually half singing and half reciting. I looked at one of our new officers. He'd just joined our outfit from the hospital, after being wounded a few months before down around the Marne. You could see the tears coming down his cheeks. It was a moment I'll never forget."

And when this former business executive told me his story, it was a moment I'll not soon forget. As he was talking, he was gazing out over the East River with a faraway look in his eyes—this seems to come easily to the elderly. It was almost as if he could see it all again—when he was a young officer, that is.

That is what this book is all about: the memories from a cross section of a generation that went to France sixty years ago. They left a country that had never before been truly involved in international power politics. They came back to a nation that could never be the same again. The results of the first postwar presidential election refuted this worldwide involvement as America tried to "return to normalcy," but it was like trying to stop a flood with a picket fence. For better or worse a country that could send two million men three thousand miles to face the greatest army that had ever existed could not return to the parochialism of 1916.

This book is not a history of what these two million men did. It is merely what a sampling of this surviving host can remember of the part they played in this historic drama.

The First Shot

> I want all loyal Americans to paste it in their hats that it was C Battery, 6th United States Field Artillery that fired that shot, and that every member of the battery did their bit towards ending Uncle Sam's first calling card into the trenches of the Kaiser.
>
> —*The First Shot for Liberty*
> CORPORAL OSBORNE DE VARILA

Shortly after I began my search for American veterans of the First World War, I read the obituary of a Robert Braley, who had died in Cincinnati, Ohio. The lead in on the notice of Mr. Braley's death stated, "Yank Who Fired First Shot in World War I Dies."

"What a shame," I thought to myself. "I would have loved to have interviewed him."

A few weeks after this old Doughboy had passed on, I was browsing through a second-hand-book shop when I spotted a book called *The First Shot for Liberty,* authored by Corporal Osborne de Varila, Battery C, 6th U. S. Field Artillery of the 1st Division. Under Mr. de Varila's name it stated, "The Yank who fired the first shot of the AEF." In this nifty bit of wartime propaganda (the corporal was brought home from the front to help sell Liberty Bonds—

he refers to the Germans in his book as the ferocious Huns), de Varila does not mention Braley. He does mention his battery commander, one Captain Indus R. McLendon, but no one else by name.

I had just about decided to give both Braley and de Varila joint credit for the first shot fired when I read the following line in Laurence Stallings' excellent book *The Doughboys:* "The gun was a French 75 and Sergeant Alex L. Arch pulled the lanyard, aiming at nothing in particular, just in the direction of Kaiser Wilhelm the II, Emperor of the Germans."

Now I had three veterans who were alleged to have fired that fateful first shot. I was thoroughly confused.

Then I was told of a Warren Ransom, currently living in Rye, New York, who had been with the 6th Field Artillery when the first shot was fired. I immediately gave Mr. Ransom a phone call to see if we could get together. He was about to leave for Florida, which made it impossible for us to meet, but he did tell me that he remembered that first shot well.

"It was Battery C, all right," he said, "and the rest of us were a little put out. I was in Battery D. We all wanted to fire that first shot, but they beat us to it."

We chatted quite a bit more about the 1st Division. Mr. Ransom, it seems, is just as proud of the old Big Red One as the rest of the 1st Division men I talked with. He also spoke in very complimentary tones about Shipley Thomas, another 1st Division officer whom I had already interviewed. One thing that Mr. Ransom was too modest to mention was the DSC he was awarded for extraordinary heroism at Soissons in July of 1918. I have read his citation; he earned the medal.

Mr. Ransom had, however, not helped me any with my puzzle on who had fired that first shot. As the months dragged on and my book neared its completion, I had just about given up any hope of getting the real facts on who had actually sent that first shell roaring toward the Heinies. Then I visited with a Mr. Jeremiah Evarts, formerly of the 18th Infantry of the 1st Division.

"No," Jerry told me, "I wasn't with the 1st Division when the first shot was fired, but I later became a good friend of Indus McLendon. Indus—a regular Army man, incidentally—was the commander of the battery that fired it. All right, here, he sent me this letter about forty years ago, you can see that he even wrote an article about that first shot."

Sure enough, there was the letter from McLendon mentioning the article he had written for the American Legion magazine in 1932.

My next step was to check out the article at the New York Public Library. My mystery was soon solved. Battery C of the 6th Field Artillery did indeed fire that first shot. Captain McLendon gave the fire command at 6:10 A.M. on October 23, 1917. The 6th was in position near the town of Luneville in the Toul Sector at the time.

As for the three men who had been credited with that first shot, here is how Captain McLendon doles out the credits: Sergeant Louis Domonick cut the fuse, Corporal Osborne de Varila prepared the fuse for cutting, Sergeant Edward Worthen loaded the gun, and Corporal Robert E. Braley laid the piece for firing. Sergeant Alexander L. Arch had actually fired the shot, but it's quite possible that the rest of the gun crew had grabbed the lanyard at the last minute. Anyway, they had all helped pull the gun into position during the darkness hours of that morning.

"It was raining," wrote de Varila, "but no other battery was going to beat the band of huskies we had lugging that gun through those shell holes."

Of course, it really doesn't make any difference who fired the shot. The important thing was that it was fired. Before November 11 of the next year, the rounds fired by the Americans would number in the millions, and when they stopped firing, the Kaiser's Germany would be a thing of the past.

The Colonel and the Sergeant

George Krahnert and Shipley Thomas

MR. THOMAS'S HOME—SHORT HILLS, NEW JERSEY—MARCH 1976
George Krahnert enlisted in the United States Army regulars in 1915. He was seventeen years of age at the time. The same year that Mr. Krahnert joined the colors, Shipley Thomas, of an old Philadelphia family, graduated from Yale College. These two men, with completely different backgrounds, met in the fall of 1917 when their regiment, the 26th U. S. Infantry of the 1st Division, was getting ready to "move in." They served together until the Armistice. This included such spots as Cantigny, Soissons, Saint Mihiel, and the Argonne. Both of them were wounded.

After the war they went their separate ways. Thomas returned to the service for World War II, while Krahnert and his wife were preoccupied with the herculean task of raising eight children. Thomas, who had been an AEF first lieutenant, rose to the rank of colonel during the Second World War. The two did not see each other from the end of World War I until the early part of 1974.

At this point, Colonel Thomas, now confined to a wheelchair, was being driven through Roselle Park, New Jersey. He noticed an auto-service garage with the sign "Krahnert's" over the door. He asked the driver to stop the car so he could inquire if there was any connection between the sign and the George Krahnert who had been his sergeant in 1918.

"You've come to the right place," he was told. "Your sergeant is my dad."

A short time later the two old buddies were enjoying a reunion over a bottle of cognac.

"Tell me, George," inquired Thomas, "did you get those medals I recommended you for?"

"No, I never did," answered Krahnert, "you know how confused things got at the end over there. I guess they forgot about me."

"George," replied the colonel, "there was no one any more responsible for our stopping those German counterattacks at Cantigny than you were. You didn't get the medal? I'll see about that!"

Colonel Thomas then began a one-man crusade against the red tape of the Pentagon.

"Actually," the colonel later told me, "I never met any resistance. It just took time."

Then, on November 11, 1975, George Krahnert, former sergeant, AEF, was honored by a full-scale review at Fort Monmouth, New Jersey. Here, at the Army's Signal School Museum, General DePuy presented him with two Silver Stars and a Purple Heart.

"Oh it was great," exclaimed Krahnert, "but what was even better was meeting up again with Colonel Thomas! He was a first lieutenant when I soldiered with him and the best in the AEF."

It turned out that Thomas lived a mere twenty miles or so from his old sergeant. Their chance meeting was the first of many get-togethers where they would break out the brandy and reminisce about the days when they were fighting the Germans. It was my good fortune to attend one of these sessions. I picked up George early one Saturday afternoon at his home in Roselle and we drove over to the colonel's apartment in Short Hills. Here we were greeted by a smiling housekeeper who bore a striking resemblance to the late actress Hattie McDaniel.

"Good afternoon, Sergeant," she said. "Oh the colonel is so looking forward to your visit."

We proceeded to the colonel's study and a most cordial welcome from the old soldier. I was immediately struck by his large collection of memorabilia from 1918 and the lack of same from his service in the Second World War. I asked him why the discrepancy.

"Oh hell," remarked Colonel Thomas, "I didn't do much in

World War II. The First War, that was my tour of real duty." The two of them then proceeded to tell me why.

First Lieutenant Shipley Thomas
Intelligence-Headquarters Company, 26th Infantry, 1st Division

Sergeant George Krahnert
Intelligence-Headquarters Company, 26th Infantry, 1st Division

> The 1st Division was digging a ditch, *parlez-vous,*
> The 1st Division was digging a ditch, *parlez-vous,*
> The 1st Division was digging a ditch to bury the Kaiser,
> That son-of-a-bitch, Hinky, Dinky, *parlez-vous!*

THOMAS: The 26th Division relieved us near Seicheprey sometime in April of 1918. While we had been there, our orders were to put only a few men in the front-line trenches. This way, you see, if the Germans threw a heavy raid at us, the losses would be small. Besides, the men in the first trenches had been told to get the hell out of there if the Germans came over in force.

Now, the Yankee Division [the 26th] had this old fool, Clarence Edwards, in charge.[1] He'd been a cavalry man and didn't know anything about modern war. And one of his colonels, "Gatling Gun" Parker,[2] was just as bad. He was supposed to know everything about machine guns, but he didn't know anything about

[1] It should be noted that Edwards has his defenders—just about every man in the Yankee Division, that is.
[2] Also known as "Machine Gun" Parker.

trench warfare. When he heard about the front-line plans, he was shocked.

"What," he bellowed, "sacrifice a single sacred foot of French soil to the Germans—NEVER! We will man all our trenches."

So he did. The only problem was the German reaction. They desperately wanted a large group of American prisoners for propaganda purposes. The policy of going into those first-line trenches in force was tailor-made for them, and it didn't take them long to find out about it. They had the high ground here, particularly a hill a short ways behind their lines. They could easily keep tabs on what was going on. They quickly put together a crack raiding party and hit the Americans in force. As I remember it, those Boche captured over a hundred men from the 26th Division.

Actually, the YD put up quite a scrap and retook all the ground that they had lost, but the damage had been done—the Germans had their propaganda tool. They took pictures of the American prisoners with their hands up and used as a caption, "Are these the men who are going to save the war for you?" Then they dropped the photos behind the French and British lines.

Well, this played right into the hands of our allies. They didn't want the Americans going into battle in division strength, anyway. They wanted to use us as replacements in their outfits. They used the Seicheprey raid to show Pershing what happened when the Americans were on their own. But they couldn't impress John J. [Pershing] with that argument.

KRAHNERT: That's right. Old Black Jack[3] wasn't going to take no crap from them. And I'll tell you something else: If the English and the French had tried to break up our 1st Division, they would have had a fight on their hands. Why, if they'd ever tried to put me in a division with those English from around London, there would have been hell to pay. If those cockneys could have won the war with their mouth, they would have done it years before.

THOMAS: George is right concerning the American feeling about going into British and French divisions. We wanted to fight in our own Army, no doubt about that; naturally, Pershing felt the same

[3] Pershing's nickname, gained when he had command of black troops early in his military career. He was also called "Nigger Jack."

way. And when they moved our division over to Picardy, near a village called Cantigny, he had his chance to show the world what we really could do.

You probably realize that John J. wasn't much of an orator, but when we first moved into that tough Cantigny front, he made a speech to the officers of the 1st Division that I don't think any of us forgot. We all gathered around him in a circle as he told us what we had to do successfully or there just might not be an American Army, as such, in France.

"You men," he pontificated, "will have to hold on until the last man is dead, if necessary. Even if your bones whiten on the fields of France, we must succeed!"

Oh ho, ho, that was a comforting thought, all right, but we'd received his message: We had to succeed at Cantigny.

KRAHNERT: Yes, well, that Cantigny was a hot spot though, even before our assault. The Germans kept throwing that damn gas at us —it was miserable. I went out into this field one morning to do you know what, and I made the mistake of using some grass to clean up. I got that damn mustard stuff on both my backside and my testicles. Christ, did it burn! My rear end still looks like it's petrified! As for the other part of my body, well, I fathered eight children after the war, so it couldn't have bothered me permanently. I never did report it as a wound—just kept bathing with GI soap.

In one way I was lucky, though. I didn't get any of it in my eyes. Colonel, do you remember that time we saw a line of men being led to the rear, each one with his hand on the shoulder of the man in front of him?

THOMAS: Yes, I do. Fortunately, the blindness the men would get from the mustard gas was almost always temporary. But it sure scared the hell out of them when they had it.

Well, the actual assault on Cantigny was as well planned as any you could think of. Robert Bullard was the divisional commander, but I've always felt that our artillery brigadier, Charles Summerall —who later commanded the division, incidentally—had a lot to do with the strategy.[4]

---

[4] Perhaps—but the later careers of many of the 1st Division officers read like an Army Who's Who—Bullard was to command the First Army; Summerall, the V Corps; and John Hines, the III Corps. Four other offi-

We did have a lucky break a few days before the boys went over. A young American engineering officer was wounded and captured by the Germans. He had the complete battle plans with him, but he'd falsified the date by a day or two. He had done this just in case he did get captured. He died while a prisoner, but we later found out that his ruse had worked: The Germans were expecting us on May 30.

The attack was on the twenty-eighth, however, and it went beautifully—a truly magnificent assault. It was led by a real fighting officer, Colonel Hanson Ely, commanding officer of the 28th Infantry. I don't think it took them more than three or four hours to reach all their objectives. But that was only the start. You could usually take a place in World War I if you used enough men and artillery. The trick was holding it. That's where my friend the sergeant comes into it. George, do you remember all that practice you had over at Menacourt?

KRAHNERT: You mean up in that church steeple, memorizing the grid co-ordinates? You bet I do! It sure came in handy at Cantigny.

THOMAS: We knew the Germans would have to counterattack. The psychological shock of being beaten by the Americans would have been devastating. Remember, they'd been pounding into their men's heads that the Americans were soft, decadent—not really any good at all. How was it going to look when the word went around that we had actually taken a key spot from them? They hit us with everything they had. But our 5th, 6th, and 7th Artillery were waiting for them.

KRAHNERT: And were they good! Their 155's could stop anybody. The 75's also—hell, our boys could handle them 75's like pistols! My job, you see, was to get out where I could see the location of their staging areas. As I remember, it was in the woods north of the village.

THOMAS: To do this, he had to work his way actually in front of our lines, and all the time dragging that damn equipment. How the

cers would command divisions. And, oh yes, the division's assistant chief of staff at Cantigny was a lieutenant colonel named George Catlett Marshall.

hell he wasn't killed, I don't know. How big were their attacks, George?

KRAHNERT: Big enough to wipe us out if they could overpower our front lines.

THOMAS: Well, Krahnert kept relaying those co-ordinates back to our guns, and they'd blast the hell out of the Germans. George, how long did this go on?

KRAHNERT: Three days; I think they tried it six times. But we stopped each attack.

THOMAS: Now, I'm not saying he did it all alone, but no one did any more to break up those counterattacks than Sergeant George Krahnert.

KRAHNERT: Well, I was a regular. I took my work very seriously. I'd gone in the Army, you see, when I was just seventeen, back in 1915. By the time the United States entered the war, I'd already had a couple of years of soldiering.

At that time I was down on the Mexican border at a place called Eagle Pass in Texas. My regiment was the 3rd U. S. Infantry, a real old Army outfit. Then when the word went around that the Army wanted to get a few regiments to France as soon as possible, myself and my good pal, Jim Clark, were two of the many regulars who volunteered. Good old Jim, just died a year or two ago, oh, he was a corker, all right, a real one-puncher. He'd had some duty in the artillery before the war, so they put him in charge of the one-pounders. When we were in combat all I had to do was relay a target back to Jim and it was good night, Fritzie.

I surely miss him. I guess most of all our old buddies are gone by now. I know Perez is gone, and so is Webber. I think the colonel over there is the only man I know from the old 1st Division.

THOMAS: Yes, George, the years go by. I can't think of anyone else left either.

KRAHNERT: But, for God's sake, Colonel, where did the years go to? Hell, we're old men now, but I don't feel that way. Why, I raised a large family, even have great-grandchildren, but it seems like yesterday that we went to war.

THOMAS: It does to me also. In 1916, when I first went to the Plattsburg camp—I can still remember the drill manual. And when they put me aboard that *Princess Irene* in 1917—hell, I can remember walking up the gangplank. Then, when we sailed, I kept watching New York City in the background—it kept getting smaller and smaller.

That ship, you see, the *Princess Irene,* turned out to be a real problem. It had been of German registry, and those Boche took real good care of us. They filled the gear boxes with emery powder. We were lucky to ever reach France.

Well, after we landed, they found out I could speak German. This sounded great to the staff, so they sent me off to a British intelligence operation they called snipers' school. Why in heaven's name they called it that I don't know. But when I joined the 26th Infantry, I was made intelligence officer. Then they told me to pick out twelve good men to form an intelligence section that would be attached to headquarters company. Nobody really knew what the hell intelligence was all about then, but I got the good men, especially George.

KRAHNERT: Colonel, you mention your trip over. How well I remember mine. It was in June of '17. We were the first bunch. I was on the *San Jacinto.* It wasn't much of a ship—a one-funneler, as I remember. We were packed like sardines. You couldn't have fit no more troops on her if you used a shoehorn.

And I'll tell you something else: I was a sergeant by then. As the ship pulled into Saint-Nazaire, I made sure I was the first man ashore. Hell, of all the Doughboys still living, I might be the first one that landed in France, as an American soldier, anyway.

THOMAS: I wouldn't be surprised, George; you were first in just about everything else.

Well, after I'd gone to all that trouble in picking my twelve good men, this old colonel called me in.

"Mr. Thomas," he said, "I don't believe in all this intelligence baloney. I'm disbanding your unit."

"Oh Christ," I said to myself. "All that work of mine for naught." I was furious; this was outrageous. I felt I'd better check with G-2. I picked up a phone as soon as I could. I can't remember whom I talked to, but he was as flabbergasted as I was.

"What?" he bellowed. "Listen, Thomas, you stay right where you are. I'll get there as soon as I can. How the hell can we win a war like this without any intelligence sector?"

It wasn't settled for a day or two, but we ended up keeping the intelligence group. Now, I bring this up just to show you how mixed up things could get when we were in France during 1917. The colonel wasn't a bad soldier; he just didn't understand the sophistication, if that's the word, of war the way it existed in France—it was a hell of a lot different than fighting the Moros in the Philippines.

KRAHNERT: You can bet the men were mad as hell when we heard we might be disbanded. We'd sized up Shipley Thomas as a man we wanted to serve with. After a few years of active duty, you can pretty well know if an officer is the type of man who will think of his men first. We'd all figured that the fellow sitting over there [Thomas] was tops. We had no desire to leave him, and we sure as hell didn't want to break up that happy-go-lucky group we had.

Oh they were really hot tickets. They were as good at finding where them Frogs were hiding their brandy and cognac as they were at finding the Germans.

And one time they really got me in the soup. One of the boys—oh, he was something, I'll tell you that—found all these bottles of champagne. Hell, I'd never had any of the stuff, didn't know nothing about it. Well, this night they'd given us beans for dinner—Christ, we was always getting beans—and we're drinking this champagne like water; you know, champagne doesn't give you any warning. I'm beginning to get a little light-headed, but I paid no attention, just kept eating those beans and drinking champagne.

Then, all of a sudden, wham, I take a Brodie, right on my face. But I still had the fork in my hand, see, and the damn thing ends up sticking in my nose. That's right, I wake up with the fork hanging out of my nose. The boys thought it was as funny as could be, but it hurt like hell. I haven't had champagne since—the hell with it!

THOMAS: Oh ho, ho, George, I should have gotten you the Purple Heart. But at least you were good boys, you didn't go to Bar-le-Duc.

KRAHNERT: *Of course not*, Colonel, that was out of bounds, haw, haw. Oh, to tell you the truth, I did sneak in there once—just to look around and get some cigarettes. But don't tell him [the author] about any of the boys who did go there. They might be still alive and so might be their wives; they'll catch hell.

I do have to ask you though, Colonel: Did you ever go to Bar-le-Duc?

THOMAS: Oc-ca-sionally, George, oc-ca-sionally, just to get cigarettes. But you did get a chance to get to Paris, didn't you, George?

KRAHNERT: I'll say I did, and that was something! I headed for this place called the American Bar. I'd heard about it from some of the boys. Well, I'd had several belts, and I was feeling pretty good—things were looking rosy, if you know what I mean. Then I went into the *salle de bain* to get rid of some of the cognac and there's this old fat gal squatting down. Hell, I thought I was in the wrong one, so I apologized and started to walk out, but she'd have none of it.

"Come on in, soldier," she said as she waved, "we all do it this way over here." She was an American, can you beat that? But it didn't make no difference to the people over there—men and women used the same toilets.

THOMAS: Ho, ho, George, that's right, and how about those small places where you had to hit the hole?

KRAHNERT: That's right, I remember them too. There was another night when I'd had several drinks and, haw, haw, I couldn't get my co-ordinates right. Oh, I'd never been able to zero in on the Heinies that night.

THOMAS: But you did at Cantigny, George, that's what counted.

Well, after they thought the men were trained enough, they sent the 1st Division into the lines. I think it was near Sommerville. It was in November of 1917. I can't remember it as being very exciting for us, but it did provide the first battle deaths for the U. S. Army in the War. The Boche pulled a raid on our 16th Infantry and killed three men: James Gresham, Thomas Enright and Merle Hays. Three men didn't mean much later on, but they surely did then.[5]

[5] Walter Guild of the 102nd Machine Gun Battalion of the 26th Division remembers hearing about this. He said the news spread throughout the infant AEF like wildfire.

After our stay in the trenches there we went over to the Toul Sector. That's where we were relieved by the 26th Division, just prior to our moving to Picardy and that assault at Cantigny where George did such a great job.

KRAHNERT: Yes, well after Cantigny came the real big fight—Soissons, where we turned the war around. But Christ, what a bloodletting it was!

THOMAS: Oh it certainly was. Actually, the battle was southeast of Soissons. We were to push over to the Soissons–Château-Thierry Road. This was the big show, for all our regiments, the 16th, 18th, 26th, and 28th. Everybody took it on the chin here. We were never really the same after that fight. We went into it on the morning of July 18. We were on the top of the line with a French Moroccan division on our right.

KRAHNERT: Oh those Moroccans, they had them Senegalese troops, they'd go over the top with rib-stickers in their mouths, looking like pirates. They were tough, but I'll never forgive them for ruining our telescopes. God, every time I think of it, I still get sore! We had two of these telescopes, a matched pair—we'd captured them from the Heinies.

THOMAS: Now, wait a minute, George, I remember when we nabbed them. The two of us had discovered where they were, across from us on the big hill. I said to you, "George, get some of the boys and go over and nail them, but no fighting. I don't want anyone killed."

And I'll be damned if you didn't do it—didn't lose a man. Oh, they were beauties, much better than anything we had.

KRAHNERT: I'll say they were, you could move 'em up and down, sideways, any damn way you wanted to. I had big hopes for those babies. But those damn Senegalese, they threw a monkey wrench in our plans.

That night our crew was sleeping in a cave. I figured if I stored the two telescopes at the entrance to it, they'd be safe. Not on your life! Those damn Senegalese came by and took them apart—threw the pieces all over the place. I guess they didn't know what they were. Anyway, the telescopes weren't any good after that. It was a crying shame!

THOMAS: Well, let's get back to Soissons. You don't hear much about it now, but it turned the whole war around. But what a price we paid! It was five of the roughest days you could imagine. Just push, push, push. I think we gained eight miles. But more than that, we stopped any chance the Germans had of another offensive.

KRAHNERT: That's right, it was push, push, push. And all the time we were trying to keep up with the infantry. Christ, it seemed every one of them Heinies had a cannon or a machine gun. They'd use those Maxims like a sickle. And they'd always shoot low. This way, if they hit you in the legs, it would take a couple of men to take care of you. If they got you in the chest—well, one man in a bulldozer could take care of hundreds. I can remember seeing one of their fire patterns hitting the ground about ten yards in front of me. If I'd been moving a little faster, I would have caught one.

The Germans did get me at Soissons, though, only with shrapnel, not a chopper. I had moved out in front of our infantry and was looking for targets when a shell landed over on my left. This ball bearing went right through my leg—I still have the goddamn thing. But thank God it wasn't any closer—it would have taken my leg off, or maybe even my head. But that was the end of Soissons for me.

THOMAS: Oh, we lost so many good men there. Of course, a lot of them, like George, were wounded, not killed—and most of those came back to us. But we were shot up ever so badly. I'll never forget my phone conversation on that last day with General Summerall; it'll show you what shape we were in. Actually, I was trying to get the divisional adjutant, but Summerall, who'd just been made divisional commander a day or so before Soissons, had grabbed the phone.

"Hello," he bellowed, "this is General Summerall. Who is this?"

"Lieutenant Thomas, sir, 26th Infantry."

"Well, how are things?"

"I have to report that we have broken through as far as we can. Our colonel is dead, our lieutenant colonel is dead, and all majors are dead or wounded. And God knows how many captains and lieutenants are down. And the situation with the men is just as bad."

"Good God, Mr. Thomas, who is commanding the regiment?"

"Captain Barney Legge."

"How is he doing?"

"Fine, sir, with what he has left."

"Well, who is his executive officer?"

"I guess I am. I'm still in one piece, anyway. We can hold, but we can't advance."

"Mr. Thomas, the 15th Scottish Division is on its way to relieve you. Tell Captain Legge when you're relieved to take the men back to such-and-such a place. I want to salute them. We'll have food there. Is there anything else we could do for them?"

"Could you get them a band? Maybe it might perk them up some."

Well, we got there—what was left of us, anyway. The old general had the band from the 5th Artillery there—they were playing "The National Emblem" march. Of course, the companies were coming up piecemeal, not all at once. The general took one look at them and turned over to the band.

"You will keep playing 'The National Emblem' march until all of the 26th U. S. Infantry has passed by."

It took more than two hours. Then, at the very end, this young lad came by; he couldn't have been more than eighteen or nineteen years old. He was marching in front of this handful of men. I can see him now, giving General Summerall a snappy rifle salute.

"Company E, 26th Infantry, sir, Pfc Smith commanding, seventeen men fit for duty."

Dear God, they'd gone into Soissons 250 strong!

[This vision from the past shook Colonel Thomas up a bit. We had to take a break while all of us consumed some brandy to get things going again.]

THOMAS: [continues] It was the end of the review, so we went over to where they had the rations. Keep in mind we hadn't had any hot food for five days. Being the Army, they had brought supplies for a full regiment. As I recall, there were hundreds and hundreds of wheat cakes. Most of the men had taken a little and then just gone to sleep. Not young Pfc Smith. He took one look at all that chow, quickly turned command of his company over to a mess sergeant, and dug into those flapjacks. He was still at it when we left. That was a pretty good outfit we had.

KRAHNERT: Oh, that Smith was all 26th, all right. During our training we'd all done a lot of that command business. The officers would leave us with a different guy in charge each time. This was so we'd be ready when the time came if we had to take command.

The spirit we had in the 26th, the whole 1st Division, was really something. Once you were a part of the 1st, you wanted to stay. Take my case. After they sent me to the hospital, I found out that they were going to shanghai me—send me over to another outfit. I could have even got a commission out of it. No sir, nix on that, I wasn't leaving my outfit.

Now, I knew there were plenty of other men from the 26th those pill pushers were going to do the same thing to. So I went over to one of them to find out how he felt about it.

"Listen," I told him, "do you know when you're discharged from this place, they're going to send you to a new outfit?"

"The hell, you say," he roared, "I come over with the 1st Division and I'm going back with it, come hell or high water. Of course, I may get my head shot off, but I'm staying with the 1st."

You know something? I was able to get a whole crew together. We just took off—went back to the 1st. Christ, some of the men still had bandages on. Hell, my own leg kept draining for the rest of the war. But leave the 1st—baloney!

THOMAS: Ho, ho, ho! That's right; I remember when George came back. We had a lot of the men do just that. The No. 1 case was none other than Theodore Roosevelt, Jr. He'd been hit in the thigh. Why, he could hardly move his leg. But he had heard we were going back into the lines, I think it was about the time of the Meuse-Argonne, so he pilfered a sidecar from somewhere and got someone to drive him up to where the 26th Infantry was. Teddy wasn't going to miss out on anything, you can bet on that.

Well, when he arrived, everybody told him how great it was to have him back. Then someone asked an awkward question:

"Ted, let's see your orders."

"Orders, hell, I've got no orders. I'm here AWOL!"

And that's the way he commanded the 26th Infantry at the end of the war, AWOL from the hospital. Oh, I suppose it had been all fixed up by then, but that's what the boys used to have to say, "Colonel Theodore Roosevelt, commanding AWOL."

But I'll tell you one thing: We had to carry him into battle. I know this is true; I helped to do it several times.

KRAHNERT: Yeah, that's when we had that mixup around Sedan. Oh were the boys riled up about that! We were all ready to take that damn place when we had to let some French outfit get the credit for it.

THOMAS: Yes, but those French had been fighting all those years. I can recall when one of their colonels came over to us—he was terribly upset.

"Gentlemen," he said, "I am from Sedan, my regiment is from Sedan, it's where we surrendered to the Germans during our last war with the Boche. God knows what my soldiers will do if you get between us and Sedan."

So one of our generals said, "O.K., brother, if it means so much to you, go ahead." It seems to me they ended up going in one side and we went in the other.

KRAHNERT: Yeah, but none of our boys felt very good when we had to leave them leapfrog us that way.

THOMAS: Well, it was almost over then, though. And that was something, when it did end! I was with Colonel Roosevelt. As a matter of fact, four of our men had been killed in the very same spot where we were now resting just a few hours before. Then this car drove up and out stepped this young lady.

"Ted," she said, "the war's over!" It was his wife. She was in France with the Red Cross and had borrowed a general's car to come see her husband. So we helped her pack Ted into the car.

Now, naturally, the word spread like wildfire. And as we were carrying Ted into the car, this Doughboy came over and buttonholed the limousine's chauffeur.

"Want to buy my gas mask?" he asked the driver.

Oh you couldn't beat the 26th; no, sir!

The AEF Division

In World War I the AEF operated with what they called "The Square Division." One of these huge units would contain four infantry regiments, each of which would have a complement of thirty-six hundred men. Two of these regiments would make up an infantry brigade, giving each division two brigades of infantry, which would constitute the fighting core of the division.

In addition to the infantry regiments there were twenty-two other units in each division. Here is the alignment of the 26th (Yankee) Division, which shows the formula for an AEF division:

1. 51st Infantry Brigade
2. 101st Infantry
3. 101st Ambulance Company
4. 101st Field Hospital
5. 101st Field Artillery
6. 103rd Ambulance Company
7. 103rd Field Hospital
8. 102nd Infantry
9. 104th Field Hospital
10. 51st Field Artillery Brigade
11. 102nd Field Artillery
12. 101st Field Signal Battalion
13. 102nd Machine Gun Battalion
14. 103rd Infantry
15. 101st Supply Train
16. 101st Engineers

17. 102nd Ambulance Company
18. 104th Ambulance Company
19. 52nd Infantry Brigade
20. 104th Infantry
21. 103rd Machine Gun Battalion
22. 102nd Field Hospital
23. Division Headquarters
24. Headquarters Troop
25. 101st Machine Gun Battalion
26. 101st Train Headquarters and Military Police

The total complement of each division would be twenty-eight thousand men. Once a division would get into combat it became impossible for the replacements to keep up with the attrition. Nevertheless, the average American division was always between two and three times the size of those of the French, British, and Germans. In their planning the practical French would normally count each U.S. division as a corps.

This discrepancy in numbers would frequently cause confusion that could result in the Americans not receiving their just due. For instance, when talking about the great British offensive in the latter part of September 1918, English writers will usually state in a throwaway manner, "Oh yes, there were also two American divisions there."

This is correct. But these two—the 27th and 30th—were equal in size to five British divisions. And on September 29 these Americans went right into the middle of the Saint Quentin Tunnel mess.

As for the fighting quality of these American divisions, they seem to have made up what they lacked in experience with enthusiasm. Ten of them suffered over ten thousand casualties, with the 1st and 2nd suffering the most; they both had well over twenty thousand dead and wounded. The other seven who lost over ten thousand men through enemy action were the 3rd, 4th, 26th, 28th, 32nd, 42nd, and 77th. There were some thirteen other divisions who suffered over five thousand casualties: the 5th, 27th, 29th, 30th, 33rd, 35th, 78th, 79th, 80th, 82nd, 89th, 90th, and 91st. The results here are quite predictable. If the division fought in both the second Marne and the Meuse-Argonne, its casualties went over the ten-thousand mark; if most of its combat was just "up in the Argonne," its losses were between five thousand and ten thousand men. There were other outfits, such as the 36th Division, that lost close to three thousand men in two weeks, and the 369th Infantry Regiment (Colored), which spent 191 days facing the Germans, but in the main it was the twenty-two divisions who each lost over five thousand men in France that carried the large bulk of the combat burden for the AEF.

The 1st Division's Vermonter

Jeremiah M. Evarts

HIS APARTMENT—NEW YORK CITY—APRIL 1977
World War I veteran Jerry Evarts followed a course that was to be so prevalent among millions of ex-servicemen in succeeding wars—to wit, he went back to school. In his case it was law school. This was followed by a very successful legal career in both his native Vermont and New York City. In Vermont he also served in the state legislative body, and in New York City he was a member of the Corporation Council's office.

"I remember my position in the Corporation Council vividly because La Guardia was going to fire me every five minutes," recalled Mr. Evarts. "He was a real dynamo."

There was another thing that Jerry remembered very well; as a matter of fact, he couldn't get it out of his mind: This was his service at Cantigny and Soissons. In 1938 he decided to put it all down on paper. The result was a beautiful little book, *Cantigny*, containing fifteen episodes from his memories of the war. It is long out of print. Anyone lucky enough to own a copy should treasure it dearly.

Mr. Evarts now lives comfortably in a Greenwich Village apartment with his charming wife of many years. His hospitality, Bourbon, and recall are all excellent.

"You know," he told me, "many years after the war I had this terrible spasm in my lower back. It was bad enough to send me to

Lenox Hill Hospital on a stretcher. Here I came under the care of a
Dr. Jordan. He was a great guy and an outstanding doctor. It took
him about a week to straighten me out. Then he decided it was
time for a little chat.

"'Mr. Evarts,' he said, 'I read that very interesting book of yours,
Cantigny. I was at that battle myself as a flier, and also at Soissons.'

"'Oh,' I answered, 'well, I can't remember seeing too many of
our planes there.'

"Then he kind of smiled.

"'Jerry,' he chuckled, 'I was in what had been Richthofen's Flying Circus. I was on the other side.'

"Oh, didn't we laugh about that! In 1918 he was shooting at me,
and thirty years later he was fixing me up. It can be a strange
world."

Captain Jeremiah M. Evarts
E Company, 18th Infantry, 1st Division

On this war men will think and write for a thousand
years. They will. And the things that will concern, interest
and fill the thoughts of the great bulk of humanity who
do think and want to know, will not be the great battles,
not the tactics and the strategy of generals and mighty
armies, but such human feelings and actions as fill these
little stories.

—ROBERT LEE BULLARD,
LIEUTENANT GENERAL (RET.),
FROM THE PREFACE OF
JEREMIAH EVARTS' PRIVATELY
PRINTED BOOK *Cantigny*.

When I went through the officers' training camp at Plattsburg the first time, they told me I was too young to be commissioned. I didn't really know what they were talking about, but later that fall (1917) they made me a first lieutenant. So everything ended up all right anyway, and they certainly didn't waste any time getting me overseas—by January, I was aboard the *Mongolia* and on my way.

When I first arrived in France, I was sent to the French infantry tactical school at Chatillon-sur-Seine. This gave me a chance to get a feel on what was really going on over there from men who had been fighting the Kaiser's soldiers since 1914. Then I was assigned to the 18th Infantry of the 1st Division of the AEF. But in the meantime, this French officer at the school offered me a wonderful opportunity.

"How would you like to serve three weeks on the front lines with one of France's finest regiments before reporting to your country's own division?" he asked. "It can be arranged."

"Oh I certainly would!" I answered.

Now, how in heaven's name he pulled this off I don't know, but I ended up spending the last part of March and the first part of April in 1918 with the 83rd French Regiment in the Argonne Sector near Vauquois. Naturally, I had no way of knowing how much fighting the Americans would be doing in that same area during the coming fall.[1]

The 83rd was also known as "The Regiment of Lafayette." Its fight at Fort Douaumont during the Battle of Verdun had become legendary. When it had been pulled out of the lines there, it had four officers fit for duty. We hear a lot in the United States about the famous old British regiments. We don't seem to realize that the French have some great ones also. Remember, that's where the term *esprit de corps* comes from.

My job here was to observe—to see what the war was really all about. After all, I was soon to have command of a platoon on the lines, which is quite a responsibility. The help I received from those French officers did turn out to be very valuable when I took com-

[1] Vauquois is the area where a feisty, bespectacled artillery officer named Harry Truman was to give the Germans hell, and a young lieutenant colonel named George Patton was to be almost killed learning the grass roots of tank warfare.

mand of my own unit. There was one of them in particular who had an uncanny knack of cutting through to the core of a matter.

"Monsieur Evarts," he would say to me, "as an infantry officer you have one all-important task: That is to go from Point A to Point B in the time allotted with as many men as possible."

Hell, some officers would take all day trying to explain that; he did it in thirty seconds.

Now, as you may know, they had experienced a great deal of trouble in the French Army in 1917—the mutinies and all that. However, this seemed to have quieted down by March of '18. One of their officers had a pretty good explanation for it.

"You must remember," he stated, "how much and for how long our Army had bled, and for results that had only succeeded in maintaining the status quo. I think," he continued, "that Nivelle's offensive on the Chemin des Dames was the breaking point. So much was expected. Then when the results ended in nothing but more slaughter, many of the men just snapped."[2]

Well, there were certainly no signs of a mutiny when I was with the 83rd. They pulled off a raid on the Germans that produced results so magnificent as to befuddle the mind. They centered in on a section of the Boche lines and came back with hundreds of prisoners. They only lost four of their own men. Can you imagine that? I had wanted desperately to go on that assault, but the French weren't going to take any chances of losing a young American officer that early in the game.

A day or two after the attack I was taken down to a front-line observation post where I met this artillery officer.

"Here," he said, "look through this telescope toward the German lines and tell me what you see."

"Two heavy-caliber guns," I answered, "that have been blown up."

"That's right, but you didn't notice the two in the distance that were intact. Our intelligence group worked on this attack in great

[2] Robert Nivelle was a very charismatic French general who led the French offensive of April 1917. The Germans knew of his plans and slaughtered the Poilu. The French suffered some eighty thousand casualties the first two days. The result was the mutiny of over one hundred thousand French troops. Incredibly, the outstanding German intelligence did not know of the disorders.

detail. They figured that the two guns that we did demolish were the ones that could butcher our men. They were right. Always remember, thorough preparation is a necessity for a successful assault."

Another thing I can recall about the French was my visit with General Maxime Weyand.[3] Apparently he had wanted to size up what a young American officer was like. And he didn't miss a trick. Oh, he was an absolutely brilliant officer. After he treated me to a delicious luncheon, he took me into an elaborate dugout. The walls were covered with detailed maps on the coming summer offensive. Obviously the French expected the Americans to play a big part in the coming fight. After we discussed the complicated strategies of moving hundreds of thousands of men, General Weyand took me outside for a lecture on deploying a platoon. He was quite a soldier.

Well, Weyand may have been thinking about the summer offensive—after all, he was Foch's right-hand man—but the immediate threat was the German assault that had hit the British Fifth Army and was driving toward Amiens. The Boche's aim was to push the English into the sea, and they gave it a very strong try. As a matter of fact, they might have done it if their soldiers hadn't liberated so much wine. Those Heinies, you see, were as worn out as the Allies. And when they started to capture villages, they had their first shot in years at some good French liquid. Half of them ended up too drunk to go any farther.

In spite of this dilly-dallying, the German drive was tremendously fierce, annihilating the major part of Gough's British Fifth Army and severely punishing their Third Army. In a dramatic move, Pershing offered everything the Americans had to help stem the tide. In reality it wasn't much—probably four divisions[4]—with the 1st Division in the most advanced state of readiness.

This was the situation then when I joined the 18th U. S. Infantry of the 1st over near Gondrecourt. My stay there was little more than a stopover. In the middle of April they piled the regiment on those luxurious 40 and 8's and headed us for Paris. Then, at a place called Pontoise, a little north of Paree, they dropped us off, and we

[3] Called Foch's shadow in 1918, he was in command of the French Army in 1940 when it was crushed by Hitler's blitz.

[4] By April 1, four American divisions—the 1st, 2nd, 26th, and 42nd—were ready.

began hiking. Our destination was the village of Villers Tournelles. This was it! We were now next to a small fortified village occupied by the Germans. It was what we called a real hot spot. The French Moroccan troops we relieved had been in and out of the damn place four or five times in recent weeks. It was named Cantigny.

My command here was the 4th Platoon of E Company. Most of its soldiers came from the Midwest, and in my books there never was a finer platoon in the U. S. Army. It served on the front lines here from April 23 until May 10 and from May 21 to June 1. And when I say "front lines," I mean it. During the six weeks or so the 1st Division was actively engaged here, the Germans threw an average of over ten thousand shells a day at us—and that's one hell of a lot.

We had our own 1st Division's three artillery regiments here also, and you can bet they returned the Boche's calling cards in spades. In addition to our batteries, the French had a regiment of naval guns several miles behind the lines. They would fire these big babies from a wooded ravine all the way across the salient to an area near Amiens. Our American artillery was coincided to fire every time the French would let go. This way we figured it would be twice as hard for the Germans to locate those French giants.

Naturally, the Germans would reply in kind against us. Christ, I don't think they let a night go by without hitting us—sometimes shrapnel, sometimes gas. They fired so many mustard gas shells one night that an actual gas pond formed in a gully. And that mustard stuff was horrible. Many times you wouldn't even know it was there until it had burned the hell out of you.

Many of our men were gassed there, including myself. I picked up a dose of what is called arsine gas. It was loaded with arsenic. If enough of it formed in the back of your mouth, it would eat through to your brain and kill you. But it was very volatile. Most of what I picked up I swallowed, so it ended up in my gut. I didn't get that damn arsenic out of my system until November. I went through that mess at Cantigny and Soissons with my stomach lined with it. Not only would it burn like the devil, but it played havoc with my bowels. I never knew when I'd be caught short.

All this gas was bad enough, but the living conditions weren't any bargain either. Our trenches were only about four feet deep, and any time we'd try and improve them, wham, over would come a 77; worse still, perhaps a 155. We had no latrines, no protection from the rain, and no real communication with headquarters—just with those damn German guns. And this was constant.

I recall one shell in particular that killed two men from my platoon and horribly wounded a third. We tried to cheer the poor guy up but with little success. He had at least twenty nasty wounds. As there was no way to get him back to a field hospital, all we could do was watch him die. It was rather rough stuff.

Well, as I think you can see, living like this could really drive you loco. And, even worse, it could discourage you to an incredible degree. Take my good friend Jim Palache. He had gone through Plattsburg with me, and we were also shipmates on the *Mongolia*. Here at Cantigny he'd ended up in charge of E Company's 2nd Platoon. After we'd spent about three weeks in that particular kind of hell, he'd begun to really feel the pressure in a matter-of-fact way. Finally, late one afternoon he gave me this resigned type of look.

"Jerry," he lamented, "my time is just about up. It won't be long now."

"Oh come on, Jim," I answered, "can that crap; you know it's bad luck."

"I know, I know, but hell, I'm telling you, that's it, and pretty soon."

Now, we were over in my 4th Platoon's trench area. You see, about every day one of us would crawl over to the other's station so we could compare notes. And on this particular day, just after he'd sung his song of woe, we spotted an airplane with French markings flying over our area about three hundred yards away. It didn't take us long to figure out that the plane was not French.[5]

"Jim," I pointed out, "can you see what that son-of-a-bitch is doing?"

"I surely can: He's laying a smoke screen on the trench where we have our machine guns."

"That's right, and look: Now he's next to your 2nd Platoon's area."

Then a high burst came over. It exploded near an apple tree right where Jim's men were. It wasn't expected to hit anyone—it

[5] A very common German trick.

was merely a range-finding. That would be where they'd zero in that evening.

"Listen, Jim," I said, "get your men and crawl over to my trench tonight. You know damn well what they're going to do."

"Thanks, Jerry, but what the hell, if it doesn't happen tonight, it'll be tomorrow."

"Aw, come on, don't be that way, come on over."

But he wouldn't budge. He felt his duty was to be in his own trench, and that's all there was to it.

Well, sure enough, at about ten o'clock the ball opened. First it was the long stuff going into Villers Tournelles, then our guns going after the Germans. At about eleven-thirty the Boche landed a 155 right on our machine-gun position. You could hear the poor guys moaning. Then a big one exploded at the bottom of the apple tree.

It took an hour or two before a relief group could get up to Jim's trench. I can vividly remember his platoon coming out because some of the men were sobbing. Jim didn't come out. And every time from then on that I began to feel I was going to catch one, I'd say to myself, "Baloney, you're going to make it!" And I did.

I felt quite badly about Jim's death. That was one of the toughest things about our existence there. You were bound to get very close to your buddies, which made it hell if they went West. And if you were an officer, you could get very protective about your men. This feeling would have cost me a court-martial one time if it weren't for the fact that the 18th had a great colonel in Frank Parker, a splendid South Carolinian gentleman. Damn it, though, I was right! Judge for yourself.

Here, let me show you in this book.[6] You can see this small trench sticking out like a salient. It was completely exposed, a very bad spot indeed. I figured the Germans had left it alone so they could use it for a prisoner-nabbing raid. I had placed a squad there under a corporal named Cesack. Now, over here I had set up a machine gun. This way, if the Heinies did hit Cesack, the gun could knock the hell out of them.

Well, one night—much to my disgust, I might add—a couple of French officers from corps headquarters came up to tell me that I

[6] Evart's book *Cantigny* has a diagram showing his platoon's trench section.

had to move my machine gun. The place I was supposed to put it made it impossible to cover Cesack's men. I tried to point out that if I did this, I'd probably lose a whole squad. But there were no ifs or buts; I was ordered to move the gun.

After they left, I gave it a lot of thought and finally said to myself, "The hell with 'em! I'm in command of this platoon, and I'm not going to sacrifice Cesack and his men for a whim." Then about two nights later Colonel Parker came up to my area. He was always moving in and out of the trenches. Parker was no dugout colonel.

"Evarts," he greeted me, "you haven't moved that Hotchkiss gun. Why not?"

"Colonel," I answered, "about a week ago I showed you where Cesack's trench is. If I take that gun away, he'll be naked as a jaybird. Would you leave him out there like that if you were in my shoes?" The colonel seemed to reflect on this for a minute.

"Evarts," he finally said, "carry on."

That's the kind of soldier Parker was. He'd go to blazes for you if you were right. But heaven help you if you were wrong.

And I'll tell you something else about Parker. He later took over command of the division near the end of the war. He was the one in charge when the 1st went through another American division on their way to take Sedan. Oh, this caused all kinds of repercussions. There was a French outfit that wanted to take it also. I was back in the States at the time, but I heard all about it. I was told that Pershing was absolutely livid—swore up and down that as long as he [Pershing] was in the Army, Parker would never get another promotion. It worked out all right in the long run, but Black Jack had one hell of a temper.

Well, back to Cantigny and another problem we had, the German air superiority. It seemed to us that their planes could come and go at their pleasure. It became a real pain in the neck for our troops, particularly as we felt so helpless about it.

Then, believe it or not, some Allied planes appeared and shot one of the Germans down; he made a crash-landing a short ways behind our lines. The pilot figured the war was over for him, so he climbed out of the plane with his hands in the air. Bang, one of our men shot him right in the heart. I was mortified and infuriated. I was going to roast the man who did it.

"What the hell's the matter with you?" I yelled at him. "You could see he was surrendering."

"Lieutenant," he answered, "the next time one of those fliers starts to shoot at us from a few hundred yards up in the sky, put your hands up; see if it does any good."

I hated what I had seen happen, but I had to acknowledge there was some logic there. I know it's pretty callous logic, but it shows you what living the way we were was doing to the minds of our men.

Take the case of Private Johnson.[7] He'd been almost killed by a shell that had blown a couple of his buddies sky high. It had been too much for him. Every time we'd get shelled after that, he'd go to pieces. I had a great sergeant at that time named James, who'd become very concerned about Johnson.

"Lieutenant," he reported, "Johnson is driving the other men nuts. They say they're going to shoot him if he doesn't shut up."

Oh this was a pretty kettle of fish. It had been raining for close to a week, and we were getting shelled every night; I had enough trouble without this.

"Send him to me, James," I said. "I'll see what I can do for him."

So over came Johnson. I tried to reason with him.

"Look, Johnson," I said, "here's the way it is. You've got to get ahold of yourself. The odds are still in your favor. I'm just as scared as you are, you know."

"I know, Lieutenant, I know," he pleaded. "I just seem to collapse when they start coming over. I can't seem to help it."

Well, I figured anyone as honest as that was no coward. I decided to keep him with me for a few days to see if I could straighten him out. He was pretty bad at first—whimpering, shaking, praying out loud, and actually bawling. But as the days went by, he seemed to snap out of it. After a week or so I sent him back to his squad, and he soldiered as well as anybody. I wish I could tell you that the story had a happy ending, but he was killed at Soissons in July. He was moving forward when he was hit.

Well, on May 28 the 28th Infantry of our division took Cantigny. They'd spent a good deal of time behind our lines practicing the as-

[7] Not his real name. The Johnson episode is described in detail in Evarts' book.

sault, and everything went like clockwork. The Germans put everything they had into several counterattacks but were stopped cold. It
was the first successful American assault of the war.

An interesting sidelight to the battle was the attitude of the
French Poilu. After our victory at Cantigny they actually started to
salute us. Most of them knew about the thousands of Americans
landing daily. They were beginning to realize that we could indeed
turn the tide.

But the Germans didn't know this. At the same time that we were
throwing back their counterattacks, the Boche were roaring across
the Chemin des Dames, heading for the Marne. The 1st Division's
biggest test was still ahead of us.

Sometime in June I was forced to turn to our doctors for some
help on my stomach. They did what they could, but it was obvious
that I needed a long rest. I ended up on a hospital train with all
these other casualties, and what a mess they were. Actually, I was
beginning to feel a little better, so I figured, what the hell, I might
as well take a little time off, then head back to the 18th.

There was another officer on the train who felt the same way I
did, so we just picked a good spot and got off. Then we ran into
some luck. A camion came by with three British sergeants, who
offered to give us a lift. We climbed aboard and soon found that
they had an ample supply of ham and whiskey. Oh this was great,
driving along and digging into the ham and drinking that whiskey.
The only trouble was what it did to my stomach. God Almighty,
was I sick! They let us off at a hotel in Beauvais, where I tried to
put myself together. I spent a week or two here. Then I decided it
was time to get back to the 18th. I knew something was probably
brewing with all the fighting that had been going on around the
Marne, but I didn't realize what I was going back to. It ended up
being the Battle of Soissons.

Now, the British can talk all they want about August 8 being the
turning point of the war, but as far as I'm concerned, it was July 18
at Soissons; there was no way the Germans could ever launch another offensive after that. But, my God, our division paid a tremendous price for those five days.[8]

The starting hour for our jumping off was 4:30 A.M. on the morn-

[8] The 1st Division suffered over 8,000 casualties during their five days
in the battle.

ing of July 18. On our right were some French colonial troops, including a regiment from their Foreign Legion, and the American 2nd Division was to the right of the French. Over on our left were our brigademates, the 16th U. S. Infantry and next to them the 26th and 28th—all four regiments of the 1st Division were involved. We were part of the XX French Corps.[9] There were three other French divisions in the corps: the 153rd, 87th, and 60th. But remember, our divisions were two or three times the size of the French ones; the heart of the attack was the Americans.

We'd all marched into position the night of the seventeenth—a dark, dreary affair, with plenty of rain and confusion. The whole idea was to make sure the Germans didn't expect an assault in force. What something like this always means is plain havoc. The men in the line don't really know what the hell is going on. I could hear all types of grousing. However, there was one thing we all knew: if we kept moving east, we'd meet the Germans. We did—shortly after dawn on the eighteenth.

We were originally in reserve, but in a push like that everyone starts taking casualties immediately. The first day wasn't that bad, though. The real carnage started on the nineteenth, when the Boche artillery opened up in earnest. They were still in a state of shock over their recent offensive bogging down, but they knew one thing: They had to stop our attack or they were in real trouble.

It was incredible, the enormous amount of artillery fire they threw at us. You could see their artillery shooting at us from across the Chemin des Dames. And, by God, I'll tell you that you never saw any heavier artillery fire against infantry than what those Germans put on us south of Soissons. I can't possibly express to you how tremendous it was! The noise from our artillery and from theirs actually blew out one of my eardrums. I saw an awful lot of artillery fire, but nothing like that. When you mention the large amount of casualties we took here, remember: Hundreds of our men were just blown to pieces. It was a nightmare! The miracle was not only that any of us survived but that we could keep moving.

Here, let me get a map.[10] Now, this village was called Berzy le

[9] Nicknamed the Iron Corps in the French Army.
[10] The American Battle Monuments Commission's map of the 1st Division at Soissons.

Sec. I was standing here on a hill looking toward the place. Next to me was the correspondent Floyd Gibbon,[11]—you know the fellow, he'd lost an eye at Belleau Wood. We could see what a tough nut our division was faced with. Gibbon was particularly concerned about one spot and so was I.

"Look, Evarts," he pointed, "that wheat field—it's loaded with machine guns. It's almost impossible for anything to get by that."

"I know, I know," I answered, "that's why they broke our first attack. It's suicidal."

At about this time a high-ranking French artillery officer came up to us. He had a few of his men with him, and they were carrying four different telephones.

"Gentlemen," he said, "I must find your chief of operations. I can demolish that wheat field if I can get his permission."

"Oh that's General Buck," I said. "He's down there setting up another attack."

You see, the artillery officer couldn't start a barrage unless our chief operations officer knew about it—our attacking group might run right into it.

Now, this was the third day of the battle. And I understand that Summerall, then commanding the division, had told Buck to go over there and take Berzy le Sec or he'd send him back to Blois in disgrace.[12]

Oh that was a dreadful thing to do. You should not have had a brigadier general down there acting like a junior officer. He had too many other decisions to make. But that's what happened. We had been moved over toward the left flank in reserve by the time they took the place, but I was told that General Buck ended up taking it with *eighteen* men. He had a rifle in his hands at the time.

We were finally relieved on July 23, after five days. During that period we were almost constantly on the attack. We'd driven the Germans back over eight miles, and in World War I terms this was a huge gain. We'd captured almost four thousand of the Kaiser's

[11] Author of *They Thought We Wouldn't Fight,* a splendid account of his experiences in France.

[12] Blois was set up by Pershing as a reassignment area for officers. Those sent there were frequently sent home, and not in good graces. The very name was hated by most officers.

best troops and killed God knows how many.[13] From then on the Americans were almost always moving forward.

The group that relieved us was the 15th Scottish Division. They marched those jocks right into the lines to the tune of bagpipes. It was a great sight, but it sure as hell was an invitation to those German gunners. Frankly, I think it was criminal. Many of the Scots were killed who probably would not have been if they had moved into their positions a bit more discreetly.

Shortly before we pulled out, I was standing on a ridge with one of the Scottish officers. All of a sudden, out of nowhere, a volley of 155's crashed down on a junction of the Soissons–Paris railroad. One minute we could see this junction, and the next one it was completely gone—those Boche had hit it right on the button. My British friend was quite impressed.

"Is it like that here often?" he asked.

"All the time," I answered, "like clockwork." Then I headed for the rear.

The battle had naturally taken a hell of a lot out of the 1st Division. We were moved over to a place called Pont-à-Mousson to tidy ourselves up and to take in replacements. The 1st still had a lot of war left; Saint Mihiel and the Argonne were just around the corner. But not for me. My stomach kept bothering me. My weight was down to 115 pounds. There was nothing else to do but go home, and in September I sailed back to the United States. It wasn't until the end of November that I was back on my feet.

There is one more thing about France that I should tell you. You may remember my mentioning a great sergeant I had named James. Good sergeants are of tremendous help to a young lieutenant. I was immensely lucky in having in James one of the very best. He was a born leader. His ability to keep the men on their toes was uncanny. When you went through what we had at Cantigny and that catastrophic affair at Soissons, it was tough enough to make sure the men kept their sanity, much less to keep them acting like a military unit.

Well, the two of us had devised a way of occupying our time in April and May during all the shelling. We'd discuss an evening we

[13] They also captured seventy-five pieces of artillery, fifty trench mortars, and five hundred machine guns.

were going to have on the town when we got back to New York
City. It would start out with a dinner at Delmonico's. We'd decide
on the wines and the courses, then we'd go into what we'd do next.
It would be a little different each time, but we'd always agree to
start at Delmonico's.

Oh, I had my dinner at Delmonico's after I got home, all right,
and many more there later. But without James. He was killed the
fourth day at Soissons. God Almighty, how I wished he could have
been at Delmonico's with me!

Vive Pair-shang

Yes, Marshal Foch, we want very much to be in the
offensive, but as an American Army.

—GENERAL JOHN J. PERSHING

During the summer of 1918 the American literary scene was
flooded with books on the AEF. In the main they were hastily put
together, overemphasizing the courage of the Doughboys and
down-playing the real horror of the war. One of these books—a
notch above the others, I may add—was *Our Army at the Front* by
newspaper columnist Heywood Broun. It describes the arrival of
General Pershing on French soil.

"When he marched down and stepped to the Quay," wrote
Broun, "there was a sudden arresting silence. Every soldier was at
salute, and every civilian too. In that tense instant a new world was

beginning, and though it was as formless as all beginnings, the unerring, dramatic, and sensitive French paid the tribute of silence to its birth."

While Pershing never created the charisma of a Patton, or the down-to-earth image of an Omar Bradley, he did "look the soldier." Standing roughly six feet, his military bearing was impeccable. This Missouri-born, fifty-six-year-old farmboy must have had the best tailor in the AEF. In every one of his photographs he looks as if he'd just stepped out of the well-known bandbox.

But what of the man—the Pershing who had fought Apaches, Spaniards, and Moros; a man whose largest pre-AEF command had been the ten thousand troops he had taken into Mexico in 1916 on a fool's errand in pursuit of Pancho Villa?

Pershing was a man of contrasts. He was vigorously demanding of promptness among his subordinates, but his own tardiness was legendary. His background of very limited means was hardly considered socially prominent, yet he ended up marrying the twenty-four-year-old debutante daughter of Senator Francis Warren.[1] He was twenty-one years her senior. President Theodore Roosevelt attended the wedding along with his daughter Alice. Pershing never denied that being the son-in-law of the senator in charge of the Military Affairs Committee aided his career.

This relationship was naturally the cause of many sarcastic remarks by his fellow officers and gained for John J. the reputation of being a very ambitious man indeed. This may have been true, but it is also a fact that he refused to allow himself to be recommended for the Congressional Medal of Honor in recognition of outstanding service in the Philippines.

When it came to personal relations, he could blow hot and cold. He made sure that his old chum, Charles Dawes,[2] who was not a soldier, became a brigadier general and the chief purchasing agent

[1] The death of Pershing's wife and two daughters in a 1915 San Francisco fire shattered the man, but he somehow managed to keep it within himself. A son, Warren, survived. His grandson was killed in Vietnam and is buried next to the general at Arlington.
[2] Later Vice President of the United States under Calvin Coolidge.

for the AEF. On the other hand, Pershing denied service in Europe to two of his former mentors, Major General Hugh Scott and ex-President Theodore Roosevelt. While Pershing could be quite friendly to his officers one minute, he could be equally aloof and unreasonable the next. He could also be quite ruthless in ending the military careers of scores of officers, both friends and foes alike. In many of these cases his decision was questionable; although he was a stickler on details in others, a little more research on his own part could have changed many of his decisions.

Take the colonel he found asleep behind the lines one morning at 10:00 A.M. The officer was immediately sacked. A little research would have shown that the drowsy colonel had spent the entire previous evening on the front lines with his troops.

Then there was Major General Edwards, long-time commanding officer of the 26th (Yankee) Division, or as his men called him, "our Clarence." Pershing relieved him of his command on October 22, 1918. Edwards had taken his Yankees overseas in September of 1917. No other American general had command of a division in Europe as long as Edwards. If he was to be fired, it should have happened long before the last weeks of the war.

There was one quality that Pershing had, however, that was immensely important to his command: This was his refusal to be bull-dozed by the French and the British. When it got down to the nitty-gritty, he could always manage to say, "I will not be coerced." For instance, when the French told him the Americans must have extensive trench training, he balked.

"Oh, they should learn about the trenches," he allowed, "but above all they must learn the war of movement. We can't win the war in the trenches." John J. knew the American people could stand casualties, but he also realized that dead and wounded Americans would have to produce positive results. He took the same firm stand on the rifle. To the French the rifle was something to stick a bayonet on—grenades and machine guns were the real killing instruments. Pershing said no. Oh the other weapons were fine, all right, but the American rifleman was to be just that, a rifleman. The Germans paid dearly for the general's thinking on that subject.

It was in the debate over the very existence of an American Army, though, where Pershing took his strongest stand; his firmness here is reason enough to put him among the great captains in American military history. Our Allies were just as obstinate in their thinking against having a separate American command. In both volumes of Pershing's own memoirs he wrote extensively on the subject.[3] The Allies just wouldn't give up—they were bound to integrate the Americans into the British and French forces. Pershing did bend some during the crisis period from March until August of 1918. But when Marshal Foch tried to make changes in the Saint Mihiel troop deployment for the campaign in September, the American commander wouldn't budge. After more than a year of waiting, Pershing had his First U. S. Army, and it was to fight as such. The time had come for the Americans to take over a large part of the battle line on their own—there could be no compromise.

What did Pershing's soldiers think of this? Well, I asked one veteran of the 69th New York Irish of the Rainbow Division how he would have felt if they had put him in a British regiment.

"Jesus Christ," he snorted, "if they'd done that, I would have gone home!"

Perhaps this example is a little on the extreme side, but the feeling among all the Doughboys was very much in favor of having an American Army; and the one man above all they can thank for the creation of one is General John J. Pershing.

[3] In Lloyd George's book this crafty old fox writes of his utter disbelief concerning Pershing's stand. Surely this wartime Prime Minister of Great Britain realized that the lack of an American Army would detract from the United States' strength during peace treaty discussions.

The Marine's Marine

General Lemuel Shepherd

HIS HOME, LA JOLLA, CALIFORNIA, JULY 1976

As overworked a phrase as "He's a Marine's Marine" may be, there is no better way to describe General Lemuel Shepherd. He entered the Corps in April of 1917 during his senior year at VMI and stayed for forty years. After outstanding World War I combat service (three wounds and a DSC) he spent the period between the World Wars all over the world—Haiti, the Far East, sea duty—there were very few ports of call missed by General Shepherd. During World War II he spent most of his time occupied in combat against the Japanese. On April 1, 1945, he commanded the 6th Marine Division as they began the vicious campaign on the island of Okinawa. Then in September, a few weeks after the war ended, Major General Shepherd took his division to Tsingtao, China, to arrange for the surrender of the Japanese forces on the mainland. Among the Japanese and the Chinese, both Communist and Nationalist, Lem had his hands full.

It wasn't over for this old salt, though. He was in the Pacific when the Korean War broke out. It was Shepherd who negotiated with MacArthur to get a Marine division to Korea.

"We didn't really have much when that debacle broke out," the general told me, "but MacArthur wanted a division very badly. He said to me, 'General, I know how good you Marines are; I saw you in France during 1918 and in the Pacific during the Second War;

you're great.' Oh, he was quite a charmer when he wanted to be, that same MacArthur," continued Shepherd. "He got his division and his Inchon landing."

From 1952 until 1956 the then four-star General Lem Shepherd culminated his Marine career with service as the commandant. He is the senior Marine officer on the retired list as of this writing. When General Shepherd dies, they'll find a globe and anchor on his heart—he personifies what they call "The Old Corps." It appeared when I visited him in the summer of 1976 that this passing will be a ways in the future. He looked as if he could still take a platoon on a twenty-mile hike. And he's not afraid to challenge a very dry martini or so when discussing his illustrious career.

My visit with the general was one to which I had particularly looked forward. As a Pfc I had joined the 22nd Regiment of his 6th Division on Guam in July of 1945. I had told him this in a letter a week or two before my arrival in California. When we met, he looked me over carefully, then shook his head.

"I'm sorry, Mr. Berry," he said, "but I don't recognize you." We spent the next two or three hours discussing the 5th Marines of the AEF. Then General and Mrs. Shepherd took a former Marine Pfc and his wife to the La Jolla Club for dinner. He's quite a guy, that same Lem Shepherd.

First Lieutenant Lemuel Shepherd

55th Company, 5th Marines, 2nd Division

ORDRE

En raison de la brillante conduite de la 4ème Brigade de la 2ème D.U.S. qui a enlevé de haute lutte BOURESCHES et le point d'appui important de BOIS de BELLEAU, défendu avec acharnement par un adversaire nombreux, le Général Commandant la VIe ARMÉE decide que dorénavant, dans toutes les pièces officielles, le BOIS de BELLEAU portera la nom de "BOIS de la BRIGADE de MARINE."

—LE GÉNÉRAL DE DIVISION DEGOUTTE
COMMANDANT LE VIE ARMÉE
[SIGNED] DEGOUTTE.[1]

Virginia Military Institute, over at Lexington, that's where I was when Wilson declared war; I was a senior. I certainly hadn't decided on a military career at this time, not at all. My family would have liked to see me go into medicine or the law, maybe even the Episcopal Church, but the war changed all this.

Naturally, after four years of a military college, we were all eager as hell to go once America got in the thing. One of the students, it might have even been my roommate, a boy named Robinson, had

[1] Order changing the name of Belleau Wood to Marine Brigade Wood.

found out that the Marine Corps would give the VMI boys a shot at commissions if they would go to Washington for a physical. So right after the declaration about six of us headed for the capital.

What a ride! We grabbed the night train, standing up all the way from Lynchburg to Washington. It seemed to me that everybody and his brother were going to the nation's capital that night. Then, of course, we were worried about the physical—it'd be awful if any of us failed. Besides, most of us had borrowed money to make the trip; you know, college boys never have any money.

Well, the physical turned out to be a breeze. This old doctor, he just thumped us a few times, checked a few things, and kind of smiled:

"Ever have the clap, Shepherd?" he inquired.

This came as somewhat of a shock to me, coming from a proper Virginia family, so I quickly answered, "No, sir."

"How about hemorrhoids?"

"No, sir."

"You'll do, Shepherd, you'll do."

Now that's a little exaggerated, but it really was somewhat of a cursory physical. You see, the Marines wanted to get into the war as a major unit, not just some small detachments, and they needed officers badly.

The next step was a review board headed by old Colonel Doyen, one of the top Marine leaders.

"Well, gentlemen," said Doyen, "you have all passed your physical. We've checked with VMI, and you're slated to graduate in June. How would you like a commission in the Marine Reserves right now?"

This came as somewhat of a disappointment. VMI was accredited, and we knew in June we would get a regular commission in the Army. Doyen must have realized this as he continued to address us:

"It'll take us a few months to get these changed to the regulars, but this way you can have your commission dated from today. You can go back to VMI and graduate—then report for active duty." We felt this sounded pretty good, and we all held up our right hand. It was April 15, 1917, nine days after war was declared.

Oh we all graduated, all right, about two weeks later. The Corps had decided they couldn't wait, so they wired the VMI commandant informing him that they needed us right away. You might say things were moving pretty fast—perhaps too fast.

We all went home to await immediate orders. A week or two went by with nothing happening, so I got ahold of Tom Holcomb,[2] the Marine personnel officer. Tom was furious, said there must have been a foulup, as we should have already reported to Parris Island; we all received our orders a day or so after that.

Parris Island was a great deal smaller in 1917 than it is now, but it did function even then as an introduction to the Corps. Our stay was short. They loaded us down with books for study on Marine functions and strategies, then gave us ten days on the rifle range. None of us was prepared for what happened next when a captain gathered us all together.

"Gentlemen," he asked, "are any of you interested in foreign duty? If you are, we can immediately accommodate you."

Please note: He did not say "France," he said "foreign duty." I had some buddies who'd gone in the Corps a few months before and were down in Haiti having a great old time. We all volunteered thinking we'd end up in one of those spots in Latin America. That wasn't exactly what they had in mind.

We left immediately for Philadelphia to join the 55th Company of the 5th Marines that was getting ready for France. Now the wheels were really turning. They'd been gathering Marines from all over as quickly as they could. Some had come up from Cuba, others from navy yards, and a great many from reserve companies in the United States—these lads hadn't even been through Parris Island. They worked us around the clock, issuing all types of gear. Then they piled us aboard the USS *Hancock*—the old "handpussy," as the boys called her—and sailed us up to New York Harbor. Here we went aboard this brand-new transport called the *Henderson* and left for France, landing at Saint-Nazaire on June 25. I'll always remember that date because it was the same day my class at VMI graduated—the graduation I'd been told I would attend.

Of course, we all felt pretty good about the whole thing. This was it. Our convoy was the first contingent of American combat troops to land in France. Along with the Marines, we had twelve or

[2] Thomas Holcomb—the Marine commandant at the start of World War II; he fought in France as a lieutenant colonel in 1918.

so thousand regular Army men who were to go into the 1st Division —I'd say there were about fifteen thousand in all.

After we landed the question came up: Where the hell are we to go? Well, we had this battalion commander, old Fritz Wise, Frederick M. Wise. And was he ever an old salt, a real "sundowner." Whenever he'd address you, it'd be "goddamn you, Mr. Shepherd" or whatever your name would be. He gave me the word. "Shepherd, goddamn you, go lay out a camp."

"But Colonel, I've never laid out a camp."

"I didn't ask you anything; I told you something. Now, goddamn it, go lay out a camp."

So I rounded up a detail and laid out a camp. You can bet your bottom dollar the first thing I did was make sure the old man had a good spot.

We had a period at this time when they really didn't know what to do with us. We were there, all right, but certainly in no shape to go into the lines. We'd keep drilling the men, trying to get them in shape, but really not doing much of anything.

One of the problems was the language barrier, but the men seemed to learn fast. You could, after all, always talk to the French with gestures. Of course, some of the men were always complaining about the failure of the French to "talk American." I can remember one time when we were on a long hike that took us through several villages. They all had their cafes, and there always was a big sign in the window with the word *bouvette*. Finally, a lad from my company came over to me with a puzzled look on his face.

"Mr. Shepherd," he asked, "I wonder does Mr. Bouvette have any daughters?"

I played it straight and asked him why.

"Well hell, Lieutenant, I'd like to meet one. Her old man must own every saloon in France!"

We all had a good laugh on this one, but I'd say one way or another, the men learned to communicate rather well.

My own situation was quite good. I'd taken French at VMI and could at least carry on a conversation if the French would talk slowly. And besides, I had a tremendous orderly then by the name of Robert Cristenbery. He'd come to me one day while we were still on the *Henderson*.

"Mr. Shepherd," he announced, "my name is Private Robert Cristenbery. I'd like to be your orderly."

"Now, that's all well and good, Cristenbery," I said, "but I've only been in this man's Marine Corps a short time. What the hell does an orderly do?"

"I'm not sure, Lieutenant, but I think it means to take care of you."

"Well, that's fine, Cristenbery; you take care of me and I'll take care of you."

That started a warm friendship that didn't end until Bob died a few years ago.

And what a peach of an orderly Cristenbery turned out to be. When we landed, the French had given the officers huge quantities of champagne. Each night after we'd been on the go all day, Cristenbery would greet myself and Lieutenant Wilson, my roommate, with a bottle of champagne in each hand.

"Champagne time, gentlemen," he'd announce, "champagne time!" After we'd polished those off, we'd go over to the officers' mess for some more. Of course, it couldn't last, but it was wonderful while it did. Years later, when I'd meet Bob, he'd still greet me with "Champagne time, gentlemen, champagne time!"

After several weeks here we were sent to a place near Gondrecourt in a small town called Menacourt. Here we were assigned to some crack French troops called Chasseurs. Known as the Blue Devils, they were supposed to be an elite corps of the French Army; and they were that. We did have some problems because all their commands were *en français*, coming from the French Army manual. You know, I can still give commands in French.

Time did start to drag through those months we spent at Menacourt. We all felt it would be a great idea if we could figure out a way to get over to Bar-le-Duc for a little fun. But the place was twenty miles or so away, and a visit there was strictly taboo. Finally, one of my friends suggested we each borrow a company bicycle and ride over. This sounded great, so we picked a time when we figured we wouldn't be missed and shoved off. We arrived in time to have some drinks and some great food. Then we almost caught it. Who do we see coming out of this hotel but a Marine colonel. If he had spotted us, we would have caught hell; boy, did we really duck![3]

By now it's starting to get dark, and one of us suggested we'd better head back to camp. We all agreed but decided we'd have one more drink. The first thing we knew it was almost midnight— now we knew we'd really better head back. Then we passed this bicycle shop with the proprietor living upstairs. Someone got the bright idea we should get this guy out of bed and buy some real good bikes. Of course, this old Frenchman thought we were some crazy Americans. But there was nothing crazy about him; he charged us sixty dollars a bike.

Now, you should have seen that old bandit when we paid him. You see, whenever the Marines would go to places in Latin America or Asia, they'd always be paid in gold—you know, coin of the realm. This was because many of the natives in those places wouldn't accept paper money; the Corps did the same thing the first several months we were in France. Anyhow, that old fellow's eyes got big as saucers. Two hundred and forty dollars in gold, hell, he hadn't seen that much since before the war. He's yelling, "*Merci! merci!*" and waving his arms; then he sticks his finger in the air:

"*Vivent les braves Americains!*" he yells. "*Vive Pershing! Vivent les Yanks!*" Christ, he should have been yelling, "*Vive le gold!*"

Well, it was a beautiful moonlit night as we started back for camp, riding our new bikes and trying to pull the old ones along. Then we heard this funny purring sound that meant only one thing: a German bomber. We grabbed our bikes and pumped into this ditch on the side of the road. I don't know why that Boche didn't see us, but I guess he didn't.

We got back to camp at about six o'clock in the morning, just before reveille. It's Sunday now, so we decided to catch a little rest. We woke up about eleven and we're drinking some coffee and you know what one of us said?

"Let's get on our bikes and head for Bar-le-Duc!" That's what he said. So back again we go to Bar-le-Duc. This time, though, we returned a lot earlier because we had to go to work on Monday.

[3] I asked the general what would have happened if later on when he was a colonel he had caught some young lieutenants doing what he had done. He said he would have given them hell.

You know, during those months of training, some of those French people were so nice to us. I can remember this old French woman in particular; she came over to us one day along with these two young *mademoiselles.*

"Pardon, *monsieur,*" she said in broken English, "but I wanted my granddaughters to see the American Indians."

Naturally, we all got a big kick out of this, so we decided to give them a tour of our company. The long and short of it was we ended up with a dinner invitation and several more of them while we were training there. As a matter of fact, the last night we were there, just before we went into the trenches, she had several of the officers over. She told us how sad she was to see us go. Then she went down to her wine cellar and came up with a bottle of brandy that was 120 years old. Then she started to sob. She had seen so many of her own countrymen go to the front and not return.

Really, as I look back, it seems to me every woman in France wore black. They had lost so many, many men. If you did see a man of military age not in uniform, the chances are he had lost a leg or something—God, how that country had bled!

Of course, we were beginning to wonder when we would get a crack at the Germans. We'd been spending all this time with the Chasseurs, and if they couldn't get you ready for combat, no one could. The group we had with us were Bretons, many of them being big blond fellows. I remember one sergeant in particular who was loaded with *esprit de corps.*

"You Marines are ze elite corps, *oui,*" he would say. "So are ze Chasseurs. We are ze best *fighteurs, loveurs,* and *drinkeurs* in all of France."

How he loved to bellow when he was training us. I can hear him now:

"*Très bon, très bon,* MAIS"—that MAIS meant "BUT," and he'd let us have it. He would have made a great Marine drill sergeant.

Well, when we did leave Menacourt, it was to spend the winter in a small town near Neufchâteau. If you've talked to any of the other men who were in France during that winter of '17–'18, I'm sure they've said the same thing: FROZEN! The only place I've known of where the Marines ever suffered as much from the cold was at the Chosin Reservoir in Korea. I don't think the sun ever did shine while we were in that French town. It seems all we did was drill and go on hikes—oh, and stand inspections. And there was one of those inspections I'll never forget.

You can probably realize what inspections meant to most of the old-time Marines. Everything was going to be perfection, and I mean, "Aye, aye, sir!" You know, I have to laugh at this even now, but this is actually what happened. We had this old sergeant who was in charge of making sure our heads were spick-and-span; they may have been slit trenches, but they were heads to him.

Well, we got the word that there was going to be some general give us one of those white-glove jobs. So the sergeant has the men dig a new trench. The ground was hard as can be, but he wanted a new head for the general. His orders were explicit: *No one*, but *no one*, was to use it until after the inspection.

Now, the night before the big day, something got into the men's chow and they all came down with the trots. Naturally, no one is now concerned with the inspection. They're certainly in no mood to stand in line, so they start using the new head. When the old sergeant heard about it, he went berserk.

"You sons-of-bitches, shit in my new head, will yuh?" he yelled. "I'll fix yuh!" He went over to where we kept the grenades and picked up a few; then he came back still cursing a mile a minute. The boys knew he wasn't kidding, so they're all trying to get the hell out of there, some of them clutching their trousers as they ran. What a sight! And I'll be damned if he doesn't throw the grenades at the new head. What a mess, everything is flying in all directions. Thank God, no one was hurt!

There were a couple of things that happened the last few months before we really got into the rough stuff that made a big impression on me. I'd even say they influenced things I did later on in my career as I advanced in rank.

One concerned our Lieutenant Colonel Wise and another Marine officer, old "Hiking Hiram" Bearss. There was really no love lost between these two, which was probably due to the fact that they were both alike—a couple of real tough old Marines.

Bearss, a regimental headquarters officer, came over one day to inspect our men. He'd grab one of our Marines' rifles, inspect it, and state, "dirty bore."

Wise would then grab the same rifle, inspect it, and yell, "clean bore."

This kept going on and on. Hell, they weren't accomplishing a darn thing. It was a small incident, but it struck home with me. You had to have harmony among your officers. I remembered that.

The second happening showed how misunderstandings can occur. I was the duty officer one night when a fight broke out between a French soldier and a Marine in a cafe. I went in there to clean all the Marines out before a riot started. Oh the woman who ran the place was furious, acted as if she was throwing a fit, told me how I would ruin her business, all this stuff—it was a dreadful mess.

Well, we'd had orders from Wise to report any such flareup to him at once if it concerned his Marines; he wanted to know about it even if we had to wake him up, and that's just what I had to do.

I felt he was going to give me hell, but he was very calm.

"Shepherd," he said (no "goddamn" this time), "sit down. I know you and the other young officers think I'm one tough son-of-a-bitch."

Hell, the old tiger was even being fatherly.

"But you know, we're going into real battle soon, battle on a scale such as I've never seen. I figure the best way to do this is with complete obedience—when I give an order I want the men to turn to. I think this way I'll be able to bring more of them out of this alive."

Of course, you couldn't argue with him when he put it that way. But damn it, why hadn't he put it to all of us in that manner months sooner instead of being so uptight? He paid for it later when he cracked up at the end of the Belleau Wood fight. He must have learned his lesson, though, because after a long rest he was put in charge of an Army regiment of the 4th Division and did a bang-up job in the Meuse-Argonne.

As a matter of fact, I spotted Colonel Wise the next year (1919) in Germany. He came running over to me with an outstretched hand.

"Shepherd," his voice hadn't changed a bit, "I've been looking for you." Naturally I became a little apprehensive.

"After Belleau Wood," he continued, "I recommended you for the DSC. Did you get it?"

I told him I had and thanked him. There was a lot of good in the old man.

Once again I had learned a lesson; in the years to come I tried to make sure my officers, particularly the younger ones, not only knew their orders but also knew the reasons for them.

Anyway, in March of '18 the spring started to come to France and with it our first tour of the trenches. It was more or less routine: a certain amount of time in the lines, then a rest while you were held in reserve. But this wasn't going to last long. Toward the end of May our real show was getting ready to start.

This is a period I can really remember vividly if for no other reason than its stark realities of war. On May 15 we had been pulled out of the lines for rest. Our next area was to be Cantigny, where the 1st Division was about to have a small and costly, but very successful, offensive against the Germans.

Things were rather quiet, which gave me a chance for some bike riding. One of these jaunts took me by this beautiful Norman-type chateau surrounded by a wrought-iron fence. And looking at me through this fence was a very pretty young girl; I'd say she was about seventeen or eighteen years old. Now, you can bet I put the brakes on and introduced myself to this "petite beauty." I could speak some French, and she knew a little English—we had a great time, just standing there talking through that damn fence. Finally I told her I had to leave, but I'd be back the next day. And back I came all ready for another session with my new friend. She's there all right, but so are Mama and Père. The conversation was a little different than the day before but rather pleasant. Oh, you know, they wanted to know all about me.

I passed the test, because just as I was getting ready to leave, they invited me back for dinner the next evening. Naturally I was all excited about this. A chance for a great meal like this would really be something. And besides, that young thing was the prettiest mam'selle I'd seen in France.

It wasn't to be. The next day was Memorial Day, so they gave us a holiday. Incidentally, that should show you how lax things were for us. I took the morning primping—I was going to look like a real Marine officer when I arrived for that young lady. Then we got the word:

"All hands, stand by for camions as quickly as possible."

Well, we all knew what that meant. When they took you out of the lines, you hiked. But when they wanted to send you up in a hurry, it was camions. I wrote out a message telling those good people I couldn't dine there that evening because of our orders and sent it over on my bike via a messenger. In the meantime I'm helping to get our company together. The scuttlebutt is flying all around. Hell, they had us going everywhere. I felt it would be exactly where we ended up. I'd read a paper a few days before that explained how the Germans had broken through the Chemin des Dames and were moving toward Paris. We were about to find out what the war was all about.

By midafternoon we were all ready, full packs, ammunition, everything, so we stacked arms and stood by our gear. You know, those damn camions didn't arrive until seven the next morning. We ended up sleeping right there on our packs. When they did arrive, wham, we were hustled right aboard—and they took off as fast as possible.

My God, what a ride, crammed into those little trucks, bumping over those roads, and most of us with our overcoats on. Hell, this was the first of June; it was hot. And the dust—we could hardly breathe.

Finally, around four o'clock that afternoon, they stopped and let us off. Then the marching started, if you want to call it that. Here we are trying to move up to the front, while all the French refugees are going the other way. It was pathetic as hell: families with baby carriages, bundles on their heads, children in their arms; old men driving carts pulled by nags; old women trying to walk with canes. It was truly the flotsam of war.

Then there were the stragglers, the beaten Poilu in groups of twos and threes. They couldn't believe it when they saw fresh troops moving up.

"Retournez, retournez!" they yelled. "La guerre est finie! Retournez, retournez—La Boche est victorieuse!"

There was one heartening sight—a division of French cavalry moving toward the front. They truly looked magnificent with their horses prancing and their guidons and lances waving. They showed us that France was still very much in the war.

I don't know how many of us who made that march are still around, but I'll bet they all agree with me—it was one hell of a dramatic experience.

Well, they halted us about midnight in this open field. We were so darn tired that no one even bothered to take off his bedroll; we all just collapsed on our packs.

The next morning they turned us to at about seven—no coffee, chow, or anything. We started marching again, this time until about four in the afternoon, when we were stopped at a place called Pyramid Farms, just off the Paris road. The French farmers had all left, so the men started rounding up all these eggs, chickens, cows—at least we had some food. But we sure as hell didn't get any sleep. This battery of French 75's had moved in next door to us. You know that peculiar crack, crack they make? Well, try sleeping through it sometime. The next morning we moved in. Our company took up a position near a place called Les Mares Farm, not far from the Lucy Torcy road.

By this time we'd gotten the word. The area was called Belleau Wood. If the Germans could break through our division, they could probably go all the way to Paris. Naturally, the French were very concerned. One of their generals [Degoutte] had asked Preston Brown, the division chief of staff, if we could hold.

"General," Brown's supposed to have answered, "those are American regulars; they haven't been beaten in 150 years!" You never know if things like that are really said, but it made us all feel pretty good.

Our orders were basic: "Form as skirmishers to withstand attacks." And that's what we did. We had to spread ourselves pretty thin because we didn't know just where they'd hit us. I'd suggested we put a dozen or so men on this commanding piece of land about two or three hundred yards in front of our lines, with explicit orders to retreat if the pressure got too hot. Just about the time the attack started I'd decided to go out and see how they were doing. Actually, when I'd cleared it with our captain [Blanchfield], I'd really been asking more or less as a form of bravado. But he'd O.K.'d it, and I was off.

Well, after I'd covered about a hundred yards or so, this huge German shell landed about six feet to my right; for one horribly tantalizing instant I saw it coming in at me. It covered me with dirt, but that's all. It was a dud. But it sure scared the hell out of me—I can still see it coming down today.

In the meantime, the Germans are attacking, and we're knocking the hell out of them with rifle fire, which was something they obviously didn't expect. The French, you see, were great on the attack and with their grenades but not much with the rifle. I guess the Germans didn't realize they were coming against Americans. We could actually hear them yelling about it.

After my dud episode I tried to find a spot where I wouldn't be too exposed but could still see what was going on. I was leaning against this tree when all of a sudden something struck me in the neck and spun me around. Well, I didn't know what the hell had hit me or how bad it was. The first thing I did was spit to see if any blood was coming out that way. When there wasn't any, I knew I'd picked up an ugly wound but nothing fatal. I went back to a field hospital, had it patched up, and returned to my company.

Now, let's leave Belleau Wood for a minute. Shortly after the war I returned to the area where I'd been hit as a member of the Battlefield Map Commission. So help me, God, there was the big tree still standing, with a grouping of seven machine-gun bullets in it. The one that had spun me around had probably saved my life. If you look and see how close it came to my jugular, you can imagine where the next one would have struck.

Well, the day after I was hit, they attacked again. Fortunately for my company, I really think they struck with their greatest strength toward the main center of our lines, not at the 55th. Once again they were stopped in most places, and, I think, once again it was the rifle fire. It only took one bullet to stop a German if you hit him. And my, how our boys could pick them off!

Now I'll tell you one you won't believe about one of our regulars, old Gunnery Sergeant Buford. During a lull on the third day of their attack one of our Pfc's told Buford that some Germans were trying to sneak through a wheat field over on our left and surprise us. Well, the old gunner had seen plenty of bushwhacking in Haiti or some place like that. Surprise him? Hell, no! He was going to surprise them! So he moved out and waited. He came back later with this grin on his face.

"Lieutenant," he chuckled, "I think I got seven."

Now, he only had a .45. I couldn't believe it, so I went over to see. There they were, laid out like cordwood.

Well, a day or two later we started to attack. And what a mess that turned out to be! What happened was old Fritz Wise got us lost in the woods. When nighttime came, we were stumbling over each other, picking up machine-gun fire from somewhere. This went on all night. At about dawn the word came to me that Captain Blanchfield had been killed and I was to take command of the company. Naturally, I started to move forward to find out where most of the men were located, when, wham, it felt like I'd been kicked by a mule; I'd picked up another machine-gun bullet, this time in my right knee. It was the end of Belleau Wood for me.

They took me back off the lines, then to a convent at Maux that they had turned into a hospital. I was lying in the courtyard, waiting my turn with the doctors, when this civilian stopped by my stretcher.

"Will you have a cigarette, soldier?" he asked me.

"You bet I will!" I answered. "I just came from the front and haven't had one for days. Thanks a lot. Could I have a pack?"

"Oh no. I can sell you a pack, but I can't give you one."

"But I have no money. I've been on the lines for the last week."

"Sorry, soldier, those are my orders."

"Then ram your cigarettes."

That obviously was the end of that!

About ten minutes later a Red Cross man came by and also offered me a cigarette. I told him the same thing about wanting a pack but that I didn't have any money.

"Pay for them?" he yelled at me. "Pay for them? These cigarettes were donated by the American Red Cross. You can't pay for them. Here, have two packs, and God bless you."

From then on I've been a Red Cross boy, and the hell with the YMCA.

My wound itself was actually what they called a clean one. But I guess I tried to move around too soon or something. Anyway, gangrene eventually set in, and I was really scared. A lot of the lads did lose arms or legs, you know. I was one of the lucky ones, though. I had to spend six weeks on my back, but it turned out all right. Actually, it well may have saved my life. I ended up missing Soissons, which was another real bloodbath.

I did get back to my outfit in time for Saint Mihiel and Blanc Mont. We really didn't have it that bad at Mihiel, but Blanc Mont was another story. As far as I'm concerned, October 3 at Blanc Mont was the toughest day of the war. And I think most of the men with me agreed.

You see, we weren't with Pershing's First Army then; we were with Gouraud's Fourth French Army. Blanc Mont was a key commanding position, and being on the far left of the Americans' Meuse-Argonne line, it had to be taken. Because of that, Pershing turned over our outfit and the 36th Division to the French. If Gouraud's and Pershing's armies were to join up, you had to eliminate White Mountain. The Germans knew this and fought like hell to keep it.

Once again the tough job was given to the 2nd Division. The Maine Brigade was to go up on the left with the two Army regiments, the 9th and 23rd on our right. They were under a tough old regular named Hanson Ely, and he really had those Doughboys fired up. If anyone wanted to question the fighting qualities of the U. S. Army, let him study what Ely's two regiments did at Blanc Mont.

The only problem was our flanks—here both brigades were to have French support, but those Frenchies were really worn out. They just couldn't keep up. We ended up taking the position, all right, but I think my company had about fifty-five men left when it was over.[4]

After we did capture the darn place, we tried to set up our lines. Remember, we had driven the Germans off Blanc Mont, but they were still facing us. I and a man named Carbo were the only officers left in our company. He was in a huge foxhole, along with a Sergeant Marcus, with plenty of room for me. Just as I jumped in, my orderly came by.

"Lieutenant," he argued, "the three of you can't be together like that; I've got a great hole about a hundred yards from here." So, what the hell, I decided I'd better go over with him.

Christ, it was cold that night. I had this flask filled with some liquor made from prunes; it was like vodka, with a kick like a mule. When morning came I crawled over to where Carbo and Marcus were, to give them some. Boy, did they need it! They were as chilled as I was. Then I went back to my own hole. You know, I

---

[4] "To be able to say when this war is finished, 'I belonged to the 2nd Division, I fought with it at the Battle of Blanc Mont Ridge,' will be the highest honor that can come to any man."

—John A. Lejeune,
Major General, USMC

don't think I had even settled down when Carbo and Marcus took a direct hit. Now I was the only officer left.

My turn came a little later. After we'd had about seven days of the worst combat you can imagine, we were relieved by the Texas National Guard. They were good boys, all right, but green. They lost a lot of men who would have made it if they'd had some experience.

We were now held in support waiting to see what they could do. I and another officer named Forbes had gone over to watch this French battery of 75's work when an Austrian 88 zeroed in on us. Poor Forbes caught it in the stomach, while I took some shrapnel in my left leg. I carried Forbes over to this trench; then my leg just completely gave way. You can see how lucky I really was again. Poor old Forbes died, but the fragment in my leg actually slid around the bone.

I spent the last few weeks back in the hospital, but I'll tell you one thing the boys later told me: The day *after* the Armistice they got the word to turn in their Chauchats and draw Browning Automatic Rifles. That BAR was so much better than that damn Chauchat. If we'd only had the BAR six months before, it would have saved so many lives.

There was one thing that haunted me for a long time after the Armistice: I'd never been in a real showdown, face to face with a German; my buddy Cliff Cates had, but I hadn't. Cates had bumped into a German officer and they both went for their pistols at the same time. Cates won. I just didn't know what I would do if it happened to me.

Well, oh, I guess it was 1925, Cates and I had sea duty together. We were ashore drinking a bit in Norfolk when he told me the story again for the hundredth time. I went to sleep that night with it still preying on my mind. Then I started to dream that I'm facing this big Prussian-looking officer.

"Put your hands up," I yelled, "you're my prisoner." Well, he went for his pistol, and I went for mine. I shot the son-of-a-bitch right between the eyes. I don't know what one of those dream-analysis experts would make about that, but it never bothered me again.

One more thing: about three years ago my wife and I visited Menacourt. There was the same small hotel we used to go to in

1917. They'd made a great many changes in the place, all right, and I pointed these out to this chipper young manager, telling him how it used to be.

"*Oui, monsieur,*" he said, "I do not remember that, but my *grandmère,* she tell me."

Of course, this didn't make me feel any younger. Then I pointed to the hills behind the village.

"And up there we used to dig trenches during our training."

"Oh *oui, monsieur,*" he answered, "the trenches, they are still there."

Can you beat that? Almost sixty years and those Frogs hadn't filled in those damn trenches!

"That Damn Y"

Pete Simmons joined the old 7th New York Infantry shortly after the United States declared war on Germany. As a member of the headquarters company he was assigned to the Stokes Mortar Platoon. The Stokes was used mainly for lobbing shells into the enemy's trenches. It was a British gun, so Pete's outfit was sent overseas a few months before his regiment, now designated the 107th U. S. Infantry of the 27th Division, to study the weapon at first hand.

Like the rest of his division, his war was greatly dominated by the "Hindenburg Stunt," the assault at the Saint Quentin Tunnel on September 29, 1918. He told me about going "over the top" while the two of us were enjoying a drink at a New York City restaurant.

"I was the smallest man in our platoon," chuckled Pete, "so naturally I was assigned to carry the seventy-pound barrel. Isn't it always like that?" he added. "Well, immediately after we started the attack, chaotic confusion took over. No one knew what the hell was going on other than that the Boche were shooting the hell out of us. My memory is as good today concerning that fight as it was a week after the battle, but even then it was a little fuzzy. I do remember an American jumping into a tank that had been put out of action and shooting down a German plane that was strafing us. The tank was no good, but its machine gun was still intact, see.

"There was one thing I remember vividly, though, and that is wondering what the hell good my Stokes barrel was in a fight like that. Hell, I was a sitting duck trying to move around carrying those seventy pounds. So do you know what I did?" (And here Mr. Simmons lowered his voice to a whisper.) "I threw the fucking thing away, that's what I did! Then I picked up a rifle from one of our men who'd already been hit, and tried to stay alive."

Pete was one of the lucky ones. He was gassed a little later on, but he came through the butchery of September 29 unscratched.

Two days later, an exhausted Pete and a buddy were sent a few miles behind the lines, where they ran into a YMCA man doling out cigarettes.

"Hello, boys," the triangle man[1] said, "glad to see you made it."

"Thank you, buddy," Pete answered. "Do you have any Lucky Strikes? We're both dying for a smoke."

"Sure, boys, here you are," and he gave both men a deck. Then he threw in a shocker.

"That'll be a franc apiece."

"What?" roared Pete. "We don't have any money; we're lucky we have our ass in one piece!"

"Sorry, boys—those are my orders. No money, no cigarettes." And he grabbed back the Luckies. Fortunately for Pete, he ran into a Salvation Army man a half an hour later and received a pack on the house.

---

[1] The logo of the YMCA is a triangle. "Triangle man" is one of the kinder euphemisms the Doughboys had for the Y workers.

Now, if this sounds like Lem Shepherd's story, this is because it is like Shepherd's story. And I was told the same type of thing by many others. For better or worse, the YMCA's mighty effort in the Great War came a cropper. While much of the criticism about it was unjust, the fact does remain that the Y never did make it with the Doughboys.

Jack Madden (his interview starts on page 372) was one soldier who, while not exactly enamored of the Y himself, did try to offer the Y a defense in a letter he wrote to his sister shortly after the Armistice.

"The main cause of the criticism," he wrote, "is the canteen. Here the organization probably is a victim of circumstances. The Y took over, at the Army's request, the sale of all U.S. goods formerly handled for soldiers in peacetime by commissaries. The U. S. Army probably realized what a difficult job it would be, so they passed the buck to the Y."

Jack's letter is basically accurate. While the Y, like any other organization, must have had its bad apples, the large majority of its workers were dedicated Americans. But to the large majority of the AEF they became "that damn Y," and after sixty decades, for better or worse, fairly or unfairly, these old-timers are not going to change their minds.

The Yalie at Soissons

Samuel W. Meek

GREENWICH SAVINGS BANK, GREENWICH, CONNECTICUT, MARCH 1976
Sam Meek is a very tough man to pin down. Among his job as chairman of the board of Walker & Company, publishers; his homes in Greenwich, Connecticut, and Vermont; and his many long trips, he keeps constantly on the go. When I originally phoned him, he was just about to depart for a long business trip to Europe. This is not very usual for a man of eighty-one.

After the Armistice this Yale graduate joined J. Walter Thompson, an advertising firm. He stayed there for forty or so years, excluding four years off for his return to the Marine Corps. He left the Corps as a lieutenant colonel in 1945.

He is best remembered at JWT, and he is indeed remembered, as a very hard-working and dynamic executive. His specialty, the international branch of Thompson, is really his legacy to the advertising world.

"Sam built it, no doubt about that," one of Thompson's top people recently told me. "He was the father of J. Walter Thompson International."

Mr. Meek is currently the only survivor of the original Board of Directors of Time, Inc. I don't feel I am telling any secrets out of school when I point out that he could easily start enjoying very comfortable retirement anytime he desired. When I asked him if he had any plans for doing this, Sam just laughed.

"Hell, if I ever stopped," he said, "I'd drop dead."

First Lieutenant Samuel W. Meek

82nd Company, 6th Marines, 2nd Division

You rushed into the fight as to a fete.

—FRENCH GENERAL CHARLES MANGIN
TO THE 6TH MARINES AFTER SOISSONS

The feeling at Yale after we entered the war was extremely pro-Allies. We all felt that great wrong had been done by the Germans, and we wanted to pitch in and help. The night after war was declared, most of the students marched over to President Pailey's house, chanting, "All out, all out." As I look back on it, I think every member of my fraternity went into one branch of the service or another; it just never entered our heads to stay out.

In my case it was the Marine Corps. Toward the end of April [17] they sent an officer to see the dean with a plan: If Yale would furnish him a list of ten men with leadership qualifications, the Corps would immediately send them down to their new base at Quantico for officers' training. The dean gave him my name—I was managing editor of the *Yale News;* Johnny Overton, the track captain; Bill LeGore, the baseball and football star; Bill Wallace, wrestling captain; Stan Burke, head of dramatics—people like that. We all accepted, and just like that, the Marines had ten new second lieutenants.

We were told to head immediately to Winthrop, Maryland, for rifle range instructions—you know how the Marines feel about rifles —then to the sparkling new base at Quantico. It all sounded great to me. The Corps were using their slogan, "First to Fight," a lot at that time. I felt the whole thing meant a quick trip to France, and it did.

Our stay at Quantico was aimed at making Marine officers out of us, and they really worked at it. It also acted as an introduction to what the Marines were all about. The actual size of the Corps was quite small when we entered the war.[1] Most of the professionals knew each other, having served together in such campaigns as the Boxer Rebellion and Haiti. Some of these salts accepted us, and some didn't. But they all accepted our rank. Actually, the so-called old Corps was much like any other group of men. After we arrived in France, some of them were extremely heroic in battle, and others were not. All in all, I think those of us who joined up for the war did just as good a job in combat as the professionals.

Well, after training, our little Yale group was broken up and sent over in different echelons; I was, however, to see my great friend Johnny Overton again later on. My unit was given sea duty on the way over, manning the guns and standing watch.

After we landed in France, we were sent up to various training areas; I was assigned to Chatillon-sur-Cher. Then it was school at Gondrecourt, followed by machine-gun training at a place called Bebilly. I guess they felt I was ready, because they gave me a few weeks' tour of duty in a quiet sector with a French unit. It's a good thing it was a quiet sector—I'll never forget the way those French officers drank wine at supper; it was incredible.

Then came the real war, the German breakthrough at Château-Thierry and the fantastic efforts to try to save Paris. The 5th and 6th Marine regiments, making up half the complement of the 2nd Division, had been thrown in near an old hunting lodge at a place called Belleau Wood. The fighting here was absolutely horren-dous. The German High Command was going all out to take Paris; they knew the Americans were landing in force now in France, and they had to break the Allies before the United States could throw a million or more fresh troops at them. And they came darn close to doing it.

Now, the Marines knew the casualties would be high, so they started to collect us from all over France. I joined the 6th Regiment

[1] About ten thousand men.

on the fourth or fifth day of the battle. This adjutant put his hands on my shoulder with this sorrowful look:

"Meek," he lamented, "we're going to assign you to the 82nd Company because they have no officers left at all." That's how bad it was!

The great acts of bravery practiced here beg description. I saw one sergeant literally climb up on the top of a machine-gun nest, driving down into the Germans with his bayonet. He was shot, but he put that gun out of commission. Come to think of it, during my entire tour of duty in France, I can't remember seeing one actual case of cowardice during a battle. Now, before we'd move into action, yes, a man would have sore feet or something else—others would want to go home. But once the ball opened, no, not once did I see a real slacker.

After the German attack had bogged down, we moved over to the offense, and the casualties kept mounting. Remember, the Germans had been doing this for four years; they were real pros. Whenever they'd find an open field, they'd pull their machine guns back into an adjoining wooded area. This way we'd have to move across the open terrain in full range of their guns to get at them. Each one of those guns—and, my God, they seemed to have them everywhere—would cost us more men.

In a movement like that you'd have to measure your gains in a few yards at a time. As the lieutenant I'd try to lead the men, but with the confusion and chaos it wasn't always possible. I'd yell out, "O.K., you men, let's go." Then, if the fire got heavy, I'd yell, "Down, down!" Hell, I didn't even know if they could hear me. Actually, when it got bad, it was kind of every man for himself. You'd be trying to move up and stay alive at the same time.

You know, several times through the years I've wondered what made us go forward like that at Belleau, and also later on at Soissons. You knew there'd be heavy casualties, that the odds were against you. I guess each man just figured it wouldn't be him; tragically, so many of them were wrong.

I think the incredulousness of the whole thing played a part. Take the time one of my men jumped in a hole with me. You'd try not to have this happen; as the book says, "Don't let the men bunch up, keep them spread apart." This makes it tougher for their guns to hit a lot of us on one sweep. Well, this guy ends up in with me, and he wants to talk.

"Lieutenant," he said, "did you know I used to be a streetcar conductor back in St. Louis?" Hell, I thought he was losing his mind—it seems like the whole darn German Army is popping away at us, and he's telling me this.

"Yes, that's right," he rambled on, "and you know what, I used to rob the city of St. Louis of all the nickels and dimes I could."

You see, it was all the complexities of the situation. In one way it was as much stark reality as you'll ever find; in another, it was all so unreal. His mind was wandering, and he just said what came into his head.

After things quieted down at Belleau, they moved us north toward Soissons, loading us into these camions one night around the middle of July. You always moved at night because of the shelling. It was dark as can be, and it seems to me it was raining. Every time we'd pass a farmer or a Poilu on the road, one of our men would holler out, "How far to Villers-Cotterêts?"

The answer was always the same: "*vingt* kilometers."

Finally, after hearing the same "*vingt* kilometers" five or six times, this young trumpeter started to laugh and looked over toward me.

"Well, Lieutenant," he said, "thank God we're not *losing* any ground!"

This broke the men up, which was perfect, as the morale was down at the bottom of the barrel. Here these guys had just been through all the hell you can imagine at Belleau Wood: seeing their buddies shot to pieces; days without food; no chance to bathe or change their clothes; and what happens?—they cram us into these camions to take us back into it.

That trumpeter—his name was Saunders—was always saying things like that. He was hell on wheels in action but really not much of a Marine when it came to the everyday routine of soldiering. I think he spent as much time in the brig out of the lines as he spent with the platoon. Then I decided I was going to straighten him out—hell, I wasn't much older than he was. What I was trying to do was be a disciplinarian beyond my age.

Anyway, I pulled him aside one day and asked him why he couldn't stay out of trouble. I went into a long spiel on how being a good Marine wasn't just being great in combat, that there were reasons for all the other rules we had—you know, all that stuff.

"Well, Lieutenant," he answered with a contented smile, "I'm always ready when the guns go off, but the rest of the time when you're out in the cold, I'm sitting by a nice warm fire in the brig." He had me stopped cold.

We finally reached the area near Soissons where the 5th Marines had made a big push. It was our job to pick up where they left off. Our 2nd Division was on the far right of the line, with some French Moroccans on our left, and the U. S. 1st Division on their left—the whole idea was to start the Germans moving backward now that we had stopped their drive.

The next morning at dawn, when we went into action, there were the Germans up to their old tricks: We had to pass through a wheat field to reach the wooded area where they were holed up. Our company had three officers when we started, but we were soon down to two. The first lieutenant had stopped a slug in his arm and was headed for the rear. Then a few minutes later I saw Lieutenant Church lying on the ground frothing at the mouth, shivering and shaking. The poor guy was shell-shocked. I put him in a hole, covering him up with several packs that had been discarded for one reason or another. So there I was, once again the only officer in the company. One of the first things I did was get rid of my pistol and pick up a Springfield. I didn't have any collar ornaments on anyway, so there was no way the Germans could pick me out as an officer.

Let me say something right now about the Springfield: It was a great weapon. Not only was it accurate, but it rarely jammed. Having very few parts, it seemed to be able to absorb the dirt—and we were always living in dirt—and still work. And that damn Chauchat,[2] it was a lousy weapon in many ways, but it was another dirt absorber. It wasn't very accurate, but it usually worked, and that's a great asset in the type of combat we were in—you could use it like a hose.

Well, we've got the same old job of moving against the entrenched Germans. Only this time we had some artillery supporting us, 75's and 37 millimeters. This is extremely important. Remember,

[2] A French automatic weapon similar to the American BAR.

while we're confused and scared, so are the Germans. After all, they knew we were moving against them. And if we break through, the best they can hope for is a prison camp.

About this time my old Yale friend Johnny Overton's company moved in on our right. As Johnny went by, he yelled out, "Hey Sam, if I get knocked off today, be sure and send my pin home to Mother." He meant his Skull and Bones pin, a secret society we had at Yale. I grinned and waved back at him. You see, we were always saying things like this. Whenever you were moving in, you'd hear someone say, "If I get it today, don't take those three hundred fives I won in a crap game last night"; or, "Don't take my watch, you ghoul." No one really means anything by it, it's just a way of nervous men trying to laugh at death. You might say it was morale talk.

Then, in about an hour, one of my men yelled over, "Mr. Meek, I'm sorry to tell you your friend Johnny Overton has been killed."

As there was another man named Overton in the outfit, I told him he must be mistaken.

Then he yelled back, "No, it's your friend, the one who told you to get his pen." He had it a little wrong—it was "pin," not "pen"— but I knew it was Johnny.

A little while later we had a regrouping in the attack, so I made my way over to where my dear buddy was. There this wonderful guy was, lying on his back with a shell fragment in his heart. I reached into his jacket, taking the pin out. Subsequently I sent it home via a Red Cross worker.

Later on I began to feel guilty about poor Overton lying out there. I contacted another officer by the name of Evans Spalding— he'd also been a friend of Johnny's. We took off one of our dead friend's dogtags, leaving the other with the body. Then we dug a hole with our bayonets. It was hard work, but we made it plenty deep enough to hold the body. We marked the spot well, making a detailed sketch of where we had buried him; then we stuck a Springfield in the ground with Johnny's helmet on the top. Shortly after the war, his father came to France and had no trouble whatsoever in finding his son's grave. They brought him back to Nashville for his final resting place. The American Legion post there is named for Johnny.

Oh, but we lost a great many good men that July 19 at Soissons. My little trumpeter was another one. The last time I saw him he was the same as always, moving about under fire, paying no attention to it at all. He was shot when trying to help a wounded buddy. How our platoon missed that trumpeter!

It seems to me just about everyone picked up some type of a wound there. I had a bullet just graze my neck, but it wasn't bad enough for me to leave the outfit. It was a horrible fight all right, but remember, after Soissons the Germans never took another forward step in France.

After Soissons General Lejeune[3] replaced Harbord[4] as commanding officer of our division. Pershing needed someone to run the SOS (Service of Supply), and Harbord seemed to be perfect. We now had over a million men in France, and the movement of supplies had become bigger than anything our country had ever seen before.

Both Lejeune and Harbord were equally good officers but completely different men; Lejeune was taciturn and distant, while Harbord was a friendly extrovert. I can clearly remember an incident that sums up Lejeune's personality rather well as far as I'm concerned. It was during a divisional officers' briefing that I attended. This Marine company commander was told to relieve a company of soldiers on the line. He promptly marched his men out as instructed, but when he arrived at the designated spot, the Army captain wouldn't budge.

"How can I pull my troops out?" replied the soldier. "I have no orders from my people. What do you want me to do, get court-martialed?"

The Marine couldn't think of anything to do but sit his men down and return alone to divisional headquarters to explain the situation to Lejeune. The general's reception was anything but understanding.

"Goddamn it," roared Lejeune, "I don't want excuses. When I give an order, I want it obeyed. You're relieved of your command!" My friend was then sent home to command a guard company at some Navy yard. The tough part of the whole thing was the poor guy was a regular, a career Marine. His whole future was ruined by something he couldn't control. I've often wondered what the hell he was supposed to have done—shoot the Army captain?

[3] Brigadier General John A. Lejeune (later Marine commandant).
[4] Major General James G. Harbord, USA.

September brought the Saint Mihiel show and the creation of a separate American Army for the first time. It also brought the end of my combat days—on the fifteenth, to be precise.

Cliff Cates and I were out trying to figure out our line of exploitation while walking down one of those white chalky roads. We had stopped to look at this map—I still have the map, incidentally—when wham, this shell exploded on our right and another on our left. We were pretty battlewise by this time and we knew the next one was going to split the middle.

"Cliff," I warned, "we just might get killed here." And this time I meant it. We instinctively hit the deck and, by God, not a minute too soon; if we hadn't, I would have been killed, not just wounded.

Well, I can't move, so I said to Cates, "Get out of here; I'm going to hide in that ditch till it blows over."

A little later I tried to walk with a cane I'd taken from a German officer, but it was no use. There was a hole in my thigh I could stick a finger in. Then this Red Cross man appeared out of nowhere. He was a big guy, and he actually carried me back to a field hospital.

I spent the rest of my days in France in a hospital, landing back in New York City in January of '19.

And what about Cates? That experience was typical of his World War I days. He was the luckiest man that ever was in the Marine Corps. He'd get his shoulder straps shot off, his leggings, every part of his uniform would pick up fragments from shells, but never Cates. I think he even had his canteen shot off one time. And it was the same at Guadalcanal in the Second War. I don't think anyone ever had the close shaves he had. I guess he was being saved to become commandant, because that's just what happened.

Good-bye, Jeb Stuart: The Cavalry

FIRST DOUGHBOY: "Do you know what is more rare than
a good meal around here?"
SECOND DOUGHBOY: "No—what?"
FIRST DOUGHBOY: "A dead cavalryman."

When World War I started, all the opposing armies were loaded with cavalry; by the time it ended, the dashing, mounted *beau sabres* had been reduced to a role somewhat above that of the carrier pigeons—and some military historians might opt in favor of the birds.

This does not mean that the value of the horse itself had been greatly diminished, just the cavalry. A good deal of the artillery, machine-gun carts, and all types of supply wagons were still horse-drawn. Motor trucks were increasingly used as the war progressed, but even by November 11, 1918, the horse was a vital factor. Many of the officers of all the services were mounted, as were the soldiers of all ranks who tended the field pieces. Actually, the obtaining of, and caring for, these horses was one of the ever-pressing problems of the AEF. Bill Cronin was a second lieutenant greatly involved in this problem for the 149th Field Artillery. I visited with Mr. Cronin during a rather vicious Detroit snowstorm in January 1977.

"You know," he informed me, "this has been a real tough winter. And that first one in France [1917–18] was also severe. Our division [42nd] arrived over there early and we went through the whole thing. The men suffered plenty, but so did our horses. We had a devil of a time getting new ones. I think we ended up buying some from Spain. It was a mess all right. We had to get them, though; just couldn't move our guns without them."

As valuable then as the horse was, the same cannot be said for those glamor boys of previous wars, the cavalrymen, and it came as a big shock to thousands of mounted Americans who had visualized riding hell-bent for election on the fields of France. It was particularly tough on the mounted troops of the National Guard. These men were normally socially prominent in their hometowns, most owned their own mounts, and their transformation into machine-gun battalions and artillery units was not usually greeted with joy. It was the unkindest cut of all for the Essex troop of New Jersey when they were turned into Military Police. One of them, Cy Currier, who now lives in comfortable retirement on Cape Cod, chuckled when he told me what happened.

"You should have heard the reaction," he guffawed, "when the boys found out they were going to be MPs. The thought of being policemen was really too much for some of them. We still had some horses, but it just wasn't the same."

There was a period when thousands of Doughboys at least saw the *grandeur* of strutting French cavalry. This was at the fighting of June and July 1918 around the Marne River. None of them seemed to have forgotten it.

"Oh, they were a magnificent sight," recalled Shipley Thomas, "with their horizon-blue uniforms, prancing horses, and military *élan.*"

The only trouble with these French troopers was that they never seemed to accomplish much. There was just no way that horses could go up against machine guns. Occasionally attempts were made to use horses against retreating Boche, but even when the Germans would withdraw, there would usually be some machine guns left to cover the movements. It wouldn't take many machine guns to utterly decimate a charging cavalry force.

In his book *The American Army in France*, General James Harbord tells of a bantam-rooster type French cavalry officer who was always going to lead a charge against the Germans and sweep the field. But Harbord never tells of it actually happening. On the morning of the attack at Soissons, Harbord, then in command of the 2nd Division, asked Preston Brown if he had seen the 1918 version of Joachim Murat. Brown just smiled.

"We'll see him when the war is over and he's lining up to get his medals," smirked Brown.[1]

Anyway, First Lieutenant Musgrave Hyde, 15th Artillery, 2nd Division, remembers his encounter with the French cavalry well.

"It was during the Battle of Soissons, and things were really confused. I was riding near Vierzy when I saw the most magnificent sight that anyone has ever seen: this French cavalry general leading his unit through a wheat field. It was like something out of another age. I assume they were moving into an attack.

"Well, later that same day a young mounted French officer appeared on the scene and asked me to direct him to our brigade headquarters. I was in the process of doing just that when the French general I had seen in the morning came galloping by. He was accompanied by three or four of his aides. You could tell by his face that he had either not been able to attack, or if he had, that he had been repulsed. He was angry.

"The young French officer with me—who was immaculately attired, incidentally—immediately rode over to the general.

" '*Bonjour, mon Général,*' he said. The unhappy recipient of these salutations gave the young officer a furious look and pointed a finger at him.

" '*Je vous en merde,*' he spit out at the lieutenant, and rode on.

"As I said, the French general was obviously unhappy over something. Perhaps it had finally dawned on this old fire eater that the day of the cavalry charge was as dead as the bow and arrow."

[1] In Major General Robert Bullard's memoirs he was even more pronounced in speaking of the French cavalry. "I felt rather sure they [the cavalry] would do no good and they did none," he wrote.

The 12th Artillery's Giant

John O'Brien

HIS HOME, LOUDENVILLE, NEW YORK, MAY 1977
Major John O'Brien found himself in command of an anti-aircraft battery in France during the fall of 1944. And he was concerned. A sergeant with thirty years of service had recently been transferred to his outfit.

"I was worried about him," recalled Mr. O'Brien in the spring of 1977. "Could an old-time regular Army man who had gone into Mexico with Pershing in 1916 relate to the modernized Army of 1944? After the old soldier had been with us a couple of months, I called in his lieutenant to find out how things were going.

"'Surprisingly enough, quite well,' reported the officer, a lad of about twenty-three. 'After all, he is an *old* bastard; he did serve in France, you know, in World War I.'

"As the young lieutenant told me this, he was staring squarely at my World War I victory medal. I was seriously considering spinning him around and planting one of my size 13 E feet right on his backside when I noticed the twinkle in his eye and his abnormally fierce effort to keep from laughing.

"'You son-of-a-gun,' I chuckled, and we both burst into laughter.

"Well, sir, that old sergeant we were talking about turned into one of the best men we had."

As I visited with Jack O'Brien at his lovely home in Loudenville,

New York, it was easy to see he does indeed have large feet. In his prime, he was six-five and over two hundred pounds. He is still very much a fine figure of a man as he nears the age of eighty.

After his return to this country, he resumed his education, graduating from Yale College in 1922. Then he went into business in nearby Albany, where he prospered. But as he found out, like so many other Doughboys, his service in France never quite left him.

"Take my wedding," he recalled. "Before the actual ceremony, I had not met all my wife's relatives. Then, at the reception, I was introduced to one of her uncles by marriage.

"'Hello, O'Brien,' he said to me.

"Good God! It was Manus McCloskey, my old colonel from the 12th Field Artillery!"

Private John O'Brien
F Company, 12th Field Artillery, 2nd Division

It was just before I went overseas in the Second War; I was having lunch at the 21 Club in New York City. Sitting across from me was General Terry Allen. He'd been sent back to the States because he thought his old World War I division, the 1st, could win the Second War single-handed. He was in the process of building up a new division (the 104th), which he later took to Europe. He kept staring at my *fourragère*, which the 2nd Division had been awarded by the French in 1918. Of course, he didn't know who the hell I was. As I walked out, I stopped at his table and said:

"General, they can't win this war without old-timers like us."

—JOHN O'BRIEN

That's right. I served in the U. S. Army in Europe during the two World Wars: in the first one as a private, and in 1944 as a major. While I feel the average American soldier did a great job in both of those scraps, there definitely were differences between the two generations.

Right off the top of the barrel you can start with unit spirit. I think the Doughboy had a great deal more of this than the GI did. Take our outfit, the 2nd Division. As you know, we had two infantry brigades, one Army and the other Marine. You can bet that there was a great deal of rivalry between these two. But just let an outsider butt in, particularly after Belleau Wood and Soissons, and the fur would really fly. I can remember when we first received our divisional shoulder patches—the Marines wore them with as much pride as our Army men did. As a matter of fact, I think the 2nd Division was the first division to get them. Why the hell we have the Indian head on them, I don't know.

Another difference was the slang. I was having a conversation the other day and I said, "Oh that's Jake with me." I hadn't used that expression in God knows how long. If you were talking about a man and you said, "He's Jake with me," it meant he was on the square. And square meant something completely different than it does today. In World War I parlance, a man who was on the square was the real goods—in other words, a right guy. This could go on all day; just let it suffice to say it meant he was "to the mustard." Haw, haw, there's another one for you.

Still another way the two generations were different were the fist fights. Oh you had them in World War II, all right, but nothing like the First War. Christ, someone was always saying, "OK, OK, let's settle this behind the latrine!"

Please remember I was 6 feet, 5 inches, and 210 pounds in those days. There weren't too many people asking me to go behind the latrine, but it happened constantly with the other men. Maybe it was because the country seemed so much younger then than it does now.

And the Australians were the same way. When we first landed at Le Havre, we were not given any passes. But another fellow and I found a hole in the wire and crawled out anyway. We went into this huge canteen they had there in Le Havre. It was mobbed. After we'd had a few beers, I went into the *pissoire*, where I was confronted by a slightly inebriated Aussie.

"Come on, Yank," he said, "let's the two of us go clean up on the whole bloody crew out there."

As there were over a thousand troops in the canteen, I succeeded in showing this ANZAC the folly of such a venture, but he was raring to go.

That brings up something that I guess goes with age. That happened fifty-nine years ago, yet I can not only remember that Australian, but I believe those are the exact words he used—amazing!

Well, let's go back to the beginning, and by that I mean 1916. I was visiting a friend of mine, Bill Carr, who was a student at Yale. [Mr. O'Brien was a student at Phillips Exeter in New Hampshire at the time.] I was there in New Haven when they called up the Connecticut National Guard for the Mexican border campaign. Bill felt it would be great fun to get involved, so we both went into the 10th Connecticut Field Artillery. You know how things like that can snowball when you're a kid. Hell, I think the first four batteries of that regiment were made up of Yale undergraduates. Then came the big disappointment. We never did get to wear those campaign hats down on the border. We ended up spending the summer training in Tobyhanna, Pennsylvania. I did get one thing out of it, though—a knowledge of, and a liking for, the field artillery. When the war came the next year, I didn't have any trouble deciding what branch of the service I wanted to enter. So, by October of 1917 I found myself down near Alexandria, Virginia, as a private in F Battery of the 12th Field Artillery, regular Army. I was nineteen years old at the time.

Due to my previous year's service I thought I knew something about soldiering, but compared to those old regulars I was as green as grass. While I was lucky enough to have two old school chums in my battery, it was the old regulars who dominated the outfit; at first, anyway. To them, you were a rookie until you had at least three years in the Army. They were professionals, all right, and heaven help anyone who couldn't learn to be like them in a hurry. This went for officers as well as enlisted men. How well I can remember the day they showed a ninety-day wonder that even those shavetails had to shape up.

Now, this young fellow was a new officer, and everybody was waiting to see how he would measure up. One of his early efforts turned into a near disaster. He had us in open ranks when he roared out the command, "Squads right!" Not a soul stirred. He yelled it out again and still no movements.[1] Finally the first sergeant took pity on him.

"Did you say 'Close ranks,' sir?" he whispered. It was one of those whispers, I may add, that you could hear on an artillery range.

Oh Christ, was that lieutenant embarrassed! Then he meekly said what he was supposed to, and all was under control. If you look at that little incident, those regulars probably did the shavetail a favor. The thing above all we looked for in an officer when we got in combat was professional competence. There is nothing that sours the men any more than a leader who would be fooling around—you know the type, one who doesn't know the score. You can bet that lieutenant paid a little more attention to what he was doing after that.

We did have another officer later on who just couldn't learn how to work with men—hell, he never was any good! But there was a time, right in the middle of some rough stuff, when he was told off in spades; I think it was during the fighting around Soissons. As I remember it, this bird was a captain attached to our outfit; he was not our commanding officer.

Well, there were about five or six of us pinned down in this ravine. The Germans were really raking us over the coals with 77's and 155's. The captain in question was one of our group. He'd already endeared himself to no one in a hundred little ways—you know the kind, a guy who always has to have some fish to fry. This time he went too far, and he picked the wrong guy.

[1] No drill order can be given when the command is at open ranks.

"McCann," he ordered, right in the heat of the shelling, "go on over near our guns and get my bedroll."

"No, sir," answered McCann, one of our really top veterans.

"What?" cried the captain. "Do you refuse to obey a direct order?"

McCann just looked at the captain with this cold stare.

"That is an incorrect order, sir. That is a personal service, sir. Army regulations do not require an enlisted man to carry those out. Besides, if the captain wants his bedroll that much, let him get his own ass shot getting it, sir." We heard very little from that officer again.

Now, don't get the wrong idea here. We had plenty of good officers—I'd say the large majority of them were tops. We had a battery officer named Martindale who was a corker. He was an Englishman who'd been a young cavalryman during the Boer War. The rumor was that he'd spent three or more years mining gold in such a remote part of Alaska that when he came down in 1917, he didn't even know there was a war going on. I can remember meeting up with him in a foxhole during another shelling episode. Unfortunately, by "meeting up" I mean that I jumped in on top of him. Remember, I wasn't exactly built like a jockey.

"Oh," I stammered out, "I am sorry, sir."

"Quite all right, O'Brien, quite all right," he answered, "drop in anytime. On your next visit I'll try and have some tea."

The greatest officer in our regiment, though, was a major whom I never really knew. He was commander of the 1st Battalion, a West Pointer, and, from what we'd heard, he was liked by everyone. And there was one occasion, over there at Blanc Mont, where we found out just what a great man he was. We were trying to take a little rest between shellings when this major stumbled down into this hole where we had our telephone set up.

"Can I get through to brigade headquarters on this phone?" he asked.

We immediately put him through. Now, mind you, we could only hear his voice, but it was obvious that the man on the other end of the line, probably the brigade's executive officer, wanted him to do something that the major was violently opposed to.

"You don't understand," he pleaded, "the Germans have occupied that area in strength. If I take my battalion there right now, they'll be slaughtered."

Then the headquarters talked for a while. And the major answered them.

"I don't give a damn about the map you have. I've just been there. It's loaded with Boche. I'll lose half my men going in and the other half trying to hold."

More talk from headquarters. It was obvious the major was getting nowhere. Finally:

"Look, you can remove me from command, you can court-martial me, hell, you can even shoot me. But I'm not ordering the 1st Battalion into that spot until we can clear those Germans out." Then he hung up.

Oh my God, we were almost in tears. The poor guy probably ruined his career, but every enlisted man within the sound of his voice wanted to cheer. He was quite a man!

Well, I've gotten a bit ahead of my story, but a good deal of my memories of my service in World War I concern officers, good and bad. I tried to use these experiences in World War II as a guideline to make me a good officer. Now, back to Virginia and 1917.

By the time I joined the 12th we'd already been alerted for a quick trip abroad. As I've told you, the 12th had a much higher percentage of regulars than most of the other outfits. Its nucleus had been formed by taking the entire 2nd Battalion of the highly venerable 3rd Field Artillery and building a regiment around it. Many of the other regulars had come from cavalry or coast artillery regiments with the inducement of a quick trip overseas.

Our colonel, a man named McCloskey, tried to keep building our *esprit de corps* by hammering into us the long history of the original 3rd Field Artillery.

"Shortly after I graduated West Point," he would say, "I joined the 2nd Battery of the 3rd in China. We were the first unit to fire on Peking during the Boxer Rebellion. We were the best then, and we're the best now." Hell, he had us believing it!

We worked damn hard that fall, trying to get ready for what was ahead. Just about the only relaxation we had came when I and my three buddies—Phil Hume, Ed Moser, and Festus Wade—could get a pass to go into Washington. We'd try and get a room at the Willard to wash the horse manure off both our uniforms and our bodies. Everything we had was horse-drawn, and you could really work up both a sweat and a stink.

Oh, and that brings up a good one. You see, the first thing we'd do when we arrived was send our uniforms and our underwear out to the cleaners. Then we'd sit around, stark naked, and do some drinking. Well, these two fellows, Charlie Lucky and L. Kitchell, who were friends of Moser's, had just been assigned to our regiment; Ed had asked them to come visit us at the Willard so we could give them the lowdown on what the outfit was like.

In the meantime, we'd grown so accustomed to our routine that we weren't the slightest bit self-conscious about sitting around balls-ass naked and drinking. You should have seen the look on their faces when they came in that room and saw us. They were a couple of good ones, though, and we all had quite a laugh about it a little later on. Both of them—Kitchell and Lucky—had just returned from a six-month tour of duty, driving an ambulance with the American Field Service in France. They were great pals to have when we went over in January of '18.

Sometime in December they shipped us up to Camp Merritt, New York, to await our transport. My parents came down from our home in West Chazy, New York, and I had a great Christmas dinner with them. I was expecting to move out any minute, but much to my pleasant surprise, we were able to spend New Year's Eve in New York City.

What a night! We just kept moving from one spot to another. I can vividly remember going into one place where one of the waiters wouldn't serve us. This was too much for one of the other waiters to take.

"Don't you know these men are on their way to France?" he yelled. Then he promptly punched the offending party right on the jaw. That's the kind of a night it was. Then, on January 10, we went aboard the *Olympic,* and it was good-bye, Broadway, hello, France.

What a trip! We were so crowded we could hardly move. As for any privacy whatsoever, it was absolutely nonexistent. There was one time, however, when I was able to grab a little rest and also realize that you never get in trouble if an officer can use you to his advantage.

It happened one day when I'd decided not to go on deck for the morning drill. I hid in the head until everyone was topside, then started to relax. It was beautiful; not a sound. It was the first time I'd been alone since we boarded ship.

Then my silence was broken by five or six officers, including Colonel McCloskey, who had decided to inspect our quarters. I jumped to attention, figuring the least I'd get was a stiff fine out of our meager pay. What I hadn't thought of was the colonel's well-known boast that he knew the name of every private in the regiment.

"Ah, ha," stated the good colonel, "Private *O'Brien*. And how are you enjoying your trip over, *O'Brien?*"

"Fine, sir, fine."

"That's fine, *O'Brien*. Carry on."

You see, what had happened was I had given McCloskey an ideal chance to demonstrate to those other officers that he did indeed know the names of the privates. I never heard a word about missing the drill.

The one good thing about that trip was the rapidity. The *Olympic* was a fast ship, so we were traveling without a convoy. We did do a lot of zigzagging but managed to reach Liverpool in about seven days. This was around the middle of January. We were only in England about a week or so before they shipped us out of Southampton to Le Havre. And they didn't waste any time with us there either. Hell, I think that time I met the Aussie in the *pissoire* was just about our only night there. The next morning they piled us on those devil's gift to transportation, the 40 and 8's, and sent us across France to Valdahon, near the French Alps. Our first morning there we were given the word by a French artillery officer.

"Soldiers, learn ze Sam-O (75's) in ze hurry. Five, maybe six weeks, you face le Boche."

We all knew this was for keeps, so we buckled down to work. French fire-control instruments, the metric system, those French maps that had all of France laid out in kilometer squares—all these had to be learned in a hurry. My buddy Phil Hume was right at the top of the class; after all, Hume was to be an honor student at MIT after the war. But right alongside of him was a man named Marty Lamb, a fellow who had never even finished grade school. This just goes to show you there is such a thing as natural intelligence.

There were a couple of things that do stick in my mind about our period there. One was the champagne. We could get all we wanted for two dollars a bottle. I knew very little about champagne in those days, so I thought this was great. After the war, when I had a chance to really get familiar with the stuff, I realized what rotgut it really was. Hell, those Frogs were screwing us royally!

The other thing concerns a Lieutenant Colonel Stimson. It seems that he was an artillery colonel who visited Valdahon while we were training. I was on KP peeling potatoes at the time when one of our men came running over to me.

"Hey, O'Brien," he said, "there's some 'Sam Browne'[2] here who wants to meet you."

Oh Christ, this would have meant that I'd have had to get all spruced up.

"Listen," I told him, "tell them you can't find me; I don't want to go through all that crap."

The result was I never met this chap Stimson, who it turned out was a friend of my father's. Oh hell, it was Henry L. Stimson, who was Secretary of War during World War II. And I had just kept peeling potatoes rather than meet him.

Well, true to their word, about six weeks after we had arrived at Valdahon, we were sent into a quiet sector around Verdun. As we were moving in, they told us we were now members of the 2nd Division of the regular Army. What they had done was put together two regiments of Marines from the Leathernecks already in France and made the 4th Brigade out of these two, the 5th and 6th Marines. Then they obtained two unattached U. S. Infantry regiments —the 9th and 23rd—and made another brigade out of them. After that they gathered regular Army units such as the 2nd Engineers from all over to fill out the division. It's still around today.

As far as I could see, it really was a quiet sector. The Germans would shell occasionally, and we would shell them back, but basically it was pretty tame. I know our battery commander's detail didn't have it very rough there. We did our job of manning the battery telephone, receiving and transmitting orders, repairing the telephone lines, and acting as runners and observers.

There was one funny story about the time a fellow named Jake Roth spent a week or so with us as an observer. The last day he

[2] Enlisted man's slang for an officer.

was to be there he called for a large barrage on a crossroad behind the German lines. We sent several shells over. After he came back, we asked him what had been going through, a large convoy? Jake laughed.

"No," he chuckled, "just one fat German sergeant. But every day I'd seen him smoking a pipe at exactly 9:30 A.M. Then he'd casually stroll over to this Chic Sales close to a hundred yards away and spend about a half an hour in there. We didn't get him with the shelling, but I think we scared the you know what out of him that morning."

The real war was just around the corner, though. We'd been relieved from our trenches the first of May and marched for nearly a week. The French countryside, where we were headed, was absolutely beautiful. While I say "marched," remember, most of us were actually riding, either on horseback or on the caissons. The rumors this time were that we would rest up for a while, then relieve the 1st Division in Picardy. This all changed when the Germans broke through around the Chemin des Dames. On May 31 they stuck us on railroad cars, guns, horses, everything, and headed us toward the Marne.

This brings up one of the most amazing memories I have of the war. It concerns one of our officers—a young West Pointer, Lieutenant Tibbitts—Charlie Lucky, and myself. This trio was let off the train early to ride ahead and help set up the area where we were going to place our artillery. We left the train at dusk and started to ride.

The confusion was tremendous, with all the civilians running away from the Germans. Yes, and some French soldiers also. We rode all night. Every now and then we'd see Tibbitts pull out a flashlight and read a map he had. But not once did we have to ask directions from the French. At about dawn we rode up to regimental headquarters near Belleau Wood. How in the hell Tibbitts did it, I just don't know—but he did. Lucky and I always referred to him as the magician from then on.

Well, this was it. Our regiment was to fire in support of the Marines until they were relieved and then get in support of whoever relieved them. The day we lined up was, I believe, June 3. The rumors were flying right and left. A fat French officer came riding by yelling, "Le Boche, Le Boche, only two kilometers away. Retreat, fast!" Hell, we had no orders to retreat, so we just shortened the fuses on our 75's and loaded up with shrapnel shells. Each battery had two machine guns. Those were also set up. Each man also had his own personal .45-caliber pistol. I hadn't fired mine in months. I think it had too much rust on it. Anyway, we all loaded them and waited.

The Germans never did break through those Marines, thank God. For the next thirty days or so, though, we were constantly in action, either heavy or light. I acted as messenger a good deal of the time. This could be real hectic, as it seemed I was always drawing shellfire. A good deal of the time I was supposed to deliver my information on horseback. I tried not to, though, because that way you were sure to be spotted by the Germans.

Those horses could be a real problem, particularly if some gas shells came over. Try putting a gas mask on one of them someday. Christ, I remember trying to do it one time under fire. It was impossible! One of those bastards just missed me with a vicious kick. Finally I just threw the masks down and yelled, "All right, you idiots, put them on yourselves!" Then I jumped into a shellhole. I don't think any of them were killed; not then, anyway.

We were losing men, though—not as many as the infantry, of course, but we were losing them, all right. I remember this Italian cook named Inco. He'd brought his rolling kitchen too close to the lines. He knew damn well the smoke from his fire was bound to draw the German fire, so he was trying to hurry us along.

"What's-a the matter?" he was yelling. "Move-a, move-a, Jesus-a Christ, move-a!"

Just after I'd filled my mess kit and cup, I heard this big one coming over. It was going to be close, so the hell with the chow, I jumped into the nearest hole, spilling everything. Our cook wasn't that lucky. It was a direct hit, and no more Inco. I felt badly about it. He was a pretty good man—for a cook, that is.

Another fellow was only with us one day before he got it. The poor guy was sent up to do his tour of duty as an observer with the Marines. He was killed before reaching them. That's the way it was when you had that constant shelling; you just never knew when one was going to clobber you.

That duty as an observer could be rugged as hell, but of course it was absolutely necessary. Each man in BC detail had to do his share. I can remember going into the front lines to take my turn at it one time when some of the Marines actually cheered me. I asked one of them what that was for.

"Well, hell," he answered, "we're afraid if we boo, you all might let one fall short." Of course, they were just giving me the business. They were a great bunch!

Now, not only was it dangerous when you'd be an observer, but it could be just as bad when you had to go out at night and try and mend the telephone wire that the German shelling had torn apart.

This brought up a problem concerning our French allies. Some nut back in headquarters got the idea that the Germans were disguising themselves as French soldiers and coming over to cut our lines at night. So the order went out to bring in every Poilu we found near our wires. You see, there was a French artillery outfit near us that would also send men out at night to fix their own wire.

Oh this was a pretty kettle of fish. How in hell were we going to get these Frogs to come over to our headquarters for questioning? I figured the best way was to tell them we had a couple of loco officers who wanted to talk to some French soldiers. And sure enough, I had the wire detail the next night, and who shows up but two of my French friends.

Well sir, I offered them cigarettes, chocolates, fruit—but without any luck. It was late and they wanted to get back to their own outfits. In desperation I even dangled the thought of a few bottles of good cognac in front of them. This seemed to make a dent. Then came the truly French reaction.

"*Mademoiselles?*" queried one of the Poilu.

Hell, I would have promised those chaps Nora Bayes if it meant they would come with me! So off to headquarters we went.

It didn't take the Frenchies long to prove that they were the real McCoy. I couldn't get them Nora Bayes, of course, or even Powerful Katrinka, but I did scrounge up all the chocolate I could and even a little cognac. I'm sure there was a lot said the next day at the French battery headquarters about the crazy Americans.

Well, we finally came off the lines the tenth of July but went right back in for Soissons. This fight was different than Belleau Wood because there was a constant forward movement. Our job was to keep the artillery moving up with the infantry. It wasn't very easy.

There is one thing I'll never forget about Soissons: a midnight trip I had to take over a field where there had been very heavy fighting that morning. My God, what a sight! The moonlight effect made it even more eerie than it would have been during the daylight. Broken and abandoned equipment was everywhere. And the bodies—hundreds of them, both German and American. They were in every possible position you could imagine. Some had been horribly mangled, while others just had one hole. Then there was the smell—a combination of powder and death. It was some trip!

They pulled our infantry out of the battle after two or three days, but once again we stayed on the lines in support of their replacements. We didn't come out of it until the middle of August. This meant that with the exception of a few days around July 10, we had been facing the Germans since the first of June. We'd lost a great many men and needed replacements. Our equipment was shot and our uniforms were in tatters, particularly mine. You see, at my size, it was almost impossible to find or steal anything. It had to be a new government issue, and none of these were coming through then.

We ended up in a village over near Pont-à-Mousson. There were three cafes in that hamlet. I think every enlisted man was in one of those three saloons our first night there—except O'Brien, that is. You see, my uniform looked like something you'd find on the Bowery. The first MP who saw me brought me back to our area under arrest. I had to march into the tent of our duty officer, who was a captain named Pell Foster.

"Private O'Brien, reporting under arrest," I dutifully informed him. He had the MP's report in front of him.

"For God's sake, O'Brien," he yelled, "when you go into the town tomorrow, hide from the MPs—behind fences, buildings, hedges, anywhere you can. But don't let them catch you again. Dismissed."

That was it. As it turned out, it was a good thing I was arrested and sent back. That night one of our men shot an MP, and there was hell to pay. We weren't overly fond of those fellows, you know.

We did have a rest during the second part of August and received some more new men. But we were back at it on September 12. This time it was Saint Mihiel. We weren't involved in that huge artillery barrage that preceded the assault because they had us right alongside of our infantry. We actually went over at about the same time they did. I've always figured Pershing's headquarters knew that attack was going to succeed, or they wouldn't have put artillery in a position so vulnerable to a counterattack.

In October our division was lent to the French for the fight at Blanc Mont. There was no tougher battle of the war than that one. You don't hear much about it because most of the Americans were in the Argonne at the time. But it was murder. It was there that the major I mentioned earlier refused to uselessly sacrifice his battalion.

Then, around the first of November, we were moved into the Argonne. If there was a scrap going on, I guess headquarters figured the 2nd had to be there. And that's where we were when it all ended.

We soon found out that we weren't going home, though; we were headed for Germany as part of the Army of Occupation. It wasn't until the summer of '19 that I finally sailed for home.

One more thing: After I did get back to the States, I resumed my education as soon as possible, enrolling at Yale College. In my senior year we played our annual football game with Princeton down in New Jersey. After the game was over, a Princetonian invited me over to his club; I can't remember which one. Well, who do I see there but Pell Foster, late a captain of the AEF. His back was turned, but I knew it was Foster. I went over behind him and tapped him on the shoulder.

"Private O'Brien," I said, "reporting under arrest."

Well, Christ, was he glad to see me! He took out a bottle of good scotch whisky—remember, this was Prohibition—and we adjourned to a private room and gabbed until dawn. Do you know that all the time I was in France I never once had a private conversation with an officer? But there was no more of that business after the war. We were just a couple of former members of the 12th Field Artillery getting together.

The Rivalry

A truckload of American soldiers drove by a platoon of resting Marines. One of the Doughboys yelled out, "Who's winning the war?"

Then another answered, "Why, the Marines are!"

A third chipped in, "Then what the hell are we fighting for?"

—A COMMON OCCURRENCE IN 1918 FRANCE

Like thousands of other World War II veterans, I did my college tour after the Axis powers were defeated. My school was Kenyon College, a little Gothic fortress of the English language in central Ohio. My roommate was a fellow named Jim Rice from Shaker Heights, a suburb of Cleveland. Jim and I would frequently travel to his house for a weekend of relaxation. Jim's Dad, Frank O. Rice, had served in France with the 33rd (Illinois National Guard) Division.

On one particular evening at the Rices' when the wassail had been flowing freely (you never left Zeta and Frank Rice's home thirsty), F.O. began to talk about his days with the 33rd. I kept trying to say something that I had read about the Marines at Belleau Wood. Finally F.O. had heard enough.

"Hell, Henry," he moaned, "I hope you're not one of those fellows who thinks the Marines won the war, while the Army stood around with their fingers up their arse!" During all the years I knew Frank Rice, it was the only time I heard that fine gentleman utter a vulgarity. But I had opened an old wound. After the laughter had subsided, F.O. acknowledged that the Marines had fought well in France, but he added, "You know, there weren't a tremendous amount of them in France."

That conversation happened some thirty years ago, but as of 1977 the thinking hasn't changed.

"Yes," I was told by many men, "the Marines did a great job in France, but they received publicity way out of proportion to the amount of men they had there."

Here the Army veterans I talked with are completely correct, but it was in no part the fault of the Marines—it was strictly a case of censorship. By the time the fighting started around the Marne in June of '18, there were hundreds of American newsmen in France. They were under constant pressure to feed their very hungry editors back in the United States. American men were fighting in France, and the folks back home wanted to know what was going on. The only problem was that the newsmen could not mention any specific division by name. They could, however, mention the branches of the service involved.

Headline after headline would blare out, "Marines and Soldiers Fighting." This put the one Marine infantry brigade on a par with several divisions of soldiers.

That one Marine brigade was undoubtedly one of the most outstanding units in the AEF. It fought at Belleau Wood, Soissons, Saint Mihiel, Blanc Mont, and at the Meuse River in the Argonne campaign. From June 1, 1918, until November 11 it was constantly in and out of some of the most brutal battles in American history. The Marine Corps suffered 11,489 casualties in France. Almost all of these dead and wounded came from their two infantry regiments, the 5th and 6th Marines. These two regiments suffered roughly 150 per cent casualties, which is frightfully harsh, but it was a small percentage of the 260,000 suffered by the AEF.

As good as the Marines were, the publicity they received was bound to create resentment. Letters to beleaguered Doughboys from back home would state how happy everyone was about the great job the Marines were doing. If the recipient of the letter happened to be a survivor of a bloody fight himself, he was bound to boil over.

And it wasn't only the foot sloggers; General Bullard once greeted John J. Pershing with somewhat of a needle.

"Well, General," said Bullard, "I see where the 2nd *Marine* Division has done another great job."

"That's an *Army* division," snapped back John J., "with Marines in it. And don't forget it!" But it wasn't really the type of thing to bother Pershing very long. When he relieved Army General James Harbord[1] from command of that same 2nd Division, he put Marine Brigadier General John Lejeune in charge. All Pershing wanted to do was to win.

But it bothered the Doughboys, and it still does. Eighty-four-year-old Musgrave Hyde, a lieutenant in the 15th Field Artillery of the 2nd Division, said to me, "Oh our Marine brigade was great, but it was no better than our other brigade, the Army one."

Then this dignified old-timer laughed and shook his head.

"I'll tell you one thing about two of those Marines that you'll find hard to believe," he added, "but damn it, it's true. After our infantry brigades were pulled off the lines at Soissons, they still left my artillery regiment there—they did that a lot. Well, a week or so after the infantry had left, I had an occasion to visit a Moroccan outfit that was facing the Germans. Oh those Moroccans, they were mean! They used to wear German ears around their necks; I actually saw that. Well, when I was in their lines, I spotted a couple of AWOL Marine enlisted men. They were embarrassed as hell when they saw me, even though I wasn't going to mess with them. One of them came over and gave me a big salute.

"'Lieutenant,' he pleaded, 'we're only here because we really enjoy going out on night raids with these fellows.' Then he pulled out this big knife and held it next to his neck and gave me a wink

---

[1] Not a demotion. He made Harbord the commanding officer of the Service of Supply.

as he said, 'They're really great with the pig sticker. Just one more night,' he continued, 'and then we will go back to the brigade.'

"'Oh sure, sure,' I said, 'go right ahead, have a good time.' Then I got the hell away from those nuts."

Mr. Hyde's Marines were the exception, not the rule. Most of the Marines were the same as the soldiers—perhaps, on the average, a little younger, but basically the same mix as their Army colleagues.

But to most of those old Doughboys there will always be a feeling of resentment against the PR the Corps received. It is just one of those things that'll never change, and it is quite understandably so.

Perhaps I can explain the whole situation with another personal experience that happened in November of 1943. I was then a seventeen-year-old United States Marine on my ten-day boot furlough, cockily walking down the street in West Hartford, Connecticut. My ten weeks' training at Parris Island had convinced me that I was the greatest thing since Caesar's legions.

As I started to cross the intersection at Farmington Avenue and North Main Street, I recognized a dear friend of my family driving by in his big Cadillac. It was the same Tom Brown that has been previously mentioned in this book. He was then about fifty-three years of age and fat. I waved at Brownie, who quickly spotted me and stuck his head out the window.

"Hanky," he roared, "go home and tell your mother you saw a soldier!" Then he laughed loudly.

Mr. Brown was one of the world's greatest people. But the vision of his old friend's son in a Marine Corps uniform automatically brought back a phrase that he'd undoubtedly said a hundred times in 1918 France.

The Fighting Professor

Arnold Whitridge

HIS APARTMENT, NEW YORK CITY, DECEMBER 1976
Of the one hundred veterans I interviewed, twelve served in
Europe before the United States entered the war. Mr. Whitridge,
who joined the British Army a week or two after the war broke out,
was the earliest of these early birds.

He spent the next two years in Flanders with the Royal Field Artillery. His father's death in New York City convinced Arnold that
he should return home to look into the family affairs. Such a separation was not difficult for an American at that time, so in January of
'17 he said farewell to the war.

Back in his own country he soon became greatly involved in
America's preparation program, and in June of 1917 he was back in
France as a captain in the U. S. Army. There he stayed, mainly as
an intelligence officer, until 1919. This second trip to France was
brighter than the first; he met a charming Red Cross lady who became his wife. Their union lasted until Mrs. Whitridge's death in
1972.

Between the World Wars he wrote, lectured, and taught, first at
Columbia, then at Yale. He was at New Haven when the Second
World War broke out and naturally became greatly concerned
when Hitler's Army pulverized France.

What concerned Mr. Whitridge even more was the attitude of a
large segment of America's college students.

"They didn't seem to realize," he recalled, "what a disaster it would be if the Nazis destroyed Great Britain. I tried my best to alert them."

His best was, among other things, a brilliant article in the August 1940 issue of the prestigious *Atlantic Monthly*. It is entitled "Where Do You Stand?" In it he points out that while he realizes most of the students are not Nazi sympathizers, they do not seem to understand what a Hitler-controlled Europe would really mean to the United States.

In 1942 this college professor once again donned a uniform and for the third time went to Europe to confront a German Army. All told, Mr. Whitridge spent close to eight years in a military uniform. However, today he looks much more at home in his study than he would on the drill field. It's a lifestyle he doesn't get from the ground. His great-grandfather was the famous educator "Arnold of Rugby," and his grandfather, Matthew Arnold, was the renowned poet and author.

It was there in his study that we visited. Along with World War I, we also discussed his article from 1940, "Where Do You Stand?" It was as apropos in 1977 as it was thirty-seven years earlier. And the soldier-professor is still concerned.

"I only hope that the Vietnam holocaust does not convince the youth of America to divorce themselves from the rest of the world," he stated. "It's a lot smaller in many ways than it used to be."

Major Arnold Whitridge
6th Field Artillery, 1st Division, AEF
Lieutenant, Royal Field Artillery, 1915–16

I wore a tunic,
A dirty khaki tunic,
And you wore civilian clothes.
We fought and bled at Loos
While you were on the booze,
The booze that no one here knows.
Oh, you were with the wenches
While we were in the trenches
Facing our German foe.
Oh, you were a-slacking
While we were attacking
Down on the Menin Road.

—SONG OF THE BRITISH TOMMY IN
FLANDERS, SUNG TO THE TUNE OF
"I WORE A TULIP."

In 1912 I cast my first vote; it was for Theodore Roosevelt and his Bull Moose Party. Indeed, Teddy would have won that election if he had received the Republican nomination. He did get more votes than Taft, you know. And Roosevelt and Taft combined outpolled Woodrow Wilson. Teddy's own tally was the largest ever recorded by a third-party candidate. As far as I'm concerned, all in all, it was one of the greatest political campaigns we've ever had.

I was attending Yale at the time, in my senior year. Naturally, all the students were pretty excited that fall, especially when William Jennings Bryan came to address us. Bryan had that real booming voice; my God, he was majestic! He didn't change my vote, but I do remember one phrase he used. It went like this:

"Taft came in with a million majority and he'll go out with unanimous consent." They don't make speakers like that anymore!

Now, you might wonder why I bring up that election in regard to the First World War, or Great War, as we used to call it. Did you ever stop to think what would have happened if T.R. had won that election of 1912? I think America well might have declared war a lot earlier than we did. It would have changed the whole course of the war.

Well, after I'd graduated Yale [1913], I went abroad. I had a great deal more studying I wanted to do, so I spent a year at Oxford. Then I decided to study in Germany, learning their language and traditions.

I must confess that was an extremely interesting period to have been in Europe. After Archduke Franz Ferdinand was assassinated [June 28, 1914], you could see the tensions building up everywhere—one thing just seemed to follow another.

But oh how naïve the people were. Each crisis seemed to bring excitement and elation. There hadn't been a major war in Europe for so many years, and everyone seemed to clamor for one. I recall trying to point out to a German what a catastrophe it might be, but he just laughed and shrugged.

"It vill not go long," he said. "Ve vill vin in a second. Besides, ze financiers vill not *let it* last long." I wonder what that fellow was thinking in 1918—if he was alive, that is.

The war did come, all right, and it changed the whole social structure of the world. When Germany actually declared war against Russia, I decided I better get out of there. I didn't want any part of the "Kaiser's *Kultur*," so I headed for Great Britain. I landed there the very day that the United Kingdom declared war on Germany.

Things were naturally a great deal different in Britain from when I had been there earlier in the summer. The country was at war, but no one seemed to know what was really happening. Anyway, a great many of the chaps I'd been at Oxford with were going into the service, so I decided to join them.

I guess the biggest issue then seemed to be Belgium. You know, in some ways we were more civilized in 1914 than we are now. The shock of what the Germans were doing to "poor little Belgium" sickened people everywhere. After the unimaginable horrors of the Nazis, the world's pretty hardened to that sort of thing now, but we weren't in 1914.

Anyway, I'd been schooled in the traditions of Dr. Peabody of Groton School: If you saw a wrong, you tried to right it. So I joined the Royal Field Artillery, and in the early part of 1915 was posted off to Flanders—and, I might add, woefully ill-trained.

At the time I'll freely admit I felt as romantically inclined about war as the next man. It seemed so natural to think of the bands and the cheering and to forget about the stark terrors that are really what war is all about.

Well, as I remember it, the only things that coincided with all the pictures that I'd seen were the horse-drawn artillery and the supply wagons. It was truly quite picturesque watching the snorting horses limbering up and drawing the caissons into line. This was something straight out of the old Civil War paintings, particularly if it was done under fire.

The same feeling applied to the supply wagons. You see, at the beginning of the war, anyway, many of the supplies coming to the front were horse-drawn. And there were certain areas, such as crossroads, where the Germans would concentrate their artillery fire. Naturally, when the horses would get close to such places, the drivers would go hell bent for election.

Oh that German fire could be devilish, all right, and they never seemed to run out of shells. But as methodical and accurate as the Boche would be, they always did everything by the book. They had plenty of spies around and they could easily ascertain when a certain road would be heavily traveled. So day in and day out, they'd shell the same places; you could set your watch by their fire.

It wasn't very difficult to pick up their pattern. As you might surmise, it was also quite easy to merely stay away from heavily shelled areas during the bad periods. Sometimes it would be weeks before the Germans would change their targets.

There was another sight straight out of a boy's concept of war—I'll never forget it. I think it was just before the beginning of the Somme battles. I was resting by the side of the road, some ten to fifteen miles behind the front, when along came the Gordon Highlanders.

Well sir, they had their pipes and drums going full blast. I think they were playing "Scotland the Brave." Their kilts and arms were swinging, and they even had their battle flags unfurled. It was an anachronism, all right, but a magnificent one.

Those poor Scotties. They were certainly shot up so many times during the war. The Germans called them "The Ladies from Hell" because of their bravery.

Speaking of bravery, that was another side of the war that I suppose you could say was romantic. And I did see many acts of unsurpassed heroics. The only trouble was it would so often end in death. I suppose that is the utmost tragedy of war—the death of so many fine men.

One of these gallant deeds concerned our battery's major, Frederick Robinson. And what a princely fellow he was! He had that absolute devotion to duty that I found in so many of the English officers.

Well, we had a building near our battery where we would store our shells. Apparently the Germans found out about it, because they zeroed in on it. They hit the building, all right, but didn't explode our shells. They did set the place on fire, so it was only a matter of time before it would blow up.

In the meantime, someone had pointed out that we had a man or two still in there, probably wounded from the shelling. The minute our major heard this he dashed into the building after the men. He was still in there when the fire reached the explosives. He was blown to kingdom come. I don't know how you could be any braver than that!

Well, to get back to when I first landed in Flanders. I was sent to a battery up near Ypres. We had the British 4.5 howitzer—a very good gun, incidentally. I was in charge of two of them. Now, remember, this was early in 1915. No one had any idea the trench war was going to last as long as it did. It was really the beginning of the three-year stalemate that was not conceived of by either side.

Take our shell supply. We were limited to ten or fifteen a day unless there was a full-scale attack. As there were long periods without much fighting, we could usually stay within our maximum. Unfortunately, the Germans weren't as badly off as we were. They seemed to have an endless supply of shells with which to pound us.

We were, oh, three or four miles behind our lines, and I'd say they were about the same distance behind theirs. I think you can safely say the normal difference between the main artillery lines would be between six and ten miles.

Of course, the munition workers back home in England were trying to beef up their workload. And a year or so later, when we fought on the Somme, we had plenty of shells. But they had made some of them defective. Somehow they'd catch fire too soon and explode. We lost two or three men that way on the Somme—poor devils, they never knew what hit them!

There was another attack the British made against the Germans quite close to our lines, but we weren't really involved in it. We could hear the guns firing, so we knew it was a major assault. It was called the Loos offensive. It ended up like all those other viciously cruel operations both sides were trying then—a few thousand yards gained at the price of enormous casualties.

I suppose the major element that developed while I was there was the German introduction of gas. I think you have to have been on the lines to realize how this initially horrified us. My God, but it was horrendous!

As I recall, it was a Canadian brigade that suffered from the first attack. Naturally, the news of their suffering spread up and down the line. As it turned out, future fears were exaggerated, but it was terrifying at first. At the beginning, you see, we didn't have any gas masks. There really was no protection at all. I had a whiff of it one time. I don't mind saying I was petrified. Fortunately, it was pretty well spent, or I would have been in real trouble.

However, gas itself played a rather minor role in my two years with the British. What I remember most is the frantic periods of action when we were constantly firing, and the long-drawn-out periods of routine. Sometimes it could get so boring you'd hope for action. Then when the fighting came, you'd hope it would end with you still in one piece.

One action that I'll never forget is the Battle of Saint Eloi in the early spring of 1916.[1] While it is called a battle, as is the Somme, Ypres, and so many others, it wasn't really a battle in the previously accepted meaning of the term. An affair like Waterloo or Gettysburg—those are battles, actions where one army is victorious and the other is either destroyed or retreats.

It wasn't that way in the First World War, at least not during the two years I spent in Flanders. Places like Ypres were merely huge pounding contests without any real winner. And this is what Saint Eloi turned out to be, though on a smaller scale.

Our job here was to reduce a small enemy salient about six hundred yards long and two hundred yards deep near the village of Saint Eloi. While the town itself was quite small, it stood at the junction of the Messines and Warneton crossroads. It seems a little odd now, but in a confrontation such as we had in Flanders in 1916, crossroads were enormously important.

Well, the village, in turn, was directly behind our lines, which were facing the salient. The key to the German position was a large earthwork called "The Mound." The elevation of "The Mound" gave a strong advantage to the Boche. It was a bonanza to their artillery observers and also their snipers.

Normally when you'd attack a position like this, you'd start off with a strong artillery barrage. Not this time. The English, you see, had spent considerable time tunneling underneath the Germans. That damn mound had been lined with explosives—we were going to blow those Germans all the way back to the Fatherland.

The operation had been mapped out to perfection. The mines were to go off at 3:14 A.M. Then, after a minute's delay to allow for the falling debris, the Northumberlands and the Royal Fusiliers were to go over. We were to coincide our barrage with the attack, first on the German front lines, then on their secondary troops. This way we wouldn't hit our men when they moved in. It also allowed us to hinder a possible German counterattack.

My major and I were to observe the attack from the top of a ruined windmill about three quarters of a mile from the mound. There was no need to map out the artillery. All the targets had been designated for days. Our function was to make sure the fire struck home.

[1] Lieutenant Whitridge, RFA, received the Military Cross for his deeds at Saint Eloi.

The charge went off exactly as scheduled. And what a sight it was to see. The mound, the eyesore that we had been looking at for weeks, just disappeared. Then the infantry went in. Everything was perfect except for the left section of the German line. We later found out that the Germans had tunneled into the ground themselves on the left and had deactivated the fuse.

Instead of the dazed and dead Germans our troops had met on the right and in the center, the left produced fully alert and poised Boche. Their machine-gun fire tore into the Fusiliers with a vengeance. We could see our men hanging on their barbed wire.

Well, for the next three days we tried to take that section, but the Germans wouldn't budge. After the Fusiliers we sent in the King's Liverpool regiment. We did manage to surround them on three sides but still couldn't capture the spot. Then we decided that the only thing was to really work the spot over with artillery fire.

Our biggest problem was the force of the early explosion. It had actually rearranged the contour of the ground to such an extent that we couldn't see the Germans from the windmill. Someone was going to have to grab some telephone equipment and move up to a very forward observation post and relay back the results of our fire. It seemed I was the logical one.

I grabbed ahold of a bombardier named Clarke. I'd worked with him before and knew how good he was. He picked up about a half mile of wire, and I grabbed the telephone and periscope.

It was pretty rough going. Ever since the assault, the German artillery had been returning our fire regularly. The whole area had been torn up dreadfully. And you never knew when some more shells would be coming our way. And remember, we were loaded down with equipment—especially Clarke, with all that wire.

We finally reached the front lines. Then we spotted a crater that would be ideal for directing our fire. We crawled into it, with Clarke still letting out what was left of the wire. Much to our surprise we found twenty-five or so of our Fusiliers in it. They looked at us as if we'd come from Mars.

"Hello, what's this, gentlemen?" asked their lieutenant. "And what in heaven's name are you doing here?"

"Why, we're going to take care of those Germans over there," I answered.

"Well, for God's sake, don't fall short; they're only fifty yards away."

And that they were. These poor devils had been manning that position right on top of the Boche for three days, staying there in the mud and filth through all that artillery and sniper fire. Many were wounded. I also spotted several large lumps rolled up on blankets. They'd paid a heavy price. But you know, there's a certain fatalistic humor about the British soldier that's hard to beat. This was borne out when I asked one of them who looked particularly used up how things were going.

"Oh just peachy, sir," he answered, "except for the bloody drainage. I'm going to write the London *Times* about it."

Anyway, we went to work, and for once luck was with us. I was able to establish communications with the major.

"Fire No. 1 gun."

"Just over and a shade too far to the right."

"Drop twenty-five yards."

"Ten minutes more left."

Then we struck home.

"That is the way I dream of them," said Clarke.

The next day the infantry went over without much difficulty and reduced the area.

Now, there was a lot more to those four days than what I've said, but the real incredible part came about two weeks later. We were relieved by then, so it didn't affect us. But the damn Germans retook all that ground. And that's pretty much what it was like, back and forth like a seesaw, a great many casualties but no one really accomplishing anything.

Well, in the fall of '16 I received the sad news that my father had died back in New York City. I felt my place was back home. So, being an American, I went to the War Office in London and obtained my release. You see, when an American went into the British Army, he didn't have to take the oath of allegiance to the King for the duration of the war, like the British did. If he had, he would have lost his American citizenship. Of course, after the war any of the Americans who had lost their citizenship by going into the British or French armies did get it restored anyway.

When I did return to New York, I found myself at real loose ends. I couldn't forget all my friends back in Flanders, and I did so desperately want to see the Allies win the war. But things kind of took care of themselves. It soon became obvious to me that it would just be a matter of time before my own country would be in it.

And if there were two men who'd been trying to get us to prepare for it, they were Theodore Roosevelt and Leonard Wood. I'll tell you a story about the former President that was told me by his daughter. It goes back to Civil War days in this country, and it concerned Teddy's father. This was during the time when you could buy a substitute and have him go into the service for you. Well, the elder Mr. Roosevelt did this—I think it was a saloon keeper's boy who went—and the substitute was killed. This haunted Teddy; he tried to make up for it all his life. President Wilson wouldn't let him go to France, but his four sons—Kermit, Ted, Jr., Archie, and Quentin—all went. The Roosevelts believed in serving their country.

Now, General Wood was just like Roosevelt. He knew how dreadfully unprepared we were for a major war and was trying to do everything he could about it. My father had known Wood, so I figured I'd better go down to Governors Island where he had an office, tell him who I was, and see what I could do.

The general greeted me very cordially and asked me what was on my mind.

"General," I said, "I've just served close to two years in Flanders with the Royal Field Artillery. I'd now like to see how I can serve my own country."

"Splendid, Whitridge," he said, "splendid, indeed. We'll make you a captain on the spot and send you to Plattsburg. We're going to be in this, all right, and you can help train some future officers for us."

So I went to Plattsburg to try and see what help I could be. I really didn't care too much for this duty; it seemed so tame compared to what I had been doing with the British. Fortunately, it wasn't to last very long. We entered the war in April of '17, and I was back in France by July.

When I first landed, they gave me unusual duty for an artillery officer—I was made APM [Assistant Provost Marshal] of Paris. We didn't have too many soldiers in France then, but each one of them was dying to see the city he'd heard so much about. General Pershing was equally determined to have them sent back to their regiments.

I'd been given a force of Marines to make sure Pershing got what he wanted. They were good troops, all right, but didn't know anything about Paris. I gave them all maps of the city and told them to meet me at different locations throughout the day. This worked out very well, I might add.

Most of the time, though, we'd just surround the railroad station and pick them up as they'd come in. My, but those poor devils were disappointed when we'd nab them. Being Americans, they soon got wise to this. They started getting off at a stop or two before the train reached the main station and walked in. This made it a lot more difficult to catch them. It was not very pleasant duty—I didn't make a very good policeman. Then, I don't know exactly when, probably in August, the 5th Field Artillery came over. I was made a major and posted with them. This was down in Alsace, near the Saint Mihiel salient.

The 5th was part of the 1st Division, along with two other field artillery regiments, the 6th and the 7th. It might surprise some people to know we had no American artillery in France at this time. Come to think of it, I don't believe we did during the entire war. Everything we had was French. I helped round that bunch into shape, and I'm proud of it. The record of the 1st Division speaks for itself.

Then, around the first of the year, I was transferred to G-2 in the I Army Corps. While my duties here took me back and forth from the front, I was no longer what you would call a line soldier.

Here, for a while, I was under the command of a delightful colonel named Williams. He was a theatrical type of a chap—one of those soldiers who found everything dramatic. I vividly remember a conversation he had with some other officers.

"Oh I have a splendid group of men under my command," said the good colonel. "Take Whitridge here, a very brave man. Why, he'll go anywhere I will." This was greeted with laughter. I never knew if he meant it as a joke or not.

The truth of the matter was we weren't in a great deal of danger. Oh we would come under shellfire, but nothing like it was for the men on the lines. But for Colonel Williams it was all very thrilling.

Shortly after I was transferred to I Corps headquarters, I was able to get to Paris for a visit. Here I ran into an old fraternity brother of mine from Yale who was serving with the French. His name was Cole Porter. It proved to be one of the most important incidents in my life, due to a few words that Cole said to me.

"Arnold," he said, "I'm giving a dinner tonight. You're not going back to your outfit until tomorrow. Come and dine."

I accepted. It was a delightful affair for me, mainly because I met a Red Cross girl from New York named Jeanetta Alexander. Shortly after that evening I received another four or five days' leave. Once again I went to Paris, this time to call on Miss Alexander. She was staying with an aunt of hers who had a home in Paris. There really wasn't much time for courting; it seems to me we spent most of our time wandering around the Métro. But events moved pretty fast in France. By the time I went back to I Corps headquarters I realized I had a pretty serious situation on my hands.

We corresponded for a while, then I put in for some leave. There was no question about it: I wanted to get married. The only trouble was I picked a dreadful time. This was the end of March 1918, and the British had just been struck very hard by Ludendorff's spring offensive. No one really knew what was going to happen, particularly the Americans.

Now, I had to get permission from our colonel to get this leave. Naturally, he was somewhat reluctant under the circumstances. After all, there was no telling what was going to happen. If the Germans did succeed in first splitting the British and French lines, and then pushing Haig's troops into the sea, what would Ludendorff do next? The colonel did consent, however, and while we didn't have much of a honeymoon, we did get married. As for the British, they managed to hold on, and while the Germans broke through for about forty miles, they did not succeed in permanently breaking the line.

There was a joke passing around the Allied troops at this time that pretty much sums up the British soldier and perhaps shows the reason why the Germans could never completely break him.

It seems that some British reinforcements had recovered a dazed Tommy whose regiment had been just about annihilated. The first thing the fellow asked for was some rations.

"Chaps, I ain't had a bite for three days," he said.

"But look, soldier," they answered him, while pointing at his kit, "you still have your emergency rations."

"Right-t-oe," he replied, "but I'm saving 'em for an emergency!"
How could you beat men like that?

After my marriage I was sent down to a quiet sector in Alsace.
My job here was to help interrogate the German prisoners. The division there was the 32nd. It was made up of National Guardsmen
from Michigan and Wisconsin. They were great troops and raring
to go. But they were quite green, and the French had some trouble
trying to show them how to play the game in a quiet sector. The
last thing the French wanted was for the American troops to stir
things up. And this was something the Yanks couldn't understand.

"No wonder this war has been going on so long," said one of the
men from Wisconsin. "How is it ever going to end if we don't shoot
someone?"

That division, I might add, had plenty of chance to do some
shooting later on.

Well, as I said, I would sit in when they would question the German prisoners. As there wasn't any real fighting going on, most of
the Boche we'd nab were fliers. And the French were masters at interrogating them.

"First, you must size up the German," they'd say. "And then either insult him or flatter him. One way or the other you can find
out all you want to know if you stay calm."

I remember one observer in particular that they brought in because he was so cocky. He seemed to be an ideal type to insult.

"Well," this Frenchman said, "I guess your Air Force is just
about all washed up. We've got your number, all right. Our planes
can shoot anything you have out of the skies. You chaps better stay
on the ground."

Oh you should have seen that Boche jump up. I can't speak German very well, but I could tell he was boasting about the Fokker
VII. Before the Frenchman was through with him, he'd told us all
about the Fokker, how many they had, and how fast they could
build them—everything we wanted to know. It was masterful!

On another occasion they brought in a pilot. You could tell right
away he was the type who looked at the whole thing as a sport. He
was shot down, so now we were all comrades to him. We immediately decided to flatter this one. The best way to do this was to
bring in a French pilot. The two of them shook hands and started
in on the bottle of cognac we'd given them.

"You know," the Frenchman said, "those planes you have are great. But how do you manage to do such-and-such with that Fokker?"

Well, they polished off that first bottle, and by the time they'd finished the second one, the two of them were going to fly together after the war. And we had once again found out everything we wanted to know.

I went back to corps headquarters sometime in July and followed the same pattern of trying to gain intelligence for the various divisions as they moved over to the offensive. This was particularly difficult during that incredible mess known as the Argonne. And that's where I was serving when the Armistice came.

You know, as I look back on it, I spent just about the same length of time with my own countrymen as I did with the British. And there certainly were differences between the two. The Tommy, you see, was pretty philosophical about things. I think he'd settled for the fact that the war would never end. As long as he could get some time off every now and then, he could accept his lot. But this wasn't the American way of looking at it. Once they arrived, they wanted to get the darn thing over with and go home. But the two had one thing in common: They were both good soldiers. The only trouble was, the Germans were good also. That's why it lasted so long.

I'll tell you one more thing about the eager Americans of World War I. I returned to the service for four years in the Second World War, and they had disappeared. I guess it was because of World War I. Anyway, the GI could fight as well as the Doughboy, but the eagerness was gone. His father had left that in France in 1918.

Theodore Roosevelt of Oyster Bay

Teddy Roosevelt, he was my man, I certainly would have voted for him in 1920 if he had lived.

—TOLD ME BY THE LARGE MAJORITY
OF THE VETERANS I VISITED WITH.

One of the strange things about World War I was the tremendous feeling that the American soldiers had for Teddy Roosevelt. While he was not officially in the government at the time, nor was he in the military, he still was the No. 1 man among the Doughboys.

"Maybe it was because we grew up with him," one veteran said. "He seemed to embody everything we were fighting for," came from another old-timer.

A third's comment was, "I can remember him vividly constantly calling for us to prepare for war, while our country was still at peace, and Wilson was pussyfooting around."

Four of my interviewees actually wrote the Army when they heard that Roosevelt wanted to raise a division and take it to France—they wanted to fight with the old Rough Rider. But it wasn't to be. There was just no way that Wilson was going to allow a political adversary to reap a harvest out of the war. It does not represent one of Woodrow's brightest moments.

Wilson's decision not to allow Roosevelt to command a division was unquestionably based on valid ground. France in 1918 was not Cuba in 1898. From a military standpoint there were many men better equipped than the former President to take a division into combat. It would also have been impossible for Roosevelt to even come close to passing a physical. But Wilson's refusal to send Roosevelt to France in any capacity was, in the words of one of the Doughboys, "small potatoes."

It wasn't only the Americans who wanted Teddy over there. At a dinner held in honor of General Joffre, this French general called for the sending of Roosevelt to France. Georges Clemenceau, France's last Premier of the war, summed up the case for T.R.'s going to France that showed keen insight into what public relations is all about. These thoughts were expressed in an open letter to President Wilson.

"At the present moment, there is in France one name which sums up the beauty of American intervention. You are too much of a philosopher to ignore that the influence on the people of great leaders of men often exceeds their personal merits, thanks to the legendary halo surrounding them. The name of Roosevelt has this legendary force in our country . . . you must know, Mr. President, that more than one of our Poilus has asked his comrade: 'But where is Roosevelt?' Send them Roosevelt. It will gladden their hearts."

How easy it would have been to make Theodore a brigadier general in a PR capacity and send him to France. Oh, he would have probably caused a few problems—Teddy could never stop talking— but our Allies would have thought it was great. Of more importance, it would have meant a tremendous amount to the American soldiers. More than eighty thousand of them were to die in France. For their sake alone, Wilson should have risen above ward-level politics.

And according to Mrs. Richard Derby, one of Roosevelt's daughters, with whom I enjoyed a lengthy phone conversation, her father would have done anything in France Wilson desired.

Wilson wouldn't budge. Theodore Roosevelt was not going to France; that was it. His sons did go, however, all four of them, and they all saw combat.

One of Teddy's boys, Archibald, is still living, in Hobe Sound, Florida. I had several phone conversations with this 1st Division veteran, but his health would not permit a personal visit. When I pointed out to Archibald that it was a little unusual for four sons of an ex-President to get into the thick of things, he laughed.

"Oh we looked at it as an exclusive war," he said. "We all knew how badly Dad wanted to go, so we went for him. He always told us to lead meant to serve."

Archie and Ted, Jr., served with the 26th U. S. Infantry of the 1st Division. They were both seriously wounded and were decorated. Son Kermit served with the British. He was awarded the British Military Cross. Then there was the baby of the family, son Quentin. When four brothers went into constant action in World War I, the chances were that they would not all come back. In the case of the Roosevelts, it was to be Quentin who would make the supreme sacrifice.

"Dad was never really the same after Quentin was killed," Mrs. Derby told me. "It was July of 1918. My four brothers were all overseas at the time, and my husband, Dr. Richard Derby, was also in France, serving with the 2nd Division. I was staying at our place off the coast of Maine," continued Mrs. Derby. "When we received the news that my brother Quentin had been shot down and killed, my father and mother also came to Maine. Dad would just stand on the shore looking out to sea, saying, 'Poor Quenty, poor Quenty.'"

Roosevelt put on a brave front. He released a message to the press that was in accord with his image.

"Quentin's mother and I are very glad that he got to the front and had a chance to render some service to his country and show the stuff that was in him before his fate befell him."

But inside, he was crushed. Six months later he died of an embolism in the coronary artery. He was sixty years of age at the time.

Most historians agree that if Theodore Roosevelt had maintained his health, he would have been a shoo-in for the Republican nomination for the presidency in 1920. If the men I talked with are any indication, he would have been elected in a landslide.

Trading Our Shovels for Rifles

William H. Houghton

HIS HOME, ANSONIA, CONNECTICUT, MARCH 1977
Ansonia, Connecticut, is a small city on the Naugatuck River. It is in that area of the state where the New York City influence has pretty much disappeared and the New England flavor has begun. It is where Bill Houghton was born and has lived most of his life.

An exception to Mr. Houghton's Connecticut days are the two years he spent with the 6th U. S. Engineers of the 3rd Division. This detour took him to France just before Christmas Day 1917, and three months later found his Company B smack in the path of Ludendorff's spring offensive around the Somme. The engineers dropped their slide rules and shovels and picked up their rifles. And that is the way it was for Pfc Houghton, either building or fighting until the following fall.

Then, on October 20, he became a prisoner of the Germans; he was futilely trying to save the life of his captain at the time. And there he remained until the end of the war. Then he did a tour of duty with the Army of Occupation on the Rhine before returning home.

Back in Ansonia he went to work for the Farrell Works, which dominate the town, married and raised three daughters, and lived the good life he had been told he was fighting for.

Now a widower, and saddened by the death of one of his daughters, he lives a rather quiet life in an apartment not far from his old homestead. He can in no way be called a violent man, but he definitely does have strong feelings about today's issues, particularly President Carter's recent pardoning of the Vietnam deserters. He does not express these views in a harsh manner; it just wouldn't be in his nature. But in a determined and calm way he airs his thoughts.

"I can't blame them for not wanting to get shot," he says. "Who the hell does? But we do have a country and a duty to it."

You can agree or disagree with him. But in 1918 he, as the old saying goes, "put his money where his mouth is."

Pfc William H. Houghton
B Company, 6th Engineers, 3rd Division

COLONEL HODGES,	FIFTH ARMY
COMMANDING, 6TH REGIMENT	S. G. 72
UNITED STATES ENGINEERS	1ST APRIL 1918

The Army Commander wishes to record officially his appreciation of the excellent work your regiment has done in assisting the British Army to resist the enemy's powerful offensive during the last ten days.

I fully realize that it has been largely due to your assistance that the enemy is checked, and I rely on you to assist us still further during the few days which are still to come before I shall be able to relieve you in the line.

I consider your work in the line to be greatly enhanced by the fact that for six weeks previous to taking your place

in the front line your men had been working at such high
pressure erecting heavy bridges over the Somme.

My best congratulations and warm thanks to you all.

[SIGNED] RAWLINSON,

GENERAL   COMMANDING   FIFTH   ARMY

It's a funny thing, but in our minds are stored memories. How in
the dickens these memories are stored, I don't know. I guess they
call it our memory bank. And it seems to me when we get to my
age—I'm eighty-one—those things that influenced our lives when we
were in our prime frequently come back clear as crystal.

For instance, you asked me if my company was one of those on
the lines when the British were hit so hard by Ludendorff's spring
push; indeed we were—O.K. Sure, I remember it, and well. As we
were engineers, we'd been sent over long before the rest of the 3rd
Division. As a matter of fact, I don't think the majority of the 3rd
had even reached France when we did our fighting on the Somme.[1]

Well, in March of '18 we were up near Peronne building bridges.
I know Companies B and D were there, and I think our headquarters outfit was with us. There were also some detachments from
other companies, but not many. You see, the whole regiment
wouldn't be working on the same bridge. We'd be moving around,
some working in one place and others perhaps many miles away.

The work had been tough. There was a general lack of proper
tools, and plenty of lousy weather. Rain is not conducive to good
bridge-work. Nevertheless, over the past six weeks we'd been able
to accomplish a hell of a lot.

Then, around the middle of March, we began to see a great
many aerial dog fights. Sometimes the Boche would win, and sometimes the English. I can recall one such scrap in particular when a
British pilot crashed near a bridge we were working on. Some of us
rushed over to try and get the pilot out before his plane caught fire.
We succeeded, all right, just before his plane blew up, but the poor
guy was dead anyway.

Then one day we saw these five or six balloons the Germans had

[1] The bulk of the 3rd Division arrived in April 1918.

sent over our lines. They had the craziest message you could imagine written on them.

"We are coming," is all it said.

Naturally, the boys gave them the old raspberries. Who could believe that they would actually telegraph their shots like that? But it was true. On the twenty-first of March a British officer came riding through our camp as if the devil was after him.

"The Boche have broken through everywhere!" he was yelling. "Retreat! retreat! Get the hell out of here!" O.K., well, that son-of-a-bitch was a spy! But the whole thing was so confusing, we didn't know what to think. The next ten days or so we moved around one hell of a lot. They had the 6th digging trenches, blowing up ammunition dumps, and fighting. Just to show you how rough it was, three of Company B's cooks were killed. And things have to get pretty bad when that happens!

We later found out that the Germans wanted to drive a big hole between the British Fifth Army and the French, and annihilate the British. But these grand plans meant nothing to us. Our big thought was to try and do what we could and stay alive. Most of our units were then under the command of a British general named Carey. He had quickly taken over several detached units such as ours, Canadian engineers, and training-school outfits in an attempt to stem the tide. They called it General Carey's "picked up" army.

About a week or so after the initial attack, Companies B and D were loaded into lorries and moved to near a place called Warfusee-Abancourt. The men all felt they'd done a good job and were going into reserve. Well hell, there was no relief. Haig had issued his famous order about dying in your tracks. I guess that's what we were supposed to do. All they'd actually done was move the Americans into another part of the line.

Shortly after settling down in the new position, Sergeant Swingle went out with a patrol to find out where the Germans were. They found out in a hurry. But of course the Germans found them also and shot the group up pretty badly. When they returned, no one could find Swingle. We sent out a night patrol after him, but they came back empty-handed.

The next morning the sergeant was located halfway between our lines and the Germans'; he was feebly waving a helmet at us. Three or four of the boys tried to get to him, but the Germans just sat back and opened up, killing two more of our men. When one of our men finally reached Sergeant Swingle, he was already dead.

In the meantime, the British had been bringing up as much heavy artillery as they could. This played a big part in bogging down the German drive, but it surely was a lulu; I think they pushed through about forty miles. But they never could really break the British Fifth Army, although they came perilously close.

Well, let's go back to 1917 and how I got involved with the engineers. It became evident shortly after we declared war that we were going to have a draft. I figured that it would be a lot better for me if I could pick my own branch, so I opted for the Marines. They told me I had a problem with varicose veins, but they'd be able to fix that, then they said to go back home and that I'd hear from them shortly. In the meantime, an uncle of mine found out about my visit with the Marines. He thought I was off my rocker.

"For God's sake, Bill," he said to me, "you spent all that time getting an engineering degree from Yale, and you want to lug a rifle in the Marine Corps. We're going to need a lot of engineers. Why the Sam Hill don't you go into a branch you know something about?" And that's how I landed at Camp American University in Washington, D.C., where I became a member of the 6th U. S. Engineers.

Now, the 6th had just been formed—O.K. Its original members had come from various engineering units of the regular Army. You know the type, the "old Army" breed. Many had campaigned in the Philippines and Mexico—one of them had even been in Peking during the Boxer Rebellion. They were a grand group, but their greeting was anything but cordial when I showed up for my first formation.

"What the hell's going on?" one of them carped. "This greenhorn don't belong here; he can't even hold a rifle in the proper manner."

Oh they all started to complain—O.K. So this old-timer called a master engineer marched me over to this other area. I think it was a parking lot.

"Houghton," this old-timer informed me, "you are now to learn the proper drilling and manual of arms as expected to be known by a member of the U. S. Army Engineers."

So for the next few mornings I had the rare privilege of being a one-man drill team right there in the nation's capital. Of course, I felt like a damn fool standing out there all alone in full view of several government office buildings. The only people enjoying it were all these stenographers looking out the windows and waving down at me. They thought it was hilarious.

Actually, they ended up being my saving grace. It seemed I was disrupting the running of the government, and finally this very official-looking bureaucrat came down to set our master engineer straight.

"Look here, Sergeant," he complained, "as long as you're trying to teach this rookie how to win the war, our girls aren't doing any work. You'll have to do it somewhere else."

Well, I think the old-timer was fed up with the whole thing by then anyway, so he decided I was ready to stand formation.

Oh, there is one more thing to tell you about my one-man drill team. One of the mornings when I was parading up and down all alone, a very official limousine drove up, and there is no one else but President Woodrow Wilson sitting in the back seat. I had enough presence of mind to come to a very snappy present arms. I don't think he even acknowledged it. But what do you expect from a Princeton man?

Then—I think it was around the first of August of '17—our battalion moved down to Belvoir, Virginia, for rifle practice and instructions in bridge building. That's where those old regulars showed how good they really were. They could shoot and they could build, all right—they were the best. One of them, his name was Biddy Boyle, took a great deal of pain with me, especially on the rifle range.

"Now, Houghton," he said, "listen to me. This Springfield has a real kick, and if you pull or jerk the trigger, you'll anticipate the kick, and your shot will go off the target. Just squeeze it—that way you won't know exactly when the kick's coming."

Why, he had me a qualified marksman in no time at all. This made me feel pretty good—especially as I'd never fired a rifle before. It also meant another three dollars a month—O.K.

That fall we moved back to Washington to await our orders to go over. And here's something for you: Every single man in the regiment received an invitation for Thanksgiving dinner from a home near Washington. Many of the families, you see, had their own sons many miles from home; I guess they hoped someone would do the same for their boys.

It was just about this time that we started receiving orders to stand formation at 5:00 P.M. with full embarkation equipment. This went on for about a week, until December 1, when the real thing happened. By December 3 we were all safely ensconced aboard the SS *General Washington,* and our journey started. I stood on deck watching America disappearing from view. It was the first time in my life I'd been out of sight of land.

Our trip took sixteen days—O.K. And this was hardly what I'd call a pleasant voyage. We ran into some very rough weather. It's bad enough when hundreds of men are getting seasick, but you can imagine how uncomfortable something like that is when you're so damn crowded you can't move. What a mess!

One of the worst times was when we'd be standing in these huge chow lines watching the men getting sick all over the deck. Fortunately for me I'd made friends with one of the regulars who knew his way around.

"Come on, Houghton," he said, "follow me." He headed straight toward the galley, where he was stopped by this real tough-looking sailor.

"It's all right, mate," he told the galley guard, "we've got to go on watch in about ten minutes." It was as easy as pie, and pie is just what we got inside the galley. It was the best meal I had during the whole trip.

The trip wasn't all misery, however. In the first place, the ship was great. It was a German boat that had been stuck in New York City since war had been declared in 1914. The Germans knew it would be easy pickings for the British Navy if it tried to make it back to the Fatherland, so they had decided to let it sit the war out in New York. We immediately took it over once Wilson declared war. We'd turned it into a troopship, but you could still find plaques on it with the name "Bremen" inscribed.

We also had some entertainment aboard—not professional, mind you, but entertainment. You see, we had about five thousand black stevedores on board, and every night they'd sing, tap dance, and put on skits for us. Remember, this was sixty years ago—things were a hell of a lot different then. For instance, one of their skits went like this:

FIRST MAN: "Oh Lordy, I'se don't want to go where dem shells is goin' to be talkin' to me."

SECOND MAN: "What do you mean, dem shells talkin' to you? What dem shells gwan tuh say to you?"

FIRST MAN: "They'se gwan tuh say, 'Nigger, yuh ain't never gwan back tuh Alabam'.'"

We also had our submarine scare; I guess every transport did. In our case it was a school of porpoises, but those Navy gunners sure blasted away at them. We really gave those sailors the business after that.

There was one more thing about the crossing that wasn't much fun. During the height of the worst storm we had, two of our men— I think they were from Company C—washed overboard. Some of our troops said they could see them for a short time, thrashing around the tremendous waves with their life preservers still on, but there was no possible way to rescue them in that sea.

Well, we reached Brest just before Christmas. Our battalion, the 1st, came ashore on the afternoon of December 23. By 6:00 P.M. they had us all loaded on those "40 *hommes et* 8 *chevaux*" railroad cars and had started to ship us toward the interior of France.

Christ, was it cold, and crowded, and also smoky when some of the men tried to light fires inside the cars. The only lucky break we had was the rather large quantities of cognac many of the lads had been able to procure during the few hours between our landing and the boarding of those damn 40 and 8's. You see, it was so bloody cold that many of the men would just keep drinking the booze until they'd pass out. Then we'd stack them like cordwood in the corner. This way the rest of us had more room to stomp our feet.

We spent the next thirty hours or so moving toward our destination of Prothoy. Every now and then we'd stop at a station and we'd pile off for some hot coffee. There'd always be a large crowd of Frenchies looking us over. Remember, this was still 1917; the Yanks were a bit of a novelty. The Poilu seemed to give us an especially cordial welcoming. But they'd eventually always get around to their favorite question:

"*Avez-vous les cigarettes?*" they'd say.

Most of the time we'd give them some. It wouldn't be until a few months later that we found out what they'd been going through, but even then we had a tremendous amount of respect for the French soldiers, particularly those wearing a Croix de Guerre or a wound stripe.

Our train ride, if you want to call it that, ended just about at the stroke of twelve on Christmas Eve. We were quickly billeted in barns and the like throughout the town. Some of the men were lucky enough to get a good Christmas dinner where they were staying, but most of us settled for coffee, bacon, a little stew, and a piece of bread. This doesn't mean the boys didn't celebrate Christmas. I don't think the cafes in the area had done such a business since Napoleon's last victory. The Doughboys from the 6th Engineers put one hell of a dent in the local supply of anything that had a kick in it.

Shortly after our arrival they put us to work building barracks all over the area. It was colder than the North Pole, but somehow we put up a great many of them.

As I told you, in February we went up around the Somme to help the English, where we found out what the war was really all about. I guess that pasting Ludendorff gave the English there in March whet his appetite, because in late May the Heinies came roaring toward Paris around Château-Thierry.

We had joined the rest of the 3rd Division by then, and we were proud as peacocks about the job our 7th Machine Gun Battalion did around the Marne the first part of June. There was only a company or so of them there, and they'd never been near combat before, but what a job they did. The real big effort, though, was made by the 38th Infantry during the middle of July on the banks of the Marne. They had a feisty colonel from North Dakota with the great name of Ulysses Grant McAlexander.[2] From that day forth they've called the 38th the Rock of the Marne; their stopping of the Germans on the Marne was one of the key actions of the war.

At the time our company was sitting on top of a hill in the woods behind the 38th digging trenches. This was going to be the next line of defense if the Germans broke through the 38th. The Jerries' artillery was really blasting us, both with shrapnel and with gas.

[2] Later a brigadier general.

The mustard gas was particularly bad on Company A—I think they had about sixty casualties from it.

Well, here we were, trying to dig these trenches when a big one landed near by, knocking down a man named Russ Williams. There was an old door lying over on my right, so a couple of us took it over to where Russ was stretched out. We picked him up and put him on this door; we figured it was ideal for carrying him to a first-aid station.

God, when we picked him up, his foot fell off. I mean by that, his foot had been sliced through and was dangling by a thread on his legging. The force of moving him had broken the thread, and the ghastly thing had just dropped. I was in a state of shock, so I automatically put the foot on the door. You do things like that without even thinking. We got poor Russ back to the station, but he bled to death.

In the meantime, all hell had broken loose down below—we couldn't see it, but we sure heard it. The 38th was putting up one of the great shows in American military history. This was the closest the Germans had been to Paris on their second Marne Drive, but they got no closer—the 38th saw to that.

The morning after the final charge had been stopped, we were ordered down to back up the 38th. My God, what a sight! Our people were trying to remove our dead, which was still tough work due to the shelling, but the German corpses were incredible; they were everywhere—both sides of the river and floating up and down the Marne. They must have charged right into our guns.

That multitude of cadavers was certainly a horrible sight to see, but it wasn't any worse than the stench that was developing. You put hundreds of bodies close together like that on a July day in France and you can imagine what it was like. These were the pick of the German Army—the ones who were going to set up the dinner party the Kaiser was rumored to have planned for July 20 in Paris. The fact that he had to cancel his shindig was due in no small way to the 38th.

Well, a few days after the stand on the Marne, we started off on the drive north in support of the 7th regiment of our division. Our job was to build more bridges, dams, work on the roads—and frequently drop our tools and pick up our rifles.

The Germans, you see, were a long way from being licked—as far as they were concerned, anyway—and they'd give up ground only if we'd actually take it.

They had a nasty habit of sticking snipers in the trees; of course, these German sharpshooters didn't have a chance, and I think they must have known it. But if they could hold us up in the slightest way, I guess they figured it was worth it.

O.K.—there was this one patrol that sticks out in my memory more than the others, and I really don't know why. We were under my old friend Sergeant Biddy Boyle. Well, there was one of these Germans up in this large tree. He opened up before we even knew he was there—I know he hit one of us, probably two. Of course, we all dropped down and started firing at him. With everyone shooting at the Jerry it was only natural that sooner or later he'd fall out of his perch, and he did. I couldn't help but think how stupid he was to do what he did, but I guess war is pretty stupid anyway.

We kept going—the Aisne-Marne offensive, the Vesle Sector—a little rest, then Saint Mihiel, and finally that gigantic operation we just called "up in the Argonne." We were always working and suffering casualties at the same time.

One of the things that kept us going was the constant stories you'd hear from so-and-so over in C Company or F Company; I guess you'd call them war stories, and I'm sure they never lost anything in the telling.

Take the time a man over in A Company badly needed a new pair of shoes—O.K. Well, he's constantly on the lookout for them. Finally he spots this Doughboy he figured was waiting for a burial party who has a brand-new pair of brogans on his feet. Well, he didn't think it made any sense to bury the shoes, so he calmly took them off and was admiring his find when he heard this roar:

"Give me back my shoes or I'll blow your head off!"

The man was dead, all right—dead to the world with exhaustion. Our Company A man returned the shoes with an awkward apology as he told the other fellow he was glad he was alive. But the next day our man was heard to mutter several times, "They were great shoes."

Another tale was about the man over in C who walked into a dugout at Saint Mihiel. The first thing he saw was a huge German sitting in a chair with his Luger-filled hand pointing at the American. Our friend immediately threw up his hands and stood there for about five minutes until he noticed something wrong with the Dutchman's eyes. Hell, the Heinie was dead, and rigor mortis had stretched his arm out. We never knew if yarns like this were true or not, and we didn't care—they were something different to talk about.

Well, my biggest moment of the war came up in the Argonne at a place called Clairs Chênes Woods on October 20. It involved several men from Company B and Captain Charles Harris. I don't think Harris was more than twenty-one or -two years of age. Someone had said he was the youngest captain in the AEF. I don't know if it was true or not, but I do know his father was Major General Harris, Adjutant General of the U. S. Army, and that he had an uncle who was a United States senator from Georgia. Charlie didn't have to be in the front lines. He could have very easily been down at Pershing's headquarters in Chaumont in a cushy job.

Now, we had moved into this wooded area the night of the nineteenth and dug in. The next morning at about seven o'clock, the captain looked at his watch and motioned to us. You know, I can see him now; he looked so young.

"O.K., men," he said, "we've got a job to do—let's go."

We followed him, moving through these woods for a few hours, knocking the branches aside. The next thing we knew we started to hear that damn rat-a-tat-tat of German machine guns. We'd spread ourselves out by this time. I hadn't seen the captain for quite a while, but I knew from the sound of the fire that he was over where the action was.

Along with the fire I could hear groans and shouts; obviously men were being hit. I had crouched down behind some trees along with a buddy of mine who had the tongue-rolling name of Harry R. O'Hara—I think he was from Indiana. Well, this master engineer came along and grabbed us.

"Look, you two," he said, "there's a wounded man over at the other side of that clearing. Here are two Red Cross bands. If you put them on, take off your cartridge belts, and lay your rifles down, the Germans might not shoot at you. And you could possibly save the guy's life."

"What the hell," we said, "why not?" And you know something, none of the Germans fired at us—we got the fellow back to a medic, and maybe we did save his life. He didn't die, I know that.

Well, we came back to the woods, where we ran into another problem. We'd brought a stretcher with us, and there was plenty of work to be done, so the sergeant grabbed us again.

"Boys," he said, "I've some very bad news. Captain Harris has been seriously wounded. He's in a trench by that road over there. The Germans have the route completely covered by machine-gun fire."

This was disturbing as hell to hear. The captain was just about as fine an officer as we had in the AEF. Then the sergeant continued.

"To get him out we have three Heinie prisoners. We think the Germans may let us get him out if we use their own people."

So, about four of us took ahold of the prisoners and started for Harris. Once again the Germans didn't fire, and we were able to get the captain. This time, though, we got lost in the woods. I guess we must have gone around in a circle, because the next thing we knew we were confronted by a large column of Germans. At first we thought they were prisoners, but a fellow named Ed Ward just shook his head.

"I've never seen prisoners carrying rifles," he said. "The only thing to do is to try and bluff them." So he ran over toward them yelling, "Hands up, hands up!" Sometimes you could get away with a bluff like that, but not this time. The Germans opened up on us. The funny thing is the only ones they hit were two of our prisoners.

When they started firing, we put the captain down and headed for the woods. But I tripped and fell, and so did Ward. While I was lying there, it dawned on me that the whole thing had happened so fast I had forgotten all about Harris.

"Listen, Ward," I said, "we've got to circle back and try and save Captain Harris." He agreed, so we dashed back, picked up the stretcher, and headed for some cover. It was no use, though; the Germans were bringing up reinforcements and they captured us.

They had one of these real Prussian-looking officers in charge of their unit. He took one look at the captain and made a motion to show us that Harris was a goner, and that we shouldn't carry him any farther.

"No, no," I pleaded, "officer, officer."

This was another story. A fellow officer was a big thing to this Prussian. At least we were allowed to carry the captain. Actually, we hated to think about it, but we did realize that Harris was in a very bad way. He had been shot in the lung, which would make his chances very slim indeed, even if he'd been in a hospital. He was still conscious, even though his pain must have been excruciating. I remember leaning over to try and comfort him.

"Well, Captain," I said, "I guess we have you in a real mess." He just gave me that boyish grin of his.

"Houghton," he answered, "I guess it's just not our day."

The Prussian officer then assigned a young soldier to us with instructions to take us back to their headquarters. Hell, I don't think the lad was over fifteen years of age—maybe not that old. Anyway, he was a nice-looking kid with a grin a mile long. It was obvious that he didn't know much about soldiering, because most of the time he walked in front of us with his rifle slung over his shoulder.

This brings up something I've thought about all my life. The Germans hadn't searched me—O.K. Well, I had a good-sized jack-knife in my pocket. It would have been a pretty simple thing to have stuck it into the lad's back. Of course, we would have had one hell of a time making our way back to our lines carrying Captain Harris. The Germans had obviously been flooding the area with troops—they were everywhere. I also figured that if the captain had any chance at all it would be at the German hospital.

But those aren't really the reasons I didn't do it. The real reason was I just didn't have the heart to kill a young boy in cold blood like that. I'd fired my rifle any number of times in combat, but that was different. All in all, I'm glad I didn't do it. There was only about three weeks of the war left; maybe the young fellow survived.

O.K.—it started to rain, which made it real tough going. We were trying to hurry because of the captain but, you know, you're supposed to have four men, not two, to a stretcher.

We finally reached their headquarters and were quickly hustled off to a barbed-wire stockade. I knew the captain was still alive when we put him down, but I guess he died shortly afterward; that is what we later heard, anyway.[3]

[3] Captain Harris was not listed by the Germans as a prisoner; therefore he must have died very shortly after reaching the German camp. According to the records of the 6th Engineers he had captured a German machine gun and turned it on the enemy when he was shot by a sniper. He received the DSC posthumously.

Now, we'd no sooner been put in the prison pen when different groups of men were escorted in. First it was my buddy O'Hara, then a man named Spillane, then Duhrkoop and Canonico—before they were through, they had about ten men from B Company. We'd run into a hornets' nest, all right.

Well, we'd only been prisoners a short time when this very overbearingly pompous German sergeant lined us up and picked out Spillane.

"Vat is your name?" he asked, then looked around at the other Germans. Why, the clown was just showing off because he knew English.

"Pfc Spillane."

"Vat is your regiment?" Then he looks around again.

"6th Engineers."

"Is you glad you are ze prisoner?"

"No!"

And that was the extent of our interrogation. A few days later the Americans started to break through, so they pulled us aboard a wagon being hauled by the skinniest-looking nags you've ever seen. They drove us a few miles farther north and stuck us in a farmhouse.

A week or so later they took us farther back to a castle called Montenidy. And then they marched us even farther back. It seems to me I spent a great deal of my time as a prisoner being moved away from the Americans. On one of these jaunts we passed through a French town where an elderly man came out and asked me in good English where I had been captured.

"Sedan," I answered, because it was the first thing that came into my head. It was a good-sized town they had marched us through as prisoners a week or so before.

Well, sir, you should have seen that old Frenchman's eyes light up.

"Sedan, Sedan," he shouted, "*Vivent les Americans!*" Then he started over to tell the rest of the villagers. Each time he'd tell someone, a new cheer would go up.

We reached our final prison a day or two later. It was a church in a village, but I'll be damned if I can remember the name of the town. But I surely remember the sandwiches these nuns gave us. At that time we were existing on a daily ration of one piece of bread and some watered-down turnip soup.

It was here that we had some fun with our German spy. It all started when one of our prisoners grabbed me by the collar.

"Have you seen our German spy?" he asked.

"No, which one is he?" I answered.

"That so-called French officer who's wearing a Croix de Guerre—on his right side. Germans wear decorations on the right side but not the French."

O.K.—remember, we'd been seeing a side of the Germans that the rest of the Yanks couldn't see. It was obvious to us that the Kaiser's war machine was just about kaput. They had everything on the lines but were just a shell behind that.

Anyway, we decided to have some fun with Herr Spy. You see, he'd always edge into any group that would gather to talk things over. The next time he did it, the boys were ready for him.

"Oh, that Kaiser's a bastard!" said one.

"And he's a fairy to boot."

"A fairy, I think he likes dogs."

Well, this went on for a few minutes, getting viler every second. We could see this bogus Frenchman getting redder and redder. Finally, one of the lads let go with a real salty accusation against the whole German Army, then sticks his face right next to the spy.

"Don't you agree?" he roared.

This was too much for the German.

"I AM A GERMAN OFFICER!" he bellowed.

Then he realized what he'd said, clicked his heels, did an about-face and marched out of the church. But you can bet the boys let him have it as he thundered out. They made what they'd been saying earlier seem tame, and they were just the lads who could do it!

The next day we had a visit from a German colonel. There was no Webber and Fields accent from this fellow—he spoke perfect English.

"Gentlemen," he said, "I'm not going to try and fool you. It's only a matter of days before you'll be heading home. I apologize for nothing. I only ask that you tell the American people the truth about your period as prisoners of war. We haven't been able to feed you much, but our men aren't eating very well either. Remember, just tell the truth."

Then he saluted and walked out. Well, here it is sixty years and another war later, and I'll still tell the truth. I did not see any ill treatment of the American prisoners by the Germans.

O.K.—on the eleventh the Armistice was signed, and on the fourteenth we were released. It was a sixty-mile hike to our lines. But when we reached them, they gave us all the corn willy and white bread we could eat. It tasted like pheasant under glass and angel cake.

When we got back to the 6th Engineers, we were told that we were going to go into Germany as part of the Army of Occupation. Oh boy, were we disappointed! But it wasn't a bad life. We had the German civilians do all the work.

While I was there, both Senator and General Harris came to see Ed Ward and myself. They had us take them back to France to see where the captain had been shot and the route we followed on the way to the prison pen. And there was his grave, almost exactly where we had put him down. He must have died almost immediately after we left him.

O.K.—about six months after the war ended, I came home. And I'll tell you one more thing: I think I sleep better, even today, because I didn't stab that German lad in the back.

The Doughboys Remembered

"*Good-bye, Broadway,*
Hello, France.
We're here to pay
Our debt to you."

If there was one thing the American became deathly sick of it was constantly hearing of the debt they owed France and, particularly, Lafayette. The famous remark, "Lafayette, we are here" never really cut much ice with the Doughboys. One of them summed up the feeling of the whole AEF when he was told his outfit was moving back in after surviving the slaughter at Soissons.

"O.K.," he groaned, "we've paid off that old fart, Lafayette. What Frog son-of-a-bitch do we owe now?"

SUCH LANGUAGE!

John O'Brien[1] was with the 110th Infantry of the 28th Division "up in the Argonne" in October of 1918. Here he experienced some of the toughest fighting of the war. Sometimes in the evenings John would find his company a mere one hundred yards or so away from the Germans.

[1] A different John O'Brien from the one whose section starts on page 99.

"We were so close to those Germans we could yell back and forth," said John. "I can remember one night when this Heinie kept yelling, '*Gott mit Us, Gott mit Us.*' (God is with us.) Finally one of our boys yelled back, 'We've got mittens too, you silly bastard. Shut up.'

"Now," continued John as I visited with him in a small hotel in Le Roy, New York, "I wouldn't use that language, never have. I was an altar boy when I was a lad, and I hate cuss words. Why, do you know, when I first landed in France, I was standing in a chow line and the two men in front of me had a violent argument. Then one of them says to the other, 'Go shit in your mess kit!' Can you imagine such vulgarity?"

A CLASH OF CUSTOMS

There were certain customs of the French that utterly baffled the Doughboys. The most bizarre of all was the manure pile in the front yard, or as it was called, the family bank account. This was a very common custom in the Vosges Mountain section of France. The size of the pile would determine the wealth of the man.

Well, it came to pass that a company of the 28th (Keystone) Division was marching toward one of these villages when they spotted an American soldier sitting by the road.

"Hey," yelled one of the Pennsylvanians, "what kind of a burg is this one?"

"Jeez," answered the resting soldier, while holding his nose, "every guy in the town must be a millionaire!"

THE PERFECT SQUELCH

One of the earliest stories I heard about the AEF came from the late Joe Murtaugh. There are other variations of this story, but I heard it first from Joe. It seemed that this young lieutenant was one of those members of the 26th Division who was sent to help train troops after his regiment, the 102nd Infantry, went through the bloodbath of Château-Thierry. It seems that Murtaugh first stopped in England on his way home, where a wounded English officer showed him around his regiment's headquarters.

"Ah here, old man," said the Englishman, "this is a cannon we captured from you chaps at Bunker Hill."

"Is that so," answered Murtaugh. "Well, you have the cannon and we have the hill!"

The Englishman answered, "Oh that's smashing! Let's have a drink."

THE SOREASSES

"I'll never forget my mental test to start my pilot training," remembered Sherwood Hubbel. "It was out at Hazlehurst Field. They had three or four officers reviewing me, with one of them giving me a verbal quiz. His first question was, "I see you went to Williams."

"Yes, sir."

"Graduate?"

"Yes, sir."

"I see you played football."

"Yes, sir."

"Phi Beta Kappa."

"Yes, sir."

"That's enough; you're in. Let's go have a drink."

Mr. Hubbel was also the one who told me the real meaning of the Aviation Section Signal Officers Reserve Corps. It was usually just called the ASSORC—so Hubbel and his friend started calling themselves "The Soreasses."

THE WHITE LIES

Niegel Chomley-Jones is very erect at ninety-three years of age, and his mind is perfect. As a captain in 1918, part of his task was to censor the soldiers' mail.

"It was the damnedest thing," remembers Niegel. "When the letters would be written in a rest area, they'd talk about the shells bursting and the machine-gun fire—you know, hair-raising stuff. It was all lies. But when they'd write home when they were actually on the lines, their letters would be very subdued. They wouldn't say a word about the Germans. Now," mused the dignified Mr. Chomley-Jones, "why do you think they turned things around like that?"

BOOM! BOOM!

When the 32nd Division went into its first tour of the trenches, it was sent into a quiet sector. Naturally, the Midwesterners of the 32nd were curious as hell to find out what was going on. Three of them actually got out of the trenches and started looking the place over. Strolling around as they were, they were getting perilously close to an area that the methodical Boche shelled each day. A very excited French Poilu came running over to the Americans yelling a mile a minute in French about the certainty of the German shelling. The Yanks didn't know what the hell he was talking about until he finally pointed toward the Germans.

"Le Boche, Le Boche," he screamed, "BOOM! BOOM! BOOM!" As he did this, he made an explosive motion with his two hands. The Americans rushed back to their trenches in a hurry.

Several veterans told me it was frequently easier to understand the gestures of the emotional French than some of the dialects and brogues of the British.

SEEING PARIS FOR ONE HOUR

Howard Baldwin was one of the many Americans who transferred from the French Army to the U. S. Air Service after his country entered the war.

In the spring of 1918 he found himself at the Paris railroad station with a full-scale problem on his hands. He had fifty young, aspiring pilots under his command, whom he was scheduled to deliver to Issoudun, about eighty miles away. There were seven hours to wait until the next train. Baldwin knew that if he gave the young men some time to visit Paris he would not get half of them back. The men had just had a boring train ride from Le Havre that had been immediately preceded by their trip overseas. They hadn't seen any girls for three weeks, and most of them had money in their pockets. After much thought, Baldwin reached a decision that would have complimented Solomon.

"Gentlemen," he declared, "how would you like to see Paree?"

The cheers, whistles, guffaws, and oo-la-las were deafening.

"That's fine," continued Howard. "Now, here's how we'll do it. Starting right now, ten of you can leave here for one hour. If you're back on time, the next ten men can go. But if you're late, the rest of the men will have to stand at attention until each and every one of you gets back. And there's plenty of MPs around here to back me up."

Well sir, do you know, not a one of them let their buddies down. I won't say they didn't bring any cognac back—hell, half of them were three sheets to the wind by the time I got them to Issoudun—but I delivered them to their new base in one piece.

The West Pointer

Mark Clark

Mark Clark is one of the foremost soldiers of his time. Graduating from West Point in 1917 (he told me that the Class of '15 might have been the one that the stars fell on, but '17 was the one the bullets fell on), he quickly rose to the rank of captain in the wartime Army.

After service in France, which included a very serious wound while serving with the 5th Division, he opted to stay in the slow-promotion peacetime Army. Then came World War II. His preinvasion landing in North Africa from a submarine is one of the legends of the Second World War.

It later became his duty to command the Fifth Army in the meatgrinding campaign going up the Italian Peninsula. Of all the World War II campaigns, the Italian one was the most similar to World War I.

As a four-star general, he was later the commanding officer of the United Nations' forces in Korea.

After his retirement from active service he became the commandant of The Citadel, a military college in Charleston, South Carolina.

When I visited the general, he was recuperating from a serious heart disorder that had necessitated the installation of a pacemaker in his chest. Nevertheless, as we sat in his office, he looked surprisingly fit.

One of my questions to the general was, "Could he see any similarities between the foot soldiers of World Wars I and II?" There was a mark of sorrow in his eyes as he answered.

"They both did what a soldier has to know how to do very well."

"What is that?" I asked.

"Die," he answered.

Captain Mark Clark
K Company, 11th Infantry, 5th Division

When the word finally went back to the United States that I had been wounded, it said I had been hit in the Toul Sector. I had to be sure everyone realized this was a section of France, not my anatomy.

My father was a regular Army colonel, class of '90 at the Military Academy. I won't say that he aimed me in that direction, but I can vividly remember a conversation we had shortly before Dad left for service in China.

"Boy," he said, "I'll support you in any college you want to attend—as long as it's West Point, that is."

And the Military Academy is just where I was when Pershing went into Mexico after Pancho Villa. God, were we excited! Naturally, we all wanted to go, but most of us realized it wouldn't be big enough to create early graduation, like they'd had in the Civil War.

Oh, we all kept in touch with what was going on, all right. My sister's husband went into Mexico, and he kept me pretty well posted.

Then came the rumblings of the war in Europe—this would be a different story. Maybe the Mexican border was just a rehearsal for the big show. And I can promise you the thought of France really had us in an uproar. You know how lads are at that age. Hell, we all thought we could win the thing single-handed.

My class was '17. We weren't supposed to graduate until June, but when Congress declared war, they quickly decided to get us out of there by April 20, which provided me with a bit of a problem. I wouldn't be twenty-one until May 1. They told me I could graduate but couldn't be commissioned until my birthday. Well, the Army followed that crazy seniority system very closely in those days—a man could be a drunk and still get a promotion if he had seniority. Just imagine how many reserves were getting commissions at that time. All of them would have time on me, and all my classmates also. I was just about the baby of the class. I must have made a good case for myself, because they relented and gave me an April 20 commission.

You know, there was one thing that happened to me at the Academy that followed me into the First World War and, as a matter of fact, into the Second World War as well. One night I was trying to do some cramming after taps. We did a lot of that in those days. You'd hang a blanket over your window to hide the light. It was sure as hell against the rules, but it was always winked at.

Well, this senior classman caught me in the act and gave me the business.

"Clark," he snarled, "you are *not* in bed properly; you are going on report."

As everyone else did what I was doing, I couldn't believe my ears.

"Is that so?" I answered. "Well, you're one son-of-a-bitch!"

That shocked this bird, but it didn't stop him.

"I'll be back after I check some more of the other men," he snapped back. "We'll see who's an SOB!"

And back he came in about fifteen minutes. You must remember that "son-of-a-bitch" was a fighting term in those days—wham, we were at it just like that. Shortly after the fight started my great buddy, McMahon, came in to see what the hell was going on; so did an upperclassman named Reed, a great friend of Taylor's, the guy giving me all the trouble. The first thing you knew they're also tearing into each other.

Much to Reed's regret, McMahon was the light-heavyweight champion of the Point. My, but Mac gave him one hell of a beating! I'm having a much tougher time with Taylor, but I'm holding my own.

Then in walks Eisenhower. He was also a senior and the cadet captain of Company F, our company. If there was one thing Ike was, it was fair. When we told him the whole story, he was amazed.

"For Christ's sake, Taylor," he said, "you mean this stupid hullaballoo happened because Clark wanted to do a little extra studying? I suggest we forget this nonsense and that you and Reed leave these two alone after this." Ike was a great friend of mine from then until the day he died.

It wasn't all over, though. Two years later ('17) Mac and I were down at Chickamauga Park where we're trying to help form the 5th Division for the AEF. Taylor and Reed are also there and, of course, they're our seniors. They started the old harassment all over again. Finally Mac and I had had enough. We cornered Reed and Taylor one night after mess and gave them the word.

"Listen," I warned, "we're in this thing to fight the Germans, not each other. But if you two don't stop treating us like we're plebes, we're going to beat the hell out of you!" They were game enough, but they knew we were right, and they left us alone.

Push the clock ahead until 1944, when I'm in command of the Fifth Army in Italy. Who do you think gets assigned to my command? No one but the now Colonel V. V. Taylor. I called him in just like I would anyone who'd been an old buddy of mine. He came in and gave me this big salute.

I greeted him with "Sit down, Taylor, glad to see you; we need good men here, it's a tough campaign." You know, the same old bullshit. Then I asked him what command he wanted, and I tried to give it to him. We never mentioned our own battles.

Now, back to the Point. In our senior year most of our bunch came to me and asked what would be good duty; this was before we'd declared war. I told them to put in for the 11th Infantry at

Fort Sheridan, Illinois. My father had served a lot of time there and had always felt it was great duty.

We all got the 11th, all right, but it had left for Chickamauga Park to get ready for France and the 5th Division of regulars. The term "regular" was really a joke. Like all the divisions we were setting up to go over, it was made up mainly of wartime volunteers and draftees. Many of the first sergeants were regulars, but they'd been privates and corporals when war was declared.

Remember, when war comes, promotions zoom. Take my case—I left the Point in April for my thirty-day furlough. At that time I was a second lieutenant. When I reported to the 11th, I was immediately made a first lieutenant. Within a month after that I was given my captaincy. Can you imagine that? Two months out of the Academy and I have command of a company!

Of course, the need for officers was tremendous. We were dealing with the old square divisions—each one would run twenty-seven thousand or so men; they were really huge. All my lieutenants were new reserve officers, and most of them were quite good. One man in particular, Iron Mike O'Daniel, was really great. Later on, in France, when I was hit, Mike took over from me. Of course, he was hit himself after I was. God, I think all my original officers were eventually hit, most of them in the Meuse-Argonne. I took Mike to Europe with me in the Second World War and also to Korea. He ended up a lieutenant general. What a soldier he was! Just died a year or two ago; they don't make them any better than Mike!

Well, here we are, a green outfit trying to get ready for an army like the Germans'. You can bet we drilled those men hard. God Almighty, how we worked those men! I drilled them, hiked them, ran them; believe me, every minute for months we were on them. I didn't want to lose any lives because they weren't tough enough.

Then, in the early spring of '18 we all piled aboard the *Leviathan* —God, I think it was the whole 5th Division on that one ship! And she was a fast one; didn't even need a convoy, she could outrun any submarine. I can't remember how long the trip took, but it seemed to me we were in Brest, France, in no time at all.[1]

Shortly after we arrived, they piled us on these 40 and 8's to head us for our training areas. They told me which town my company

[1] The 5th Division landed in France on May 1, 1918.

would be billeted in and to be sure to get them all off at the right spot. It wasn't as easy as it sounds. In the first place, good old Company K was spread throughout the train. Then we were trying to keep the men sober. The damn train would stop at each town, and the Frenchies would run over to the train and sell the men wine. It was really one hell of a mess!

Finally, we're out in the middle of nowhere, and I'm told to take K off the train. Then they gave me this little map and told me to march them to a town named Fresney, down in the Vosges Mountains. I started them off in what I hoped was the right direction, and God Almighty, we made it to the right town. This farmer came out to greet us, telling us he was the mayor. He had to be the richest man in the town because his house had the biggest manure pile in front of it. Iron Mike and I moved in with him, hoping the wind would blow in the other direction.

The town itself had about one hundred or so people in it. As we were the first American troops they'd seen, they really fell all over us. You see, they'd be getting a franc a day for every soldier they put up in a barn, and more for each officer in the homes. Then there was the wine they were going to sell to our men. Hell, they were going to clean up!

Now, my rolling kitchen had come with us—so I had enough food for two days. But my problem was I didn't know where the hell the rest of the division was. What was I going to do in two days? Besides, we hardly had any ammunition. This was a so-called quiet sector, but what if the Germans pulled a surprise attack?

Well, I told the officers to have no formations until I had things squared away. Then I borrowed a bicycle from the mayor and started out pedaling in search of battalion headquarters. Fortunately, I ran across one of our dispatch riders, who told me which direction to head in, and I succeeded in finding Major Kingman, a grand old-timer. He was really too old for combat, but at least he'd taken us this far. Kingman sent me over to regimental headquarters, another ten kilometers away. Here I really caught the devil. This old colonel looks me up and down and bellows:

"Clark, how did you get here?"

"Why, Colonel," I sputtered out, "I rode a bicycle from Fresney, about twenty kilometers away."

"I know you did, you damn fool," he growled, "and how do you think it looked to the French to see an American captain riding a woman's bicycle?"

I was flabbergasted. What possible difference did it make how I'd gotten there?

"Well, Colonel," I tried to explain, "I have little food left and a very modest supply of ammunition; I had to get here."

"Oh you'll get your supplies all right," he replied, "but don't ride that damn woman's bike back. Walk, do you understand? All twenty kilometers!"

"Yes sir, Colonel," and then I saluted and started back. I walked that silly-looking bike until I was out of his sight, then I started pedaling as fast I could.

You know, I hope I'm not being too hard on an old-time officer such as he was, but we had so many of them back in '18. World War I was really the first modern war, and many of these old career types just weren't ready for it. Back at Chickamauga we had a major we had nicknamed "footsie." The only time you'd ever see him was every now and then when we were hiking. He'd drive up, get out of his car, and stop the company. Then he'd make a few of the men take off their shoes. He'd look their feet over carefully, tapping them with his swagger stick, nodding his head.

"Oh that's fine, Captain, absolutely fine," he'd mumble, then drive on. We wouldn't see him again for a few weeks. Now, feet are important, all right, but there is more to being an officer than worrying about a soldier's dogs—and certainly a lot more than what kind of a bicycle you're riding. So many of these old-timers were just out of it when it came to the tactics of the type of war we had in France.

Well, we received our supplies, then started a two- or three-week training period. You know, rifle practice, bayonet drill, twenty-mile hikes every day. We couldn't waste a minute, because we knew what was ahead.

Then the word came from headquarters: We were "moving in." It's just impossible, sitting here in Charleston, fifty-eight years later, to visualize the excitement this created, but it was absolutely electrifying.

"Full marching gear, men," I told them, "it's our turn now." You could feel the tension in the air.

Actually, my company was one man short. The poor devil, he just didn't want to go. He'd deserted just before we left New York, but I'd had him sent over on the next boat. I thought he was just a loner that we could rehabilitate. Of course, we all felt he'd gone AWOL again, but we were wrong—he'd walked over to the woods and blown his brains out.

The rest of the company was ready, though, and we took off for the trenches. Now for the amazing part. Just before we went into the front lines, I received new orders from regimental headquarters. Major Kingman was sick, and I was to take the battalion into combat. Poor Kingman, he was too old to even be there, but he was all soldier. Anyway, here I am, twenty-two years of age and I have command of a thousand men in combat. The area was called Saint-Dié in the Vosges Mountains.

This was what they called a quiet sector. But the Germans had a nasty habit of frequently sending over shells whenever they knew an American outfit was moving in. This was in Alsace-Lorraine, where the Germans had hundreds of spies. Hell, they knew the 5th Division was going in, and where, before most of us did.

I had no sooner disposed of my three companies in the lines, holding the fourth for reserves, when they let us have it. Being young and eager, I felt I should start inspecting the units to make sure no one panicked. That's when I caught it; the divisional history says I was the first man in the 5th wounded. It was bad. Shrapnel hit my right knee, shoulder, and, worst of all, right near the spine. I'll always remember the date, because it was our first day on the lines: June 12, 1918.

They tried to patch me up on the lines, then rushed me back to a hospital. It was the French who evacuated me; as a matter of fact, they evacuated my watch, revolver, and just about everything I had. They did quite a job of surgery though, very, very skillful—that spine business can be tricky and quite dangerous. I can't say too much about the treatment those French doctors gave me.

In the meantime, the word had gone back to the States that I had been killed in action.[2] My father immediately tried tracking down the details. When he got the real facts, he started a very quick and very successful ploy to have me moved to an American hospital.

[2] Not rare. Captain T. W. Brown, F Company, 102nd Infantry, had his false death notice framed in his office.

The American hospital was more like home, particularly the nurses. You can't imagine how great it was to talk to women from the States. They soon had me in a wheelchair and were pushing me all over the place. It was first-rate!

Then one day this young nurse came to me with some good news indeed:

"Captain," I can still remember her pretty smile, "the French officers have a place called the Lafayette Club right next to the hospital. Anytime you want a ride over there, I'll be glad to do the honors."

This was the best word I'd received in quite a while; the next day I took her up on it. There we were, the young lady doing the navigating and I'm sitting back like King Tut. She wheeled me right up to the bar in this place and said to the bartender:

"The specialty of the house for Captain Clark, who's been badly wounded in combat."

"Oui, oui, mademoiselle, pour le gallant capitan," replied the bartender as he poured me this "porto flip." As I remember, it was loaded with port, egg, cream, nutmeg, and, I think, brandy. It was quite a delicacy.

Well, this nurse and I had two or three of these, and maybe one or two more. It was the first alcohol I'd had since before I was wounded, and, naturally, I'm now feeling like I can lick the Kaiser, Hindenberg, Ludendorff, the whole German Army. On the way back I was very gallant and insisted that the pretty nurse ride in the wheelchair with me doing the pushing. Here I am, wobbling on one leg, pushing this wheelchair and bowing to everyone passing by. The officer of the day witnessed this whole scene and naturally put me on report. Boy, I thought the commanding officer was going to have me shot at sunrise!

Shortly after that very pleasant sojourn, they figured I was at least ready for limited duty, so I was assigned to general headquarters of the First Army to serve under Colonel John Dewitt—the same Dewitt who later incarcerated the Japanese on the West Coast after Pearl Harbor. He was a good officer, even though he certainly made a tragic mistake when he started those camps in World War II.

We were part of I Corps then, under the command of Major General Hunter Liggett, who was later put in charge of the whole

First Army in the Argonne. Liggett was "old Army," and when he heard that a Captain Mark Clark was at headquarters, he called me in.

"Clark," he inquired, "are you any kin of Charlie Clark?"

"Yes, sir, he's my father."

"Well, God Almighty," exclaimed Liggett, "I was serving with Charlie in the 9th Infantry when you were born. It's great to have you with us!"

You see, even though we now had well over a million soldiers in France, I represented that small group of men who had soldiered together in the old Army. Don't get me wrong about Hunter—he was old Army, all right, but he was one of the great generals of the AEF. He had many more men under him than Grant or Lee, and the Meuse-Argonne battle was bigger than any battle of the Civil War. Yet only the real historians can even tell you who he was.

My job was to reconnoiter the areas where our troops would be moving, making sure the railheads would be established for each division every day. This was when we were preparing for Saint Mihiel. God, did I make charts! They're over at The Citadel's museum; you can go see what a job this was. This type of movement for a mobile army was something new for us. When you read that Pershing finally had his own army, just think what this meant— transporting half a million men from all over France.

Then came the Meuse-Argonne. Now it was a million or so men we were trying to get into the line. First we had to move them by train. This meant all that trouble between the single-gauge and the broad-gauge track, then the setting up of the trucks to take the men as far as possible. With twenty men in each truck, you'd need well over a thousand of them to a division. And all the time you're trying not to have traffic jams on those roads. Another question was: Where the hell are you going to get the trucks?

For six or seven weeks we were concerned with this, moving men in and out of the Meuse-Argonne. We had to also make sure there was transportation for the wounded—we had well over one hundred thousand of them there, and plenty of sickness also. Believe me, it was one hell of a job!

Here I was, still at it on November 11 when I got the news. Actually, I was not too far from my old outfit, the 11th Infantry, at the time. My, but they'd been shot up there, just dreadful, perfectly dreadful![3]

I had a car, so I maneuvered over to check on some old buddies. There I spied one of the real swell fellows the 11th had: Dan Boone. What a peach! Boone was a great big guy from Memphis, one of those men who always had a laugh for you. He later had a big job with International Harvester; I think he ran the whole South for them.

Well, I grabbed Dan and gave him the facts.

"Look," I pointed out, "the Armistice has been signed, you can sneak away for a while. Let's go over to Nancy and help them light up the town!" Boone thought this was a great idea, so we headed for the fun. You should have seen it. I think we were the first Americans there. The way those Frenchies fell all over us was marvelous. They had been part of the war for so long. Hell, it was just a short time before that they felt the damn thing would never end, and if it did, they certainly never thought the Allies would win. Christ, everyone had a bottle of wine, and they kept insisting we take a drink. What a time! It was hilarious, unbelievable! I can't remember everything that happened, but it was a real barn-burner; and I do remember one particularly beautiful French girl.

And you know, that night came up again just a few years ago. I'm in charge of the American Battlefield Monuments Commission—Pershing was the first one given the job, then it was George Marshall, now it's my turn. Well, in connection with this position I had an occasion to spend some time in Nancy, I think it was in 1972. Oh my, but they gave me this great reception, with the mayor telling everyone how wonderful I was, ending his flowery remarks with the question, "General, is there anything we can do for you?"

Now it's my turn to talk. I thanked him for all the baloney he'd said about me, then I thought I'd have a little fun.

"Monsieur Mayor," I chuckled, "you don't know this, but I first came to your fair city on November 11, 1918, from the Meuse-Argonne, with the express purpose of helping you light up your city. And I remember specifically this very pretty mademoiselle."

[3] The 5th Division suffered over nine thousand casualties, the majority in October 1918, being particularly hard hit going against the Kriemhilde Stellung. Included in this number was Sam Woodfill, whom Pershing called the outstanding "old Army" soldier of the war.

Well, you can imagine how all those French began to get interested now.

"And I was wondering," I continued, "if you could possibly see if
she could be located."

Then I went on to describe her in detail. You wouldn't believe
what happened next. The mayor got all excited, started waving his
hands all around and said:

"Monsieur Général, Monsieur Général, we will find her, we will
find her!"

Well sir, he called the chief of police, the fire department—hell,
half the people in the town. I'd only done this as a joke. How were
they possibly going to find her? But God, how they tried! I think
that hopeless search excited Nancy as much as the Armistice had
fifty-four years before.

Well, back to '18. There were several things from the First World
War that influenced the rest of my military career.

One was the stand Pershing took about having an American
Army. He was constantly under pressure from the English and the
French to send the Doughboys into their outfits as replacements,
but he stood firm. And he ended up with his own American Army
at both Saint Mihiel and the Meuse-Argonne.

Now, believe it or not, I ended up with the same problem in
North Africa. The British—oh they were slick—set up this headquarters that I think was just to attract our troops. They wanted to
use them the same way they had wanted to in '18. They had this
general named Anderson, and was he tough to deal with, not an
easy guy to get along with at all, AT ALL!

I was Ike's deputy here, with my job being to keep the peace. As
a matter of fact, I just had a dream about it the other night. I was
complaining to Ike about what the British were trying to do, and
Ike, that wonderful diplomat, just kept patting me on the shoulder.

"Oh Wayne"—Ike always called me Wayne—"for Christ's sake,
keep your shirt on," he warned. "Pershing wouldn't let them take
him over, and we're not going to either—it'll be all right." And it
was.

Another lesson I learned was to try to keep the peace between
line and staff. Peyton March[4] and Pershing weren't exactly buddies,

[4] Chief of staff in Washington during most of the fighting.

you know. Take the Sam Browne belt.[5] March wouldn't let the officers wear them in the United States. It was such a petty thing, but nothing compared to what they did to our commissions when we returned from France. All the overseas officers reverted to their original ranks the minute they landed back home, while it seemed most of those who hadn't gone to France were able to keep their new ranks. We all felt this was a little way March had to take a swipe at Pershing.

They used to tell a story about three of Pershing's generals who were knocked way down in rank when they hit the dock back home —they used to call these men BA's, for "Busted Aristocrats." Not only did these three get demoted, but they were also ordered to attend the commanding general's staff school. This was definitely a school for subordinates.

The three of them were in class one day, listening to a lecturer who hadn't been to France. Of course, the three BA's felt the spit-and-polish teacher didn't know what the hell he was talking about. So subsequently one of the three fell asleep and started to snore. "Sleeping beauty," incidentally, had been a major general in the AEF but was a captain back home.

"Captain," ordered a very irritated lecturer to the man on the snoring officer's right, "will you *please* wake your friend up!"

"Hell no, Colonel, you put him to sleep, *you* wake him up!" chuckled the other BA.

It's all funny now, but it wasn't then. I think all of us in World War I realized that bad feeling like that is not good for an army. In contrast to March and Pershing, Ike and Marshall worked as a great team.

But the thing above all that I kept remembering in World War II was, let's make sure the Germans know they're licked this time. Oh we put a small Army of Occupation across the Rhine in '18, but we didn't do enough. I remember watching a parade in Coblenz the first part of '19. If any German civilian refused to take his hat off when the U.S. flag went by, an MP would walk over and knock it off. Now, those Boche knew who'd won the war, all right, but so

[5] First Lieutenant Joseph Cummings of the 1st Division left France in April of 1918 to come back and train troops. He had to take off the belt immediately upon landing in the United States.

many others didn't. Perhaps if we'd done in '19 what we did in '45, we wouldn't have had a Second World War.

One more thing about the First World War. On my way home in the spring of '19 I was loaded with dough. You know, I lost every cent of it to naval officers playing poker. Christ, they were good; I guess they'd had a lot of practice during the war. Anyway, I landed in New York City and called my father, who was then in command of Fort Jackson. I'll never forget that conversation.

"Boy"—he still called me boy—"is that you?"

"Yes, Dad."

"Well, are you going to come see us?"

"You bet, as soon as you send some money. The Navy cleaned me out in a poker game."

Well, Dad got me some money, and after two years "Boy" was back with his family.

Sam Woodfill of the Regular Army O

John Gilbertie stands about five-four. It must have been quite a sight when this Sicilian-born Doughboy stood alongside of the six-two lanky mountaineer Alvin York as Pershing pinned the Distinguished Service Cross on each of their blouses. They both had won their medals for outstanding heroics in the Meuse-Argonne while serving as sergeants in the 82nd Division. York's deeds made him the best-known civilian-soldier in the AEF. They even made a Gary Cooper movie about York which, according to Gilbertie, didn't quite make the grade. That's what this delightful eighty-three-year-old gentleman told me, anyway, while enjoying a luncheon at Manero's Steak House in Westport, Connecticut.

"I don't think they did a good job on those battle scenes," he stated. "They just didn't show the confusion of the Argonne. But I guess you couldn't really do that in a movie. I know that after that battle was over, they told me we gained five hundred yards in two weeks—that's what it was really like. And another scene they weren't right about was the medal-giving. They showed Pershing giving York the Medal of Honor in France; York got the DSC in France, he didn't get the Medal of Honor until he came home. You can bet on that—I should know; I was with him in France."

Well, wherever York received the CMH, he did get it, and Pershing called him the greatest civilian-soldier of the war. But who was considered the No. 1 AEF soldier of the old regular Army—those "forty miles a day, on beans and hay, in the regular Army O" boys? Pershing had something to say about that also. There was no question about it as far as the general was concerned: It was Sam Woodfill of the 5th Division.[1]

Sam was a farmboy, born and raised along the Indian Kentuck Creek in Jefferson County, Indiana. His father had fought in Mexico as a mere lad and was a captain in the Civil War; Sam was brought up swinging his father's saber. When the trouble with Spain erupted, he traded his Pa's sword for a Krag rifle and was off to the Philippines. As they used to say in the service, Sam "found a home," particularly with his rifle. The Krag evolved into the Springfield, and Woodfill developed into one of the best shots in the Army.

He was serving on the Mexican border when the United States entered the war. It was a move that ended the tightly knit life Woodfill and roughly one hundred thousand other regulars had been experiencing. America needed commissioned officers in a hurry. After almost twenty years of soldiering, Sam was made an officer and a gentleman by an act of Congress. Then his government put Woodfill to work helping to form the 5th Division. It was

[1] John J. would get an argument from the supporters of Sergeant Dan Edwards. This 1st Division machine gunner cut his way out of a shell entrapment by amputating his own arm. Dan still managed to march his four German prisoners to the rear.

no mean task. The 5th was officially to be a division of regulars, but in fact it was nothing of the sort. Other than Woodfill and a few others, it was just like the rest of the outfits being formed; it was loaded with citizen-soldiers. One of these rookies was Italian-born Johnny Pulcino. Sam had taken a particular liking for Pulcino, but no matter how hard Woodfill tried, he couldn't get Johnny to master even the rudimentary aspects of his rifle. This flaw in Pulcino and all the other weaknesses in the new men worried Sam. He knew what lay ahead, and he wanted mightily to bring as many of them back home as he could.

The big show for the 5th Division was the Meuse-Argonne, and for Sam it was the area near the Kriemhilde Stellung. The Argonne campaign was filled with actions of small groups of Americans fighting equally sized bands of Germans. It seemed to follow the same pattern: The Doughboys wanted desperately to capture a small plot of land that the Heinies were equally desperate to hold. There was only one way for the Americans to accomplish their goal: Reduce the German machine guns. At this task Woodfill was to become a peerless master.

It all started for Sam at 6:00 A.M. on October 13 when he moved his men into no-man's-land. The Germans' Maxims, as always, were waiting for them. They tore cruel holes in Sam's ranks. He jumped into a shellhole to try to size up the situation. He picked the wrong hole. The damn place was loaded with lingering mustard gas. Woodfill stayed long enough to locate three groups of Boche. Then he proceeded to work himself into a position where he could bring his Springfield into play. Before he was through, Sam had eliminated five German gun crews, using his rifle for most of them, but also chipping in with his automatic and even a German pickax. He didn't quit until he collapsed from the gas he had inhaled earlier.

They moved Sam back of the lines to the hospital at Bordeaux, where he almost died from the pneumonia that set in. Still worse for Woodfill was the tally sheet on his men who were killed; above all there was Johnny Pulcino, the young immigrant who still didn't know one end of the rifle from the other. Realizing that the advance was to be rough, Sam had sent Pulcino back of the lines on stretcher detail. Nevertheless, a German shell found Johnny sitting in a dugout. At least ten people told me that there was just no haven in the Meuse-Argonne.

As for Sam, his fame, including the Congressional Medal of Honor they gave him, was short-lived. He found out that the only way he could protect his pension was to revert to the rank of sergeant and serve out his thirty years.

When World War II came along, the U. S. Army was once again crying for officers. They dusted off Sam's file and brought him back, this time as a major in charge of one of the largest rifle ranges in the country. If anyone could teach the GIs how to fire a rifle, it would be Sam.

The Machine Gunner from Hartford

Philip H. Hammerslough

HARTFORD GOLF CLUB, WEST HARTFORD, CONNECTICUT, NOVEMBER 1975
Phil Hammerslough joined Troop B in Hartford shortly after the
United States entered the war. Horses weren't exactly his favorite
relaxation, but many of his best friends were part of the troop, so
Phil felt it was the outfit for him.

"I was a very happy man when we were told that machine guns
were to replace the horses," he told me, "but the rest of the men
were all broken up."

He landed in France in October of 1917 and went all through the
American participation in the war, serving in action at the Second
Battle of the Marne, Saint Mihiel, and the Meuse-Argonne. He returned to Hartford, Connecticut, in April of 1919, where he went
into the family's wholesale tobacco business.

Phil's real joy in life is the study of antique silver, a subject in
which he is recognized as one of the country's leading authorities.
He has had many books published on the subject.

During his days at Hartford Public High School, Mr. Hammerslough was captain of the track team, his specialty being the
one-hundred-yard dash. When I asked him what he could run that
distance in today, he answered, "Run it? Hell, I'd have trouble
walking it!"

Pfc Philip H. Hammerslough
101st Machine Gun Battalion, 26th (Yankee) Division

I was nicknamed "Agile" because I was nowhere to be found when the hard-work details came up.

You must realize that when we actually did go to war, very few people in this country knew what it was all about. Really, no one had any idea what the actual fighting was like. I had a great many friends in old Troop B, and all I knew was they were going and I wanted to go. I felt that if I didn't go, the world would come to an end.

Actually, I was about a quarter of an inch under the height requirement, but the doctor told me to try standing on my tiptoes. This came back to haunt me later on. One night in the spring of '18 we were standing in a trench with the rain coming down like hell and the shells coming over us when one of my buddies looked over and laughed:

"You, you goddamn fool, you stood on your tiptoes to get into this mess!" He was right. What I would have given to have been back in Hartford.

Of course, I never figured it would be like this when I joined the troop. They had just come back from the Mexican border, and they never forgot it. Even over in the trenches those who had been on the border felt they were the real soldiers and we were the rookies —they were always bragging about their days as horse soldiers.

Now, the government knew that cavalry would be no damn good in France, so they turned us into the 101st Machine Gun Battalion; then we became part of the Yankee Division. Our job was to be a mobile machine gun battalion. We had these converted Ford ambulances. Whenever any area would get hot, they were supposed to rush us in as support. The problem was that in many front-line sections the shellholes and woods made it impossible to drive. When the Saint Mihiel salient drive came, we had to march 18 kilometers at night. The gun and the tripod weighed a total of 110 pounds; then we had all that ammunition. It was one hell of a load! Fortunately for us, this wasn't one of our tough fights. Most of the Germans we saw here were surrendering; they were everywhere, yelling *"Kamerad."* The toughest thing about Saint Mihiel was what we saw. We climbed this hill, reaching a spot where we could look down into a large valley. In the distance you could see these two or three villages that the Germans had set fire to before they left; it was a magnificent sight, but horrible at the same time.

Our battles weren't all that easy, though. One time, near Verdun, I can remember firing the Hotchkiss in support of our infantry when this German shell landed on my left. It killed one of the men on our gun and wounded another—he later died also. I didn't get a scratch, but it seemed like my heart stopped beating for fifteen minutes.

Then there was Château-Thierry—to me that was our toughest fight! This time the Fords took us toward the front, driving past "Machine Gun" Parker, who was in command of the 102nd Infantry. He had that crazy grin of his and was yelling, "Go get 'em, boys! Give 'em hell, boys!"

We all thought Parker was a little nuts, anyway. When we arrived in France, he had this review of the four battalions, making us fire over his car as he drove by. Then he yelled:

"I've brought you over here to get killed, and that's what I'm going to do!" Parker was always cheering the boys up like that.

Well, the trucks dropped us off near the front, where it was our job to support Major Rau's[1] battalion of the 102nd Infantry—that was also a Connecticut outfit, you know. It seemed like we'd been driven through the whole 26th—a battle can be confusing as hell to

---

[1] Rau was killed the second day of Château-Thierry.

a private, but I think we were leading the advance of the Yankee Division.[2]

The first thing we knew, the shells were flying so fast we could only move forward on our bellies, crawling through this wheat field, trying to find a place to set up our guns. The Germans were letting loose with rapid fire—mainly their one-pounders—and they were hell! A fellow named Hezekiah Porter was over on my right. I could see him out of the corner of my eye. Then this shell landed, and he completely disappeared. Can you imagine that—seeing a buddy one minute, then a minute later he's gone? I still have nightmares over that one!

We weren't always fighting, of course. Sometimes the boredom and the filth of the trenches could be rotten also. We spent about six weeks in this way in May and June of '18. Each trench section had dugouts with bunks. You'd take your turn standing in the trenches, then go back into the dugouts. The bunks were all full of cooties. During these six weeks I never took a bath, and the only extra clothing I had was one pair of socks. When we left that area, everyone was lousy, and most of us had scabies. They took us to this medical center where they could scrub us with wire brushes. Boy, did that feel good! And they took all our cruddy clothing and burned it. Did it stink!

You know, there's one thing I'll always remember about the war—and that's how mixed up things could get. Now, when they first sent us into the trenches, we'd hoped to get Browning machine guns, but we ended up with Hotchkiss. Well, when we relieved this French outfit, they'd had our gun dismantled. They were in such a hurry to get out they left it that way. None of us knew how to put it back together; we'd never seen it done.

Not knowing what to do, we decided to go to sleep. The next day an officer came by.

"Where the hell's your gun?" he yelled.

"We can't put it back together," one of us replied. "Can you?"

You know, he couldn't either. We finally got someone to show

[2] "The motor machine-gun battalion of the 26th, taking the place of cavalry, was given the right of way through the troops by Major General Edwards—a very brilliant stroke with all the romance of any cavalry charge." Frederick Palmer, *America in France* (New York: Dodd, Mead & Company, 1918).

us how, but just think what would have happened if we'd been hit by the Germans that night. We would have been helpless.

It was at about this time that an order came from Pershing's headquarters stating that on certain days all Jewish men had to have matzo. Our sergeant got this order and he called me over.

"Phil," he pleaded, "you're one of only two Jews in the outfit; do you have to have matzo?"

Now, keep in mind the food we're getting from these rolling kitchens wasn't exactly Delmonico's, so I said to him, "Listen, Sarge, matzo is better than most of this crap we're getting. Put down that half the outfit is Jewish; the boys will love matzo." I got a big kick out of this—old Troop B, the blue bloods of Hartford, being half Jewish.

Nothing happened until around October. We're then in some pretty tough stuff around Verdun when the sergeant yells, "Hey, Agile, your matzo is here." Sure enough, two big loads of matzo had arrived. The boys all ate it until the Armistice. Haw, maybe that's why we won the war!

The only other Jew was Rick Wise. He was a great pal of mine. Poor Rick, he was a child of calamity. Everything happened to him. On the boat coming over, he had a bad case of boils. Can you imagine being on one of those jammed troop ships with boils? After we arrived in France, he caught the measles—then it was pneumonia. We used to have a lot of arguments trying to figure out what was going to happen next to Wise.

When we first heard the yell, "Gas attack, gas attack," everyone put on his mask except Wise—it turned out he didn't know how to. None of us knew what really was happening when Wise yelled, "Help me, help me, Sergeant Brown; I'm sinking fast!" Then he fell down. I figured I could take my mask off for a few seconds and try to get his on right. You know what? There was no gas at all. You can imagine how we all gave Wise the raspberries after that. Every day someone would yell, "Help me, help me, Sergeant Brown; I'm sinking fast!"

Later on, the Ford Rick was driving took a direct hit. Rick picked up fourteen different shrapnel wounds, but he came through. Then I heard the boat he went home on went aground off Hoboken. To top it off, he fell on the gangplank, trying to get off the boat, and sprained an ankle.

It's a funny thing: I haven't concentrated my thoughts on the war for years, but it all comes back. Take that time after we came out of the lines for a rest—it was in a little town near Bar-le-Duc. Most of the men went over to Bar-le-Duc and got paralyzed. I was on guard and I couldn't go.

That night I was resting in this large room where we were staying. They had put the 6th, 7th, and 8th squads in this one big room. Pretty soon the men started to filter in; most of them could hardly stand up. They were staggering in, a few at a time, then they'd cork off on their bunks. Howard Manning was one of them. Manning's only problem was he was in the wrong room—Howard was in the 9th Squad. Anyway, he's really plastered and doesn't know the difference. He said to me, "Phil," as he lies down on my chest, "you don't mind if I sleep here, do you?" Now, Manning was a real big guy; he'd played center on the Yale football team, you know. What the hell could I say?

Then this little guy comes to the door and bellows out, "Who the hell's in here?"

I yelled back, "The 6th, 7th, and 8th Squads."

"Izzat so?" the little guy answered. "Well, I can lick any of yuh!"

Then Manning rolls off my chest and starts to crawl toward the back entrance. When he got to the door, he stood up and put his finger to his mouth.

"Sssh," he says, laughing all the time, "I'm going to get the hell out of here before that tiger gets to the 9th Squad."

The next day some of the boys were talking about some girls they'd met. You never knew if they were telling the truth or not; you know how soldiers can get in lying contests about those things. I think most of them were as scared about catching something as I was. I don't think I even talked to a woman in France. In the first place, if the girl wasn't a whore, she'd only speak to the officers, not the privates; they'd always look for the bars on your shoulders. And if she were a prostitute, look out!

My brother-in-law was a doctor who had gone over in June of '17 and was serving with the British. Well, when he heard my outfit was getting ready for France, he wrote me this long letter about all the VD.

"Phil," he wrote, "you sure as hell better watch yourself when you get over; these girls are really loaded with VD—you'll catch something and the damn thing will fall off." That was enough for me; I stayed away.

After that rest near Bar-le-Duc, we went back into the lines. I think that was just before Saint Mihiel, where I "captured" my machine gun, and that's another story.

A couple of us were walking through the woods when we stumbled onto this "grim reaper"; the Germans were in such a hurry to get out of there they'd just left the damn thing. I figured it would be great to send home, but so did this lieutenant who came waltzing by. He told me to get it crated and sent to company headquarters. Well, I got it crated, all right, but for me, not him. I left it with the mayor of this small town, gave him some money, and told him to send it via American Express to Hartford after the war.

Then I had to face this lieutenant who's roaring like a bull, wants to know where the hell his machine gun is. I looked at him with this angel face and said, "Gee, Lieutenant, right after you left, I was put on this work detail. When I returned, the damn thing was gone." He grumbled a bit, but what could he do?

Shortly after that we moved into the Meuse-Argonne campaign down near Verdun—I think we were on the southern tip of the line. That's where we were when Pershing relieved General Edwards. Oh my, but the men were absolutely furious. We all loved General Edwards; you always felt he was concerned with the division and everyone in it. Now, I don't know if this was a rumor or not, but we heard there had been bad blood between the two going back to their days in the Philippines. The word was that Edwards had been Pershing's commanding officer and something had happened between the two. Actually, we were too busy worrying about the Germans to do anything about it, but after the war, we booed the new general when he tried to give us a speech. You'll note that Edwards has a statue in Hartford, not Pershing.

Well, as I was saying, we were down near Verdun, trying to push the Germans back. We kept hearing all this latrine talk about an armistice. But, hell, every time we'd hear a rumor, the Heinies would send over all these shells; they didn't seem licked to us.

Then, early in the morning of November 11, I was sitting in this dugout called Château Toto (it means Hotel of the Cooties) when this Doughboy came running by yelling, "There's going to be an armistice! There's going to be an armistice!" At that exact time a German shell landed close enough to make us hit the ground.

The fellow next to me laughed and yelled, "Stick the armistice up your ass; come on down here before you get your head blown off."

About an hour later an officer came by and told us it was on the level; the whole thing would be over at 11:00 A.M. You can bet we stayed down in that dugout until we heard them blow that whistle. I wasn't going to be the last guy to catch it. The funny thing is when it was over, there was no cheering or waving, or anything like that —just an exhausted silence.

After that—well, you know the Army, the first thing you know, they had us doing all this darn drilling; and I mean all the time. We didn't give a damn about that stuff; all we wanted to do was go home.

Now, headquarters, you see, wanted to keep the boys out of trouble. They even sent an order around that anybody who had been to college could take courses in England or France. We had this great guy in our outfit named Northey Jones, who'd been a whiz at Trinity College. He came over to me one day while we were waiting for chow.

"Agile," he asked, "I want to take some courses in economics over in London. Can you lend me five hundred dollars?" Well, Foggy (we called him that because he wore such thick glasses) was a wonderful fellow; I had the money, so I lent it to him.

After he came home, Foggy (he paid the money back, incidentally) went to work for J. P. Morgan. Well, about fifteen years ago I was reading *Life* magazine and there's a picture of my old buddy Foggy. He's become a senior partner at Morgan Stanley and is shown giving a check for $67 million to the Burlington Quincy Railroad. So I said to my wife:

"Dear, there's the guy I lent five hundred dollars to. Can you imagine that!" We both had a great laugh out of that one.

You know, I'll tell you one more thing the war did to us: It taught us to swear. Before I went to France, I never used bad language. Then we started to use words like "fuck" for everything and thought nothing of it. This came home to roost when mother met me as the boat docked back in the United States. She was crying and hugging me, and then she said:

"Philip, what port did you leave from?"

"Brest," I answered.

"Oh that's awful," she sighed. "I've been reading in the papers how dreadful that place is."

"Now, mother," I consoled her, "don't believe what you read about France. Most of it is a lot of horseshit." I know I shocked her, but she didn't say anything.

And, oh yes, do you remember about my captured machine gun? Well, about a year or so after I got home, I received a phone call from the Old State House telling me they had something that had arrived from France. I went down to pick it up, and this elderly man looked at me suspiciously.

"Now look," he said, "we can't let you have a machine gun; besides, it'd cost you a fortune for duty."

Then I put on my angel face and started to plead.

"My friend," I said, "do you know how I captured that gun?"

His eyes widened as he said, "How?"

"Well," I said in a low voice, "it was at Château-Thierry. That gun was holding up our outfit. My buddy and I jumped on top of this machine-gun crew and finished them off with our bayonets; my buddy was badly wounded, but we saved the rest of our company."

It was too much for the old-timer; I thought he was going to cry.

"Son," he said, "you can have this gun if I lose my job!"

I felt bad about my little lie, but I felt I'd earned the machine gun.

The Spirit of the Guard

The Civil War left a lasting influence on more aspects of American life than any other event in the history of the United States; one of these was the development of the National Guard. Almost all the fighting from 1861 through 1865 was done by state regiments, both North and South. Many of the units that had been created for the war remained intact after Appomattox, while the pre-Civil War militia regiments gained in stature. The men who made up these regiments were usually civilians who enjoyed a night out with the boys. America was infinitely less mobile before World War I than it was to be after the conflict—there just weren't as many diversions then as there are now. Many of these weekend soldiers used the Guard to get away from an overworked housewife who would take her own frustrations out on the old man.

When Congress declared war on Germany, thousands of Americans who belonged to the National Guard were eager as hell to go to France in 1917. The Spanish-American War had been a bummer for the Guard. It just didn't last long enough. The Mexican border episode had ended up being a colossal bore, but it did whet the men's whistle for France. The Guard felt that World War I would be different, and it was.

One man, whose story can well stand for all the members of the Guard, who had been waiting for years for something such as the Great War, was Boston's Bill Drohan. Long a member of the old 9th Massachusetts, he was well past combat age, and physically he was a wreck—the boys called him "Disability Bill." But, by God,

Bill was going to France or die trying. His regiment had helped form the 101st U. S. Infantry, which in turn had become part of the 26th (Yankee) Division. Bill was the officer in charge of the regiment's wagon train and also a court officer in South Boston. He had a lot of strings, and he was willing to pull every one of them to get overseas.

Everything ran smoothly until just before the division was to sail. Then an order came down from headquarters replacing Bill with a young lieutenant from a machine-gun company. But the brass didn't reckon with Drohan's ingenuity. He merely assumed that he was supposed to change places with his replacement, so he presented himself to the machine-gun company's captain (Bill had known the captain's father) and started to help get the men ready for the trip. When the company did sail, Bill made himself scarce to an extent that would be the envy of James Bond.

He followed this same policy in France but was soon spotted walking down the street in Neufchâteau by none other than Clarence Edwards, the major general in charge of the division.

"Say," Edwards said to his aide, "isn't that old 'Disability Bill'? I thought we left him in Boston. Give him an immediate physical examination, and unless he's in top shape, send him home."

The next day Bill received orders to report to the hospital for the examination. It just happened that the officer who sent out the order had known Bill for years; he was to be examined by Major Fred Bogan, another old chum of Drohan. The next day Bogan spent about thirty minutes checking Bill out.

"Bill," the major intoned, "you have cirrhosis of the liver, a bum ticker, high blood pressure, and doubtful lungs, and I'm not even finished with the examination."

"Look, Fred," pleaded Bill, "I might as well die here as in Boston, and God, how I want to go to the front." This went on and on until the major gave up.

"Oh hell, Bill," he said, "get out of here, go on back to your outfit. Don't blame me when you drop dead."

The weeks went by, and the 26th prepared for its entrance into the lines at the Chemin des Dames. Then, once again, General Edwards came into the picture. On a very cold morning he spotted Bill trying to walk down a company street. Drohan also suffered from arthritis, and the bitter winter of 1917–18 greatly aggravated his condition.

"Oh no," the general cried, "not Drohan again. I can't believe it." Then he started to laugh. "Look," he told his aide, "tell old 'Disability Bill' to come to my quarters after dinner—I want to have a few words with him."

That evening the two old soldiers enjoyed an after-dinner cigar: Major General Edwards, whose life had been regular Army, and First Lieutenant Drohan, a veteran of forty years in the Massachusetts National Guard. They got along famously.

"You're a great guy, Bill," the general told Drohan, "but we have some real rough stuff ahead of us. I'll tell you what I'll do. I'm having a dinner for some shavetails tomorrow night. Come on over and tell these kids what the outfit's all about. Then, in a few days, when we go into the lines, you can move up. It's to be a quiet sector, and it shouldn't be too rough. But after a few weeks of it, you really have to go home."

Sure enough, the next night Bill showed up and really laid it on thick to the new lieutenants. His parting shot was, "And remember, your men come first; that's what being an officer in the Massachusetts National Guard is all about."

A few days later, old "Disability Bill" faced the Germans. He experienced a little artillery and machine-gun fire, and even had to twice put his gas mask on. Then he went home to Boston. The 101st would have to go through Château-Thierry, Saint Mihiel, and the nasty bit around Verdun during the Meuse-Argonne fighting without "Disability Bill." But when they came back home in the spring of 1919, there was Bill to greet them. He died two weeks later.

The Down Easterner

Russell Adams

HIS HOME, PROVIDENCE, RHODE ISLAND, FEBRUARY 1976
Russ Adams was born on a farm in Woodstock, Maine, in 1892. His father was a sea captain, so Russ spent most of his growing-up years on his grandfather's farm while his father was out to sea. When Russ was about twelve years of age, his dad took him on a trip to Cuba.

"And don't you think I wasn't a big thing around Woodstock among the other kids when I came back from that jaunt," he told me.

Naturally he was. There just weren't too many youngsters taking a trip to Cuba from Maine at the turn of the century.

After the war Russ settled in Providence, Rhode Island, where he went into the meat business.

"I used to do a lot of business with the other men in the American Legion after the war," Russ recalled. "We had a great bunch of fellows in those days."

Today a widower, he's living in pleasant retirement in Providence and still riding a bicycle when weather permits. His biggest problem when I visited him in January of 1976 concerned his relations with his granddaughter.

"It was that damn World Series last fall," he remembered. "I'd been a Boston Brave fan all my life until some damn fool moved the Braves out of Boston. Then I started a-rootin' for the Red Sox.

But when the World Series came along, well, that old National League feelin' came back, and I was a-rootin' for the Reds against the Sox.

"Well, my little granddaughter—oh she's a corker—well, she's a real Sox fan. And when she found out I was pulling for Cincinnati, she said, 'Oh how could you? You're a bad granddaddy!'"

Ay-ah, Mr. Adams, ay-ah!

Sergeant Russell Adams
Company B, 103rd Infantry, 26th (Yankee) Division

I'm from Woodstock, Maine. You probably never heard of it, but it's seventeen miles from Rumford Falls.

—SERGEANT ADAMS

It was the barrage that counted; it meant everything to the infantry. Take Saint Mihiel—I don't think our whole 1st Battalion had more than a handful of casualties in that fight. This was because we'd plastered those Germans for four hours with artillery before we went over. I can really tell you what happened; you bet I can. You see, I'd been out on a patrol the night before; I'd seen all this barbed wire the Germans had set up. I was scared to death when I thought what it would be like to charge through it. Then we had that barrage starting at 1:00 A.M. on September 12. Why, all that barbed wire just disappeared—t'wasn't nothing to it.

On the t'other hand, Hill 190 at Château-Thierry—that was another story. We had no artillery there; it was just going against those Maxims. We had 29 men left out of 180. Now, most of them were wounded—not killed, mind you—but it was pure murder without the artillery.

Well, you want to know why I went to be a soldier. You have to go back to 1916, when that fellow Villa was raising the old Harry down on the Mexican border. I was working in Rumford at the time, driving back and forth from Woodstock in this Ford Tin Lizzie of mine. I'd given my friend Harold a ride into Rumford one Monday morning. We were about a half an hour early, so the two of us were standing there punching the bag when up walked Jim Bisbee, a lieutenant in the 2nd Marine Infantry of the National Guard:

"Boys," he asked us, "how would you like a trip down to the Mexican border?"

"Ay-ah," I said, "but Jim, how the dickens are we going to do that? It's a long way from Oxford County [Maine] to Mexico."

"Why, join up the Army, boys, and I'll guarantee you that within two weeks you'll be down on the border. And I'll buy you a breakfast to boot."

"Well, Jim," I answered, "sounds good to me. Besides, I need a good breakfast—how about you, Harold?"

"Hell, I always wanted to see Mexico," answered Harold. And you know, that whole thing didn't really end for almost three years.

Well, Bisbee was right. In a few days we were sent to Augusta, then Portland; there we boarded trains for Laredo, Texas. That train ride was no bargain, don't you know—but it was a hell of a lot better than those 40 and 8's we had in France.

Now, we never did go into Mexico—Pershing did with his regulars, but not the National Guard. Oh, our job was a snap. We would check cars crossing over from Mexico around Brownsville, looking for arms going in or out. The papers down in Maine were playing it up big, like we were in a war, but really it was a picnic.

My station was at a place called Powder Ranch. We had about twenty men here, just enough for two baseball nines, so we played a lot of ball. Our lieutenant was a man name of Coolidge, but hell, there t'weren't anyone but us around for miles. He was a Rumford lad, so you could say he was just one of the boys down there. It was great fun for a while; then we started to get bored. Oh, everybody was squawking all the time. Wilson finally called us home *after* the

November election. We all figured he was afraid to bring us home sooner; he wasn't going to get many votes from those boys.

Now, I'm no international genius, but I always figured that our going down there had nothing to do with Pancho Villa. The government just wanted to see how quickly they could put a Guard outfit together so they could give us a little training. The size of our Army then, don't you know, didn't amount to a hill of beans. If we did have to fight in France, Uncle Sam would need some soldiers in a hurry.

Well, we finally did get home, and those war rumors started to fly thicker than the potatoes in Aroostock County, and I'm beginning to take them seriously. I hadn't been really interested in what was going on in Europe before that. Why, hell, when the damn thing broke out in '14, I was more concerned with the Braves. They'd been in last place on July 4 and still gone on to win the National League pennant and whip Connie Mack's A's in the World Series. Most of the folks in my neck of the woods had been Red Sox fans—Rough Carrigan, the Sox manager, was from Maine, don't you know, ay-ah over there in Lewiston. Not me, though; I was for the Braves.

Well, it was different now. Company B was made up of Rumford boys, and I was one of them. If the 2nd Maine went, I was going. Then that Kaiser started to sink our ships; darn fool, that's what he was. We were just going to have to show him a thing or two. And you can bet we were ready when it came. Now, the regiments were sure big in those days; ours ended up well over three thousand. It included the whole 2nd Maine, most of the 1st New Hampshire, and some companies from a Massachusetts regiment. Then we were sent over to Westfield, Massachusetts, where they turned us into the 103rd Infantry, assigned to the 26th Division.

They had the division spread all over New England: the 102nd was in New Haven, Connecticut; the 101st in Framingham, Massachusetts; one machine-gun battalion in Rhode Island, and another one at Niantic, Connecticut—we were all together down near New York City to start going over in September. Of course, this information was to be kept under your hat, but everybody knew about it.

Then I got a shocker: I came down with the measles. I thought it was curtains for me, figured I'd be left behind. But, you know, I was only really sick a day or two, so when I heard Company B would be leaving shortly, I went AWOL and reported to my captain.

"Adams," he said to me, "how in hell did you get here?"

"Oh I skipped, sir," I answered. "I haven't been sick for a week. Why, I'm at the hospital playing basketball every day. I don't want to lose Company B."

"Do you think you can sneak back tonight without getting caught?"

"You're darn tootin'!"

"All right, Adams, if you can get away with it; I'll see you go with us—don't want to lose a 'border man.' But if the company all get the measles, I'll kick your arse all the way back to Rumford!"

Well, I made it, and it's a good thing—two days later we left for New York City.

Some of the boys had hoped to see a little of the Big Apple—I hear they call it that now—haw, haw, but it was no soap. They stuck us on this small boat and started us toward the battery. I can remember one of our boys saying, "This is it!"

Well, remember, I'd been to sea several times with my father and I knew we weren't going to France on that boat.

"Listen," I said, "t'ain't no way this tub can go overseas."

Sure enough, a little later we tied up alongside of this big British boat, the *Celtic*. We got offen our boat, walked right through the pier, and went aboard the English ship. Then, quick as you can say Jack Robinson, we were off.

Oh that *Celtic* was a fast boat. But they had to keep slowing her down so we could keep in the convoy. I'm sure she could have outrun any U-boat if she had been alone, but they didn't want to take any chances.

Our quarters were down below, four bunks high. A lot of the men were griping, but it didn't bother me any. And the food—most of the boys were sore as hell about that, but I thought it was great. Then again, I'll eat almost anything, always have. And I don't lose my temper very often—maybe that's why I've lived to be eighty-four. I will admit I found the waiting in line a chore. One morning I waited so long that when I finally was finished eating, it was time to get in line again for the next meal.

Well, we landed in Liverpool sometime in October; then they shipped us to a place called Camp Borden near the British base at

Aldershot. You know, I think we were just about the first Americans they'd seen; many of them thought we were Australians because of those big campaign hats we all had.

The next step was France, I'd say about ten days after we'd landed at Liverpool. Now, there was a bad trip, even I will say that. Damn cattle boat, that's what they put us on—and the Channel was choppy as the devil. But it was a quick trip, just a few hours and we landed at Le Havre.

Plans for the divisions had been set up long before we landed. Our training area was to be over near the Vosges Mountains. Well sir, it took over three days for those 40 and 8's to get us there; why, we spent more time sitting on the railroad sidings than we did traveling. I told the boys who'd done all the bellyaching aboard the *Celtic* to grumble all they wanted about that train ride; it was awful!

Our regiment was billeted in a town called Liffol-Le-Grand, with the rest of the division in surrounding towns. It was here that our training really got down to brass tacks. There was a French regiment there that was supposed to be resting, but they pitched right in to help us.

I can remember one night when they'd gone out into this wooded area as if they were Germans. Our job was to find them. Oh we went after 'em, all right, but the first thing you knew they had us completely surrounded. This was to show us not to be led on that way, and not to bunch up the way we were. On another night they planted one of those spiked German helmets. Of course, our boys scrambled to get it when this Frenchman jumped out from behind a tree.

"Boom, boom," he's hollering, "ze helmet she go boom, boom."

The Germans, you see, were always wiring things like that. If you picked them up, you'd be apt to get blown back to New England. What these Poilu were really trying to teach us was how to stay alive. And they did one wonderful job, you can rely on that.

I was a corporal by then, in charge of a squad. Well, I didn't know all there was to know about soldiering, I'll tell you that. But I had a man in my squad named Mike McQuade; he was a real soldier.

We didn't know much about Mike, 'cept that he'd spent several years in the British Army serving in India. But he never threw it around, nothing like that. He'd always keep his eye on me, and if I'd seem puzzled I could always count on him.

"Now, Corporal," he'd say to me, "I'll bet you've thought of this already, but don't you think we should do it this way?" or "Corporal, back in India one time we did such-and-such and it worked." Well, you can bet I'd always do it Mike's way. He'd forgotten more about soldiering than I knew.

Well, you might say, why was I the corporal and not Mike? It was the liquor; yes, sir, the liquor. Oh Mike loved it. The boys used to say, "If there's a nip in the air, McQuade will find it." If anyone had something on his hip, it would be Mike. Why, whenever we'd be ordered to move, the search would be on for McQuade—check all the barrooms. And sure enough, we'd find him, all right, either tipsy or stone drunk. One of us would get his pack and another his rifle and helmet. We'd sober him up by marching him along and pouring water in his face. But drunk or sober, he was the best soldier I ever saw.

Of course, we weren't always training. There was plenty of time that fall and damn cold winter to get to know the people of Liffol-Le-Grand. You see, this was 1917; we were the first Americans these folks had seen, don't you know. I won't say they didn't try and make a dollar out of us, 'twasn't that go, but we seemed to get along hunky-dory.

I will say we were mighty good to them. Almost all of their menfolk were away or dead, with the women doing a good deal of the farming, so we used to pitch in whenever we could. Some of the boys helped with t'haying, while others unloaded coal and firewood. Oh we had some bad numbers—you always do—but by and large we were on the square—just a lot of farmboys a long way from home.

Personally, I ran into a stroke of good luck while I was there when I met up with old man Bouchair. Seems a little funny for a man like me to call someone an old man, doesn't it? But I'll tell you, no matter how long you live, you just don't think of yourself as an old man.

Well, Monsieur Bouchair was the owner of the barn a few of us were billeted in.

And what do you think this old-timer did? He asked us to come and sleep inside the house. Not only that, but we slept upstairs in the bedrooms with a cozy, wood-burning stove while he was down-stairs. On Sundays he'd cook us a full-scale meal just like down home. The old man was quite a cook too. And friendly—you couldn't beat him. We'd heard he'd lost his son early in the war, but he never talked about it.

We had our chance to pay him back a little at New Year's Day. The YM had this big party with music, singing, prize-fighting, a lot of things. We decided to take our friend and try and show him a little fun. Oh but he had a bang-up time, laughing, singing, even drinking a bit more wine than he usually did. And did he ever love the prize fights—why, I don't think he'd ever seen one before.

That New Year's party was just about the end of our frolicking. The next month we moved into the trenches at Chemin des Dames. There'd been a lot of fighting there at one time or another, but it was supposed to be quiet when we turned up. It was sure funny the way they'd do it, setting up those practice areas. Oh the Germans were there all right, just down the road a piece. But outside of some shelling and patrols, both sides were using it for training or resting, don't you know. It might just be that's why the Germans had their big breakthrough there in June—nobody was expecting it.

Of course, we weren't exactly kissing cousins with them. We lost our first man here, Harold Sweeney. Poor Harold, he was from New Hampshire. They have a park named after him in Manchester.

And as far as I'm concerned, Sweeney was murdered. Here's what happened. I was standing in our trench trying to watch out for the shelling. Then I figured there was something fishy going on, so I started to face the other way. This puzzled the hell out of Joe Arsenal, who was also a Rumford lad.

"Adams, you dang fool, the Germans ain't over there."

"You're the dang fool, Joe," I told him, "those shells are coming from the French."

Well, do you know something? They were. We found out the next day that a German spy had snuck behind our lines dressed as a French officer. Then he'd gone around raising up the elevation on the artillery pieces. It didn't take much of a change to drop those shells in our lines. A French sergeant had finally caught on and they made short work of Fritzie, but it didn't do poor Harold any good.

We spent several weeks here at Chemin des Dames; then they

moved us over to the Toul area, a much more active sector. They piled us into those damn 40 and 8's again, but not for long. We ended up hiking most of the way, covering more than ninety miles on our dogs in about five days—and most of the time it was raining.

The 103rd area was near a place called Apremont, with the rest of the division stuck up and down the line. The routine was the same as near Soissons, and so was the mud; it was like a quagmire. The difference was in the activity—here the war was twenty-four hours a day, and you needed plenty of luck.

Take the time of the gas attack. We'd put our tour in and had headed for the rear. You know, 'twasn't more than a few hours after we'd left that the Germans threw over a gas barrage, caught most of the boys from Company D by surprise. It was mustard, the kind that would burn you all over. It toasted the hell out of a lot of those fellows. If the Heinies had thrown that in just a little earlier, it would have been Company B that caught it.

Then there was Lieutenant Burke from Waterville. He'd not come across with us, but had moved in as a replacement one night when we were in the Toul sector. The morning after his arrival he decided to take a look around. God, I don't think he was in the lines an hour before a sniper caught him between the eyes. The shot seemed to have come from a bombed-out barn near the German lines. I rested my rifle on top of a sandbag and watched to see if anything was stirring. Sure enough, a few minutes later I saw this German peeking through this caved-in window. I took my time, waiting to see if he'd really show himself. He did and I fired. I think I got that one. Of course, you never know, but we weren't bothered from that dang barn any more. Anyway, it could have been me that German picked out, but it was the lieutenant. Some of us went through the whole thing while others, like Burke, only lasted a couple of hours.

It was the 102nd that really caught it while we were at Toul. They were a few miles away, at a place called Seicheprey. The Germans threw two or three thousand of their best men at them in a surprise raid. The Connecticut boys really put up a scrap, finally driving them out. One of their cooks even split one of those Fritzies half in two with a meat cleaver.

We ended up spending more than two months in the trenches near Apremont. It was now the middle of June, and we'd been at the front or marching for more than four months[1]—why, we were just petered out.

According to Joe Latrinsky,[2] we were going everywhere but the North Pole for a rest. But in the meantime, those Dutchmen were raising Cain over on the Marne—'twasn't nowhere to send us but there. This time it was to be a place called Château-Thierry, and our biggest party of the war—ay-ah, it was our toughest scrap, all right.

The first thing we did was relieve the Marines who'd been doing all that fighting 'round Belleau Wood. They weren't going to get any rest either—no, sir, they were going over near Soissons to hit the Germans there. It was all to be part of the Second Battle of the Marne, the real beginning of the end for the Kaiser.

Our part was to move nor'east through an area called Lucy le Bocage. Oh it was a big battle, all right, one of the biggest. But to me it was just this wooded area where we were, a hill where the Germans were, and close to half a mile of wheat field in between. There must have been a better way to do it than the one we used, but we were brand new to this open-warfare way of fighting, having spent all that time in the trenches.

Anyway, the way we went at it was to hit them head-on—first it was to be Company C, they were from Livermore Falls [Maine], as I remember, then the Rumford boys. Oh those poor devils from Livermore. They went a-running out of those woods with the sunshine lighting up their bayonets, and those Germans started mowing them down. We were to be the second wave, but we hadn't gone very far before we were the first wave—that's how bad the men from Company C had been hit.

The Germans, you see, had these machine guns that they would swing up and down our lines. It was a miracle any of us got through.

I'll tell you what saved me. You see, when I was a boy on my grandfather's farm, I used to love to run through the fields. And when I'd come to a little hill—cradle knolls, we used to call 'em—I'd always run right up it, never around it.

Well, there was this mound directly in my path. Instead of avoid-

[1] The 26th spent 205 days in the front lines. This is exceeded only by the 222 days of the 1st Division.
[2] Captain of the latrine—it means a rumor.

ing it, I went straight up. At that very moment the Germans shot the hell out of us. I could hear my old friend Joe Arsenal yell out, "Corporal Adams, Corporal Adams, I'm hit, I'm hit," just as I climbed that knoll. If I'd been on level ground, I'm sure I would have stopped one.

As it was, Mike McQuade came over to me after we'd taken the hill and pointed to the bottom of my leg.

"Christ, Adams," he said, "you're hit. Look at the bottom of your puttee."

Sure enough, there was a red line going across. A bullet had grazed me, just barely breaking the skin above the ankle. If it hadn't been for the mound, I would have been hit in my gut.

And McQuade, wasn't he fit to be tied! One bullet had ricocheted off the top of his rifle, then bounced off his helmet; you could see the dents in both places. But the thing that had his dander up was his canteen—the Heinies had shot it clear off. I don't know what he had in it, but you never heard Mike curse a blue streak about water, and he was cursing now. Oh that McQuade, he was a caution!

Well, just before we reached the Germans, they started hightailing it out of there fast as they could. We shot several of 'em, but our orders were to hold the hill in case of a counterattack. Besides, we were beat—we were in no condition to chase 'em, and there weren't enough of us left, besides.

We did capture their machine guns and several of their men. One of 'em was an English-speaking officer.

"Brave men," he kept saying, "brave men. How did you get through ze fire? Good soldiers, good soldiers. If ve only had our men of 1914 mit us, zen ve have ze real fight!"

Well sir, those Heinies they had with them in 1918 were tough enough for me. Most of the machine guns we'd captured were out of bullets; they'd fired at us right up until the end.

Their counterattack never came, so we started chasing them. Now, keep in mind I'm only talking about our unit. The other regiments in the 26th had also had a bad time. All up and down our lines the Yankee Division was shot up. I can't remember exactly when, but within a week after our charge, a Pennsylvania National Guard outfit (the 28th Division) relieved us. We weren't sent to any rest area, but we could catch our breath.

Shortly after this I was sent to gas school at Gondrecourt for about a week. On my way to the school I skipped the train I was on so I could spend a day in Paris. I wasn't after any wild time; I just wanted to see the city. And that's a tough thing to do if you only have one dollar on you—it took a Maine man to do it.

I arrived there after dark and spent the night at a YM. The next morning I ran into "Honest Pierre's" sightseeing tour. And honest he was! I saw most of the city for the grand sum of twenty cents. Then I ran into some MPs, told 'em I must have gotten off at the wrong station, and could they help me get to Gondrecourt.

The next week I learned all there was to know about a gas mask. My job was to be gas sergeant when I returned to Company B, so I had to be an expert. I'd be in charge of all the masks. You can imagine what would happen to a man if his mask wasn't working when we had an attack.

I got back to the 103rd in August and hardly knew the place. We'd received all these replacements, mostly from Texas and Philadelphia. The boys from the Southwest were all right, but not the ones from Pennsylvania. Now, I'm not saying they weren't good men, only that they didn't know one end of the rifle from t'other. Some of them had been drafted only a week or two before they went over.

Now, naturally, this affected the whole division. We had plenty of New Englanders left, but you couldn't say a company was from such-and-such place anymore. We had plenty of war ahead of us, but we left something there at Château-Thierry.

Our next big show was Saint Mihiel. As I said earlier, this was a picnic compared to Château-Thierry. It was too bad all our fights couldn't have been like Saint Mihiel. After that one was over, we kept at it until the end of the war, mainly over near Verdun. It was that nasty day-to-day stuff where you try and push 'em back yards at a time. Our position was just about the extreme southern end of the line. Most of the fighting that got into the headlines was closer to the Argonne Forest, but we were doing the same thing they were —keeping the pressure on them, hoping they'd crack.

It was down here that I finally caught it—mustard gas in my private parts. Oh I was scared! It was the damnedest thing. Nature called, and I'd moved away from the boys to do my duty. I'd no sooner settled down when that darn stuff came right off the ground

to hit me, and it really smarted. That was the trouble with that
damn mustard gas. It could settle and you wouldn't know what had
happened until you were really burned.

They got me back to the hospital and covered my testicles with
this creamy solution. Every day the doctor would check me for de-
velopments. Finally he told me I was at the critical stage.

"Adams," he said, "your testicles are loaded with scabs; DON'T
touch 'em! If any of 'em start to drain, I'll have to operate—and
that's bad."

Well sir, that night I tied my hands to the bed when I turned in.
I didn't want to do any scratching while I was sleeping. I kept this
up for two or three days—and each morning the doctor would
check my privates and nod with approval. On the fourth day he
gave me this big smile:

"Adams," he grinned, "you're all right; I don't have to take your
KNOCKERS off!" Now, I promise you that was exactly what he
said, ay-ah, exactly what he said.

By this time the war was over. They sent me back to the 103rd to
wait until they shipped me back. I decided I'd go back to Liffol-Le-
Grand and see my old friend Monsieur Bouchair. When I'd left
there almost a year before, I'd given the old man my silver watch
and one hundred francs for safekeeping. I figured that if I was
killed, he could keep 'em; if not, I'd go back and pick 'em up.

Well, when I returned, one of his neighbors told me that the
good man had died just before the war ended. Before he had
passed on, he'd given my stuff to his niece to hold for me. He'd told
the neighbor to be sure I knew about it. Now, remember, he'd told
that neighbor it was a watch *and* one hundred francs.

Naturally, I went over to see his niece. Oh she said she was glad
to see me, told me how much her uncle thought of me, then gave
me the watch.

"*Merci, mademoiselle,*" I said, "and the hundred francs?"

"*Mais non, monsieur,*" she answered, "a watch, no francs."

"Well, *c'est la guerre,*" I said to myself. I didn't mind losing the
money. What bothered me was how awful that grand old man
would have felt if he knew that his niece had put one over on me.

We finally received orders to go home in April. You can't imagine
how great we felt, particularly the old-timers. They decided to give
us all a physical before sending us home. They didn't want us

bringing anything back with us, I guess. After mine was over, the doctor put his right hand on my shoulder in this fatherly way.

"Adams," he said, "I have some bad news. Somewhere along the line you've picked up some phosgene gas in your lungs, and it's done some damage. If you take it easy, don't smoke, eat well, and get plenty of rest, you might live until you're thirty-five or forty. If you don't, you could go anytime."

I'll be eighty-five on my next birthday, and I've worked hard all my life—still shovel snow and ride a bicycle.

The Great Raid

On April 20, 1918, the Germans launched a massive trench raid against the 26th (Yankee) Division in the Toul Sector. Most of the men who took the brunt of this attack were members of the 102nd Infantry. They were manning the trenches near the town of Seicheprey[1] at the time. It was an accepted premise of World War I trench warfare that if you threw enough troops at a certain area of the line, you could break through. This raid was no exception. The Germans crushed the two companies they were concentrating on and pushed into Seicheprey. Whether or not the Germans intended to hold the town depends on whom you are talking with or whose prose you are reading.

Anyway, they only stayed in the town about an hour and were forced to fight just about every minute of that time. Then the New Englanders of the YD recaptured all the ground they had given up. This was the biggest fight the Americans had been in up to this

[1] Pronounced "sea-spray" by the Doughboys.

time, and it ended up causing a much bigger furor than it would have produced a couple of months later.

Walter Guild, with whom I visited in Orleans, Massachusetts, was serving in the 102nd Machine Gun Battalion of the 26th Division at the time.

"We were in the village of Xiuray at that point," recalled Guild.[2] "This was only about a mile from Seicheprey. I can guarantee you that those Germans concentrated everything on one area. We were shelled, but I didn't see a single German soldier. But they surely hit those Connecticut men [the 102nd Infantry was the Connecticut regiment in the YD] a hell of a clout."

That the attack was a surprise is beyond question. What is open for discussion is whether or not it could have been stopped immediately. The German attack was spearheaded by a group called the Sturmbataillon. These elite troops were specialists in the quick thrust across the line. Then they'd be followed in by regular troops. Each attack was planned thoroughly and practiced to perfection. The best defense against them was a counterattack. To make the position of the Americans even tougher, Seicheprey was a salient. For those front-line troops to have stopped the attack would have almost been impossible.

Now, if, as some military historians have claimed, the Germans had originally planned to grab up a large batch of prisoners and dash back to their lines, why did they continue on into Seicheprey where they were bound to run into more resistance? They already had their prisoners before they went into the village.

Major Rau of the 102nd worked fast. Cooks, truck drivers, orderlies—anyone he could get his hands on—were thrown into the firefight. He had even armed twenty-five men from the 1st Division who had been under arrest since their own outfit had been pulled out of the area two weeks before, and sent them into the fight. A great many of the 160 Germans who were buried after the battle were killed in Seicheprey itself. One thing is indisputable: the Germans would have been better off if they had done their killing and

---

[2] Guild served throughout the war as a corporal. He stayed in the Army and was a colonel in World War II.

capturing outside of Seicheprey and immediately withdrawn. It was like a man knocking someone down with a sucker shot and staying around to see if the fellow would get up. In this case he did.

As it ended up, while both sides claimed a victory, it was really a standoff. The important thing for the Americans was that their green troops were able to quickly bounce back after being blasted. This is a difficult thing for troops to do in their first fight.

The Germans did their best to turn it into a great success, and from the prisoner-taking standpoint, it was. A total of 157 Americans were hauled away. They probably became the most photographed and exhibited POWs of the war. The Boche said nothing of the 103 prisoners the Americans captured.

One of those the Germans nabbed was the late Joe Nolan[3] from Hartford, Connecticut. He was actually taken back to Berlin and put in a cage. His head was shaved, and he was dressed up like an Indian. Then he was shown to the German people as a ferocious American savage—the type of man who would ravish the German people unless the Kaiser's troops won the war. The only trouble was that Nolan was 5 feet, 6 inches and weighed all of 125 pounds, soaking wet. He was about as ferocious-looking as Little Orphan Annie!

[3] A corporal in the AEF, Nolan later became a brigadier general in the National Guard.

The Artist Hero

Merritt D. Cutler

HIS HOME, NORWALK, CONNECTICUT, MARCH 1976
The 7th New York National Guard Regiment in 1917 was one of the swankiest military clubs in America, and, according to Mr. Cutler, it *was* a club.

"I doubt if I could have got in it before the war," Merritt said. "You really had to know somebody. Many of the swells that were in it found some excuse to get out of it when the war came along, but there was also a lot of blue blood shed at that Hindenburg Line."

That there was a lot of the regiment's blood shed at the Hindenburg Line, particularly on September 29, goes without question. Cutler's I Company suffered 166 casualties during the war; 121 of them occurred that single day of September 29. It was rugged as hell.

Mr. Cutler's life after the war has been as eventful as his days in France. For almost sixty years he has been a practicing artist and sculptor. He recently sold a wooden falcon to an old friend, John Huston, the film actor and producer. Mr. Cutler was one of the national amateur doubles champions in tennis in 1931 and has authored a book, *The Tennis Book*, published in 1967. He has also written several books on art, two of which are still in print.

About twenty-five years ago Merritt decided to take up golf; within two years he had a six handicap.

In November of 1976 Mr. Cutler lost his wife of some fifty years. He soon found himself at loose ends, so he decided to take a trip to Mexico. He drove there alone, which isn't too bad when you are almost eighty.

Sergeant Merritt D. Cutler
I Company, 107th Infantry (7th NYNG), 27th Division

> Don't sigh, don't cry-ee
> Baby dear, wipe the tear from yer eye-ee
> It's hard to part, I know,
> But I'll be tickled to death to go.
> Don't sigh, don't cry-ee
> There's a silver lining in the sky-ee;
> If a Nine Point Two gets its eye on you
> Turaloo, napoo—good-bye-ee!
>
> —BRITISH WAR SONG
> SUNG BY MERRITT D. CUTLER

Oh but the 7th New York, you see, was a very snooty outfit before the war. They used to call it the "kid gloves 7th," and that's just about what it was. You had real trouble getting in if you weren't part of the 400 or at least had a lot of money. If you look at one of its rosters—say, around 1913—you'll see nothing but English and Dutch names. I guess today you'd call it a WASP outfit, and well-heeled WASPs at that.

My older brother had gone down to the border with it in 1916 when they first started to let the barriers down. I joined up right after war was declared. I knew I wanted to go to France, and what could be nicer than going with a bunch of men you knew?

Then the government got smart. They realized that if the regiment really took a pasting, you'd be practically devastating a certain group of men. It wasn't because many of the men were wealthy. They did the same thing to many National Guard outfits all over the country. In the Civil War most of the regiments had strong local flavor, you see. And certain villages and towns lost half their male population.

So, they started moving men in and out. Of course, we'd been federalized by now—our new name was to be the 107th U. S. Infantry, part of the 27th Division. And we were to suffer exactly what they were afraid of at the Hindenburg Line stunt, only now the losses were spread over men originally from several New York National Guard regiments. The ironic part was that several of our men, including the poet Joyce Kilmer, went into the 165th Infantry, the old 69th New York Irish. Their division, the Rainbow, suffered more casualties than ours did. On the other hand, they never had one day as bad as our September 29, 1918, show; then again, no other American regiment did during the whole war.

Along with the lads from the 69th, we traded off with the 10th from Flushing and the 1st from Middletown. We called the boys from Flushing the "clam diggers," and the Middletown men the "apple knockers." Of course, we were all integrated, but in many cases your best buddies remained the fellows you'd started out with, at least until the Saint Quentin charge; after that there weren't enough left to make any difference.

Well, they decided to ship us to Spartanburg, South Carolina, for training. You should have heard us cheer when they told us this. We'd be spending the winter in the sunny Southland. What a shock this turned into! It was the coldest goddamn winter they had in the history of South Carolina—sunny Southland, hell; it went below zero a couple of times.

By this time I'd been made a corporal, with not a single old 7th man in my squad. They were all "clam diggers" and were they tough! One of them, a man by the name of Jim Fottrell took particular delight in giving me the business. When I'd give an order there would be good old Jim, shaking his finger at the rest of the boys.

"Now, Corporal Merritt Cutler wants us to do something, lads," he'd crackle, "and he's from the exclusive 7th Regiment—La-de-da Boys." Then he'd kind of wriggle his hips. Everyone would roar. As that comedian says on television, "I was getting no respect."

It reached a boiling point on one of the coldest nights of the winter. I was sitting on my bunk writing a letter when zap, I got hit on the back of my head with a shoe.

"Oh I'm so sorry," apologized Fottrell. "I was aiming at one of the ruffians from the 10th."

"That cuts it, Fottrell," I roared. "The two of us outside."

Now the whole tent goes into hysterics. You see, I weighed 126 pounds, and Fottrell came in at about 180. Besides, Jimmy was actually a professional prize fighter. Nevertheless, I knew damn well that if I didn't stand up to him, I was lost. So out to the company street we went, dressed only in our underdrawers.

It was a moonlit night—that I remember for a certainty because I spent most of the next five minutes or so looking up at the sky, flat on my back. I wish I could say as in one of those old Frank Merriwell books that I thrashed the villain. But the truth of the matter was, Jimmy knocked the bejesus out of me. Christ, I must have gone down about six times. I had a black eye, a fat lip, a broken nose, some loose teeth, and a swollen jaw.

Finally, after I tried to get up for about the seventh time, Fottrell came over, picked me up like a baby, and carried me back to my bunk. Then he turned to the rest of the squad.

"Anyone who has the guts that Cutler has," he announced, "can be my corporal anytime. If anyone disagrees they can come back to the company street with me." There were no takers. From then on, I had no trouble with anyone. Of course, I had to let Jimmy give the orders for a week or so—I couldn't talk.

About two months after my go with Fottrell I had the biggest break of my life. Someone got the bright idea that our division should have some camouflage men, so they started putting together a special squad of creative types who had some connection with painting. I'd been studying at Pratt Institute before I enlisted, so I volunteered. I must confess that the whole thing was somewhat of a lark, but what a deal it turned out to be.

They rounded up twenty of us, under the command of a captain who'd been a sign painter in New York City and told us to go to it.

None of us, including the captain, knew a goddamn thing about camouflage, but it got us out of all the drilling and what have you.

Well, the captain got us all together and tried to give us a lecture. Then he gave us our orders.

"All right, you men," he instructed, "pair off in twos, with each team putting something together that would fool the enemy." Then he took off.

I picked Harry Hull, the brother of Henry Hull, the actor, as my partner, and we went to work. We decided to put together a fake stump, the type that you could move around and hide just about anything in. Three of the other teams decided to do the same thing, so we had a little competition.

I'll say one thing: By God, we didn't fool around. We figured that if we came up with a beauty, we might end up with a seventy-two-hour pass or something like that. First we took some real bark off a tree and wired it to a cage we had. Then we actually planted it in an area that had a lot of other stumps—really, you couldn't tell the damn thing from the others. We even had a little trap door on the bottom that you could crawl in or out of.

Then came the big inspection team, headed by no less than Major General John O'Ryan, the divisional commander. I crawled into our masterpiece while Hull went over to our leader and challenged him to pick out the artificial stump.

Our captain thought this was a great idea, so he walked over to O'Ryan.

"General," he said, "our Corporal Cutler is out there in a phony stump. I can't tell which one he's in. Can you? Of course, General," he continued, "I have taken special pains with Cutler; he's one of my best men."

Well, that was a lot of horse manure; he hadn't helped us one damn bit. But he knew we had a great stump, and he wanted to get a little gravy out of it.

O'Ryan thought it was a splendid idea, so the whole crew of them trudged out to the field. I was completely hidden in our stump, but I could hear them coming.

"Captain," sputtered O'Ryan, "if you're giving us the business, you'll be sorry. All these goddamn stumps look the same to me." Now our captain is obviously getting worried—maybe we didn't have a stump there after all.

Please keep in mind that I can hear every word they're saying. It's all I can do to keep from laughing. Then when they were only about ten yards away, I jumped out with a great big "BOO!"

First there was shocked silence, then laughter and applause. O'Ryan in particular thought it was hilarious.

"Great job, Cutler," he barked, "great job indeed! You fooled the hell out of me. You'll hear more about this."

The general, you know, was quite a guy. He was just about the only National Guard divisional commander who could get along with the old Army types, which was due to the fact that O'Ryan could get along with anybody. He had graduated from both the Army War College and the Army Staff School. None of the regulars had anything on our general.

He was also true to his word—that little stump episode really affected the rest of my World War I career. As a matter of fact, when I went back into the service as an officer for World War II, I found out there was mention of the stump in my permanent military file.

Anyway, I knew I had a good thing going, so I decided to play it for all it was worth. I had our company commander detach me from my squad and make me I Company's camouflage expert. Each day I'd pick up a few men from the company and give them a detail. Oh, I'd ask them to rig up a dead horse or hide an artillery piece, something like that. I once even had them build a fake hill we could hide something behind. Then, at the end of the day, I'd examine what they'd accomplished.

Now, having most of the day off, I had a chance to do just about what I wanted. To make matters even better, my good friend Jim Streitcher was working on the divisional paper. Between the two of us we managed to have a very pleasant tour of duty.

Jimmy's the one, you know, who wrote the Dere Mabel books. They started out as a series of articles called "Letters from a Rookie." Then some publisher heard about them and put them in a book. Before he was through, the sales went into the millions. The country was starving for material about their sons, particularly on the lighter side.

Really, for us in those days, his books were funny. This rookie would always be fouled up, and he'd write his girl about it. I remember one letter where he said, "Dere Mabel, thanks for the mittens you sent me. If I have my fingers shot off, they'll be great!" Then a soldier named Bill Brech would draw a picture of a hand with a mitten on where the fingers would be sticking way out.

Another buddy I had there was a Chinese named Alex Kim. His mother had been the first woman member of her race to graduate from an American college. His whole family was very successful. I think they brought the soybean to the United States, or something like that. Alex himself had graduated from Columbia, which was a very rare thing for a Chinese back in the teens.

He had a sad tale to tell, though, one that made him very morose a great deal of the time. While at Columbia one of his classmates had taken him out to the Hamptons for a weekend. There he met his host's sister and had fallen madly in love with her. True to the old melodramas of that period, her family had stepped in and broken up the romance. They were real upper-crust; their daughter wasn't going to marry any Chinaman. Alex never got over it. We were all itching to get to France, but no one as badly as Kim. He transferred out of the division into chemical warfare, knowing this would get him to France ahead of the twenty-seventh. It did.

Our turn finally came in May. They moved us up to Camp Stuart, Virginia, where we boarded the USS *Susquehanna*, a gift from the Kaiser. She was formerly the *Rhein* and had been seized in a U.S. port when war was declared. The officers, as to be expected, got the staterooms, while the enlisted men were down below. We called our spot the Black Hole of Calcutta. Christ, it was awful—men getting seasick all over the place, moaning and groaning, really bad. It took over fourteen days to reach Brest, and you can bet there wasn't a single unhappy Doughboy when we landed.

Now for the crazy part. We had spent the better part of a year training in the States, with special emphasis on physical fitness. Most of the men were hard as a rock when we boarded ship. But those miserable fourteen days in the hole knocked the hell out of us. The men just had to be hiked back into shape—and hike we did.

Brest is a long way from the northeastern section of France, and it was hiking all the way. We went through one French village after another day in and day out. Those darn packs and your rifle and ammunition weighed about eighty pounds. Why, each one of us was almost a walking general store. The items the men hated to carry the most were the extra pair of shoes and the tent poles. We had all been given two pairs of these hobnailed boots when we left the States. They were really great. The only problem was you couldn't wear them out. I spent my entire time in France wearing my original shoes. Yet I was supposed to carry this extra pair at all times. You can bet I disposed of them early in the game. As a matter of fact, French children would usually follow a group of marching Americans like sea gulls following a ship. When the Yanks would throw stuff away, these *enfants* would grab it up. Hell, you might have some old Frenchman wearing Doughboy boots today— that's how great they were!

Most of the divisions arriving in France when we did were sent down toward the southern end of the line, but not us. Our orders were to join the British on the northern section. Actually, we spent our entire service with the English, never becoming a part of Pershing's Army. Of course, he was still our overall commanding officer, which brings up an interesting story.

A group of us were sitting by the roadside in July or August when this staff car drove up. We hated those "brass buggies"—they never meant anything good. And if it had been raining, they'd whizz by splattering mud all over you. Well, this one stops right in front of us, and out jumps this spic-and-span young second lieutenant. Christ, he looked as if he'd just walked out of Brooks Brothers' uniform floor.

"Attention, you men," he snapped, "prepare for inspection."

I'm sure you can realize what a pain in the ass something like that was, but, what the hell, we started to fall in. Then I noticed the four stars on the license plate. It was old Black Jack himself coming over to see how the 27th was doing.

Naturally, I was quite concerned. Remember, I'm still the camouflage man—no squad roll calls or reveilles—just trying to do what seemed pleasant. The reason I was with this group was my sketching. I had this huge sketchbook that on the surface was supposed to be ideas for camouflage. What I was actually doing was preparing a book on the Doughboys that I could develop after the war.

Well, Pershing goes up and down our lines, shaking his head. I guess we weren't military enough for him. When he reached me, he really seemed appalled, particularly when he saw the sketchbook.

"What do you have there, Corporal?"

"Oh this is just my sketchbook."

"Sketchbook, sketchbook," he thundered, "what the hell do you think this is, an art school? You're in the United States Army, soldier. Give me that sketchbook." Then he handed it to the lieutenant. I never saw it again. You know, I often wondered what happened to it. There was so damn much stuff in that book.

By this time we're getting pretty close to the front, and we're certainly getting to know the French people. Oh the privates and the noncoms aren't visiting with them as much as the officers, but we're seeing them every day. That's why I always get a big kick out of movies like *What Price Glory?* where you have a big romance between a sweet *mademoiselle* and one of the men.

Hell, I only spoke to a woman alone once or twice during the entire war. I did have a chance for a rendezvous or two after the war, but by that time I was too interested in getting home. Who knows? Maybe I was a little retarded in that area in those days.

I'll tell you one thing I definitely didn't do was go into one of those crummy whorehouses they had. Those lectures they'd given to us back in Spartanburg had really gotten to me. You know, all those pictures they showed us of men with their noses falling off—yes, and other things also.

We marched by one of those bordellos up near Belgium. Christ, it just looked dirty, and I can imagine what it smelled like. There was a line waiting for service about a quarter of a mile long. You could see French, British, and American soldiers all waiting for a quick roll in the hay. The rumor was they'd even caught a German soldier or two trying to buy a little. No sir, sex on the assembly line wasn't for me.

In the meantime, it was getting close to the time when we were to begin doing what we'd come over for. It started for us in both an amusing and a sad way on July 14, Bastille Day. Some British troops were staging a cricket game in this field while we were having a baseball game in the same place. Everyone was having a great time when one of the English yelled, "Here comes a Jerry!" Sure enough, this German bomber flew over us. He didn't succeed in hurting anyone, but he sure broke up the ball game.

That night we had an opportunity to watch one of the English concerts put on by a Professor Matt and Company. About halfway through, an unscheduled show-stopper appeared. It was an American soldier from one of our colored labor battalions all dressed up in a clown suit. To top it off, he's appearing in whiteface—turning the tables on our minstrel shows. And how the boys loved it when he started to sing these London music hall ditties in a cross between an American darkie and an English cockney accent. One of them became a great favorite of mine. It went like this:

> Oh for a roley-poley
> That Mummy used to mike,
> A roley-poley puddin' duff
> Roley-poley that's the stuff,
> Only to think about it
> Mikes my tummy ike.
> O Lor' lumme!
> I wants my Mummy
> An' the puddin' she used to mike!

What we didn't know was that while we were watching the black man's act, my own I Company was having its first battle death. We had been constantly moving up some of our officers and noncoms to spend a day or two with the British in the front lines. One of them, Corporal Billy Leonard, an original 7th Regiment man, was killed by shellfire the night of July 14. It was quite a shock to us all.

Then, sometime in the first part of August, the whole outfit moved into the lines near a place called Dickebusch Lake. The night we moved in, the English were moving out across the way from us. I can still hear them now.

"Hie, Yank."

"Welcome aboard, Yank."

"Don't stir up Jerry."

"Yank, you shoot at 'im, he'll shoot back twice."

It was all supposed to be secretive as hell, but the next morning the Germans hung out this big sign, "Hello, 107th Infantry. We are the 15th Division of Prince Ruprecht's Army." After over a year in the Army it was frightening to realize that you were only fifty to a hundred yards away from some men whose main aim was to kill you.

Some of the boys had been a little puzzled by what the English had said, but they soon found out what it was all about. The British outfit we relieved had been the Sherwood Forester. They were a crack outfit who'd bled a lot and were what you'd call "trench-wise." Anytime we'd fire, they'd just fire back. It didn't get you any-where, and someone might get killed.

The artillery was the same way. The only difference was our ar-tillery would fire at their trenches, and their artillery would fire at us. Every now and then a German shell would land in Dickebusch Lake. The damn place was loaded with decomposing bodies. No matter which side they would have belonged to, they all smelled the same.

And the flies were brutal. This was August, and it was hot as hell. We had these woollen uniforms and puttees that were stifling. Of course, we all had cooties. No sir, I can't think of one pleasant thing about trench life, except your relief. It seemed to me we'd spend about a week there, get pulled back for a week, then go back up.

During one reserve period we had a chance to see Sir Harry Lauder, the great Scotch entertainer. Harry had lost his only son near where we were earlier in the war. From that time on he spent almost all his time putting shows on for the soldiers. He came out with that funny cane of his singing "Roaming in the Gloaming," "Mary, My Scotch Blue Belle," "The Wiggle, Waggle of His Kilt"— all his old standbys. There must have been a lot of men from Glas-gow in the crowd because he brought the house down with his "I Belong to Glasgee."

But your time out of the lines seemed to fly by, and your time in the trenches seemed an eternity. My second tour gave me a chance for my first patrol. A British lieutenant took seven or eight of us out on a prisoner raid. It was nighttime, of course, and we crawled through the wire and headed for the first German trench. What a surprise we got when we reached it. There was one solitary middle-aged German soldier guarding this stretch. He was loaded down with weapons, though, looking like one of those one-man bands they used to have.

He took one look at all of us, shrugged his shoulders, and stuck up his hands. We headed back with him, but by now the Germans knew something was up. They opened up with machine guns and artillery. We all hit the dirt but the poor German. He just stood there and was cut in half. So we returned to our own lines, rather shook up and no prisoner.

A few nights later one of our other companies sent out a patrol that ran into real trouble. They had to break up and try to get back as best they could. The last one to attempt to come in was their lieutenant. He'd been badly shot up, particularly his jaw, which was broken. The sentry, of course, didn't know this, and when the lieutenant couldn't give the password, he put a bullet in his stomach. Things like that really break you up when you hear about them, but they happened all the time.

I couldn't get over how much smarter the Germans were about that trench business than we were. Everybody knew that either side could take any part of the first trench line anytime they wanted to. You couldn't really hope to set up any kind of a defense before the second line at the earliest. By putting well-armed men up front, they weren't going to be badly hurt when we came over.

The worst shelling we received here came from those damn Mieniewaffers; this was a trench mortar they could elevate to a certain degree and drop into our position. Its shrapnel was devastating, but its concussion was worse. Most of the shell-shock victims of World War I weren't what we'd call today battle fatigue. Real shell shock was the actual scrambling of a man's brain by concussion. If you've ever seen a man actually lose his wits through shelling, you'd never forget it. The poor guys became jibbering idiots.

In the meantime, I'd been developing this progressive rash on my chest. When it became intolerable, I went to our medic to see what could be done. Well, for Christ's sake, I had, of all things, scabies. That's an infection caused by improper nutrition, normally occurring when you're living in filth. They gave me a pass to take a train back to a base hospital. They fixed me up in pretty good order, and I started back to I Company.

Then I made an incredible discovery: Now, I'm not saying that everybody in the 107th was perfect; far from it. Look at the racket I had worked out with the camouflage routine—I was no rosebud. But I had stayed with the outfit during the shelling and patrolling. The thought of shirking the combat had never entered my mind, and I think most of our men felt the same way—not half the chaps I met on the train. They'd discovered what I called the choo-choo train racket.

Here's how it worked. They'd figure out some way to get back to a base hospital. Then when they'd get their travel orders to return to their unit, they would board a train with no intention of getting off at the right station. Eventually some MP would catch up with them, but they'd just play dumb, say they'd missed their stop for one reason or another, and could the guard help them get back. Well, they did have legitimate orders, so the MPs would feed them and send them on their way. It was a pretty simple thing to change the date on your orders, so the slackers would keep doing this for weeks. I guess their only problem was to make sure they didn't run into the same MP twice. You know, if I'd realized what kind of hell I was going back to, I might have done the same thing.

I did return to I Company, however, and shortly after I got back, a new recruit showed up. Oh he was unshaven, disheveled, and looked like something the cat dragged in.

"Where the hell's I Company?" he asked. He looked as if he'd been riding the rails for weeks. He was so done in I had to look closely to see that he was a Chinese. It was my old buddy, Alex Kim, AWOL from his chemical unit.

"That chemical warfare is all a lot of baloney," he told the company. "All I do is sit back in Paris and shuffle papers. That's not what I came to France for. Everyone knows there's going to be a push, and I want to go in with the old 7th."

"Oh for Christ's sake, Kim," answered our captain, "I can't let you do that; you don't belong to our unit anymore. I'll have to put you under arrest and send you back." Then he looked around and saw all the men staring at him.

"The hell with it, boys," he sighed, "someone get him a rifle; he can stay."

When we did go over the top on September 29, Kim was one of the first to get it—he was cut in half.[1] I often wondered what the parents of his old girlfriend thought when they heard about it. And the girl, did she pine away like a broken-hearted heroine in a Dickens novel? Probably not. I'm sure she married a stockbroker.

Well, it wasn't very long after my return that the show started. It was to be part of Foch's tremendous drive to push the Boche back to Germany. Pershing's Army, down on the southern end of the line, would strike in the Meuse-Argonne, while the French would be going against the center. We would be striking at an area in the

---

[1] Corporal Alexander Kim is officially listed as killed in action, Company I, 7th NYNG (107th U. S. Infantry). He also received a citation from General O'Ryan.

British section called the Saint Quentin tunnel. It was one of the most heavily fortified positions on the whole Hindenburg Line. I guess they figured if we could really get the Germans on the run before the snow set in, we could finish them off by the spring.

Our attack area was stretched along a twenty-mile front. Along with the 30th Division,[2] we made up the II U. S. Army Corps. There were British troops on either side of us, with some splendid Australians coming in on our rear.

Well, after moving around for two or three days, we settled down on the night of September 28 about a mile from the front. We were told to try and get some sleep, but I doubt like hell if anyone did. We were down to light marching packs and all the ammunition we wanted. This wasn't going to be a parade.

They woke us up the next morning at about two-thirty. We were told it might get a little sticky before the day was out but not to worry—along with the artillery we would be supported by twenty tanks. These were a new weapon to us, but we figured they'd do a bang-up job on the German machine gunners. Do you know that not a one of those tanks even reached the barbed wire? Every single tank was knocked out. Those poor devils didn't have a chance.

We jumped off at dawn, moving into a valley between two hills. It was foggy as hell, and when the shelling started, you could barely see at all. I don't think I'd taken two steps before the Germans opened up. We had been told not to run toward the Germans or we'd catch up with our own artillery. Well, I don't know whose artillery it was, but shells were dropping right and left. The only thing I could concentrate on was to keep moving—don't let your buddies think you're yellow; I think I was more concerned with this than with the Germans. The British had given us a big half tumbler of rum before the charge, and thank God for that. The Americans would have never done that.

After the artillery came their machine guns. They had them in fixed positions maintaining a field of fire. As I saw more and more of our men go down, I developed this incredible desire to get one of those pillboxes. Finally—I have no idea how long it took—I worked around behind one of them. I dropped one of my Mills gre-

[2] The 30th was a National Guard division from the Carolinas and Tennessee. They were very good troops.

nades in the rear opening. I'm not a violent man, but I can remember my glee when the grenade exploded. It horrifies me now, but I was in such a state of shock that nothing mattered but the killing of some of those Germans. Before that morning was out I know I put half a dozen or so of their machine guns out of commission.

I must have been hit sometime in the morning, but I don't remember it. My real pain was coming from the barbed wire. You know, it was never strung in a straight line—you had acres and acres of it in all directions. Our tanks were supposed to have knocked it out, but as I told you, they were all destroyed.

The only great thing we had working for us were the shellholes. The area had been fought over so long, it looked like something out of *Dante's Inferno*. I'd keep jumping from one of these holes to the next one. And so would my buddies. At the beginning of the advance I could keep track of my direction by the heads that were bobbing up or down from these holes. Then, as the hours went by, I began to see less and less of them; finally, none.

I hadn't seen Kim get hit, but I did see Fottrell go down. My old buddy, Jimmy the prize fighter—it was dreadful; it looked as if his whole jaw had been shot away. And there were so many others. They'd just become figures going down, like pins in a bowling alley.

Sometime that afternoon it dawned on me I couldn't see any more Americans; to top off my confusion, I'd been hearing fire behind me. The Germans, you see, had dug such an elaborate tunnel network they could send reinforcements to the area we had already charged over.

In the meantime, the Australians had mingled in with the Germans in the rear. Everyone was shooting at someone. To make it worse, the shellholes were loaded with wounded men from the 107th. Christ, what a mess!

Well, I decided to look for some Americans, so I started jumping from hole to hole. I'd lost all conception of time, but I think it was about nightfall when I found a lad from Company I named Blanchette. The poor guy had a real bad leg wound, with half the bone sticking out. I spent several hours trying to comfort him. Then a man from another company crawled into our hole with a bullet in his stomach; he was in even worse shape than Blanchette. Honestly, there were so many wounded Americans there, many of them dying, but others who could be saved if they could be attended to. I knew I had to get a stretcher somewhere and move these poor guys to a field station.

I drove a bayoneted rifle into the ground and stuck a helmet on its top—this would help me locate the spot. Then I left for help. Fortunately I ran into some Australians and was able to get a stretcher. One of the Aussies didn't want any part of going into that mess, but his buddy said, "Sure, Yank, I'll go; we're in this bloody thing together."

Well, I can't remember how many trips we made, but there were several. The first stop was for two friends. Both men were still alive, and we got them back to an aid station. I know Blanchette lived, but I don't know about the other fellow—he was pretty far gone when we left him.

The amazing part of the whole thing was what happened next. After fighting all day, spending that time in the shellhole with the two men, and then going back and forth to pick up our wounded under fire, I was told to lug rations to the men out on the line. I did it, of course, then I saw the sergeant in charge giving me a funny look.

"Cutler," he said, "look at your leg. You've been hit."

I looked down, and one of my puttees was soaked. When I unraveled the darn thing, I found it full of blood. Fortunately for me it was a clean wound, but it did mean the end of the battle for me. Incredible as it sounds, I don't know when I was actually hit; it was probably when we first moved against the machine guns, but I never felt it.

They sent me to a hospital in Calais, patched me up, and in about two weeks or so headed me back to the front. Just as I rejoined the company, Captain Leland told me to turn around and head back. I'd been ordered to take a short course, after which I'd be commissioned a second lieutenant.

The funny thing about that venture was that I didn't become an officer until World War II, twenty-three years later. We finished the course on November 9. Then they gave us a little pep talk and told us we were all second lieutenants. Three days later they called us together to tell us it was all a mistake, the war was over, so they didn't need any officers. No one really cared at that point; all we wanted to do was go home.

Well, it's all a long time ago now. We didn't actually take the tunnel—the Australians accomplished that. But we'd softened it up for them, and if you ever want to find out how good the 107th was, ask the boys from "Down Under"—we had a mutual admiration society.

One more touch: A few years after the war I was standing on the corner of Madison Avenue and 47th Street in New York City when this fellow walked up to me.

"Hello, Cutler," he said. "Want to go a few rounds?"

I almost fainted. "Holy Christ," I answered. "Is that you, Jimmy? I thought you were killed on the twenty-ninth."

It was Jimmy Fottrell, and what a job they'd done on his jaw and face. But as great a job as they'd done with the plastic surgery, they couldn't erase the scars on his mind. He wasn't the same Jimmy, no doubt about that.

For several years a group of us from Company I used to meet annually at Keene's Chop House on September 29. I told Jimmy about it, and he started to join us. Then he disappeared. We later found out they had to put him away. I'm afraid he'd left more than part of his jaw in France. As a matter of fact, it was a miracle any of us kept our sanity after the Hindenburg Line stunt.

Some Others Who Went

Of the two million Americans who went to France in World War I, many were bound to achieve prominence after the war, especially in politics and the military.

The No. 1 AEF veteran was President Truman. While Harry could not credit his ascendency to the White House to his World

War I record, his service in France played a large part in his early political career in Missouri. Truman's command—Battery D, 129th Field Artillery of the 35th Division—was part of the Missouri National Guard. The local Guardsmen had a way of sticking together after the war. It is also quite possible that the thirty-fourth President developed a good deal of his salty way of speaking in France. The Argonne was very fruitful territory for profanity and obscenities.

Two other World War I veterans tried for the presidency but didn't make it: Alf Landon, who served but did not get to France, and Wendell Willkie, who did go overseas. Willkie was among that large contingency of artillery officers who were slated to play a big part in the mid-November offensive that was canceled due to the Armistice.

Leverett Saltonstall, longtime U.S. senator from Massachusetts, was also in the same category, according to Frazier Wilde.

"Lev was in my artillery outfit of the 76th Division when we went over in July of '18," said Wilde, "but we never really got into anything. We would have, though, if the war had lasted much longer."

Wilde was typical of the several very successful postwar businessmen whom I interviewed in that his memory of the two years he spent in the military when he was a young man was excellent. Although he was to become the chief executive officer of the giant Connecticut General Insurance Company, and also a very important figure in the national financial hierarchy of the Republican Party, he could still remember such minor incidents as a conversation he had with his unit's chaplain after he landed in England.

"We were one of the few groups to go through London," recalled Frazier, "and I vividly remember all those man-starved English girls cheering us. Our boys, who hadn't talked to any young ladies in quite a spell, were just as interested in the whole thing as the English women seemed to be. I was standing next to our Catholic chaplain at the time. Oh he was a great man. I'm not a Catholic, but we all loved that guy!

"Well, he just kept taking the scene in, and he finally turned to me and stuck his finger in the air.

"'Frazier,' he said, 'I fear for the honor of the regiment.' Then we enjoyed a hearty laugh."

Other political figures who went were Coolidge's Vice President, Charles Dawes, and the well-known senator from Illinois, Everett McKinley Dirksen. This colorful solon was a balloonist, or, as they were called, a "gas bag" man. Senator Dirksen passed on in 1969, so I obviously couldn't interview him, but I did speak to another balloonist, George Cobb of Greenwich, Connecticut.

"We would get a Croix de Guerre and a furlough if we were shot down by the Germans," recalled Mr. Cobb. "We all had parachutes, and the Boche would almost never shoot at us as we were descending.

"Most of those gas bag men were heavy drinkers, though," continued Mr. Cobb. "I remember these two in particular who were always boasting about all the liquor they could consume. So the French set up a drinking contest between the two. I'll be damned if they didn't both pass out at the same time. There was a lot of *d'argent* bet on the match, so the passing out just wouldn't do. The two of them woke up. One of these lushes promptly got sick, while the other calmly went over and poured himself a drink.

"'Le victor,' cried a Frenchman and held up the hand of the still-thirsty gas man."

Then there was Fiorello La Guardia, the Little Flower, the mayor of New York City, who used to read the funny papers on the radio when the newspapers were on strike. As a major in the U. S. Air Service, La Guardia served both in France and Italy. Sherwood Hubbell, later a gunner on a Hadley Page bomber in General Trenchard's Independent Air Force in France, remembers Fiorello well from the period that Hubbell also spent in Italy.

"Oh he was a great little bombastic guy, always strutting around and smiling," said Hubbell. "And how those Italians loved him! He may have been an American, but he was one of their own to the Italians."

Another man to become prominent in American politics who went to France, as a U. S. Army colonel, was Frank Knox, who unsuccessfully ran for the vice presidency on Alf Landon's ticket and was a World War II Secretary of the Navy under Franklin Roosevelt. According to Grantland Rice, it was Knox who cut through the red tape and helped the famous sportswriter get home in 1919.

FDR himself also managed to go abroad in 1918, and it almost killed him. As Assistant Secretary of the Navy under Woodrow Wilson, this astute young politician could see the publicity value of a trip to France to check on his famous Marine Brigade. While there, this future President contracted the flu, or pneumonia (probably both), and almost died.

Unlike the Civil War or World War II, no man emerged from military service in France with a record that could put him in the White House. General Pershing would have undoubtedly accepted a nomination for the presidency, but the "Iron Commander" just didn't have the needed charisma to sell himself to the American public. As so many of the Doughboys put it, "I wasn't about to vote for a man who kept our regiment waiting three hours in the rain so he could review us."

There was a future American President who gained national prominence during World War I, but not in the military; this was Herbert Hoover. First he set up the commission for food relief in Belgium; then, after the United States entered the war, he headed up the United States Food Administration. To "Hooverize" meant to save food for the people in war-torn Europe. After the war he returned to Europe to direct the feeding of millions of people. Ironically, it was Herbert Hoover, a Quaker, who gained the most politically out of the Great War. On the other hand, two of the war's finest combat records belonged to Colonels Theodore Roosevelt, Jr., and "Wild Bill" Donovan. They were both defeated when they ran for governor in New York State after the war.

As for the military, most of the senior officers in World War II and even Korea had been part of the AEF. Naturally, all 1917 career officers were anxious to get to France.

"We all felt," General James Van Fleet told me, while relaxing in his beautiful Polk City, Florida, ranch house, "that our careers would be hindered if we didn't go to Europe during the First World War. But hell, look at Omar Bradley and Ike—they didn't leave the States in 1918, and it certainly didn't hurt them. They were both classmates of mine at West Point in 1915," continued the general, "and I know how badly they wanted to get into it, but they had to wait for the Second World War before they could go over."

Most of the other leading military figures of World War II did get to France during World War I. George Patton, Douglas MacArthur, Mark Clark, and George Marshall were all members of the AEF. It was Marshall's outstanding staff work, first as a member of the 1st Division and later at Pershing's general headquarters, that so greatly determined Marshall's future. While General Marshall undoubtedly possessed one of the truly great military minds in American history, he never held a line command in action. It was the greatest disappointment in his life.

It was at the level of divisional commander in World War II where the combat experience in World War I paid off. Such generals as William Wyman, Andrew Bruce, Fred Walker, Terry Allen, Clarence Huebner—the list goes on and on—fought in France in 1918. The junior officers of World War I were indeed the combat leaders of World War II.

And it did not apply only to the Second World War generals. Fifteen of the men I interviewed returned to the service for World War II in ranks ranging from captain to colonel.[1] These men have a very unique organization called The Retreads. Its membership is open only to those who served in both World Wars. I attended one of their meetings in 1976. When I pointed out to one of them that it was unusual to find men who had served against both the Kaiser and Adolf Hitler, he just laughed.

"Nothing unusual about us," he said. "We just wanted to finish what we started in 1918."

[1] Four of those I interviewed served in World War II as generals: Lemuel Shepherd, Mark Clark, James Van Fleet, and Edward Curtis.

The Lafayette Pilot

Reginald Sinclair

HOTEL BERKSHIRE, NEW YORK CITY, JUNE 1976
There will always be an aura of glamor attached to the Americans
who flew with the Lafayette Flying Corps. Raoul Lufberry, Ted
Parsons, Frank Baylies, Nordhoff and Hall (and the two seem to
always go together), Tommy Hitchcock (probably the world's
greatest polo player), Vic Chapman—their very names seem to con-
jure up the last of the romantic aspects of war—if shooting down
another plane in flames, or suffering the same fate, is glamorous.

But there was something about them that will never come again.
Maybe it was because they were mostly all young, or that a large
majority of them had just left college, or that so many of them had
known each other back home. Perhaps it was their seemingly unmilitary manner, but whatever it was, they did shoot down 199 planes.

One of these men was Reggie Sinclair from Corning, New York.
Born to the purple, as Reggie puts it, "I've always been independent," he picked the way he wanted to fight. And fight he did,
and very successfully. Credited with three official victories, he
strongly suggests he had more. He does this in such a casual yet
factual way, it is impossible to doubt him.

While never hating the Germans, "they were doing the same
thing I was," recalls Mr. Sinclair, he hastened to go back into the
service for World War II. This time he picked the U. S. Naval Air
Corps, where he was made a commander. When he reported for

duty at one station, his French wings and decorations were questioned by a young officer.

"What are those, Commander?" asked the officer.

"Well, these are my French aviator's wings, and this is my Croix de Guerre with three palms, and . . ."

"Oh you can't wear those on an American uniform around here!"

"Is that so!" replied Commander Sinclair. And then Reggie set the young fellow straight. It must have been a beautiful sight to see.

Adjutant Reginald Sinclair
1st Regiment, French Foreign Legion, Spad 68

> *Quand Madelon vient nous servir à boire,*
> *Sous la tonnelle on frôle son jupon,*
> *Et chacun lui raconte une histoire,*
> *Une histoire à sa façon.*
> *La Madelon pour nous n'est pas sévère,*
> *Quand on lui prend la taille ou le menton*
> *Elle rit, c'est tout l'mal qu'ell' sait faire,*
> *Madelon, Madelon, Madelon!*

The funny part of my becoming an aviator is how close it came to not happening at all. The first time I went into a plane, you see, was a complete disaster. But it ended up just like being thrown from a horse—you know, you have to get right back up on him or you're finished.

Here's how it happened. It was July of 1913, and I was visiting my mother at the Clarendon Hotel in Daytona, Florida. There was a woman there named Ruth Law, who was what we used to call an aviatrix. She'd give you a three-minute ride in a Wright Model B for twenty-five dollars. I only had ten, so I asked my mother if I could borrow the rest from her. She acquiesced, so I was off on my airborne jaunt.

Now, that old-timer was a single-seat plane, so I had to sit on the lower wing—no seat belt or anything like that—just sit on the wing with my feet on the same bamboo rod that hers were on, hanging onto two straps. Well, we took off with the wind out of the north.

The problem was she went right under the clouds, which was the bumpiest place she could go. God, it was uncomfortable—I can't say I was frightened, but it certainly wasn't any fun. She got caught in a wind situation, and we ended up landing on a deserted beach several miles north from where we had started. Then we took off again, this time downwind, and got back one hell of a lot faster than it took to get to that beach. That was enough for me, the end of my flying career. Then Ruth's husband (he was also her manager) came over to console me.

"Well, that wasn't very good, was it?" he said.

"To tell you the truth," I replied, "I don't know. I've never done it before."

"Now, listen, young man," he continued, "you come back after four this afternoon and we're going to give you another ride—this one on the house."

I came back on schedule, and they were true to their word. By this time the sun was low and the air was as smooth as a ribbon. She took me over the city of Daytona and, let me tell you, there was all the difference in the world between the two flights. If she hadn't taken the trouble to give me that Annie Oakley, I probably would have ended up in either the artillery or infantry.

Well, at the time I was a freshman at Yale but just about to resign. I'd had an altercation with one of the professors at New Haven that had reached an impasse, so I said to hell with it and quit. My father, along with a man named Emory Houghton—who had married sisters, incidentally—were founders of the Corning Glass Works, so I went home to go to work for the family firm.

Then in the spring of 1916 I saw an article in a periodical saying that the Aviation Section of the Signal Corps was taking applications from civilians to learn to fly. Well, some of my school chums had gone to France to fly with the Lafayette group, and others were already learning to fly with our forces. I know that Hobie Baker was training with the Signal Corps and so were Buck Church and Cord Meyer. Baker had been ahead of me at St. Paul's School in Concord, New Hampshire, but Meyer had been on the crew with me at SPS, and Church had been on the freshman football team with me at New Haven.

The situation looked attractive, so I applied, and this started the biggest run-around you've ever seen. After waiting quite a while, I finally received orders to report to St. John's Military Academy in Manlius, New York, for an examination. So I reported as requested, and seemed to do well on both the oral and physical tests they gave to me under the supervision of this old-line cavalry officer. Nobody seemed to be overly interested in the thing, so I finally approached this horse soldier.

"Well, what do I do now?" I asked.

"Oh you just go home and wait until you hear from Washington."

It seemed to me I was being given the old don't-call-us-we'll-call-you treatment.

Finally, in the early spring of 1917, I received a letter from the War Department written in what today we'd call Pentagonese. Why, it was just a lot of gobbledygook. I didn't know what to do, so I went down to Governors Island in New York City, where I knew the Air Service had a depot. Here I ran into a Captain Milling.

"Sir," I asked, "could you please translate this for me? I don't know what it means."

He read it and kind of chuckled.

"I don't blame you for not understanding this," he answered, "but what it says is you're not going to be ordered to active duty at this time."

I guess he sensed how darn disappointed I was, because he continued, "You know, if you could get in to see Brigadier General Squire in Washington, he could get you an educational waiver. Your problem is we're only taking men with a college degree at this time."

So I trotted down to Washington, where I called up Senator Wadsworth, an old friend of the family and a great guy. Well, first he got me an interview with Lieutenant Colonel Saltzman. I gave him my story, and he seemed to be impressed.

"Young man," he said, "we can pull a few wires here; you'll be all right. I'll get the general."

Naturally, I'm beginning to feel confident now. Hell, I'd told my story so many times I've really got it polished. Then in walked the general, a red-headed fellow with a big red beard. He was quite busy, you see, because by this time we'd just declared war, and I figured if he was willing to see me, everything would be all right. So, as I'd expected, he kept nodding his head when I expressed my desire to fly against the Germans.

"Young Sinclair here," he said to Saltzman, "really wants to get into the thick of this thing. Give him a note to Major Bolling up in New York City so he can go over with the first group that ships out."

So then I went back to New York to see Bolling, and once again I seemed to impress someone, but I still had a problem.

"Sinclair," he said, "I can take you over as a mechanic, even make you a sergeant, but I can't promise you what will happen when we get there."

"Mechanic!" I replied. "I don't want to be a mechanic; I want to be an aviator."

Bolling seemed to muse about this for a while; then his eyes lit up.

"I know what you can do," he said. "Go see Mr. MacAnerney; he can get you into the Lafayette Flying Group in the French Army. You can take your training with them, then switch over to our Air Group later on."

Well, my next step was to see Mr. MacAnerney, where I finally got some action.

"Can you sail on Saturday?" he asked.

Oh this really caught me off guard. After all my maneuvering, here it was.

"Gee," I said, "maybe in about two weeks or so—I do have to put my affairs in order." Then came the craziest thing of all!

"Fine," he said, "then you can spend a week down in Newport News, Virginia, with the U. S. Aviation Section learning the basic aspects of flying." The long and short of it was, I went down there with the group I couldn't get into, actually did some flying, which they weren't doing, and ended up not only landing in France a couple of months before they did, but flying in combat about four months before they even got close to a German.

Well, if you wanted to go into the Lafayette Flying Group, you presented yourself to Dr. Edmund L. Gros, the guiding light of the Americans who had come over to either drive an ambulance or fly a plane in the service of France. You see, the only way you could fly was to enlist in a French regiment; then you went on detached service with the French Air Service, but officially you still belonged in your original regiment. In my case, it was the 1st French Foreign Legion.

After you enlisted, you'd go to Alvord as a second-class soldier, where you'd learn to fly, first with Bleriots and then with Caudrons. After this you'd get your military pilot's license and be sent to advance school at Pau, and be made a corporal, I might add. At Pau you'd fly the Nieuports and learn acrobatics. The final step took you up near the front for work on the Spads.

That was it. The next move was to a squadron. In my case, it was Spad 68 near Toul. I was still a corporal, as one couldn't make sergeant until you had 40 hours of actual combat flying—and after 140 hours of flight time against the enemy, you could be an adjutant, which was quite similar to being a warrant officer in the American Army.

Now, when I say I went to Spad 68, the word Spad is used here to mean squadron or, *en français, escadrille*.[1] It took four escadrilles to make a combat group. The most famous escadrille as far as Americans were concerned was the Escadrille Lafayette, Spad 124. And any American who flew with the French is said to have flown with the Escadrille Lafayette. This isn't correct. I didn't fly in Spad 124; neither did Frank Baylies nor Dave Putnam. But the 124th was made up of practically all Americans, while mine had only one American other than myself. So if someone says his father flew in the Lafayette Escadrille, and you can't find his name listed in the records of Spad 124, look for him under the Lafayette Flying Corps. We're all, including the boys from the 124th, listed there.

[1] While in America it is pronounced es-ca-drill, those who flew in the escadrilles pronounce it es-ca-dree.

Well, back to when I joined Spad 68 and an ironic thing that happened. Some of the fellows who had trained with me figured that they weren't quite ready for pursuit flying, so they decided to opt for Bréquets until they really got the hang of things, then they'd transfer to the Spads.

The sad part was that this meant daytime bombings behind the enemy lines. And several of the men who did this were killed while flying the Bréquets. A close friend of mine named Bluthenthal was one of them. He'd been an All-American center at Princeton and was just a really splendid fellow. But he wanted to try the Bréquets before the Spads, and he ended up getting killed on a bombing raid in June of '18.

Well, I started flying in combat on the Spads in January of 1918 and spent the next nine months at it. All in all I logged over two hundred hours of actual combat time, and I was never wounded. Oh I wore out nine planes, but I was never actually hit.

There was a good thing about wearing out a plane, though—you'd frequently get a forty-eight-hour pass to go to Paris and pick up a new plane. And that usually meant a pretty good time. There was one time, however, when a trip to Paree ended up causing me a lot of grief.

On this particular trip I headed for one of our favorite spots, the Chatham Bar Hotel. You could always count on meeting several fliers there and also many of the American newsmen—they'd be there looking for a story. But we had an unwritten law that we wouldn't tell these men about our flights. Oh they were great fellows, all right, but if you told them anything, they'd exaggerate it beyond belief.

Besides the fact that a lot of the Americans would gather there, the place had a great bar and excellent food. So I'm standing there having a drink, anticipating a great meal, when up walks this newsman named Wales or Wills. I'd just been credited with my first official victory, so naturally I was feeling pretty good.

"Here, Wales," I said, "have a drink."

"Thanks, Reggie," he answered, "and what can you tell me about that big moment you had the other day?"

"Oh come on, you know we don't go into details on those things; it's against our code."

As far as I was concerned, that was the end of it But remember, this was February of 1918—these birds didn't have much in the way of American combat to write about; you might say they had to innovate.

And did Wales go to town! Christ, you'd think I was destroying the whole German Air Force. Naturally, the boys gave me quite a riding about this, but that wasn't the end of it. You see, he'd said I did this in partnership with another American—a flier who wasn't even in our escadrille. I knew the chap, all right, and he was a nice guy, but I'd never flown with him. Then this other flier was moved to another sector, where he was killed. I didn't know any of the details except that he was dead.

Well, his folks back in Illinois were upset, naturally. And according to what they'd read in the papers, the poor guy was my great buddy. So they wrote me to find out what had happened. I answered the letter, all right, trying not to hurt their feelings, but pointing out I just didn't know anything about what happened.

Was this the end of it? Of course not. They bombarded me with letters the rest of the time I was in France. I guess they just didn't believe me. Oh they must have thought I was dreadful, but it was all the fault of that darn reporter.

Now, you note I said earlier "my first official victory," because I'm rather sure I had one in January, but the credit was given to another pilot.

It happened on one of my early patrols. I'd taken a sortie behind the German lines along with this French pilot. He'd only been in our Spad a day or so, but he was a sergeant because that was his rank in the artillery regiment he'd come from.

Well, we both had the 150-horsepower Spad (this was before we received the 220), with one gun, a Vickers, mounted on it. So we headed out full of beans, just looking for trouble, that's all.

We found it, all right; two two-seaters with three fighters in formation. Oh we were both eager as hell, so we went after them. One of the Boche fighters peeled off to the left, and the Frenchman went after him. Then another German went to the right, and I went after him.

Well, he kept turning and going under me and I kept making passes at him—I must have made five, firing each time. I'd try and lead him, keeping in a position where he couldn't fire at me—I don't think he ever did get a round off. Finally I went into half an outside loop, trying to get a killing shot in. At the same time I was hit on my goggles with hot oil because my mechanic had put too much of it in the filter right in front of the windshield. Of course I couldn't see, so I had to grab a rag and clean off the goggles. By the time I was squared away, the German had disappeared.

After this I headed for home. When I landed, my French friend was already there—and I may add, he had put in no claims. Naturally I hadn't because apparently when the German went down, my goggles were covered with oil.

Then our captain heard that a German plane had been shot down between the lines, so he walked over to the two of us.

"Ah *monsieurs*," he said, "who shoot ze plane down?"

My friend still didn't put in a claim. I didn't know what to say, so I tried to explain what happened. The trouble was that then my French was still straight from St. Paul's School, and the captain's English was even worse. He wanted to give us both credit, but he'd just received a call from an artillery officer who said there had only been two planes involved, a German and one of ours.

Anyway, what happened in the long run was we both received a Croix de Guerre, and the French sergeant received the credit.

Another time when I might have had credit—but I really don't know this time—occurred over near Saint Mihiel. I was flying with my good friend, a Frenchman named Gutterman, when we ran into a two-seater. It was obvious that this Boche was under orders to take photographs, so of course we had to knock him down. But each time one of us would get close he'd turn and go back over the German lines.

Finally, after a hell of a lot of maneuvering, we got him in a position where we could come at him from both sides. In the meantime the sun had just about set down below, giving us a dark background if we looked toward the ground.

Then, wham, like a bat out of hell, this American came roaring up from beneath the German, firing a mile a minute. Actually, I could see his incendiary bullets before I saw him—that's how bad the light was. This was the end of the German, all right; he headed for the ground with the American in hot pursuit. I had to admire the way this unknown pilot had moved in—that was the way you were supposed to hit a two-seater, from underneath.

After the kill, Gutterman and myself headed back toward our

field, which was over near Bar-le-Duc. It was so dark they had to put flares on the field so we could land. We told our story to the captain and waited to see what would develop.

The next morning we got the word. The American had gone all the way down with the German, landed, and spent the night guarding the downed Boche. Under the circumstances it would have been difficult to deny him the credit. And as I said, his maneuver had been perfection. When we found out who the Yank was, we could understand it—he was Frank Luke, one of the truly outstanding pilots in the American Air Service.

Luke, however, like so many of the great ones, had a fault: He'd tackle anything, any time. I think it was a case of just getting overconfident. He was shot down himself a little later on behind the enemy lines. He tried to shoot it out with some German soldiers, using his pistol western style, and was killed.

One of my close friends, a fellow named Frank Baylies, was the same way. He was a New Englander from New Bedford, Massachusetts. His twelve official victories were surpassed only by Raoul Lufberry among the Americans who flew with the French.

Like myself, Jules decided not to switch to the Americans when the United States started to build their own air force over at Issoudun. My reasoning was simple: They'd given me such a runaround when I tried to get in that I just couldn't get excited about it. And there was also the fact that I was happy with the Frenchman I was flying with. After all, we were fighting the same Germans.

Oh that name Jules—that's what we called Frank Baylies—heaven knows why, but we did, and that wasn't his name at all.

Jules went West on June 17, and right in front of my eyes—I'll never forget it. I was in a group of five Spads when we spotted about the same number of Pfaltz. This was near Saint-Dié, around the old Marne salient.

After we sighted the Germans, Gutterman and I peeled off and sailed into one of them. Both of Gutterman's guns jammed, but I kept going and shot the enemy plane down. Incidentally, we had the 220 Spads by then, with the two guns instead of one.

But just after I'd sent my German down in flames, I saw this Spad going down at a tremendous speed with a Fokker on his tail—he was obviously trying to shake the German, but he'd run out of luck. It was my buddy Baylies. He was a great pilot, all right, but too strong, too aggressive. Dave Putnam had seen him a short time before in a dogfight with four Germans. And Putnam was the same way. He was another New Englander who shot down eleven or twelve planes but was himself killed around Saint Mihiel a few months later. He had gone after five Germans at the time.

That fighting in June and July, when Baylies was killed, was the worst I saw. Remember, the Germans were sure they were going to win at this time. And they put everything they had into the air against us. I remember that we had to move our field away from Château-Thierry when they got too close.

In the meantime we'd been losing a lot of planes, so they'd sent me into Paris to pick up a new one. I would frequently be given this assignment because, frankly, I was a darn good pilot—with all the hours I flew in France, I never had a crackup. This was on July 13, and I was due back at the field on the morning of July 16.

After I arrived in Paris, I ran into an old buddy named Rufus Rand; I think he was from Minneapolis. We took a room at the Hotel Crillon and had a great time that night. The next morning we went over to the Place de la Concorde on the Champs-Élysées to watch the big parade. The place was mobbed, so we climbed up on a statue to get a good view. We were sitting there, right under the horse's hooves waving at everyone and having a great old time. By this time I'd really learned to speak French; hell, I was even thinking in the language.

Then the parade started. Well, I had never been moved by anything before the way that procession affected me—and I haven't been since. Those Poilu who had been bleeding all those years, and the band playing "Madelon." And there were my own countrymen also. I'd been told that many of those Doughboys had already done a lot of fighting and were going back to the front the next day. I knew that men from the 1st Division and the 2nd Division were there; in just a few days they were going to see hell at the Battle of Soissons. I just couldn't take it.

"Rufus," I said, "I don't know about you, but it's too much for me. I'm going back the minute this is over." Well, I could see he was as choked up as I was.

"Reggie, you're reading my mind. They may need us." Ruf wasn't at my field, but he was in the thick of it also.

I got back that night and heard some astonishing news. One of the men in our spad was Marshal Foch's sister's son. His mother had written and told him that the Germans were going to launch a big attack the next day. Foch knew we could stop them and had already planned a counterattack on July 18. Can you imagine that? I wonder how many other people knew it.

Well, the Germans were on the north bank of the Marne when we went out the next morning on dawn patrol. There were two French brothers in our formation of five planes whose home was right where the armies were fighting. We flew right over it. Everything was fine except there was a huge shellhole in the roof. Christ, those boys were angry!

On the way back we saw about seven pontoon bridges that the Germans had set up.[2] We reported this to our captain, a Frenchman named Baille. The minute he heard this, he jumped up.

"*Mon Dieu, mon Dieu*," he shouted out. Then he ran into his plane and took off after those bridges. He raised hell with those Boche until they hit him twice in the neck with ground fire, might have even been rifles, that's how low he was flying. Amazingly enough, he lived. Now, be sure and mention him—he was a real hero!

That ground fire could be nasty, all right, particularly when you flew low. But, believe it or not, we used to tease their artillery. We'd get up five thousand meters or so over sea level, then slow down. Well, the German gunners would send up a burst, trying to judge our speed as they'd attempt to lead us. We'd figured out that when we were that high, it'd take the shell about thirty seconds to reach us. So we waited until they thought they had us bracketed, then we'd increase our speed about forty or fifty miles an hour—this way the killing salvo they'd send up would land behind us.

Of course, it was a pretty dangerous game, and one time they almost caught up with me. I was up all alone, playing that little farce, when wham, they fired one that just missed me, right under my right wing. Oh Christ, I could even taste it! I don't know if it was blind luck or if they'd figured it out. Anyway, I high-tailed it out of there and headed home.

[2] It was here that the 3rd U. S. Division earned their name "The Marne Division." They held.

When I returned to my base, I found out how close it really was. The concussion had taken the cloth from the under part of the wing. The ribs were still there, but a large part of the wing was bare.

But you know, as I look back on all that combat flying I had, it's still the men I remember most. Two of the great guys I haven't mentioned were Bill Wellman and Tommy Hitchcock. Wellman is the one who became a famous movie producer after the war, just died a year or so ago. I can remember when he brought out his film *Wings* about fifty years ago. He invited a bunch of us to its preview —of course, in those days most of us were walking around. And you know what he did? He had all the ushers dressed up in Foreign Legion uniforms. He was quite a showman, and a crackerjack pilot also.

Then there was Tommy Hitchcock—now, Tommy was only seventeen years old when he joined us, just a baby, but a darn good flier. He's the one, you know, who was shot down and captured, then taken into Germany. And he was one of the very few men who actually escaped from Allemande. They were moving him from one spot to another, and he jumped from the train and made his way into Switzerland. He even had to swim a river or two to get back to France. He surely looked like something the cat dragged in when he got back to us.

Haw, haw, here's something else I'll tell you about Tommy. I took him to this private club we had in Paris; he'd never seen anyplace like that before. And that's all I'll tell you about that club except that I saw Raoul Lufberry there on several occasions. That was a private spot, and if any of the old-timers read this, they'll know what I'm talking about.[3]

Another thing I'll always remember is what great guys those French pilots were. And it's a funny thing, but even though they had been allies of the English for all that time, they seemed to greatly prefer the Americans. Of course, there'd always been a certain amount of jealousy existing between the French and the English. I can even remember a little song they had that ended up, "Let's go piss in the ocean and embarrass the British fleet."

[3] No matter how hard I tried, this grand old eagle wouldn't tell me any more about "the club." For all I know, they might have gone there to shoot pool—but, personally, I don't think so.

But you could feel the great affection the French had for the Americans fighting for them, particularly when we'd go into Harry's and Ciro's, the restaurant right across from Harry's, and the Crillon Bar. When I was at the front, I used to wear this old raccoon coat I'd had at St. Paul's, but when I went to Paris, I tried to look like a soldier—I think the French liked that.

Well, the French Army had a system called permission. This meant you were entitled to a ten-day furlough every four months. If you came from outside of France, you could save them up for a year; then you were entitled to thirty days. When I saw Frank Luke that time, I had already earned my thirty days. This bothered one of my American buddies.

"Reggie," he said, "we've all heard of pilots going down with their permissions in their pockets. Go on home; there'll be plenty of war left when you come back." I went home, all right, in October, and that's where I was when it ended. As I was still in the French Army, I returned to France to get my discharge and to bid *adieu* to my comrades.

And you know something? I ended up with the scare of my life. Just as I boarded this French ship to come home for good, I came down with the flu. I went to the ship's doctor, and all he did was paint my throat with iodine—but it worked. Wouldn't it have been hell to die on that ship after all that flying!

Sex and the AEF

Banging away on Lulu,
Banging all the day,
Where 'm I going to get my banging
When Lulu goes away?

—DOUGHBOY SONG, 1918

In September of 1918 there were less than two thousand cases of venereal disease in the AEF. That total represents under .001 of the American troops in France and is an extremely low ratio. As France was loaded with both whores and VD, it's a figure that is indeed puzzling. Surely those lonely young men should have been easy pickings for the prostitutes but they were not.

First, there were their moral standards. Time and time again, veterans told me how often they thought of going after a woman, but then they'd think about Susie back in Springfield, who was faithfully knitting the mittens that never seemed to fit, and they just wouldn't get around to going tom-catting. If the war had lasted another year or so for the Yanks, it probably would have been different. Cy Currier's story is a perfect example.

"After the Armistice," related Cy, "I had a chance to get a week's leave down near the Riviera. While there I was resting in my room when this darling little French maid came in to tidy things up. She kept dusting the bureau and shaking her cute little fanny; God, was I tempted! But I was engaged to a girl back home, and I wanted to stay pure. I finally gave the pretty *mademoiselle* a franc and went out and had a drink.

"Now let me tell you the payoff," laughed Cy. "Just before I left for America, I received a telegram telling me that my fiancée had given me the business and married another guy. Boy, was I sore! You know," he continued, "I thought about that little French girl just the other day, but what the hell, she must be about eighty years old now, just like me."

Another reason for the low VD rate was General Pershing. He was no purist, but he knew that a syphilitic Doughboy wasn't going to kill any Germans. He tried to close as many bordellos as possible, but being a realist, he also furnished a plentiful supply of prophylactics for his soldiers. While he knew it was impossible to completely abrogate the sisters of sin, he was also aware of their high VD rate. If the boys had to have their women, protection would be furnished. And they'd better take advantage of it, because a diseased soldier would not only be forced to submit to very painful treatment, but he'd also be hit with a rough military court-martial.

One of the best examples of the disease problem that concerned Pershing comes from the same faithful Cy Currier, who was a private in Company C of the 29th Division's Military Police.

"We received orders to rush over to a certain town that had a particularly bad red-light district," Cy recalled, "and we naturally wondered what the problem was. We knew there was another MP company in the town. So, I asked our top sergeant what the panic was all about.

"'Oh Christ,' answered the top kick, 'all the jaspers in that other outfit have the clap.'"

With all the efforts made to prevent it, many of the men still did manage to find sex. It was just too available, other than at the front lines. Many of my veterans did tell me of experiences, but it was almost always something that happened to a buddy, not to themselves.

"We had this guy in Company G," one old Doughboy told me, "who simply walked up to this nice-looking lady in Nancy and asked her for it. She just smiled and told him no, she didn't do that type of thing, but to wait a few minutes and she'd get him a girl. I'll be damned if she didn't come back with one—it cost my friend five francs."

One of the veterans who made no bones about the whole thing was a wonderful guy named Morry Morrison. Perhaps this was because he never married. It all started when I asked him if he'd ever been to Bar-le-Duc.

"Oh yeah, sure," acknowledged Morry, "that's where they had them cat houses; some of them girls were real young, and pretty, too, you see.

"Yeah," he continued, "we had MPs there, but they were just there to keep the drunks from fighting, you see, and to make sure no one didn't hurt the girls.

"You had the girl for thirty minutes for five francs, but most of them fellows didn't last more than five minutes; they hadn't seen a girl for months, you see. Some of them had been wounded, you see; I remember seeing one guy trying to climb up them steps on crutches."

I finally asked Morry the big question: How about Sergeant Morrison? Did he also patronize the girls?

"Sure, of course," he laughed. "What do you think? I had to get rid of my tension too. And I'll tell you something else: I'm seventy-eight years old and I still have a girlfriend. I'm not through yet, you see."

And bully for you, Mr. Morrison!

The First Ace

Douglas Campbell

HIS HOME, GREENWICH, CONNECTICUT, JUNE 1976
This gentleman is credited with being the first ace in the United States Air Service and also with being the first member of the United States Army to shoot down an enemy plane. His being the first ace is a matter of official record, but Mr. Campbell denies the second part of the above statement.

"Alan Winslow beat me by about thirty seconds," stated Doug. "There is no doubt about it."

At the time this all happened, Mr. Campbell was a member of the legendary 94th Aero Squadron, World War I's leading American flying unit. Of course, you will always get an argument from any members of the 95th Aero Squadron on this, but the record does show the 94th with 69 victories, No. 1 in the AEF. Along with such aces as Weir Cook, Hamilton Coolidge, and Reid Chambers, Doug had the good fortune to share his service in the 94th with Eddie Rickenbacker, or as Doug called Eddie, "one in a million."

After many years in an executive capacity with the W. R. Grace Company, which included a long period in Latin America, Mr. Campbell now lives in Greenwich, Connecticut. He, like so many of the other veterans, is bothered by that scourge of the aging, arthritis. It makes it difficult for him to get around.

They had a festive gathering of World War I fliers in Colorado Springs a few months after I met with Mr. Campbell. I asked Doug at the time if he was going to attend. He told me that he didn't think so, that it would really be quite a chore. And what a shame—I'm sure there was no one there that the rest of those old eagles would have rather seen than Doug.

First Lieutenant Douglas Campbell
94th (Hat-in-the-Ring) Squadron, 1st Pursuit Group,
U. S. Air Service

Lieutenants Campbell and Winslow were overwhelmed with cablegrams from all parts of the United States. . . . It was particularly fortunate for the squadron that such an extraordinary success should have marked the very first day of our operations.

—*Fighting the Flying Circus*
CAPTAIN EDDIE V. RICKENBACKER

While at Harvard I had eagerly read all the exploits of the Americans in the Lafayette Escadrille—you know, Lufbery, Rockwell, Jim Hall, all those fellows. There seemed to be something glamorous about the air war, something you probably couldn't put your finger on, but it seemed quite different from the holocaust that was the way of life for the foot soldier. It gave me this tremendous desire to fly—and to fly against the Germans; they seemed to be the bad guys.

Well, you can imagine how I felt when I actually did fly with Eddie Rickenbacker on my first patrol; particularly as our leader was none other than Raoul Lufberry himself—Luf had transferred from the French Air Force into the U. S. Air Service after we had entered the war.

It occurred on the morning of March 6, 1918. Luf had announced that he was to take a jaunt over the German lines and that he wanted Rick and myself to accompany him. You can imagine how much excitement this created. Boy, were the other men jealous! Both Rick and myself tried to act nonchalant, though—after all, it was just another flight. The only difference was this time we might meet some Germans.

The flight itself took close to two hours, taking us over the trenches in the Champagne sector. We ran into some archie[1] but nothing else spectacular—at least it seemed that way to me. After we had landed, Luf came over to Rick and myself.

"Did you men see anything?" he asked.

"Nothing unusual," replied Rick. I agreed.

Luf continued his quizzing. "How about any other planes?"

I answered in the negative, and Rick also shook his head. Then Luf started to chuckle.

"You birds are all alike. If you don't learn to see right, you're not going to last long."

Well, you can imagine how puzzled we were. We didn't know what the hell he was driving at. He didn't keep us in suspense very long.

"There were a couple of times when I could see Spads, and then just as we turned away from the German lines, there were four Albatros about two miles away. There was still another one much closer. You've got to *really* keep your eyes alert when you get on top of their lines. Those Boche will try and draw you over every time."

Naturally, we felt Luf was throwing mud on our parade. We thought we'd be the cocks of the walk. After all, he had picked the two of us to go up first; he certainly took us down a peg or two.

What he was actually talking about was learning how to see up there. Try it yourself some time. If you focus in on a certain spot in the sky, you're very apt to miss what is going on to your right or left. But if you sort of use a vacant stare, don't focus in on anything,

[1] World War I slang for anti-aircraft fire.

you can detect movements you wouldn't see otherwise. Of course, you have to keep moving your head around constantly, keeping in mind not to focus in on a spot unless you see something. You just look for a blur. When you detect this, then you focus in. It was a good way to stay alive.

Well, almost a year had gone by from the day Wilson declared war until that first flight. My original plan had been to graduate Harvard, go over with one of the ambulance groups, and then work my way into the French Air Force; our entrance into the war had changed all that. Now I could try and enter the aviation section of the U. S. Signal Corps—this seemed to offer the quickest way to France. And that joining up is a story in itself.

You see, they closed the college for our class the end of April. First they gave us these easy exams, then mailed us our diplomas. There was no commencement ceremony—it was as simple as that. This way we were available to go into service at once—which was just about what everyone did.

As I've said, I wanted to go into the Air Service, but the problem was to find it. Yes, that's what I said: The problem was to actually find the Air Service. A few of us went over to the Army recruiting office in Boston, where we met these two regular Army sergeants.

"Air Service," said one of them. "I know we have one, all right—I remember seeing a couple of our planes down on the Mexican border, but I'll be damned if I know how you join it. Try Washington; that's all I can tell you."

So we headed for the nation's capital, still trying to find out how we could become U.S. pilots. We arrived in Washington on a Thursday night and spent all day Friday looking, to no avail. Finally, on Saturday morning, we located a Captain Tom Milling in a rented one-room office in a downtown building. Milling was one of our pioneer fliers. I guess you might say he was the head of the Air Service recruiting force. He took our names and told us we'd be hearing from him. I went back to Cambridge, where I got a job working for the Burgess Aircraft factory in Marblehead. A manufacturer of seaplanes, they were one of the few aircraft factories in America in 1917.

Well, I'd say it took about ten days before I received a telegram to report to Portsmouth, New Hampshire, for a physical. There wasn't much to it; you could almost say they'd decided to take me before I'd arrived. Then it was ten weeks of ground school at MIT, after which it was aboard the old British ship *Orduna* and a trip to Europe.

We landed at Liverpool toward the end of July, and zip, we were quickly shuttled off to Southampton. Here we stayed for a few days at these beautiful villas that had been owned by wealthy Germans; naturally, the British had taken over for the duration. We weren't there very long, though—we had come to Europe to fly, and they wanted us in France as fast as they could get us there.

Then came my biggest disappointment of the war. After they had sent us across the Channel, they assigned ten men from our group to become glorified office boys at the new air headquarters in Paris. Oh I suppose it could have been called good duty, all right, but it broke our hearts. We'd come over to fly, not shuffle papers. It was a pretty sad moment when we said good-bye to the rest of our crowd. They were on their way to Tours to learn to fly.

There was one good thing about our duty, though—that was the reaction of the French people toward the American soldiers. Oh how they loved the Yanks! We'd travel around in these open cars. Remember, the Americans in Europe then wore those old-style campaign hats. When we'd drive by, they'd easily recognize those big sombreros.

"*Les Americains, les Americains,*" they'd yell. "*Vivent les Americains; vive Wil-son!*" They certainly made us feel welcome.

After about two months of this I was sent to the new air training base at Issoudun. By this time I'd been made a first lieutenant but still hadn't been behind the controls of a plane. Heaven knows why, but they'd actually made me the adjutant of the camp. I didn't know a damn thing about all that Army paperwork and neither did my boss, Captain Jim Miller. But we did have this old-line regular Army first sergeant named Tuttle; he'd been doing this type of work for years. God, we'd have been lost without him!

Shortly after we had taken the place over, they sent us a group of American pilots for advance training on the Nieuports. The problem was they'd sent them too soon. Why, we hadn't even built the barracks. These pilots, all of them officers, had to actually build the place. Back in '17 the RAF was called the RFC, for Royal Flying Corps. We also called these men the RFC, but it stood for Royal Flying Carpenters.

Well, we got the place built, and the men started their work on the Nieuports. We had three types then: the twenty-three meters, which meant it had a twenty-three-square-meter wing surface; the eighteen meters; and the fifteen meters. It was on these that I finally learned to fly, with their rotary engine—you know, the kind where the crankshaft stands still and the cylinders revolve around it. This was one time that being adjutant had its advantages. I could take a plane up anytime I wanted to. I was able to catch up with the other pilots in no time at all. As a matter of fact, I soon had more flying time than most of them.

Of course, our biggest problem was the lack of what I guess you'd call a military style. None of us had really experienced much of it— we were running a pretty loose ship. Then, I think it was in November, we had a surprise visit from General John Pershing himself, no less. God, but he was horrified! He personally spent about ten minutes out on the field showing Captain Miller how to salute.

Then he asked to see the barracks. Now, as I've told you, most of our living quarters were built by the pilots themselves. Many of them were still pretty bitter about it, while most of them also felt a special proprietary air about it.

Well, it was just after lunch when Miller took old Black Jack into one of the barracks. The pilots were lying around, some half in uniform and some in their underwear, reading, snoozing, you know, taking a little siesta.

"Attention," yelled Miller as he opened the barracks door.

And from the back of the room came this very irritated voice.

"Who the hell for?"

"For General John Pershing, that's who for!"

Now, you can imagine how that little scene set with Pershing. The man who had yelled was named Fitzsimmons. I don't think they ever roasted him for it, but shortly afterward Carl Spaatz came down to take charge. It was the beginning of the military side of the U. S. Air Service. This did give me a chance to get out of the adjutant's job and be just what I wanted—a pursuit pilot.

Then, around the first of March, a bunch of us were sent to Villeneuve, where we became part of the 94th Aero Squadron. This is where Rick and I took that first patrol with Lufberry.

It was also at Villeneuve where the pattern of losing pilots to the Germans began.

As I've told you, I'd been with Jim Miller for several months. Jim was a little older than the rest of us. He'd already been established in business in New York City, where he had a home and family, when he came to France.

Well, Jim had been put in command of the 95th Aero Squadron, which was to fly with the 94th until the end of the war. Like all of us, he was raring to go up and meet the enemy. Around the middle of March he got his chance. There was a French Spad squadron near us that had some American officers attached to it. They agreed to let him fly a patrol with them, following the same basic route that Rick and myself had flown a week or so before. Apparently Jim had encountered a formation of Germans and torn right into them. He didn't return.

A month or so later we heard that he'd been shot down, badly wounded and died shortly afterward. While I'd known pilots who were killed in accidents before, Captain Miller was the first one shot down by the Boche. It had a lasting impression on all of us. From now on it would be for keeps.

Well, the squadron waited awhile for planes; when they finally arrived, they had no guns. In the meantime, the Germans were smashing at the British in their big spring offensive. All hell was breaking loose. At one time they were said to be only eighteen miles from our field. Planes with no firepower were useless, so they moved us over to Epiez. It was here that we received all types of new instruments for our planes and, above all, our Vickers guns. Then they moved us to this French aerodrome a mile or two east of Toul. Once it was evident that we were to be the first U.S. squadron to actually fly against the Germans in combat, we decided we should have an insignia. Our commanding officer, Major John Huffer, suggested we use Uncle Sam's top hat. We thought this was great. Then we decided to put a ring around it. And that's how the Hat-in-the-Ring name came about. It stood for the squadron that was to score more victories than any other U.S. one in the Great War. I wasn't there for the last one, but I surely was for the first.

Let's go back to the night of April 13, 1918. The whole 94th was buzzing with excitement—the next morning was to see the first official patrol by our squadron. Captain Dave Peterson was to take up Reed Chambers and Eddie Rickenbacker. I was to be on alert with Alan Winslow. This meant the two of us were to stay by the phone, ready to take off at once in case of an emergency. You can imagine how disappointed I was not to be picked for that flight, but I was to get my chance sooner than I thought.

The next morning we watched them take off. I can remember one of them yelling back at us as they left:

"Be on the alert, boys. We're sure going to stir up some Boche!"

Actually, their trip was quite uneventful. The weather was extremely bad, forcing Peterson back to the field early. Chambers landed at another aerodrome, and Rick had trouble landing.

Just about the time Eddie was landing, we got the call:

"Two Boche planes, two Boche planes approaching the field." I think it was about eight forty-five the morning of April 14.

Well, Winslow and me both jumped into our planes and took off. You know, I don't think I was two hundred yards off the ground when I spotted them—an Albatros and a Pfalz. I can still see those Iron Crosses—it was the first time I'd ever seen a German plane.

I can't remember many details of the maneuvering, but I can remember the other fellow, the one in the Pfalz, starting to shoot at me. I began to zigzag, and the first thing I knew, I found myself underneath him. I kind of stood my plane on its tail and started firing my Vickers. Some of my bullets probably hit his fuel tank because he began to descend, with flames coming out all over. I do know Winslow got his first, though; I could see his victim going toward the ground out of the corner of my eye, while I was still pumping bullets at the Pfalz. I guess it had to be very, very close, though; after all, the two of us were only off the ground 4½ minutes.

It was really great for the morale of the whole squadron: two of us going up like that and knocking down two Germans that quickly. I don't think we were ever more than a thousand feet off the ground at the outside—the whole squadron had ringside seats.

And here's something for you: Jim Hall, the author, was in our squadron.[2] He was shot down around Saint Mihiel in May of '18 and taken prisoner by the Germans. Well, I ran into Jim shortly after the war. He told me about this French air officer who did great work as an artist, particularly on air combat scenes. I remem-

---

[2] James Norman Hall—co-author with Charles Bernard Nordhoff of *Mutiny on the Bounty* and *The Hurricane,* among others—both served in the French and the U. S. Air Service during the Great War.

bered the chap somewhat, as he'd been one of our instructors at Issoudun. I gave Jim all the details of what had happened, and I'll be
damned if a few months later I didn't receive through the mail the
painting you see over there hanging on the wall. Here now, look at
the picture. I think it's a good one, all right, but he does have a few
mistakes. He did his homework on the terrain, though. He probably
got out some air maps on that because he's got the ground just
about right. There's the Marne-Rhine Canal and the Moselle River
—and the road from Toul to Pont-à-Mousson; he does have our
aerodrome on the wrong side of that road, but other than that he's
right.

His biggest mistake is the numbers on the plane. He's got mine
marked No. 3 and Winslow's No. 10, when actually it was the other
way around. My kill is going down in flames, all right, but he has
plane No. 3 shooting at it. Of course, a Pfalz and an Albatros look a
lot alike. I actually thought I was fighting an Albatros, but after it
crashed they told me it was a Pfalz—it means sparrow in German.

I honestly don't know if the pilot of the plane I shot down lived
or not, but I know Winslow's was captured. However, the truth of
the matter does remain, and I'd like to set this straight, I'm sure
Alan got his first. Yet, I'm always introduced as the first U. S. Air
Service pilot to shoot down a German, but 'tisn't so.[3]

You know, the two of us used to kid a lot about it after the war,
right up until 1936, when he died. The poor guy, he'd later been
shot down around Château-Thierry behind the Boche lines. His
right arm had been badly mangled, and the Germans had to ampu-
tate it under some pretty primitive conditions. The whole thing
took a lot out of him, no doubt about that.

After the war he went into Pan Am with Juan Trippe and that
crowd. Part of his job was to travel all around the world setting up
landing rights. Then, at a very young age, he had a stroke; I can't
remember just when, but it hit him pretty badly. He did recover
and went back with Pan Am, taking those long trips again.

Well, on one of them, when up in Montreal, he fell out of a hotel
window. There was a lot of talk about suicide, but I never believed
it. Hell, I'd seen him just a week or so before, and he seemed in

[3] The author asked this aging pilot if he'd settle for a tie on the whole
thing. He laughed.

great spirits. Besides, if you're going to kill yourself, you try something with a greater potential than jumping out of a *second*-story
window—and that's exactly how far up he was when he fell. He'd
just opened these french doors on the window. I'm convinced he
had an aftermath of the stroke or maybe another one, and just
keeled over.

Well, getting back to France, we started to fly patrols pretty regularly after that. Actually, it was what you'd call a quiet sector, but
if you went up enough, you were bound to find some Germans. I
managed to do this quite often, shooting down my second plane on
one of our forays.

Then came May 10, one of my most pleasant days in France in
one way, and also one of my most heartbreaking in another.

My brother Wallace, who was serving over at Gondrecourt in the
engineers, had told me to expect him for lunch. This was great—I
hadn't seen him for months and was really looking forward to our
meeting. To top the thing off, I downed No. 3 that morning, a two-
seated Rumpler—and besides, it had gone down behind our lines.
This meant I could take Wallace over to see it. And what a kick he
got out of it—I can still remember his grin when we met.

"Christ, Doug," he chuckled, "thanks a lot for shooting a German
down in honor of my visit—maybe I should come more often."

Then we motored over to see the Rumpler, picking up some sou-
venirs of my third victory.

Now, you know, they have those good-news-and-bad-news stories
these days; well, I just gave you the good news. The bad news also
awaited my return from the bout with the Rumpler: Raoul Lufberry, the idol of all us young pilots, had been killed that day. I
found out the hard way a few days later that we couldn't brood on
such things, but it surely was a shocker. The reason I couldn't be
too despondent over Luf's death, you see, was another loss I
suffered the same week.

John Mitchell[4] had come over to France with me and had also
been one of those ten glorified office boys I talked about earlier.
Add to that the fact that he had been a pal of mine at Harvard, and
you can imagine how close we were. Well, a few days after Lufberry's death, I returned from a patrol to find out that Mitchell had

---

[4] General William Mitchell's brother.

been killed in a landing accident at Columbey-les-Belles. I was heartbroken, no doubt about that. The truth of the matter was you played a dangerous game by becoming too fond of the other pilots —you paid a heavy price when they caught it. And remember, we'd go up just about every day—it was kind of a Russian roulette.

Of course, staying detached was easier said than done. This was particularly true as our group was just about as great a bunch of fellows as you could ever find—I can only remember one bad apple in the whole barrel. I suppose today they would have all types of excuses for the lad, but to us he was just plain "yellow." Actually, it wasn't that he was a bad person, he just didn't want any part of combat. Then, one day he went out on a patrol and didn't come back. The rumor was that he had deliberately flown over to a German aerodrome and surrendered. I later heard he'd survived the war, but never tried to contact any of the squadron ever again. Oh well, I guess you have people like that.

Now, toward the end of May, I was still going up whenever the weather permitted—and by this time looking for No. 5. This would make me the first American ace who'd done all his flying with the Aviation Section of the U. S. Signal Corps. Oh I got it all right; I got it in a way that really showed me what war was all about.

It was a Rumpler, and it was a tough fight, I'll tell you that. My guns jammed at one time, so I had to try and keep away from the Germans while I fixed them; that's a trick in itself. It's especially true when facing a Rumpler, where you have both the pilot and the observer shooting at you—the pilot's gun was set up so he could shoot it only when facing you, but the observer's was mounted so he could cover the tail and the sides. Well, we went through a hell of a lot of maneuvering and firing when the observer ran out of ammunition. I'll be damned if he didn't hang his empty cartridge belt over the side, stand up with folded arms, and glare at me—in other words, he was saying to me, "All right, I've done my best, do your damnedest!"

Naturally, I didn't relish the thought of shooting at this brave, unarmed chap. But I had no choice. The Germans had been photographing our artillery positions. If they returned to their lines with those photos, it might mean the loss of many American lives. Besides, the pilot was still capable of shooting me down, and he was showing no indication of ceasing his lethal efforts.

My big advantage lay in the superior maneuverability of my Nieuport 28 as against a Rumpler. With the observer out of the fight, it was a matter of coming in from behind and blasting their plane. I succeeded, and they soon went down. Both of them were goners. I didn't take any joy out of killing those brave men, but even with the so-called glamor of the air service, it *was* war; no matter how you slice it, it's not a very pretty affair. I was soon touted as the first U. S. Air Service ace, but it was not a position I would hold long—nor was my air combat career to last much longer.

On June 5 I ran into another Rumpler. This time I was too brash, that's all there was to it, just too damn brash. Besides, the German pilot was a good one. We had a real go at it, all over the sky. I just couldn't get in a position where I could put in a telling burst. Then the observer's gun stopped firing. I figured either his guns were jammed or that he'd run out of ammunition. I don't know, maybe he was decoying me. Anyway, the next time the pilot started to turn, instead of turning with him, I went in for the kill. Then the observer opened up—one of his bullets went right by me and hit a wire behind my seat. It was an explosive cartridge, and part of it ended up in my back, taking the skin off my spine as it went in. It felt just as if someone had given me a swift kick.

In the meantime I must have disabled the Rumpler, because it took off for the German lines. It never made it, crashing in no-man's-land. This was my sixth[5] and last victory.

After I landed, I went over to the hospital, where they took the steel out of my back. I spent a few days there, then they let me have a few days off in Paris. Of course, I headed for the Hotel Crillon, which was a great hangout for the American fliers. Then I'll be darned if I didn't come down with the flu. This laid me low for a couple of weeks, after which they sent me down to Biarritz to

[5] Rickenbacker always claimed that Campbell was one of our greatest pilots, and that there was a seventh victory that Rick is *positive* Campbell achieved but wasn't credited for—all this between April 18 and June 5, 1918.

recuperate. Well, believe it or not, I picked up a bad case of pto-
maine poisoning down there. I was beginning to feel jinxed.

Then, around the middle of July, I received a tremendous disappointment: I was selected to go back to the United States to train
new pilots. God, I was heartbroken. The 94th was going through all
that rough stuff on the Marne; I wanted to be with them. I even
went to see Benny Foulois[6] to try and have him do something
about it but had no luck.

After I reached the States, I was given a leave, then sent to San
Diego to train pilots. I never gave up trying to get back to the 94th,
and finally succeeded just as the war ended.

The years have flown by since then—why, there've been almost
sixty. Surprisingly enough, though, I think there're about eight of
the old 94th left, or were last I knew. There's Maloney down in
Florida, and Eddie Green, I think he's there also. Bob Cates, he got
two or three Germans, he's over in Spartansburgh; Ordway is in
Washington, D.C.; and Harold Titman, he's there also. Harold's the
one who lost his arm around the Marne and was later ambassador
to Peru; Snow is alive, and so is Roy Prince.

And there's plenty more from different outfits. Reginald Sinclair
from Corning, New York—he flew with the Lafayette Group—he's
still around, I understand. He stayed with the French the whole
time but used to fly over to Toul and have breakfast with us every
now and then—must have wanted some American cooking. Out of
that original Escadrille Lafayette (Spad 124) there's only one left,
though—Charley Dolan—I understand he's living in Hawaii.

I think of these comrades quite a bit, especially when Hollywood
does a film trying to show what flying in 1918 was like. Most of
them are a lot of crap. Take one I saw recently called *Blue Max*. It
had some great flying scenes, but the rest was ridiculous. This German flying hero has an affair with the general's wife. Haw, what a
joke! And then another scene has two pilots doing stunts under a
bridge after a patrol. In the first place, they wouldn't have had
enough gas left—then they'd be too darn tired. The only thing
they'd do would be inspect the planes for damages, then take a
nap.

No, I just don't think there's any way you can really re-create

[6] Brigadier General Benjamin Foulois, one of the very early U. S.
Army pilots.

what flying in combat during World War I was like—we old-timers will take it to the grave. But don't worry, we're tough old birds, all right—we'll be around for a while yet!

Jim Van Fleet and the Sight-seeing 6th Division

Jim Van Fleet was a young second lieutenant with the 3rd U. S. Infantry down on the Mexican border when the United States entered World War I. Like all the regular officers, he expected to go to France very quickly. But it didn't work out that way. He became a machine-gun officer in the 6th Division and didn't reach Europe until the middle of July 1918. There were several other divisions that arrived in July of '18 and saw a great deal of combat, but not the 6th.

"We ended up in the Vosges Mountains," Van Fleet told me, "and while we spent about six weeks on the lines, our total casualties were quite small (486 men) compared to the other divisions.

"There was one thing I did learn there, though," continued Van Fleet, who was to be one of America's truly great combat leaders in World War II, "and that was the true value of machine guns and the proper use of artillery. How these two weapons are used in combat can often determine the outcome of a battle.

"We had our lighter moments too," recalled Van Fleet. "I remember this spinster lady from the Y.M.C.A. who was assigned to us. She seemed quite old to me then, but I guess she was only about forty. She was actually quite a fine person but a little too proper for the front lines.

"Oh what a shock she received when she found out that she had to share a privy with a French family. She came storming over to me.

"'Captain,' she stammered—I was a captain by then—'you'll have to have some of the men build me my own convenience.' So, lo and behold we had to build this lady her own Chic Sales. Of course, the boys got quite a kick out of this.

"The payoff came after the war, though," the general told me. "Several of the officers and men had a chance to visit the Riviera, and so did this Y.M.C.A. lady. Well, after they came back, our Y.M.C.A. lady came to see me again.

"'SIR,' she indignantly said, 'I met one of your officers on the Riviera and he made advances toward me.'

"I couldn't believe what I was hearing. I felt like saying that she should have considered herself lucky, but I didn't. I told her that I'd look into it right away. It was all I could do not to break out laughing.

"Well, I looked into it, all right, and you should have seen how embarrassed that young lieutenant was.

"'You must have been out of your head,' I said to him.

"'Oh I guess I was pretty drunk,' he answered. That was it."

It was after the war ended that they really moved the 6th Division around. According to the records, they marched them across most of France.

"The sight-seeing 6th, that's what they called us," Van Fleet said. "They'd marched us plenty during the war, but what they did with the 6th after the Armistice must have broken some records."

Today, at eighty-five years of age, the general has some interesting ideas about the American soldiers.

"They can be great," he said. "Take my World War I outfit. Oh how they wanted to get into that Meuse-Argonne scrap! We were headed there right at the end, some of the men were even pulling our equipment by hand. And look at the job the GIs did in World War II and in Korea also.

"The world is different now, though, and we have to adapt to it. I was sent to Greece to try and stop the spread of communism there in the late 1940s. And we did. More importantly, we did it without the use of a single American rifleman. I'm rather proud of the job that was done there. We just can't keep sending large bodies of troops into combat anymore. There has to be a better way."

When the General Was an Ace

Edward Curtis

HIS HOME, ROCHESTER, NEW YORK, FEBRUARY 1976
When you arrive at the Rochester airport, you can notice a plaque in honor of Rochester pioneer airman Ted Curtis. It is quite proper for this upstate center to acknowledge Ted in this way. Not only was he one of the U. S. Air Service's first aces in World War I (six victories), but he also returned in World War II, where, as a major general, he was Carl Spaatz's chief of staff.

Ted's roots go very deep in this city, where taxi drivers have become millionaires by investing early and wisely in first Eastman Kodak and then Xerox securities. The general has such cherished memories of Rochester as taking golf lessons from the young golf pro at the Country Club of Rochester, Walter Hagen.

After the war, Ted went to work for Kodak. He ended up as the vice president of their International Division, a very key part of this multinational giant.

He lives today a couple of four-wood shots from the country club where he learned golf at a very young age.

First Lieutenant Edward (Ted) Curtis

95th (Kicking Mule) Squadron, 1st Pursuit Group,
U. S. Air Service

It was generally conceded that the 95th had the finest
bar on the Western Front.

No, I can't say there was any great feeling on my part against the
Germans in the autumn of 1916. I don't think you had the repulsion
in the First War that you had in World War II; you just can't compare the Kaiser to Hitler. As a matter of fact, the president of my
college, old Harry Augustus Garfield, was supposed to be pro-Ger-
man. Maybe he was, maybe he wasn't, but when Wilson did go to
war, Garfield went to work for the government in Washington.
After all, his father had been President of these United States. I
think he just didn't want America involved, and there were a lot of
Americans like him.

My own feelings were more plain curiosity than idealistic. Here
it was, 1916, and the biggest event in the history of the world was
going on in Europe. I just didn't want to miss it.

Then I heard about the American Field Service from this gentleman in Williamstown. He told me that I could sign a contract with
them, proceed immediately to France, drive a French Army ambulance for six months, and then come home. Well, this sounded
great; I figured I was going to learn a hell of a lot more about life
there than at Williams College. I was right!

I landed in France in January of '17, quickly finding myself up near Verdun in Sector 15. The big battle was over, but we had plenty to do, and the German shelling kept it interesting. It all seemed a little tame later on when I was flying against Udet and his "Flying Circus," but not at the time.

President Wilson changed all this in April, when America entered the war. Then it became merely a case of finishing out my contract and moving over to the U. S. Army. My only question was: Doing what?

I'd really had no great interest in aviation, hadn't even been up in a plane, but I'd seen enough of the French Poilu to know I'd just as soon stay out of the infantry. Besides, there was a great deal of glamor connected with the Air Service that you didn't have in the rest of the branches. I guess I just figured that it would be more fun doing my fighting in the sky than in the trenches.

The amazing part was the ease in which I was accepted. Remember, flying was very much in its infancy at the time. I guess they figured that anyone who had driven an ambulance for six months would be easy to teach flying to. The physical was the funniest part of all. Once the doctor found out I had two legs, two arms, could see, and could walk, I was in.

First they sent me to Tours to train with the French. This gave me a little edge on the rest of the Americans. At least I had fifteen hours of flying time when I went to the new field at Issoudun; the rest of the Americans had never been in a cockpit when they arrived. You know, when I think of it, I'd only had a total of forty hours' flying time when I first took a Nieuport into combat. Today you need more than twice that much time just to get a pilot's license.

Well, Issoudun was as dreadful a place as you could find. Muddy beyond belief, dreadful food, never enough planes to go around, and the constant accidents—hell, we were losing men right and left, and we weren't even in combat.

Then there were our two top officers, Major Carl Spaatz and his aide, Captain Wiedenbach. Things were so bad we labeled these two birds "the twin German spies," and only half kiddingly at that. Now, I'm sure you realize that all Spaatz ended up doing was leading the U. S. Strategic Air Command in World War II—I should know, I was his chief of staff then. As for "Vie-denbach," as we called him, he was another interesting case. His father had been an officer in the German Army, which was enough for the boys to be suspicious about. After the war he changed his name to Willoughby —his mother had been a Willoughby from Philadelphia—and ended up Major General Charles Willoughby, MacArthur's No. 1 aide in the Pacific. German spies, indeed!

It was at Issoudun that I first met Rick, probably the greatest all-around ace we had. He was a real good pilot—not a great one, but a good one. And what a shot—I think he was the best shot I ever saw! Actually, the word that best describes Rickenbacker is professional; God, he was calculating. He spent hours studying and practicing. Most of us took it in a hit-and-miss fashion, but not Rick. Maybe that was because he was older than most of us, must have been all of twenty-seven or -eight.

There was another pilot about Rick's age who was somewhat of a hero to all of us, named Raoul Lufbery. If anyone stood for the romantic side of the air war, it was Luf. We never knew for sure what he'd been before the war, and the mystery just added to the mystique about the man. Whatever he'd been, he wasn't an insurance salesman; Luf was a real swashbuckler.

His ways, including his accent, always seemed more French than American. This was particularly true about the women. If the weather was bad, a few of us would go over to Luf's room, where he would read to us some of the letters he was constantly getting from women all over France. They were sizzlers, all right. The mam'selles really went for this guy in large quantities, and he could accommodate most of them.

When it came to flying, it was another story: He was all business. He'd been a legend in the Escadrille Lafayette, where he'd knocked down sixteen or seventeen Germans. You can imagine how this made him look to us, a bunch of college kids who'd never even seen a Fokker.

His death in May of '18 was a real blow to the whole group, particularly as many of us saw the darn thing happen. This German observation plane came over our field at Toul, trying to get some pictures. The first thing we knew, Luf showed up, jumped into a Type 28 Nieuport, and took off after him. This was a beautiful flying machine, but not great for combat. You see, it had a gas tank on either side of the cockpit; if Fritz could put a slug in one of those tanks, you were a goner.

We all saw Luf take a pass or two at this German; then his guns seemed to jam. He pulled out of combat for a while, trying to straighten them out, then went back for the kill. That's when the German put one in Luf's gas tank. We were all horrified—God, it was awful watching this man we all thought was so great going down in flames. That was the one thing we were all concerned about—going down in flames. Actually, he jumped or fell from the plane on the way down. We never really knew which, but what difference did it make? He was dead, and that's all there was to it.

Now, let me tell you something that happened a month or so before we lost Luf that you'll find hard to believe. Our outfit, the 95th, had been formed and became the first U.S. squadron to fly patrols, even though we never crossed our lines. There was a simple explanation for this: We had no guns. Can you imagine that? I don't know what the hell we were supposed to do if we ran into any Germans. Ask them for tea, I guess.

After two weeks of this, we were sent to gunnery school. In the meantime, the 94th (Hat-in-the-Ring) Squadron went into action *with* guns. Doug Campbell and Alan Winslow of that distinguished group had the distinction of scoring the first kill by an American aviator while flying with the U. S. Army.

Then we returned, raring to go. The 94th and 95th became the 1st Pursuit Group; we would fly together for the rest of the war.

And what a lucky break we had! The first month or so we flew in combat (May of 1918) was comparatively quiet. This was of vital importance, because it allowed most of us to learn the ropes and stay alive. A little later on, when we hit the real rough stuff around the Marne, the new pilots took a tremendous pasting—we'd had on-the-job training, and they hadn't.

It was in May that I had my first victory, and it showed how lucky I was. In training they'd always told us to hit a two-seater from underneath—this way the gunner in the second seat couldn't get a good shot at you. So here I am flying along and admiring the scenery when I spotted this Rumpler biplane. I got excited and just rushed down on top of him as fast as I could. Luckily, the gunner was a lousy shot, or he would have nailed me. I might point out that it was made bloody clear to me that it was hardly a classic victory. I never went in on a two-seater that way again.

Then came the big stunt around the Marne. That, I think, was the toughest air action the Americans had. People don't seem to remember what a close thing that was. We had to move our field two or three times, ending up at Fontainebleau, really at the gates of Paris. The Germans sent the best they had against us there—Ludendorff knew he had to take Paris or lose the war.

We'd fly two or three missions a day, returning to the field just long enough to fuel up and take off again. I knocked down three more Germans during that stretch, but I also had a devilishly close call. One of Udet's boys stuck a bullet in my radiator, draining all the water out. I had to make a forced landing, barely reaching our lines. You know, that was a clever trick of the Germans. It always seemed our dogfights were behind *their* lines—that made a big difference if you had to go down.

The Marne was the first time the Americans did any ground strafing. The Boche were crossing the river in these pontoon boats. We'd fly right down into them, blasting away. Thank God we had our Spads in time for the Marne battle—it wasn't as maneuverable as the Nieuport, but it was sturdy as hell, built like a brick house.

It was here that we lost Quentin Roosevelt, and what a wonderful guy he was, totally unpretentious—he never made a big thing about being Teddy's son.

We never really knew what happened, but I can surely tell you it was one of the big fights of the war. Johnny Hamilton had taken our patrol up, looking for Germans. Then his motor went on the bum and he headed for home, leaving me in command. Shortly after we crossed the Marne, they came out of nowhere—Christ, but the air was full of Fokkers. To tell you the truth, each pilot was busy looking out for his own hide—none of us saw Roosevelt go down.

Shortly after we returned to our field, I noticed that Quentin wasn't with us. This happened to a lot of the pilots, but you could usually count on the lad showing up later on. For the next day or two the same question was on everyone's lips: "Have you heard anything about Quint?" Then the Germans dropped a note over our field telling us he was dead. I think they also sent down his boots. It was a sad day for the 95th.[1]

After the Marne I had a chance to take a few jaunts to Paris. I must admit that very few of the pilots were teetotalers; God knows I wasn't. I can only remember once or twice going into combat with a hangover; this was a very, very hazardous act, but I can't say the same about Paree. We used to head for a spot called Harry's—you might say it was somewhat of a pilots' hangout—and a great little place on the Rue Caumartin; I can't remember the name of it, but you could always count on catching up with all the latest news there. Now, don't misunderstand me: We weren't a bunch of drunks. On the other hand, each time we went up, the chance of not coming back was there. I didn't know a single pilot who escaped having his plane shot full of holes, and most of us had emergency landings somewhere along the line. When we had a chance to let off steam, we were bound to paint the town red.

It was around this time, just before Saint Mihiel or shortly afterward, that one of the craziest episodes of the war occurred to the 96th Bombing Group.

We had developed bombing tactics for the Rhine cities. This was light-years away from the type of bombing we did in World War II, really unsophisticated. The objective was to hit the Rhine cities—the areas where most of the supplies were coming from to refurbish the Western Front.

Well, the 96th was a Bréguet bombing group, up North with Trenchard's independent group. Six of them took off one day aimed at the Rhine under the command of Major Brown—I think they were going after Cologne. A tremendous wind came up, blowing them all over hell—this would happen every now and then; the planes in '18 just weren't built to resist noticeable wind changes. What happened after that gets a little fuzzy, but all six ended up landing on a German airfield.

Naturally, the Dutchers thought this was hilarious; here they have all these pilots and Bréguets without firing a shot. One of the

[1] The Americans captured the area where the Germans had buried Quentin shortly after his death. His grave became somewhat of a shrine for the troops. The generation that made up the AEF idolized Theodore. In a way, they were all Teddy's boys.

Germans must have had a sense of humor, because he sent back the following message:

"Thank you very much for all these fine planes and pilots, but what the hell are we going to do with the major?"

Most of us had a laugh out of it, but not Bill Mitchell; he was furious. Billy was a real interesting man. He'd tell you he was the best pilot, shot, horseman, hunter—really, the best everything—in the Army; and the funny thing was, he was usually right.

He knew exactly what he was doing after the war with all that court-martial business. Mitchell knew he didn't have much of a chance. What he really wanted was to let the country know that air power would play a tremendously important part in any future wars; in this he succeeded, but we still weren't ready for World War II when it came.[2]

Our next show after the Marne came at Saint Mihiel—it was just as easy as the Marne was tough. I think the Germans were really surprised there; all they wanted to do was draw the troops back to where they could set up a strong defensive line, and that's exactly what they did at the Meuse-Argonne.

This campaign was a different story. The Germans had the Fokker 7 here, which I feel was the best plane I flew against in France. I've always felt they knew the jig was up by the time the American offensive started, but, my God, did they fight tenaciously, both in the air and on the ground. We could look down and see the Doughboys trying to push the Dutchers back, a yard at a time. The terrain, particularly in the Argonne, was one hell of a bad place to have to fight.

The big difference between the Marne and the Meuse-Argonne was the style of German fighting. Earlier in the year they had been on the offensive; by October it was defensive. They were still plenty tough, however. I don't think you could say that the German Air Force really did crack; they were a viable unit right up until the Armistice.

Sometime during the Argonne fighting, I picked up a DSC. The word came down that GHQ wanted a pursuit pilot to dash well behind the enemy lines, take a reading on their movements, and re-

[2] Brigadier General William Mitchell resigned from the Army in 1925 after his court-martial conviction. World War II proved him a true prophet, indeed.

port back to the field at Vaubecourt.[3] As it was very risky business, they asked for volunteers. Hell, I think our whole squadron volunteered. Anyway, we had to draw straws to see who would go. I won.

The next morning I took off with all the gas I could carry, flying straight for their lines. I flew quite close to the German border, then went up and down the rear-echelon lines. Everything was headed north. It was evident to me that the Germans had no idea of a real counterattack in France—Germany, perhaps, but not France. Fortunately I didn't run into a single German plane, but I surely ran into "Archie." After I turned in my report at Vaubecourt, I took a look at my Spad: it was riddled!

Along with November came bad weather and a lull in the air fighting. On November 7 we heard this motor overhead. We ran out to see what nut was trying to fly in that weather. It was a totally unexpected German Fokker 7. Our mechanics started to throw rocks at it, and one of our pilots let go with a .45. Then we pleasantly noticed that the bird was coming for a landing. He puts the machine down just like the book says you should, calmly walks out of the plane, and looks around:

"*Mein Gott,*" he utters, "you have captured Metz!" Then he started to laugh, and so did we. He knew darn well it wasn't Metz. He also knew the show was just about over, and he didn't want to get it the last day. None of us blamed him. He was the last German we saw during the war.

If you ever go down to the Smithsonian Institution in Washington, D.C., take a look at the Fokker 7 they have there. It's the same one our German friend presented us just before the war ended.

[3] The 1st Pursuit Group's final aerodrome of the war.

"The Early Birds"

I have a rendezvous with Death
At some disputed barricade
When spring comes back with rustling shade
And apple blossoms fill the air.

—ALAN SEEGER

On July 31, 1914, Wilhelm von Schoen, Germany's ambassador to France, was in trouble. He was under strict orders to return himself and his staff of ninety Germans to Berlin. His problem was simple: He didn't have enough cash. And with war about to break out, his credit rating was close to zero. Then the United States, in the person of their ambassador, Myron Herrick, came to the rescue. He shepherded von Schoen over to the Morgan-Harjes Bank in Paris; here Herrick drew five thousand dollars, which he promptly loaned to the German. In short, the mighty Kaiser's plenipotentiary fled Paris, kit and kaboodle, on a handout from Uncle Sam. It was one of the few things the United States did for Germany during the entire war.

As for the Allies, that was, to use a 1914 term, a horse of a different color. The very bank where Herrick obtained the five thousand dollars played a very heavy hand in sponsoring the Norton-Harjes unit, one of two such operations that furnished hundreds of ambulance drivers for the French Army. The other group was the American Field Service. By the end of 1916 the AFS had sent to France eighty-nine Harvard men, twenty-six Yalies, and eight Princetonians; in all, some fifty colleges were represented in their ranks. Between the two ambulance services, the amount of Americans who went runs well into four figures. On the grave of one of them, who was killed by shellfire, is written: "Richard Hall, A Friend of France."

How many Americans went to Europe to serve the Allies before the United States entered the war in one capacity or another is an unknown figure, but several thousand must have gone.

It all started in France immediately after the war broke out. A group of young Americans called on Ambassador Herrick to find out if there was any way they could join the French Army and still maintain their citizenship. Herrick quickly went to his legal file and came up with the answer.[1]

"Yes, gentlemen, there is," the ambassador informed the young Francophiles. "Join the French Foreign Legion. And it's just what I'd do if I were your age." Woodrow Wilson may have been calling for strict neutrality back in the United States, but his diplomats were not always in line with Wilson's thinking.[2]

Many Americans took the ambassador's advice, including New York City-born Alan Seeger. This Harvard graduate became somewhat of a poet laureate of these expatriates. While he was to have his "rendezvous with Death" near the village of Belloy-en-Santenne in July of 1916, he did manage to last almost two harrowing years on the Western Front. Due to the extremely large amount of publicity he received in the United States, the death of this 1914 François Villon helped forge the inexorable link between the Ameri-

[1] In the long run, no Americans lost their citizenship by fighting for the Allies. For instance, the late Thomas McAllister served with the AFS and the French Army, both in their artillery and air service. He did not switch to the AEF. In later life he was a judge on the Michigan Supreme Court.

[2] The movie theaters were soon placing the following notice on the screen just before the news report started: "The President has called for strict neutrality. Please do not hiss." It didn't work; not in the eastern section of the United States, anyway. The German soldiers were always given the raspberries.

cans and the Allies. The Central Powers never did have a chance in the United States.

Of even greater use to the Allied cause were the Americans who flew with the French. Many Yanks also flew with the British forces, but they never received the attention back in America that those who served with the French Service Aeronautique did. They were the American glamor boys of the war until the AEF arrived in France. They even had their own squadron, originally called the Escadrille Américaine. But the Germans carped so much that the name was changed to the Escadrille Lafayette.

In addition to this one escadrille, close to two hundred other Americans flew with the French. One of them, the late George Dock, told me that there was some jealousy felt toward all the notoriety the Lafayette received, but he added, "What the hell, we were all doing the same thing. And besides," he continued, "when we'd get together at the American Bar in Paris, it didn't matter a damn what escadrille you were in." All told, sixty-five Americans were killed flying with the French. This figure does not include the hundreds of Americans who served in French escadrilles after the United States entered war while they were members of the U. S. Air Service.

One man who really went the rounds was Howard Baldwin. He originally went overseas in 1916 as a member of the Norton-Harjes group. Then he transferred to the French Air Force. During the first part of 1918 he followed the example of so many other American fliers and switched to the United States Air Service. Here he first went to the air base at Issoudun and then was transferred to the Italian Front.

Today, Mr. Baldwin makes no bones about the fact that the West Point officers, many of whom were not fliers, got under his skin. "Too many of them who knew nothing about flying were always giving orders," Howard told me. "Christ, they even had a guy giving us instructions in brushing our teeth." He succeeded in getting transferred to a British squadron, where he flew the S.E.5a. "And what a great plane that was!" he remembered. He ended up getting shot down in no-man's-land on August 8, 1918. Fortunately, some

Kilties reached him before the Germans could, and he spent the rest of the war in a British hospital.

Mr. Baldwin told me one of the great stories of my travels. It seemed that there weren't enough troops to make a good showing for the Americans in the July 4, 1917, parade in Paris, so Pershing sent out the word that any Americans serving with the French should show up and march.

"Boy, did we look like the Rinky Dinks," said Howard, "all kinds of uniforms, but we had a great time. That night we all went to a superb banquet like only the French can have—great food and plenty of wine. We all were a little tipsy when the toasts started. One of the Americans grabbed Charlie Kinsolving and told him to get up and say something; Charlie was a great guy, one of those fellows who always had something to say. He stood up and started to laugh.

" 'Gentlemen,' he chuckled, 'I find I have nothing to say, and that's really unusual, because my father is a bishop and my mother is a woman.' Oh how those Frogs loved that; they really broke up. You know," continued Baldwin, "it was at this time that one of Pershing's colonels, Charles Stanton, said, 'Lafayette, we are here'— that was all over the newspapers, but it was Kinsolving's remarks that the French people loved; you heard it everywhere."

Baldwin, who also served in World War II, was one of my first interviews. Close to two years later, I found out that Charles M. Kinsolving was hale and hearty in Carmel, California. I immediately gave him a call to try to confirm Howard's story.

"Oh yes," Charlie said, "I must confess to that one—we had a great time that evening."

Then he talked of his days in France. "I was like most of us," he said, "sometime in 1918 I switched over to my own country's Air Service. It was when I was squadron commander of Aero Squadron 163 that Carl Spaatz said of me, 'Hell, Kinsolving, you're the only man I know who can strut sitting down.' " He sounded as if he was still strutting—more power to him.

They were a great breed, these early birds. I can't say they normally went to France through any great moral indignation. They did, however, play a big part in creating sympathy for the Allies. But most of them never forgot they were Americans. Musgrave Hyde was a perfect example. He was studying architecture in France when the war broke out. Over the next three years he served as both an ambulance driver and artilleryman. "I was too tall for a pilot," said Hyde, who had been six-five in his prime. After Pershing landed in France, Musgrave went over to the general's headquarters to present himself.

"There were Poilu all over the place," Hyde said, "and they weren't going to let me in without a pass. I put on my sternest look and showed my 1912 pass to the Polo Grounds, signed by John McGraw. They presented arms, and I walked in."

The Midwesterner

Earl Goldsmith

It was called the Iron Brigade. It was the 1st Brigade of the I Corps
of what Bruce Catton has called Mr. Lincoln's Army. One would be
hard put to find another Civil War unit with a finer record. It was
made up of volunteer regiments from Wisconsin and Michigan.[1]
These two states would unite again in World War I to produce a
superb military organization. This time it would be the 32nd (Red
Arrow) Division.

Earl Goldsmith was a part of this division and its great midwestern heritage. Born in central Wisconsin, he first ventured outside of
his native state when he went down to the border with the Wisconsin National Guard. The next three years found him traveling over
a good deal of the United States and across the Atlantic Ocean to
France. Remember, this was before the mass communications of
today. There were no air lines, TV, or even radios. The main outlets
to the rest of the world for a teen-age Earl Goldsmith would have
been a Wausau, Wisconsin, newspaper and the silent movies. It is
only natural that the events of 1916 to 1919 should have made a
great impression on Mr. Goldsmith. They did.

When it was all over, he returned to Mesonine and went to work
in the town's paper mill. There he stayed until his retirement some
forty-four years later.

[1] There was also an Indian regiment in the Civil War version.

My visit with Mr. Goldsmith was in many ways like most of the others. When he first started to recall his experiences, he was quite factual and unassuming. But when he really got going, his eyes lit up—it was almost as if he was once again moving North from the Marne.

The conclusion of our interview still found me with two hours to kill before my trip back to Milwaukee. I asked Goldie if the two of us could go somewhere and drink a little cognac.

"You know," I reminded him, "just like you did in France."

"Oh I don't do that much anymore," he answered, "but the best place in town is the airport. I'll drive you over, and I may have one."

Well, we not only had a luncheon, but also three cognacs apiece. It was great! He talked more and more about France, and even told me a few things he made me promise *not* to put in the book. Unfortunately, I keep my promises, but a couple of his stories were tremendous.

Then I finally realized something that in other interviews I had not quite been able to put my finger on. Sure, I was having a great time—hell, I'm a history freak. But Goldie was also enjoying himself. You see, it's really not much fun to be eighty-one years of age. And for a few hours he was twenty again. When he left that airport, his shoulders were thrust back, and his stride was jaunty. I would have felt sorry for any of the Kaiser's Prussian Guards he might have met on the way home.

Sergeant Earl Goldsmith
G Company, 128th Infantry, 32nd Division

How could I forget the war? It got me my wonderful
wife, who I'm still lucky enough to have.

It was 1916, you see, and I was down on the border
with the 3rd Wisconsin. This friend of my sister wrote
to tell me that if I'd write to this girl in Wausau, she'd
write back. This started a correspondence that lasted till
I returned from France. Then I married her.

—SERGEANT EARL GOLDSMITH

Yes, there were a great many German-Americans in our outfit—
some people even called us the *Gemutlich* boys—but that didn't
make any difference to us. Take my father: He was born in Germany, but he looked at himself as an American. I can tell you something that happened while I was still in high school over in Wausau
that will show you what I mean. I wanted to get a job clerking in a
shoe store. As a large segment of the trade was German-speaking, it
would have helped me a lot if I could have learned some of that
language, so I asked Pa to teach me.

"Listen, son," he answered, "I left Germany to get away from all
that stuff they have over there. Why, you could get pinched for
looking sideways. You're an American; just speak the language they
have here, that's enough." So I never learned much German.

Well, you want to hear how it all started for me, the war and all that, and it sure is an innocent tale. The long and short of it was I wanted to go to camp. It was back in 1915, and I had just come out of a bowling alley when this high school chum of mine came along.

"Goldie," he said, "let's go over and join the 3rd Wisconsin National Guard. They'll be going down to Camp Douglas shortly, and we can give it a try for two weeks."

I was working for the Curtinson-Yale sash and door factory—they tore it down years ago and put in a shopping center—and I was bored as hell. Douglas was in Sparta, over near the Minnesota border. It seemed like it would be fun, so I decided to go along.

Then we got a jolt: The sergeant told us it was too late to sign up for camp. Of course, we was pretty broken up. You know how it is when you're nineteen and you have set your heart on something. I guess it showed, because the sergeant became interested.

"Listen," he said, "there are always some men who don't show up. Why don't you assume their names and come along? The main thing we're interested in is having as close to a full company as possible." And that's how we got in, under someone else's name. Of course, we changed it shortly afterward, but that's how it all started.

And when we were ordered down to the border the next year, I was elated. In 1916, you see, I had never been outside of Wisconsin. The thought of going to the Wild West was really something! We soon found out that Texas in the middle of July, with the temperature at 116 degrees, was anything but fun—particularly when you're wearing woollen uniforms. We used to think a lot then about the time on the trip down when we stopped by this lake in Oklahoma and all went skinny-dipping—we would have loved to have done that in Texas.

You see, we never did guard the border. We just maneuvered in Texas. There were several Wisconsin outfits with us, the 8th Illinois [redesignated the 370th U. S. Infantry in France, a good outfit]— they were black troops—and three or four National Guard regiments from other states. One of our movements down there—a round-trip hike from San Antonio to Austin—was the biggest maneuver ever held in this country up until then; we had twelve thousand troops. I think what we learned down there helped us a lot when the big thing came along.

They shipped us back home in December and mustered us out,

but called us right back in March. This was just before war was declared, and the state of Wisconsin wanted someone guarding the locks around Lake Superior. Then, a few months later, they sent us back to Texas—this time to Camp MacArthur, near Waco; it was named after Douglas's father, Arthur, a Civil War hero from Wisconsin.

It was down here that we found out what kind of a man our General Hahn was, when he interrupted a little gathering we was having behind the latrine.

Actually, I have to go back to our Lake Superior days to explain the situation. We had been doing this guard duty at the locks for about two weeks when a company of lumberjacks joined us—and they was lousy. Naturally, we all ended up catching those damn things and had to go through a real long delousing process. Then, several weeks later, down at Waco, my company started to itch again.

Oh was everybody angry—each man blaming the other. Hell, you had no way of knowing who'd caught them first. What difference did it make, anyway? You couldn't help it.

Well, there was these two in particular who was calling each other everything in the books. Finally they'd had enough.

"All right," one said, "you son-of-a-bitch, come on outside; we'll see who's lousy."

"Suits me fine, you crud," the other guy answered, "behind the latrine."

Now, we all thought this was great, so we formed a line to watch them go to it.

Then, I'll be damned if this car don't drive up and out jumps the general.

"What's going on here?" he bellows.

"Oh it's two of the men, General," replied one of us, "they're having a difference of opinion, and they decided to fight it out." The general looked us all over slowly—of course, we all thought we'd catch the Old Harry. Then he starts to go back into his car, turning toward us with one hand on the door.

"Urump, urump," he sort of grumbles, "good idea, good idea, but save some for the Germans." Then he drove off. When he got to France, he took over the division, and the men thought the world of him.

Well, we spent several months at Waco, training every day; a lot of us were beginning to feel we was ripe. Then the orders came along to move out; we was to board trains for the East Coast. I think it was shortly after the beginning of the year when they hustled us aboard a troop train, and we were off. It seems to me crossing the country took four or five days, something like that. Anyway, we landed at Camp Merritt in New Jersey to wait for our ship. Then one of those little things happened that was to be important as hell to Company G later on, but I didn't think much of it at the time.

Now, you had four platoons in a company then, adding up to about 250 men. Well, two of Company G's platoons had to be quarantined at Merritt; someone had come down with diphtheria. This was pretty serious in those days, serious enough for us to sail without them.

And what a difference this made. You see, things weren't good at all when we reached France. First they started working us with the SOS (Service of Supply); then they told us we were to be a depot division. This meant we'd keep doing this kind of work and that our men would go piecemeal into other divisions—in short, there'd be no more 32nd Division. Well, when they took all of Company G's privates away and sent them to the 1st Division, they couldn't take the two that had been quarantined, because they weren't with us. And by the time they arrived later on, the orders had been changed about the 32nd—we were to stay as a division. Of course, the men who'd left never came back, but at least half my company was still made up of central Wisconsin men.

You know, looking back on that whole situation, it's hard as hell to see how they could have done that to us—take those men away, I mean. Why, many of them had been on the border with me. God, how we hated to lose those men! My wife's brother was one of them. The poor guy got his leg pretty badly shot up with the 1st Division later on, came home a cripple.

The toughest part was when the men left—you know, seeing all those buddies leave like that. Boy, did I tie a beauty on—I drank all the brandy I could get my hands on. I'd just been made a sergeant, and it's lucky I wasn't broken. I was supposed to take a wood-loading detail out that day, but I ended up falling flat on my face. Luckily, a buddy of mine filled in for me, and I got away with it.

In the meantime, old General Hahn is fighting like hell with headquarters trying to get Pershing to let us stay as a division. Then we got us a helping hand from, of all people, the Germans. You see, they'd gotten themselves quite a bunch of soldiers from the Eastern Front because Russia wasn't in the war anymore. And they was raising a big ruckus with the British, so Pershing figured he better get all the divisions he could into the lines as soon as possible.

By this time our boys from them other two platoons had joined us, and were they a mess. My good buddy Casey Jones, you see, he was with them, and Casey was pretty good at nosing things out. Well, these two platoons had been landed in England first, then taken on an English boat across the Channel. Now, this boat was also carrying a cargo of scotch whisky for the English troops and, wouldn't you know it, Casey and the boys located it. What a high old time they had!

Now, we didn't really look at things like that as stealing, particularly if it involved the French. Why, I can remember when they first paid us in France; they took so many francs out of each man's pay. They claimed, you know, that we had lifted a lot of wine from some cafe and that they had to pay the guy for it. I hadn't taken any and, at that time, I didn't know anyone who did—so we figured if that's the way it was, we could play that game too.

Another thing was them prices: They had one price for us and another for their own. So we'd always get to know some woman pretty good and have her go do the buying. We'd end up with two or three bottles instead of one, and better stuff, too. Then someone figured out that their smaller freight cars would usually have some wine in them. Some of the boys would go right inside them and grab some bottles, and if it was in casks, they'd tap 'em right there.

Well, I guess it seems funny now, but after we'd been in France awhile, we were itching to get to the front; we figured we hadn't come over there for drilling—and were we sick of that. I can recall one time when quite a bunch of us went to the medic saying we had diarrhea and couldn't turn out for the drilling. He just smiled and gave us some pills. We got away with this for a while; then they ran out of pills, so we were told we'd all have to take this castor oil. Now, that was a different story; we sure got well in a hurry.

Then in May they moved us over to Alsace for trench training on what they called a quiet area—but there were plenty of German soldiers over in their lines using it for the same thing. Why, we could hear them Heinie bands playing at night.

Those Alsatians were a lot different than the French we'd been with before. Some of them considered themselves French, all right, but I think most of 'em just figured they were Alsatians. And some of them figured they was Germans. While we was there one farmer had actually plowed his field so it was pointed like an arrow right at this concealed anti-aircraft gun the French had. They used to send dogs back and forth from the German lines with messages. I saw plenty of them when I was in the trenches. Of course, I'd fire at 'em, but never hit any—God, they were fast!

One of the good things about this sector was the beer; don't ask me how, but the Alsatians could actually get this great beer from Germany itself. We all drank it 'cept this British sergeant we had with us.

"It might be piezen, matie," he warned. Well, poison or not, we thought it was great!

Oh he was quite a guy, that Englishman, though. We had a lot of trouble understanding him for a while—you know how fast those cockneys talk—but once we caught on, we got along fine. One of the boys even told him we'd probably have to hire a translator to deal with him.

"Translator, yuh bloody bloke," he answered, "I'm the one what's talking the bloody King's English." And he said all that in about one second.

Then there was the thing about the Kaiser. We were all drinking when one of the boys yells, "Fuck the Kaiser!"

"Fuck 'im," answers the Englishman, "'ow yuh going to do that? yuh can't get near 'im!" He took the Doughboy literally.

Now, you see, we didn't spend all our time there drinking beer; our job was to hold that section of the line, and we did. And there was one little thing that happened there that really stands out in my mind. For some crazy reason, a buddy of mine named Nelson and myself decided we wanted to get off a few good shots at some Germans. I guess we were just feeling pretty tough or what have you. So we got ahold of a couple of telescopic sights and started to maneuver into an area where we figured we could get a good bead on the Germans. Well, while heading into this area, we crossed

through this beautiful raspberry patch. Oh this was it—the hell with
the war. We filled our packs with raspberries and brought 'em to
the officers' mess. We told the cook he could make a pie for the
brass if he'd make one for us too.

You know something? Through the years I've thought a lot about
that—we were sure some kind of killers. But damn it, I'd rather eat
raspberry pie than shoot someone every day of the week. Wouldn't
you?

Now, it wasn't always quiet while we were there. There was one
night when the Germans pulled a big raid on the French Senegalese troops on our right. They were colonial troops, black as tar,
with those fez hats and the red pants. And they were fierce, great
with those knives they had.

It was the kind of a raid you really had to look out for because
the Germans were bound to spill over onto our lines. And they did.
We were in support at the time, but they soon leapfrogged us into
the line. This was the first time we'd been in anything, so we're
firing like mad wherever we thought the Germans were. It was then
I realized how hot the barrel of those Springfields could get—why,
it was like to burn your hand off. But it was a beauty. A lot of the
men who came over later had Enfields and Remingtons. We were
lucky; we had that Springfield.

In the meantime we're all getting low on bullets, so we started to
go toward this dugout where the ammunition was; the problem was
the damn door was bolted. We had this man in the outfit, you see,
who was a little retarded; none of us could figure out how in hell
he'd gotten into the Army. And what he done was go hide in the
dugout that had the extra weapons and ammunition. Oh Lord, how
we had to plead with that guy to open up. It's a good thing the
Germans didn't hit us with strength at that time; we would have
been in the soup.

And you know, they still didn't send that poor imbecile back. It
wasn't until we got into the real stuff later on that they finally did
something about him.

I can't remember which town it was, but we were really catching
it. And this poor soul is moaning, yelling, singing—just raising hell
in general. Well, finally Lieutenant Harris walked over and gave
him a tremendous whack in the behind with an entrenching tool.

The nut just got this tremendously hurt look on his face and started to whimper. Then they sent him back.

Now, you don't want to confuse a retarded man like that with some of our lads that just snapped. I can think of one man in particular. He went through all those tough fights we had in July and August. Then he finally collapsed. It was one morning when the fire had been really deadly. Why, the poor guy just sat down and started to bawl like a baby. He was no coward, mind you; he was just as much a casualty as if he'd been hit by one of their Maxim machine guns.

Well, back to the trenches and all that boredom. Most of the time our biggest excitement was rat shooting. God, were they big! Some looked like small dogs. The trick was to try and make them jump when you hit them. But don't kid yourself—they weren't very good neighbors.

Oh there's one thing more I want to tell you about the trenches. Haw! Haw! It's amazing how something like this sticks with you, but I can vividly see it now. You see, when we was on the front lines, you'd kind of relieve yourself as best as possible. But when you was back farther, especially in the third lines, you had a regular privy trench. Now, one of the areas would be near where the women would pass by on their way to the fields. Well, we'd be sitting there, right on that "ole six-seater," waving away at 'em.

"Bonjour, monsieur Américain, comment allez-vous?" they'd yell, grinning like hell.

"Bonjour, mademoiselle," we'd yell back, "très bien; et vous?" They'd carry on a regular conversation with us. Can you imagine that going on back in Wisconsin? I'll say not!

Well, musta been around the first week in July when General Pershing came to see General Hahn. We knew we'd been in the quiet sector long enough, and we'd heard about all the fighting that the Americans had been in down around the Marne. There wasn't no doubt about it: They needed us, and we were ready. I can recall this one man, oh he was so sure we were headed for Italy, but I think most of us knew it would be the Château-Thierry front—and it was.

The last German drive had been stopped in the area a week or so before we arrived. Our job was to be part of the huge counterattack. I think you can honestly say that the gates of hell opened up for us for the next six weeks.

One of the reasons I think it was so vicious moving North was the caliber of Germans we had against us. They still had those tough Prussian Guards, and they were rugged.

I don't want to get ahead of my story, but sometime in September I left the outfit to go to school at Langres—I didn't get back to the 128th until the latter part of October. I wasn't back very long before I had to go to the hospital with pneumonia. But it seemed to me that the Germans I saw in the Argonne were much quicker to surrender than the ones in July and August. It was back there that a French general gave us the nickname "Les Terribles"—someone said it was because we took so few prisoners. Maybe so, but I didn't see many of them trying to give up—no sir, not many at all.

Well, I guess it was the last week in July that we started the big move. They call it the Aisne-Marne, and then the Oise-Aisne, but it was all one big push to me. A little rest for a day or so, but mainly one big move. And there was one thing that was everywhere—the stench of death. You can ask anyone who was there. God, it was awful. All those dead animals. Yes, and the men also. Remember, it's July and August I'm talking about. I don't mean to be too dramatic, but the stench never left you.

And what those shells could do to someone's body—God, just turn it to nothing! Then there were other times when just one little piece of shrapnel could do the job. I remember one time when there were three of us in this ravine. Casey Jones was on my left, and a fellow by the name of Chatfield was on my right; he was an American Indian from around Ashland in northern Wisconsin. A big shell came over and landed in front of us. I didn't think it was close enough to be a bad one, but I'll be damned if one piece didn't hit Chatfield in the side of his head. He'd just turned to talk to me, so his face was pointing in my direction. It must have driven clean through to his brain, because the poor guy was dead; he looked just like he'd gone to sleep.

Then there was the time when I got knocked cuckoo. My good buddy Nelson was in this hole with me when the concussion from a shell actually picked us up and set us down.

"The hell with this place," yells Nelson. "Come on, Goldie, let's vamoose!"

So we ran over to this deeper hole, but the exact same thing happened again. Then we made a dash for a sunken road we could see about thirty yards away. And just as we got to it, another big one knocks us down into the road, where we kinda slid along like someone was pulling us. And then we saw a whole bunch of our boys lined against the side of the road. Once they saw we weren't hurt, did they ever give us the old haw-haw, really the business.

"Where do yuh think you're at, Goldie," yells one of them, "back home on a sleigh ride?"

And you know, just after he said that, another one came by and took his foot off. He lived, all right, but we didn't joke much after that.

I guess we all had to take our turn at it; some were lucky and some weren't. I shed my drop of blood like the rest, but I was one of the real lucky ones. And so did my buddy Nelson—he took a bad one in the groin near Juvigny. Thank God he survived.

My case could have been called comical if it wasn't so damn painful. One of our own shells had hit against a tree, with the shrapnel going in all directions. A piece of it just nicked the tip of my finger, forcing this large drop of blood to form. I didn't even report it, but that goddamn finger was sore for a week.

I surely didn't hold it against the 32nd's artillery, though, no sir—they were good, damn good; they were paying back those Heinies in spades most of the time.

Now, here, look at this map [in the 32nd Division's history], you can see our line north—straight to the point; that's why they called us the Red Arrow Division—because we shot through every line the Germans put in front of us. First we started from north of Château-Thierry and moved up to Fismes, going through a bunch of villages in between.

See St. Giles? That's where I almost got it when we were having that house-to-house business—that was nasty as hell. I'd just jumped into this caved-in house trying to get some cover when a shell came and knocked over what was left of the walls. I was almost buried, but I jumped out just in time.

Fismes—that was another hellhole; I spent a good deal of the time here by the railroad track. I can't say we had it too bad there near the Vesle River; I think the 127th Infantry took the real pasting there.

That's how you'd do it in a drive like that. One regiment would relieve another one. Then you'd usually go in a battalion at a crack. Eventually your whole division would be relieved for a short time, and that's what happened to us at Fismes; I think that Pennsylvania bunch [the 28th Division] came in.

Now, when you were moving like we were, there was no way for your rolling kitchen to keep up with you. And when you'd come off the lines, the orders were for the kitchens, no matter what outfit they was from, to feed you.

There was one time when we hadn't eaten for four days other than a little hardtack we had taken in with us. Well, we got pulled out of the line and marched four or five miles back. Yuh know, we stopped and ate at every one of those damn kitchens we could find. The first one gave us what we called "slumgullion." You see, the cook would get issued a quarter beef. Now, that's a lot of meat, but not when you're trying to feed a whole company. So he'd put hunks of it in a pot along with just about anything else he could find. God, you'd end up with things you'd never heard of, but rarely the same thing twice. But I'll tell you one thing: It tasted like pure roast beef after four days of nothing.

The next kitchen was a little better—they had what we called "monkey meat."[1] It wasn't real monkey, just very stringy beef, not good on American standards, but edible. And that's what we did all the way back—it was feast or famine, all right.

We'd no sooner finished what they call the Aisne-Marne than they put us in General Mangin's famous Tenth Army. Oh I guess we had maybe a week or so of trying to clean up, but we couldn't go nowhere. It was back to that same old push. And it took us to the village of Juvigny.

Oh there was a hot spot! This was one place where the 128th took the brunt of it. We went into the town from the left, where it seemed those Germans concentrated their fire. That's where I had the flap over my revolver cut right offen my holster. We took the place, all right, on August 31—but those Heinies didn't want to leave us do it.

On the next day we were still going at it. It was the worst day of the war for my platoon. The Germans had several machine guns

[1] Monkey meat was corned beef from Argentina. Some Doughboys will still swear, "The hell you say, it was monkey meat."

left around the town, and we had to knock them off. There was one of them that our bunch had to take, and we tried it head on. God, it was slaughter! They just kept mowing us down. But Lieutenant Harris, what a great guy he was, kept trying to rally us until he was cut in two. Then I had to take over the platoon. I got us all into this old trench to take a count. Of the forty who had started against that damn Maxim, there was only twelve left.

"Christ, men," I said, "if we couldn't take it with forty men, we're sure as hell not going to do it with twelve. We're going to hold."[2] So we stayed put until that night, when some Algerians relieved us.[3]

That affair at Juvigny was just about the end of the real war for me. We were taken to a rest area before joining the First U. S. Army in the Meuse-Argonne, but before we were to be sent back into combat, they ordered me over to infantry command school at Langres. Then when I did join 'em again, toward the end of October, I was hit with the flu and was back in the hospital when it all ended.

I do know the 32nd had the hell shot out of it there for the third time, and right up until November 11 too.

When I finally did get well, I could have gone back to the outfit—they were over at the Rhine in the occupation—but all I wanted to do was go home, so I ended up beating the boys to Wisconsin; of course, there weren't many of the old Wausau boys left in the 128th then, anyway.

Now, as the years rolled by, some of the things we did have faded, but not many; something like that has to stay with you.

And there's one thing I never could get out of my mind. When I was in school at Langres, I met this sergeant from the 1st Division who had a huge, ugly-looking scar on his arm. I asked him how he got it.

[2] Goldsmith received the Croix de Guerre for taking over command after Harris was killed.

[3] The 32nd Division's history tells of the brutal fighting at Juvigny on August 31. Then it says of September 1: "Further attempts were made to improve the position of our advanced elements on September 1 and a number of troublesome machine-gun nests were cleaned up." I gather the word "troublesome" was an understatement. Incidentally, Goldsmith's Company G had 105 casualties at Juvigny.

"I traded bayonets with a Heinie; he left his in my arm, and I stuck mine in his throat," he answered.

Well, I never had to use no bayonet on another man. I shot at hundreds and probably hit some, but there's something impersonal about that. But to bayonet someone—thank God, I never was faced with that!

Oh there's another thing I should tell you about, our "Last Man's Club." After the war those of us from this area who had gone into the 32nd formed into a group that would meet once a year over at the VFW in Wausau—you know, kinda reminisce. We bought this very expensive bottle of wine that we put in the safe. The last man alive was to drink it. Then, about ten years later, we took a look to see how it was doing: The damn thing had been stolen. Finally one of us confessed: It was my old pal, Casey Jones. Said he didn't want it to spoil. Oh you couldn't beat Casey!

"Buddies"

We drunk from the same canteen.

—CIVIL WAR SONG

While all the veterans I talked with constantly referred to their buddies, the No. 1 memory concerning his chums belongs to Enos Curtin, a veteran of the American Field Service and the Field Artillery of the AEF. He also remembered an incident that occurred during World War II that concerned another one of the veterans I interviewed and thus earns a place on these pages.

It seemed that in 1944, when the then Lieutenant Colonel Curtin was serving with U. S. Army Intelligence in England, he was invited to a dinner at a country manor house. Several other American officers were also in attendance, including an Army Air Corps major general. The two-star officer was to share a room at the mansion with Colonel Curtin.

Well, the dinner was a smashing success. Curtin didn't say anything about the food served, but he did mention that much more scotch whisky was available before the dinner started than was still around when the evening ended.

An important matter the next day back at his base necessitated a 6:00 A.M. rising on the part of the general. This was particularly tough on this fellow because, like the rest of the officers, he undoubtedly was suffering from what is commonly called a hangover. A more fortunate Curtin had the day off.

Later on in the morning, Enos received a phone call from the general.

"Enos, I was so foggy when I woke up this morning that I went to the bureau and calmly put my watch on my right wrist and, just before leaving, must have put your watch on my left one. I was the only man at our staff meeting who could tell time from either direction."

The 1944 watch borrower was none other than Major General Ted Curtis, Carl Spaatz's chief of staff in World War II and a U. S. Army aviation ace in World War I.

Both Curtis and Curtin are really quite pleasant men, and it's easy to see why they would be friends. As a matter of fact, it would be hard to see how anyone who knew him would not be a friend of Enos Curtin. And his buddy from World War I, Bob Brooks, must also be a great guy.

"Oh Brooks," Curtin told me, "what a colorful character he was! Now, take the time we were in a replacement camp in France—we were both second lieutenants at the time. Oh but we were so goddamned bored, it seemed like we were going to spend the war there, when Bob came up with an amazing idea.

"'Enos,' he said, 'there are about two hundred artillery officers around here. The only way we can get noticed is if we either rape a girl or go AWOL. We both know we can't rape any of these girls— they're too goddamn willing! So, what do you say, let's take a couple of days off and see what happens.'

"The next day we pulled out and thumbed a ride to this town about twenty miles away. We had a great time. A day or two later we thumbed a ride back to camp. We knew that we'd be missed at dinner, and we were right. The next morning we were called up in front of the colonel. Bob knew this was going to happen, so before we reported we'd polished our Sam Browne belts and everything else to this tremendous shine. Then we practiced the correct military salute for half an hour. When we walked into that office, we looked like something out of the King of England's household cavalry. Then Bob gave the colonel some cock-and-bull story—I can't remember exactly what it was—but we got off scot free. Two weeks later we were promoted to first lieutenant.

"Now, if you're going to pull the stunts that Brooks was always talking me into, what you had to really be was lucky, and this was particularly so on one of our escapades that happened just after we landed in England, on Christmas Eve 1917. They sent us to Liverpool to await transportation across the Channel. It wasn't exactly Bob's style.

"'The hell with this,' he said. 'I have it on good authority that we won't be leaving here for at least a week. Let's go to London and spend a few days at the Savoy.'

"So off we go to London and have a bangup time for a few days. We found a couple of pretty young ladies who didn't have anything to do, so we took them to dinner and the theater. Then we went back to Liverpool and, oh Christ, we found out our unit had left for Southampton to board ship for France. Well, we were now really in trouble—if our outfit sailed without us, there'd be hell to pay. So Bob gets ahold of a taxi driver and we offer him a lot of money to drive us all the way to Southampton. The driver gets so excited that the damn cab broke down when we were only halfway there. Then we had to get another guy with a car to finish the trip. But, damn it, we arrived at Southampton about fifteen minutes after our men had left for France. We figured what the hell, nothing we can do now, so we took a room at the Hotel Southern or Western, I can't remember which, figuring we'd turn ourselves in the next day. Once again we were lucky enough to meet a couple of nice girls, and we're having a great dinner when in walk several officers from our outfit. Oh they'd started for France, all right, but they spied a couple of submarines and had headed back to Southampton so they could pick up some destroyers the next day. We had some tall explaining to do—Brooks was tremendously good at that—but our hide was saved because that ship had to turn back.

"Bob's greatest trick was the time he really gave it to the regulars. You see, there always was a certain amount of animosity between the reserve officers and the regulars in World War I. Those regulars, they thought they were really something! Well, I'd gone to MIT, and Brooks was a Yalie—hell, we didn't think we were dummies!

"It all happened when we were on a troop train traveling toward the front. The regulars were all in this real nice car on the very rear of the train, while we were on these third-class coaches. Oh, this really burned Brooks up!

"'I'm going to fix those bastards, you just watch,' he said. 'I've had a belly full of them.' So he gets ahold of this Frenchman who's working on the train and he gives him three hundred francs to disconnect the last car out in the middle of nowhere. The trainman made it look like an accident, so no one was ever the wiser. But those regulars had to sit out there for a whole day before anyone could come and get them."

This was the type of thing that Mr. Curtin liked to reminisce about. He talked very little about the physical aspects of his 1916 stint as a driver and even less about his days firing in combat as an artillery man. It was a conversation mainly about his friends.

There was Harold Willets, who had gone over with Enos in 1915 as an ambulance driver and then transferred to the French Air Service.

"I couldn't get into flying because I weighed too much," Curtin stated, "but my buddy Willets did. He was shot down and captured, but he never stopped trying to escape. As I recall he finally succeeded the day before the Armistice. Then he went back into the American Field Service for World War II, and I'll be damned if he didn't get captured again by the Germans. He might have been the only American who was an American POW in both wars."

And there was Jim McConnell, who hated everything the "Kaiser's *Kultur*" stood for.

"Jim went over with me as an ambulance driver in 1915," Enos told me, "but he was one fellow who really wanted to do more toward defeating the Germans than driving an ambulance, so he switched over to the Lafayette Escadrille.

"Then," continued Curtin, "I ran into him after he'd become a flier. We were drinking at a bar in Paris when he laid out his true feelings.

" 'I really hate those bastards,' he said, 'and what they're doing to France. If I'm ever in a to-do with one of them and I run out of gas, I'm going to crash into that son-of-a-bitch.'

"Now, not long after we talked, that's exactly what he tried to do, but he missed the German. Then he made a crash-landing and survived. But the next time it happened, he hit the Boche straight on, and they both were killed. I don't know if that's what the records say, but I have that on good authority."[1]

So that's the way my interview with Enos Curtin went—one hour and a half of recording tape on the friends he had during his two trips to France in the First War and his overseas tour in World War II. One of his last references was once again about his good buddy, Bob Brooks.

"I think it was about 1925," Enos said, "when I received a phone call from Bob's wife. It seems that my old buddy wanted to take her on a trip to Europe. She was delighted with the prospects of such a jaunt, but she wanted to know if I would please use my good counsel to persuade Bob to take more than one suit of cloth-

[1] James R. McConnell was from Carthage, North Carolina. He was one of the original members of the Lafayette Escadrille. There is a statue to his memory on the University of Virginia campus. He is officially credited with shooting down three German planes.

ing on the trip. I did my best, but Brooks—who, incidentally, was quite independently wealthy—would have none of it.

"'Oh for Christ's sakes,' he moaned, 'the next thing you know she'll want me to take a dinner jacket.'"

Two Lads from Texas

Wendell Martin and Alphonzo Bulz

MARRIOTT HOTEL, DALLAS, TEXAS, MAY 1976
I first learned about the Veterans of World War I in early 1976 through their New York commander, Dorothy Frook. This remarkable woman is a practicing lawyer, publisher, and author. She was a yeowoman in the U. S. Navy during World War I, working mainly in the naval recruiting program. She recited for me the following verse, which she used during the Navy's enlistment drives.

> Here's to the Kaiser,
> That wormy old cheese,
> May the swell in his head
> Fall down to his knees.
> May he stub his toe
> On his watch on the Rhine,
> And break his damn neck
> On his Hindenburg Line.

It was through the Veterans of World War I's Dallas chapter, called the Big D Barracks, that I was able to visit with Alphonzo Bulz and Wendell Martin. These two Doughboys from Texas both served with the 36th (Texas) National Guard Division in France. Growing up in western Texas at the turn of this century, they were just about as close to frontiersmen as I could get.

After the war Al Bulz became very successful in the printing business. He is still quite active in his firm. Wendell Martin entered the construction business and spent a good deal of time in Latin America.

Mr. Martin is the current quartermaster of the Big D Barracks. There is a sad note contributed by Mr. Martin in the chapter's monthly bulletin. It goes like this: "Be a buddy to a buddy and attend all the funerals you can. This is our duty to our buddy. You may be next."

Private Wendell Martin
B Company, 111th Engineers, 36th Division

Private Alphonzo Bulz
M Company, 143rd Infantry, 36th Division

Before the cowboys were relieved on the Aisne, company commanders had to restrain men who wished to swim the river and carry the Lone Star flag into Hindenburg's last line.

—LAURENCE STALLINGS, *The Doughboys*

MARTIN: We make a number of talks at the local high school here in the Dallas area to tell these youngsters what World War I was like. You know, until we start talking, they can't believe any of the boys from 1918 are left. Why, the World War II veterans are old men to these kids.

BULZ: That's right, they call us "vintage," and that's all right. We are. I tell them, "I know, I know. I'm an antique, but let me tell you what it was like over there, chasing those Germans before your daddies were born." Then some little girl will always ask me why I wanted to go.

"Why, honey," I'll answer, "I just wanted to see what them mam'selles was like. Now, they was all right, but nothing like the pretty girls back in Texas."

Now, these kids love it when I tell them that. Oh they laugh and cheer; I get 'em in a good mood, you see.

"But I'll tell you one thing," I'll continue, "there was one night over there, up in the Champagne sector when the shells were bursting and I was plumb scared. And I said to myself, 'Al, you're only eighteen years old; you could still be back at Rosebud High School, getting ready for a Saturday night dance. Now just what in hell are you doing here?' "

MARTIN: Yes, you have to be a little light when you start. I'll usually open up with the story about the potato masher—that's what we used to call those German hand grenades. You see, we took over this area where the German crown prince had once had his headquarters.[1] Those Germans had skedaddled in such a big hurry that they'd left most of their equipment behind.

We'd just received a bunch of replacements then, most of them raw recruits from the East Coast who'd only been in the Army a month or two. Well, one of those damn fools picked up one of those potato mashers and pulled the pin. Luckily for us one of our old-timers grabbed it fast and threw it away. And you know where it landed? Right in a German latrine! Hell, the place was still ripe! You can imagine what it smelled like with all that stuff flying around.

Just at this time our Captain Coghill came running up, all in a frenzy.

"Gas attack, gas attack," he's yelling, "put on your masks, and don't forget the horses; get those masks on the horses; we need them!" You can bet we never let old Coghill get over that one.

Of course, the reason we make these speeches is that we don't want these youngsters to forget what we did, even though I don't

---

[1] Montfaucon—in the Meuse-Argonne—a very tough nut to crack.

think the government really remembers. Just the other day I was talking to this friend of mine at the VA.

"You know," I said to him, "the government owes me three hundred thousand dollars—they tell me that's the difference between having a college education and not having one. I was all ready to enter the University of Texas, I was accredited, when the war came. We never did get the benefits they got after the Second World War, and I didn't have a chance to go to college."

BULZ: Why, I never even finished high school over at Rosebud. You see, we didn't have the radio and the TV the way we do today. Why, we got our information from what we used to call the "drummers." Don't have them anymore, not the way we used to, anyway. These were the salemen who'd go through all the towns in places like West Texas selling all the merchants their merchandise. They would paint such a dark picture on what was going on over there that we all felt the Kaiser was going to invade America. And all those awful things the Germans were doing to the Belgians— cutting the fingers off the men so they couldn't pull the trigger on a gun and raping all those nuns and all that. Then we'd hear how they were riling up the Mexicans so that they'd want to fight us. I was only seventeen then, but I thought I'd better go over there and fight so I wouldn't be no slave to any foreign country.

Of course, my family wasn't about to let me go, so one day I stopped off at the baker's shop on my way to high school. He was a good buddy of mine, so I left my books at his shop and told him to hold them for me because I was going to be gone a couple of days. A couple of days—that was a funny one. I was gone about two years.

Now, I didn't have any money, so I went down to the railroad yard and hopped a freight train to Waco, then grabbed another to Fort Worth. I told the recruiting sergeant there I was twenty-one. I lied, you see; I had to to get in. I told them I wanted to join the infantry so I could fight those Germans, and they said fine.

Well, when my daddy found out where I was, he came down to get me to come back home.

"Al," he pleaded, "we need you at home. What do you want to go over there to France for, get all shot full of holes? We love you at home, boy."

"No, Dad," I answered, "I don't want to go back home. I want to go to war, show that Kaiser he can't fool around with Americans."

Poor Dad, he tried so hard for about an hour to get me to go home. But finally he gave up.

"Well, son, if that's the way you feel," he said, "remember one thing: If you love your God and your country, and if you do your duty, you'll come back safe." And he was right.

MARTIN: I was a little older than Al, but I felt the same way. And my mother didn't want me to go either. My brother had been the first one in West Texas to enlist. The minute he heard we were in it he rushed down to the post office and had the postmaster swear him in. Mother felt one was enough. But I had to go, and that's all there was to it. So I took myself down to Abilene, enlisted, and was sent to Fort Worth, where they were making up the 36th Division out of the Texas and Oklahoma National Guard units.

BULZ: And you should have seen some of those Indians from Oklahoma. Wow-ee, weren't they something! Some of those rascals had oil money, and they'd get ahold of some firewater; would they have a high old time! They'd do war dances right there in the camp. I don't know if you've ever heard an Indian war whoop, but its a cross between a scream and a yelp. Hell, they'd be at it all night. A bunch of us complained because we couldn't get any sleep, but we didn't get nowhere at all.

"They're just blowing off steam now," this officer said to us. "Just wait till they get to France. They'll be the best ones we have."

And you know, he might have been right. They were great when we went into the Champagne sector. They'd jump out of those foxholes, screaming those war whoops and yelling in the Cherokee and the Choctaw and all those languages. I think the Germans were scared to death of them. I remember this one officer we captured—he was petrified.

"Vhat kind of men are zeze?" he asked us. "Zey are vild men; ve can't fight mit vild men!"

The ones in my company were mainly the Osage. They used to love to talk on our telephones, and they'd talk in the Osage. We used to wonder if the Germans could ever interpret those calls. If they could, it would have confused the hell out of them.

MARTIN: Now, while we were at Fort Worth, our general was a
man named Greble—old "Swagger Stick" Greble, we used to call
him. He made the officers carry these swagger sticks all the time—
keep their hands out of their pockets. A lot of the noncoms started
carrying them also; as a matter of fact, they started calling our
outfit the swagger-stick division. But maybe they should have been
calling us the stay-in-Texas division instead. Do you know, we
spent a whole year there. We were really itching to go over. Then,
finally, in July of '18, we got the word that we were going. By this
time Greble was gone, and we had a Major General William Smith
in command. He was the one who took us over and stayed with us
through the whole thing.

Well, they stuck us on a troop train, and we headed for the East
Coast. You should have heard the rumors. You know, latrine talk,
that's what we called it—news flashes from the fourth hole on the
right. One was that we were going to Russia. I don't know who
started that one, but it sure had the boys scared. One of the men
kept telling everyone that it got so cold there we'd all freeze to
death. Of course, it was all hogwash. Like everyone else, we were
headed for France. We boarded ship around the middle of July and
landed in *la belle France* about two weeks later.

BULZ: That's right, I think the whole division went over in the
same convoy. Ours was an Italian boat, the kind they had been carrying cattle in. These sailors told us how great it was going to be,
all the wine they were going to give us. Wine? Colored water, that's
what it was; they probably charged Uncle Sam for champagne.

MARTIN: Oh I'm sure they overcharged the government. God
knows the French did after we landed. They'd ring the village
church bell when we were approaching one of their towns. That
meant the Americans were coming; you know, give them a chance
to jack up all their prices on cognac, Benedictine—hell, anything
they could sell us. Then after we'd leave, they'd bring the prices
down again.

And they were vicious on their claims. Let's say some of the boys
wanted to have a fire. They'd go out and "borrow" a little wood
from some of these Frogs. Why, they'd put in for a cord. Sometimes
we wouldn't take anything, but they'd still put in. I must confess,
though, most of the time we did take something.

BULZ: It was even worse on the food. We had this cook by the name of Klump. Well, old Klump was my cousin. He could get the flour and gravy, so I'd go out and "borrow" a chicken, maybe two. Why, those Frenchies would say we took a flock. If we'd grab a bottle of wine, they'd say it was a barrel. We'd start the robbing, but they'd finish it. We didn't care; we was hungry—we wanted something good to eat, and that old boy Klump, he could sure make it good.

And those barns they'd put us up in, they weren't any bargains— no, sir. And they were getting a franc a day for each of us. We'd be right there with the cows and the hawgs and the manure. My, but those places could really be gamey!

I can remember one of them a little special because of this one boy we had in my company. Well, he was a real country boy, don't think he'd ever had shoes till he joined up with the Army. Now, he could go just like a hawg—you know, sowee, sowee. He fooled us all night long. Just about the time we'd get back to sleep, he'd start making like a hawg again. Finally one of the boys caught on. We told that farmboy that if he didn't shut up, we were going to make him sleep with the pigs; then he shut up.

MARTIN: Well, let's go back to when we first landed. Al stayed with the division, but they took our outfit, the 111th Engineers, and sent us to corps headquarters. You see, most of our officers and a lot of the men were graduate engineers. Our job was to work on the roads and the bridges—trying to keep the area near the front open. I carried an automatic, not a rifle, and I never did fire it at the Germans. But for sixty-one straight days I was in range of the German artillery. You can bet there were a few things you had to learn in a hurry if you were going to stay alive, particularly during the night shelling.

If we were in the field, which was most of the time, we'd try and find real soft ground to bivouac in. Not only was it easier digging, but the soft earth was more apt to absorb some of the shrapnel. Then you'd try and dig as deep as you could without risking a cave-in. When you'd finally try and get to sleep, you'd lie on your stomach with your pack on top of you. If any shrapnel came at you, it might land in the pack. That happened a lot.

Then there was your helmet. You'd lie it lengthwise so it'd cover your head and your neck—maybe this would absorb some shrapnel also. Of course, nothing meant anything if you took a direct hit— you was going West, and that's all there was to it. I think that's the way most of us felt; if your number was up, it was up. If you didn't look at it that way, you'd go nuts.

BULZ: After the 143rd Infantry landed, they started to really harden us up, brought over these English fellows to teach us what it was all about.

"Love Mother Earth," they'd say to us, "love Mother Earth, if you want to live to go 'ome. And when yuh attack, don't bunch—if someone gets too close to yuh, tell 'im to get the bloody 'ell awaye. Those Jerries will always fire at a bloody bunch!"

"And another thing," they'd say, "don't try and do it all with one swipe. Go five, ten yards, no more—then go back in Mother Earth and wait a little bit."

Well, I can tell you, he was right. We lost so many of our men in October around Blanc Mont because they *didn't* stay down or because they tried to go too far at one rush. It was too bad, but that's the way it was. Green, that's what they called us, green troops, and I guess we were. But those English did help us plenty. I reckon you could say they probably saved a lot of lives.

I'll tell you one other thing about the English, though, and it had nothing to do with what they were teaching us.

It happened over at Is-sur-Tille when this minstrel show came to entertain us. All the Americans were sitting on one side of the hall while all the English was on the other. Hell, I don't think those English even knew what a minstrel show was. Anyway, it started off with a little dialogue between the two end men.

"Mr. Bones," one of them asked, "does you know what de AEF done stand for?"

"No," says the other one.

"After England Failed, Mr. Bones, dat what it stand for." Well sir, that sure cut it. All these limeys started to swing on our boys, and, of course, our boys started to swing back. It was one sweet hell of a brawl—but not for me. I said to myself, "Al, you're here to fight the Germans, not the English," and I high-tailed out of there.

Well, we finally got the word to move up. We was going into the Blanc Mont area to relieve the 23rd Infantry of the 2nd Division.

Good Lord, were they ever torn up, shot to pieces, but they'd done quite a job. This was not actually in the Meuse-Argonne. It was kinda sticking out on the left end of the line, and we were under this French general, Gouraud, who had their Fourth Army.

They took us up as far as they could by train, then it was shank's mare the rest of the way. You couldn't really go by truck—the roads were too tore up by the shellfire.

How well I remember when we got off that train to march up. They had this other train going in the opposite direction. Hell, it was filled with wounded Doughboys going to hospitals—must have been hundreds of them. And they were amoaning and crying. Poor devils, must have been shot up bad! As we got closer and closer to the front, and the guns got louder and louder, I kept thinking about those lads in the train, wondering if I was going to be one of them.

Our rolling kitchens couldn't keep up, so we was eating mainly corn willy and prunes—you know how thirsty that corn willy makes you. And the Germans had poisoned most of the wells—they'd do that—yes, sir, they would. I can't remember not being thirsty at any time those two or three weeks we was in the Champagne sector.

After we reached the front line, our job was to keep pressure on those Germans; you know, push, push, all the time. It was jumping from one foxhole to another, trying to stay away from their shells and machine-gun fire. Why, they would camouflage those grim reapers by putting them right up in the trees—we'd usually lose some men before we'd know where they were.

Then we had a breakthrough. I think there was one day when we went about fifteen miles. By then we were close to the Aisne River, which was one spot those Germans wanted to hold. I can remember a bend in that river we called "Riley's Nose" [Rilly-aux-Oies]. Here it was really bad—we lost a great many good boys there.

When we finally chased those Heinies to the other side of the river, some of our men wanted to swim across and keep chasing them. But old Bill Smith [the West Point major general in command of the 36th] told us we had done enough for a while—I reckon they wanted to let us rest our dogs after all that chasing. I remember one newcomer coming up and asking if we'd seen any Germans. One of our old-timers just smiled.

"I seen 'em running thataway," he said, pointing to the other side of the river.

After that fight, they put us in reserve. I guess we was to go into a big push near Verdun around the middle of November.

Then, on November 11, when we were getting ready to go back in, this Frenchman came driving by on one of those crazy motorcycles they had.

"La guerre est finit! La guerre est finit!" he's ayelling. He's driving that darn bike all over the road; probably had a heap of that good French cognac.

And you know what I did? I got down on my knees. I was thinking of all those good old boys we'd lost chasing them Germans a few weeks before. And I prayed God, thanking him I'd been spared —and that I wouldn't have to be a servant to the Germans, and that Americans wouldn't be slaves. I was mighty thankful to God, and I wanted him to know it.

MARTIN: Of course, just because the war was over, it didn't mean we could all just pack up and go home. Far from it! I went back to playing in the band. Then I had a once-in-a-lifetime chance to really see Paris. We had played for a big staff officers' dance where they had loaded us up with all the wine we could drink. We all got a little tight, but we played them one hell of a dance, I'll tell you that. A few days later they gave us all a five-day pass to Paris.

Well, we had this man in our outfit who was a preacher. He decided we should all go to the opera, but we couldn't get tickets. Then we went to some kind of a French burlesque show. You should have seen the preacher's face when he realized what type of a place we were in.

"Why boys, those are scarlet ladies," he whined. "This is nothing but a bawdy house."

We all got a big chuckle out of that. Then someone said, "That's right, Deacon, but back home we call 'em cat houses." Even the preacher laughed at that.

Shortly after that, we separated. Then I went into one of those outdoor urinals. They were the damnedest thing—you'd be standing up, relieving yourself, and smiling at the ladies walking by. They couldn't actually see what you were doing, but they could see your head and feet.

As I'm standing there, I smiled at one mam'selle who I thought was a real honey, and she kinda smiled back. Well sir, as I walked out of the "pieswa," I noticed this MP looking me over. Then he gave me a wink—he knew I'd been giving the eye to the pretty girl, you see.

"She's OK, buddy," he said as he nodded his head, "she's clean."

The reason he did this was because of the VD. It could be something fierce. But apparently he knew this one was on the up-and-up.

Well, I started to talk to her, you know; a little French, a little American. She was on the square all right, and we got along famously. I had taken a room at the YMCA, but I didn't see it for three days. But I sure did see Paris. I'd won over two thousand dollars in a blackjack game, and we went through that faster than lightning hitting a stump. We saw Napoleon's tomb, the Champs-Élysées, the Eiffel Tower, and all those places, all right, but she also knew all these out-of-the-way places where the Doughboys normally didn't go. She was the real goods, and we had a right bang-up time!

BULZ: We were in the same boat as Wendell. They couldn't send everyone home at once, so they tried to find things for us to do. Our colonel, a man named Hoover, decided we should be more military; the first thing he did was send out an order saying we all had to get real short haircuts.

Say, you should have heard the boys howl. I was mad as hell myself; I had real nice curly locks in those days. [Mr. Bulz is now bald.] But the ones who really yelled were the ones from the Texas plains. How they wanted to keep their long hair!

Well, one of them walked into our barber shop fit to be tied.

"I got to be scalped, boys—that goddarn old fool Hoover says so," he growled as he headed for one of the seats.

Now, you know what? Colonel Hoover himself is in the shop for a shave, with a towel over his face. He threw that towel down on the floor and jumped out of his seat with his face as red as a tomato.

"Lord God Almighty," yells the lad with the long hair, "it's the colonel!" You can bet he high-tailed it out of that shop like the devil was after him. He might be still running!

We weren't all military then, though. This was the time when we had our best chance to meet some girls. Most of it was pretty innocent stuff, for me, anyway—just an eighteen-year-old boy trying to pitch a little woo. Some of these meetings were kinda funny, particularly one night over at Is-sur-Tille. I met this young thing down at the YMCA. We were getting along just great, so I decided to walk her home. Well, we got to her door, and I started a little old Texas necking.

"We call that kissing," I cooed.

"No, here come Pa," she answered.

Well, you can bet I ran out of there. I didn't want some old daddy coming after me. I got back to the Y and told the boys what happened. One asked me if I was sure she hadn't said *"ne comprends pas,"* meaning she didn't understand. You know, that was what she had said. I sure messed that one up!

It wasn't all funny, though. One time when I was walking down the street, this girl asked me to go into this house with her. Like a damn fool, I went. When we got there, these two big Frenchies were waiting for us.

"All right, soldier," this girl snapped, "give us all your money, or I'll holler ze rip!"—She meant rape, of course. I had about twenty francs. I forked it over pronto and ran as fast as I could.

Then, about three weeks later, we had to all stand in formation and watch them hang this young Doughboy, who some woman claimed raped her. It was the worst thing I saw all the time I was in France. Why, he wasn't much older than I was. How do I know some girl hadn't pulled the same stunt with him? But they hung him, all right, and we all had to watch. That was the type of thing the folks back home weren't hearing about.

After that I did a lot of convoy duty on trains going all over France. Some of those French girls would come right into the freight cars. They'd do anything with the boys to get some apple butter, or prunes, or cigarettes—whatever we had. I stayed away from them, though. I kept thinking of the poor old boy they hung. I didn't want anything to do with that kind of woman.

I met plenty of the nice ones, though. The French girls were the same as anywhere else. Some were what we used to call sweet, and the others weren't. If I'd meet any of the nice ones, I'd tell them to write me in care of Rosebud, Texas. Do you know that when I finally did get back home in the middle of 1919, I had a stack of letters waiting for me from all over France. Did I ever think I was a

Casanova! But in 1920 I married this sweet Irish girl here in Texas, and I've been a happy man ever since.

MARTIN: I did the same when I got home, but I had a bad deal: We were divorced a few years later. I have a nice one now, though, have had for over forty years.

There's one thing I'd like to finish up with. If I had it to do all over again, I'd still go to France for my country. But I wish that Congress in Washington would think a little bit more about the World War I veterans. We went when the country needed us, and some of the old-timers need the country now.

Law and Order

It was during the Argonne fighting, I had to leave my job of trying to keep the road open to pick up this Doughboy from our division [the 29th] who had taken it on the lam. Hell, he was only a kid, just scared, that's all. I didn't blame him.

—CY CURRIER, C COMPANY, MP

At this late date it's easy to imagine that all the Americans in France were heroes, but of course this is not true. Like every other military host, there was an ample supply of rogues included within the AEF. But thanks to an order instituted by President Lincoln during the American Civil War, not a single Doughboy was executed for a *military* offense—rape and murder, yes, but desertion or cowardice, no—not legally, anyway. The Civil War order called for the actual presidential signature on every military execution warrant. American Presidents are just not going to make a habit out of shooting some lad who deserts in the face of the enemy. In the four years of World War II the United States only shot one man for desertion, Private Slovik, and this poor unfortunate has become a martyr to as many people as Sacco and Vanzetti.[1]

If or if not any soldiers were executed out of hand by the authorities will always remain a question mark. But of the executions witnessed by the men I visited with—and five veterans stated they did see one—all were for murder or rape.

Most of the men I talked with, however, not only did not witness an execution, but also weren't even aware of any. Surprisingly, though, there were three men who told me of definite murders occurring within their division. They did not mean possible situations in combat where an American could have been shot by his own people, but out-and-out behind-the-lines affairs. One of these slayings concerned a very unpopular sergeant who was simply tossed overboard in the middle of the Atlantic. The men in the late sergeant's platoon were then not fed for two days while an investigation was conducted into the deceased's disappearance.

"He was my platoon sergeant and a real bastard," a veteran told me, "and while I didn't witness it, I always felt I knew the men who did it." The old-timer who related this to me did not want his name connected with the incident, but he did add, "Believe me, it happened, and nobody shed any tears."

Jack O'Brien was not as reluctant to identify himself concerning the shooting of an MP after his regiment (12th Field Artillery) had returned from almost constant fighting in July and August around the Marne.

"I wasn't in the cafe where it happened," O'Brien told me, "and

[1] In reality the United States has always had the most lenient attitude toward the military in the world. For instance, 450 men within the United States were given sentences ranging from ten years to death in the 1917–18 period. Their crime was refusing to enter the service after the government decided they were not legitimate conscientious objectors. None was ever shot, and by mid-1920 all were freed.

it's a good thing for me because I was sore as hell as it was. My uniform was all beaten up from Belleau Wood and Soissons, so an MP had sent me back to camp. I don't know if it was the same guy or not, but one of those behind-the-lines heroes later went into this spot where a lot of our boys were letting off some steam and tried to throw his weight around. Someone from our regiment finally took the MP's own revolver and shot the poor guy dead. Oh there was hell to pay, but everybody really clammed up. I never found out myself who had done the deed, and you can rest assured the authorities didn't."

Phil Hammerslough claimed that a similar thing happened concerning one of the infantry regiments in the 26th Division, only this time it was premeditated. It seems there was one MP whom many of the boys hated, and just before the division was to sail for home, a party, or parties, unknown did the unpopular fellow in.

These were the sensational happenings—the things that would always be remembered. But what about the actual overall justice of the AEF? Well, according to Fletcher Reid Andrews, it was quite outstanding.

"Of course," this retired dean of Western Reserve University's Law School told me in his Shaker Heights, Ohio, home, "I can only speak for my own division, the 37th. It was the Ohio National Guard outfit, and I do think we had a pretty high type of soldier. But you're bound to have some problems in any group of twenty-eight thousand men, and we had our share. One thing I am sure of is that the docket was more crowded when we were off the lines than when we were near the front. And the 37th saw plenty of action both in the Argonne and on that little jaunt we took to Belgium the last few weeks of the war. Everyone was too busy to worry about minor infractions then; we were more concerned about the Germans. It was when we would be in a rest area that the trouble would come. You know, some French farmer claiming that someone had stolen his pig or made eyes at his daughter, things like that, or AWOL cases, and fights—what you'd really call minor affairs. Most of the time the charges would be reduced and the soldier would end up with a few days' confinement or an extra work detail. We weren't really trying to see the men get in trouble—we needed them—but if soldiers have a lot of time to sit on their asses, problems can arise.

"Now, I wasn't a lawyer then, mind you; I'd just graduated Dartmouth College when I went into the Army. I was the divisional sergeant major in the adjutant general's office, and I was familiar with most of the offenses, particularly the major ones. I think the various stages that the serious ones had to go through made it mandatory that the accused get a fair shake.

"First the soldier had to be charged, and we were always reluctant to ever do that. Then an investigating officer would check out the charges as thoroughly as possible and then recommend to the commanding officer of the division if the thing should be dropped or not. If the recommendation called for a trial, the general would take still another step—that is, contact the division's judge advocate for his opinion. If everyone was still in agreement, then, and only then, would a general court-martial be declared. We had serious cases, all right—no doubt about it. As a matter of fact, I believe one of our men was actually sentenced to death, but the sentence was later reduced by either Pershing or Washington.

"Honestly," continued Dean Andrews, "I do feel that the military justice as practiced by the United States during World War I was as fair as it possibly could be. And I'll tell you something else: I went to Washington, D.C., as a colonel in World War II, and it was still good."

Punching the Bag with the 69th

James Minogue
William Carroll
William Fleming
James Vail
Nick Martino

69TH NEW YORK ARMORY, NEW YORK CITY, APRIL 1976
When the American Civil War broke out, New York City was the
haven for thousands of Irish immigrants. Driven from their island
home by famine and British persecution, they were fast becoming a
force to reckon with. They even had their own regiment, the 69th
New York. Led by a charismatic, revolutionary leader, Thomas
Francis Meagher, they left their dead all over Virginia. Perhaps a
Confederate rifleman summed up their service best as he looked
out at the mass of blue-clad bodies that covered Mayre Heights at
Fredericksburg and remarked:

"Them lads with the green sprig on their hats, they got the
closest to the wall."

In 1917 the sons and grandsons of the potato faminers, and a
great many newer arrivals, once again brought the 69th into action
against an enemy. And the 69th's Doughboy doesn't have to stand
one inch behind the Army of the Potomac version.

Picked to represent New York State in the Rainbow Division,
they landed in France on November 1, 1917. And they didn't come

back until May of 1919. In between these two dates they suffered over thirty-five hundred casualties, which is just about the number of their original complement.

Today, some six decades later, their ranks have thinned greatly. But once a month a score or so of hearty veterans gather at the 69th Armory for a get-together; I had the great privilege of joining them there one Sunday.

The high point of this visit was sitting down with Jim Minogue to talk about the war. During our discussion four more of the old 69ers joined us. I said very little, just let the tape run. It was an historian's dream.

They talked of Colonel Donovan, Father Duffy, Joyce Kilmer, and most of all about a lovable rogue named Mike Donaldson. Holder of the Medal of Honor, it seems Sergeant Donaldson would have furnished an ideal part in a film for the late Victor McLaughlin.

I've made no attempt to state who said what. After all, as one of them said, "We were like a big family."

Punching the Bag with the 69th

My, how the men were grousing. Honor or not, we didn't want to go into Germany. The war was over; we wanted to go home.

Then, just as we reached the border, we spotted this beautiful rainbow hanging over a German hill. And didn't the boys make something out of that, being part of the Rainbow Division and all that. Then the band changed

from playing "The Yanks Are Coming" to our own tune.
It made us think of all those ghosts that were marching
with us. It was enough to make you straighten your
shoulders. It's called "Gerry Owen."

—A WORLD WAR I VETERAN OF THE 69TH

"John McGraw, you know, the one who managed the Giants, he
knew we'd be going over soon, so he invited the whole 69th to the
Polo Grounds to see a ball game. Jeez, I'll bet half the regiment
went! Some of the lads took their rifles, others their packs and cartridge belts. McGraw loved the 69th, and so did most of New York.

"As for myself, I probably was rooting for the visitors. You see, I
was raised in Ireland's largest county, at least it was then—it's
called Brooklyn, New York. I was a great Dodger fan and didn't
give a damn for the Giants. But I did like John McGraw, so did
most of the boys in the 69th. We called him Mugsy.

"Well, Irish Town was not far from Ebbets Field, and when I
was a kid, every Saturday afternoon we could, we'd head for the
ball game. I think it cost a quarter. Then, after the game, we'd walk
over to Duffield Street to the public bath; for two cents you'd get a
towel, some soap, and a hot bath. It'd make us look clean for Mass
the next day. And a lot of the kids who went with me ended up in
the 69th.

"The 69th, you see, was quite a thing to the Irish kids, narrow
backs and greenhorns alike. We'd hear about their great record in
the Civil War and Thomas Francis Meagher and Michael Corcoran.
So I guess it was natural that when war came, I would want to go
over with them.

"Now, there was some change in the outfit after they made us
the 165th U. S. Infantry. We were full at about two thousand at the
time, almost all Irish, but they'd decided to make an AEF infantry
regiment thirty-six hundred strong. So they moved men into the
69th from the 7th, 12th, and 14th regiments of the New York National Guard. The funny thing, though, was that many of the new
men were Irish also.[1]

[1] Probably correct—on the AEF death roll of the 165th are seven
Kellys, five McCarthys, and four O'Neills, O'Briens, and Brennans.

"The matter of the name change from 69th to 165th didn't really concern anyone—we simply paid no attention to it. Oh we were the 165th U. S. Infantry, all right, but you always had 69th N.Y. in parentheses. Let me ask you one question: Did you ever hear a real New Yorker call Sixth Avenue the Avenue of the Americas? Of course not!

"What did concern us, and we were proud as peacocks, was the Rainbow Division. We were told that twenty-six units from twenty-six different states were to make it up, and that we were to represent New York. This was due to the fact that the 69th had even outhiked the regulars down on the Mexican border the year before. Oh we were good, all right, and so were the others in the Rainbow, the regiments from Ohio, Alabama, and Ioway—and the 149th Field Artillery from Chicago, Reilly's boys, they were the cream of the crop.

(At this point Bill Fleming, late a sergeant in the 69th, walked in.)

"Here, Bill, join us. I want you to make sure I don't make any false statements."

"Oh I know you will; the truth is not with you—but I'll verify it anyway."

"Bill was our champion runner. He's a Tipperary man. He learned to run fast tear-assing through the bogs at night."

"Oh I'm a Tipperary man, all right. I came to this country in December of '16 and I was back in Europe in November of '17—Tipperary men work fast.

"And speaking of Tipperary reminds me of when I met Father Duffy walking down the company street at Camp Mills before we went over. Yuh know, he'd always walk with his hands folded in front of him, meditating on things not of this world. That's the way it seemed, anyway, but he still spotted me.

"'Good morning, my son,' he said, 'and where are you from?'

"'Why, the Bronx, Father.' But in those days I had one hell of a brogue.

"'No, son,' he answered, 'not immediately, but before that.'

"'Oh Tipperary, Father!'

"'I thought so. And your name?'

"'Bill Fleming, Father.'

"'Well, Bill, the Tipperary men are all fine. God bless you!'

"And he resumed his walk, communicating with the Almighty.

"Now, I didn't see him again for almost a year. Then I met him walking down a road in the Baccarat section of France. There he was, the hands folded in front, looking up at the heavens. Nothing had changed at all. But what a shock he gave me!

"'Why, hello, Fleming,' he said, 'how are all the good bog jumpers in Tipperary?'"

"Oh the man was uncanny. He was better than Jim Farley."[2]

"Yes, he was that, and there was another side to the man: his aloofness under fire. I think he felt that if he were to be killed, it was because the good Lord wanted to visit with him."

"And don't forget his sense of humor. Do you remember his story about the wounded man next to the Ourcq?"

"You mean Jack Finnegan?"

"The same. The Ourcq, you see, was hardly a river on American standards—more like a creek."

"Oh if you spit in it, it was an addition."

"That it was. Now, poor Jack[3] had taken a nasty wound and was lying near the Ourcq when along came the good Father."

"Oh he was always looking for the wounded men."

"Yes, he was. Well, he spies Jack and goes over to give him a drink from his canteen. Oh Jack was a man with a great thirst all right, but not for water, unless it had a stick in it. So he says to the Padre,

"'And what do ye have, Father?'

"'Why, water, my boy.'

"'WATER! Sure, give it to the Ourcq—it needs it more than I do!'"

(At this point along came Jim Vail.)

"Sit down, Jim. We're telling this man all about the old 69th, starting at Camp Mills."

"At Camp Mills, you say. Did yuh tell him about Harlem Tommy Murphy?"

"Jeez, Tommy Murphy, there was one for yuh, the renowned prize fighter."

"Oh he was a good boxer, no doubt about that. Well, he comes

[2] The late Sunny Jim was renowned for not forgetting a face or a name.
[3] Finnegan died of his wounds.

over to the camp and says he wants a commission—he wanted to give us all that physical training. His only problem was he didn't want any part of the real fighting. Of course, they told him no soap on the commission, but he could give us training."

"Yea, that's right, but all he'd do was give us boxing gloves and tell us to go to it."

"That's right, and he got the bejesus knocked out of me. I was lucky I wasn't killed! A whole crew of us, you see, had gone over to The Goose's on Washington Street."

"Oh The Goose's, I remember that night; The Goose was an uncle of Paddy Connor from my company."

"Now, naturally, when you went to The Goose's, you'd really tie a package on. Oh but we had a Branigan that night! So the next morning my mouth felt like the inside of a motorman's glove, and my gut wasn't any better, don't you see. I didn't think I was long for this world.

"And wouldn't yuh know it, that's the morning this goddamn Murphy makes me put the gloves on with Jimmy Hackett. Well, Christ, not only was Hackett bigger than me, but he had what you'd call a secret weapon. He'd been with us the night before, all right, but he had a kettle back at the camp, and he'd had a couple of stiff belts that very morning. The son-of-a-bitch thought he was Stanley Ketchell. Oh didn't he kick the living hell out of me!"

"Haw, haw—that he did! I remember it well, but Murphy got it himself later on."

"Oh yes, he did all right, from Eddie Manning."

"Manning, yuh see, was a professional fighter himself. I think he fought under the name of Tommy O'Kelly, but Murphy didn't know this. Well, Murphy would frequently put the gloves on with some of the boys. And, of course, most of us couldn't lay a glove on him."

"Oh he knew the science of the ring, all right."

"So this one morning, Murphy picks on Manning. And Eddie, he plays it dumb, but he's waiting for his opening. In the meantime, Murphy is toying with him, pointing out to the rest of us the little tricks he's using.

"Then, wham. Eddie tags him."

"Oh he knocked him out of the ring."

"And after that we never saw hide nor hair of Harlem Tommy Murphy."

"Oh you never saw such a crazy outfit. It was like a big family. Now, take Bill Fleming here, he married the drum major's daughter. She's a little bit of a thing,[4] but her father, John Mullins, oh he was an enormous man. He couldn't sit in a regular chair. Why, when he'd take those drum sticks, he'd raise 'em so high in the sky, he'd hit the clouds. And by God, when he'd strike that drum, yuh could hear it in San Francisco.

"John didn't go over with us, though. I guess he was a little old. But they wanted to keep it in the family, so they made his son John the drum major."

"And wasn't there another of old John's boys—Fergie, I think his name was—who went over with us?"

"Yeah, Fergie went too. But you know, if we stop to talk about all the brothers we had in the outfit, we'll be here the night."

"That we will; let's go back to those boxing matches. Do you remember when we had a special program of 'em and they also had the clown who was trying to show us that pain didn't exist?"

"Oh Jeez, haw, haw—yuh mean the nut with the needles?"

"That's the one. Well, this clown stands up, I think the whole Rainbow was watching, and he puts this needle through one side of his cheek and it comes out the other. I don't know how the hell he did it, but it made my cheek ache just to watch him. Now, can you imagine that—trying to show us that pain didn't exist! Oh we had some characters, all right, but no one fell for that."

"Speaking of characters, do yuh remember Chicago Higgins?"

"Oh the one with the long legs—why, he could kick just like a chorus girl!"

"That's the guy. Now I remember this time when Chicago and myself were lying in a pup tent, it was right after the Ourcq fight, see. Hell, we'd really been shot to pieces, and almost all our noncoms were dead or wounded. We did have this one corporal left called The Dutchman. I don't know where he'd come from—maybe from under a rock—but he didn't seem to get along with anyone,

---

[4] Mrs. Fleming was at the armory, and she's a handsome woman today. Bill Fleming surely had some competition for her hand.

and especially Higgins; apparently they'd had some kind of a row back in the border days.

"Well, The Dutchman comes over to where we're lying.

"'Private Higgins,' he greets us with, 'get a shuvel.'

"'For what?'

"'To dig a latrine, that's for what! The sanitation conditions are deplorable. We must have a latrine.'

"'Oh for Christ's sakes, Dutchman, we're moving out tomorrow.'

"'Do what you're told: GET a shuvel.'

"'Fuck you, you Dutch bastard!'

"'Listen, Higgins, you're talking to a noncom. I'll run your ass up!'

"Well, while they're going at it tooth and nail, up walks Jerry O'Neill, the first sergeant.

"'All right, boys,' says O'Neill, 'I've got some news. Higgins here is your new sergeant.'

"Jeez, I thought Chicago would have hysterics. Then he bellows out, 'The sanitation conditions around here are deplorable. We've got to dig a new shithouse. Dutchman, get a shuvel.'

"Of course, that's what you call the lighter side. But that fight on the Ourcq, north of Château-Thierry, was no lark, you can count on that."

(At this point Nick Martino walked in.)

"Oh here we have another. Nick Martino, our Irish Dago, and one of the best men in the regiment. Sit down, Nick, this man is writing a book on the AEF."

"Ooooh—well, that's right, I'm Italian, but I was raised in Irish Town in Brooklyn, just like Minogue. Why I wanted to go over with these crazy Micks, I'll never know, but we had one hell of a regiment.

"Now, I think you were mentioning the Ourcq River. How well I remember that, particularly that awful shelling we took—it seemed to last for hours. Here I was trying to dig a hole with my mess spoon—honest to God, that's all I had—when up pops Bill Ritter.

"'Let's dig a hole together,' he says.

"So I answered, 'Wait a minute, Bill, they're supposed to be ten yards apart.'

"'The hell with that,' he said. 'Here I have my bayonet; let's start.'

"And I'll be damned if he doesn't dig a hole with the bayonet, and we jump in."

"Yeah, but Bill was a skinny guy."

"I know that, but the damn hole still had to be big enough for the two of us. Then the big stuff started to come in. Christ, was I scared! And so was Bill.

"'Jeez, this is horrible,' he says. 'Let's pray together, the "Our Father" and the "Hail, Mary."'

"Oh we started, all right, but each time one came close, we had to start all over. You know something, we never even finished one 'Our Father,' much less a 'Hail, Mary.'

"Finally, I started to laugh. You see, I'd received a letter from my mother a short time before. In it she'd told me about this notice she'd received for me to go into the Italian Army. I don't know how things were on their front, but they couldn't have been any worse than around the Ourcq."

(Bill Carroll joined us here.)

"Now, here's a good one, Bill Carroll. And after the war he was a mounted sergeant in the New York Police Department. Join us, Bill, I'm about to tell this man about Mike Donaldson."

"Oh there was a character."

"I'll say he was!"

"All right, all right, you two call him what you like. But do you remember that night years ago, in this very same room, when it used to be a bowling alley, when someone called him a phony in front of Terry O'Connor?"

"Oh God, Terry O'Connor; he's been dead these many years."

"Well, O'Connor said, 'A phony, is he? I remember that night up near Landres St. George in the Argonne. There I was, lying out in no-man's-land with me face half shot away. And I'd be there still but Mike crawled out there with all that shelling and picked me up in his arms and carried me back.'"

"Now, no one says he wasn't brave—why, the man knew no fear. Didn't he get the Medal of Honor! But you know what a con man he could be. Take that time he sent Hylan a telegram congratulating him on being elected mayor. We were the only New York outfit in France then, so Hylan sends Mike a wire back thanking him. Then Mike went around showing everyone the wire.

" 'Oh it's just a wire from my good friend the mayor,' he says."

"And didn't he do the same with Elsie Janis when he heard she was coming over. I'll never forget it when he walked over with her reply.

" 'Good news, boys,' he boasted, 'Elsie has just sent me a wire saying she's coming to France. Of course, she'll be looking me up.'

" 'Oh yeah?' someone said. 'Elsie who?' And Mike said, 'Elsie Janis. Is there any other?' Then he calmly walked away."

"Oh he was a pip, all right. He could wiggle the devil out of his tail."

"What about his old sparring partner, Teddy Roosevelt?"

"Haw, haw, that's right. He was always talking about Teddy."

"Then there was that time with Colonel Howland. Mike, you see, wasn't much of a military man. And the colonel caught him out of uniform this day and started to chew him out. Now, Mike is smart enough to be humble at a time like that. Then he got shrewd.

" 'Colonel,' he says, 'you know I've been around prize fighters all my life, and you remind me of one.'

"Well, naturally the colonel loved that.

" 'Yes,' continued Mike, 'it's Bob Fitzsimmons you remind me of most of all. You have shoulders just like him.'

" 'You think so,' said the colonel. 'You're Mike Donaldson, aren't you? And you have the DSC, I know that!' From then on Mike had his way with Howland."

"Oh he was a shrewdie, all right, but he couldn't fool Major Donovan. Oh Christ, Donovan put the gloves on with him one time—Donaldson couldn't touch him."

"Yeah, and he surely set Mike straight when Donaldson went AWOL."

"Didn't he though."

"Mike snuck off, yuh see, figuring he could get away with it with Howland. Well, the Marine MPs caught him in Paris and took him to the guardhouse. Naturally, Mike gets quite indignant.

" 'You can't do this to me,' he yells, 'I'm Mike Donaldson.'

"So the Marines kicked the shit out of him, made him scrub the floor with a toothbrush, and sent him back. But by this time Howland was gone, and Mike runs into Bill Donovan. Well, Donovan's a colonel now, and he knows we're about to go into the Meuse-Argonne. Naturally, he doesn't want to lose Mike when we're going into a fight, so he calls me over.

"'Here,' he says, 'take this man out and make him dig a hole ten feet by ten feet.'

"So I marched Mike over to this field and he starts digging. Well, you know what a loafer he was; it took him the whole day. I'd already missed lunch when I reported back to Donovan.

"'All right,' says Donovan, 'now make him fill it up.'

"Jeez, I ended up missing dinner also."

"But Mike was a joy to be with—Christ, he'd keep you laughing all day. I remember shortly after the war they had me in the division hospital. The mustard gas I'd picked up in my eyes was acting up, and I was scared. Well, in walks this medic with Donaldson. I don't remember what was wrong with him, but he wanted no part of a ward.

"'Here, here,' he yells, 'I demand a room.' Of course, the medic just laughed.

"Well sir, for the next week he kept us in stitches. There was this guy from the Ioway regiment in the bed next to me—his name was Glen Ordt from Guthrie. He'd never seen anyone like Mike; Jeez, he laughed so hard he wet the bed."

"Oh but Mike never changed. I remember one time many years after the war. I was a mounted sergeant in the Police Department with my area up near the Forest Hotel where Mike was staying."

"I thought he stayed at the McAlpin."

"Oh he did, but they'd put him out; he didn't pay any rent.

"Well, I'm riding down Forty-ninth Street and there's Mike standing with a couple of guys, and he spotted me.

"'Here's my old buddy,' he yells, 'my old sergeant from the 69th. He was a leader of men then, and he's one now.'

"Why, I was never his sergeant; I wasn't a sergeant in the 69th, but he didn't care. Then a few weeks later he spots me again.

"'Sergeant,' he says, 'I'm on my way to Washington; I'll be back with thousands of dollars, but I'm a little short now; could you lend me a couple of hundred?'"

"Haw, haw, that was Mike, all right. But he did have connections."

"That he did. Why, when they wanted a Medal of Honor man to

ride with Mrs. Harding in the President's funeral procession, who do they pick but Mike."

"That's right, and look at all the publicity he got. I was told that the editors had been instructed by William R. Hearst himself to put Donaldson's name in the Hearst papers every chance they could."

"He was always being written up, all right. But you know, you could take Mike. I had seen him one day, you see, and he'd hit me up for a couple of bucks. Then, when I bumped into him a few weeks later, I was ready for him.

"'Mike,' I said, before he could open his mouth, 'I'm up against it. Could you let me have a few bucks?' Do you know, he gave me every cent he had."

"Oh that was Mike, all right. Of course, he's been gone for years, but how I'd love to see him come through that door."

"Oh hell, we had a lot of laughs, all right, but remember, we saw as much fighting as anyone."

"We did that!"

"You see, it depended on which battalion you were in on a certain day. One battalion would be on the line, another in support, and a third in reserve. If it really got bad, the battalions would be leap-frogging over each other."

"Yeah, and that's just about what happened on that sunken road in the Argonne."

"Oh God, everyone caught it there. We were supposed to take this area, but we had no artillery. And they had acres and acres of that goddamned barbed wire."

"Jeez, I'll say so. We left a lot of good men hanging on that wire."

"And that clown Summerall,[5] he's sitting back in corps headquarters on his fat ass wondering why we can't move. Why, we couldn't move because we'd had the hell shot out of us. Then he [Summerall] moves all these big guns up. Why, they had them lined up hub to hub.

"Well, they pulverized that barbed wire. Then Summerall calls in the 2nd Division to take the place. Oh they had no trouble atall. But why should they? There was no goddamn wire. And the artillery had knocked the hell out of the Germans at the same time."

---

[5] Major General Charles Summerall—the 1st Division loved him, apparently the 69th didn't.

"Oh that attacking we did in the Argonne was nasty, all right, and so was the Heinie artillery. It's funny, though, the things you do remember about something like that. Like the time I ended up in a shellhole with Fred Garrison, you all remember him, he'd been a soldier of fortune down in South America—you know, the guy whose family had money."

"Garrison, I'll say they did! His family had been in New York before the Indians."

"Well, I'm telling him about this beautiful girlfriend I had back home. Now, she wasn't as pretty as the woman I married; she'd be here tonight, but she's off her oats, but that other one was a looker, all right. Anyway, I can see Garrison is more concerned with the shelling than my girl in Brooklyn.

" 'Listen, young fellow, and listen good,' he said. 'Never trust a woman, and that's the truth.' Then some more shells came, and we both shut up.

"Well, I ran into Fred back in New York City four or five years after the war; he wanted to know what had happened to the girl I'd had back home.

" 'Oh Christ, Fred,' I told him, 'when I was in France, she went into the Follies. She had no time for me when I got home. How about you? Did you ever get married?'

" 'I wish the hell I hadn't,' he answered, 'I should have followed my own advice. I married, all right, and she took me to the cleaners —my home, money, everything. She even got this portrait that had been in my family for generations. I got drunk one night and tried to sneak into my own house to get the damn thing back. The bitch caught me and had me thrown into the hoosegow. If it hadn't been for Bill Donovan, I'd still be there.' "

"Oh some of those talks in the shellholes in the Argonne were something, all right. We had seventeen straight days of it, and it rained every one of them.

"On one of those nights I ended up in a hole with a new lieutenant who had recently joined us. Well, he was brave enough, but he'd just received a three-hundred-dollar money order from home, and he was afraid he'd get killed before he could spend it. Oh I could see this was bothering the hell out of him.

" 'Listen,' he finally said, 'can't we give each other some small wounds, just bad enough to get the hell out of here for a week or two? We can have a big time with this three hundred and then come back. There'll be plenty of war left.'

"I was tempted, but I told him I guessed that wasn't such a smart idea. Then I went off for a while, and when I came back, the poor son-of-a-bitch had been buried by a shell."

"Oh that was one thing that scared the hell out of us all; we'd had a lot of men buried alive. The very thought of it was horrifying."

"Well, I started to dig as fast as I could, and I got him out just in time. When he realized what had happened, he tried to laugh, which was very hard because he'd cracked two or three ribs. 'The Heinies did it for me,' he kept laughing, 'the Heinies did it for me!' It was painful as hell, I could see that, but he was going to spend that three hundred."

"Oh the shelling could be hell, all right, particularly when it was raining all the time. But I still think the charge at the Ourcq River was the worst time the Shamrock Battalion[6] had. And we were shelled there also. Poor Jim McKenna[7] was killed in that advance and never touched. It was the concussion, you see; there were three or four of our men laid out together, and not a mark on them. And those machine guns, they were everywhere."

"Yeah, and don't forget Joyce Kilmer; he got it there also."

"Now, there was a beautiful man! Of course, he could have gone to the OCS and become an officer, but he didn't want to leave the 69th."

"And they wanted him for *The Stars and Stripes* also. Not Kilmer; he wanted to stay with Donovan. . . ."

At about this time the ladies joined us, and the 69th broke camp for the evening. But they'll keep meeting until man's mortality catches up with them. And that will be too bad, because when they go, a piece of New York City will be gone forever. And a wonderful slice of Americana will go with it.

[6] The 3rd Battalion, but all three could have been called Shamrock battalions.

[7] The 3rd Battalion's major—a very popular officer.

The Immigrants

Yuh bet I'm glad I went. I'd seen what living in Russia was like. This country was different.

—MORRY MORRISON, 53RD PIONEERS

One of the most interesting statements I obtained during my travels came from an old AEFer who had been quite successful in later life. It went like this:

"I had just graduated college in 1917 when I applied for a commission in the Army. I figured it would be one hell of a lot easier if I put down on my application that I had been born in the town that I had been living in since the age of four. Hell, no one bothered to check anything—I was soon off to France, where I spent the next year and a half.

"After it was all over, I registered as a voter, showing my separation papers as proof of citizenship. It's probably a little late to nail me now, but I was born in Canada. Let's say that the mustard gas that I picked up near the Meuse River made me a citizen."

This gentleman will not appear in the statistics concerning the foreign-born members of the AEF. How many men followed his example will never be known, but some 17 per cent of the AEF were acknowledged immigrants.

One of these turn-of-the-century European newcomers to America who went to France was Herman Levine. Suffering from extremely bad vision in one eye, Mr. Levine could have probably stayed out of the Army, but he had found conditions so much better here than in Russia that he sincerely felt a strong obligation to serve his adopted land.

"It wasn't always easy," recalled a very alert eighty-three-year-old Mr. Levine. "First there was the food problem—you see, my family was Orthodox. It wasn't bad when I was at Camp Dix because my father would bring me kosher food in the evenings. But when I left for overseas with the 78th Division, the real trouble started. I was able to take plenty of food aboard, which came close to lasting the whole trip. But the last day or two I was hungry as the devil.

"When we landed at Le Havre, they took us to this large mess hall. It was early in the morning, and they had rustled up a great deal of bacon for us. Now, you know how great bacon smells when it's cooking. Well, I decided then and there that I just had to bend a few rules for the duration."

Another Russian-born Jewish immigrant I visited with was Morry Morrison. This veteran of both World Wars talked a great deal about both his early life under the Czar and his days on Hester Street in New York City.

"I was about five years old when they came and took my father away for the Japanese War. He was a tailor, you see, but they stuck him in the infantry, and he was killed. Things were very bad for Jewish people in Russia then, and my mother, she didn't have no way to get any money, so we snuck out of Russia to get to America, where my older brother was. We had to carry our food in bundles and get more from other Jewish people as we moved along, you see.

"Yeah, well then we get to Ellis Island and then we came to Hester Street, yeah, yeah, that's right, Hester Street. Boy, were things different here—no fear, that's the difference, no fear, see. I went to school and learned all about Washington and Lincoln, and being free. I also joined the Boy Scouts. We used to go to Van Cortland Park and put up tents; it was great. They taught me how to play the bugle. That's how I got to play the cornet, see.

"In 1917 I joined the 47th Brooklyn National Guard. My mother, she didn't want me to go, see, 'cause she was thinking of my father, but I figured this country was different from Russia; it was worth fighting for."

John Gilbertie also spoke highly of America.

"My father left Sicily and went to Westport, Connecticut, when I was five years old," John related, "and two years later he sent for the rest of the family. I was working when the war was declared. I remember someone telling me I couldn't get drafted because I wasn't a citizen, but I didn't care nothing about that. This was my country, and I went down and enlisted.

"I can still remember when I left home," John continued. "There was a trolley line in those days between Westport and Stratford, where the assembly place was. I got all dressed up, and so did my father. My mother put some food in a brown bag, yuh know, real good Italian food. Then my pappa and me got on that trolley. We didn't say much on that trip. I guess we were both thinking a lot. When we got to Stratford, Pop told me to remember I came from a good family. Then he kissed me and asked God to protect me in Italian. There were tears in his eyes, and in mine too, when he walked back to the trolley."

Germans, Irish, Polish—no matter what country the man I talked to had come from, it was always the same. "Sure I went. Why not? It was as much my country as anyone else's, wasn't it?" Of course, two of my Irish friends allowed as how they would have been just as happy if the English hadn't been on the same side, but it really didn't bother them much.

And it didn't seem to bother the two German-born old Dough-boys I visited with that they were going back to fight against their old homeland.

"I was living in Yorkville[1] at the time," said John Schultz, "when I left for the 82nd Division and later the Argonne. Yorkville had plenty of Germans then, but I can't remember no Kaiser lovers at all there. Hell, that's why they'd left Germany, to get away from

[1] A once very heavily German-populated area on the East Side of Manhattan.

people like him. I knew plenty of other German Americans who went to war."

Schultz is certainly right. There were hundreds of new Americans who marched against the Fatherland, many of them in such midwestern divisions as the 32nd and 89th. They piled up a great record, as did the other immigrants. Two of these foreign-born soldiers that I talked to, Gilbertie and Jack Herschowitz (born in Romania), were awarded the Distinguished Service Cross. New York City's Irish-born old 69th compiled one of the great records of the war, while the 77th Division, which probably had as large a contingent of new Americans as any unit in the AEF, gave American history the legendary Lost Battalion. It was a period when the United States was indeed the hope of the world. These immigrants wanted everyone to know that they were part of it.

O'Neill of the Ourcq

Richard W. O'Neill

HIS HOME, BRONXVILLE, NEW YORK, AUGUST 1976
What makes a hero? This is a question that has baffled the sages since the beginning of time.

Why does a George Dilboy, 103rd Infantry, 26th Division, shoot it out face to face with a German machine-gun crew and, although mortally wounded, keep firing his Springfield rifle until the Germans are annihilated, thus undoubtedly saving the lives of several of his buddies?

Or a Thomas Pope, 131st Infantry, 33rd Division—what is his motivation when he jumps into another Maxim nest, flashing his bayonet and accomplishing the same results as Dilboy?

These men must have surely realized that their chances of survival were small. Yet they performed acts of extraordinary heroics far beyond the call of duty. They both were among the ninety-six members of the AEF to be awarded the Congressional Medal of Honor.

Another Doughboy to receive the CMH was Dick O'Neill of the 69th New York Irish. When I visited with Mr. O'Neill, I could not help but ask him what was going through his mind on the morning of July 28, 1918, when his heroics near the Ourcq River earned him his country's highest award for bravery.

"Well," he said, "Donovan [Major, later General, William Donovan, commanding officer of the 1st Battalion, 165th Infantry] had sent me out in charge of a mission of great importance. The success or failure of this mission would determine, in all probability, if or if not a good many of my buddies would be alive at day's end. This was uppermost in my mind when the scrap began. As for the action itself, it all happened so fast I can't really tell you what I was thinking. But I can tell you one thing: I had no desire to get killed. Who the hell does?"

Then he changed the subject. "Oh that Donovan," he snickered, "you know, I served with him again in World War II. He asked me to show up for a briefing one time at the Washington Airport. I ended up in Brazil. What a man he was!"

Most of O'Neill's civilian life was spent in the steel business. Today, as he approaches his eightieth birthday, he lives in a very pleasant Bronxville apartment and enjoys his retirement. He does make regular trips to the Veterans' Administration Hospital to allow the doctors to keep track of some 1918 German lead that he is still carrying in his body.

"Why," his charming wife told me, "it was just a few years ago that some shrapnel came so close to the surface that I took it out with tweezers."

Dick told me the story of his show near the Ourcq River. I also checked the official records; Dick O'Neill is modest.

Sergeant Richard W. O'Neill

B Company, 165th Infantry (69th NYNG), 42nd
(Rainbow) Division
Holder of the Congressional Medal of Honor

It is only natural, I suppose, to be proud of being the recipient of our glorious nation's highest military award, but it has always been my honest contention that when an individual is chosen to be the recipient of that award, it is a grateful nation's way of recognizing the overall fighting qualities and selfless sacrifices of *all members* of the Unit in which the recipient served, especially the *sacred combat dead.*"

—DICK O'NEILL

What an outfit we had! Of course, I'm bound to be biased, understand. But really, there was something a little special about the old 69th. Maybe it was because of the large amount of Irish-born in the regiment. They had known how hard it was in Ireland, and they had a particularly strong feeling toward America. I think most of those who had come from the other side felt that way. My mother was a native New Yorker, but my father was a County Clare man. When he first left Ireland, he went to Liverpool, England. Hell, he used to work fourteen, sixteen hours a day, trying to make ends meet there. He did much better in this country, and he appreciated it. And so did most of the men who came over.

Of course, they felt they were a little special. Oh they accepted those who had been born here, but they did call us narrow backs. And were they characters! I remember one time in France, before we went into the trenches. I had just received several packages from home. One of these was a carton of cigarettes. Now, I didn't smoke, and these four or five Irishmen eying me and the cigarettes knew it. They turned their backs and started to talk in hush-hush tones—they sounded like people who had learned to whisper in a boiler factory.

"That Dick O'Neill, he's the finest sergeant in the 69th."

"The 69th, yuh say—in the whole goddamn division, I say!"

"The two of yuh are wrong—it's in the whole American Army. He's a fair man, and a brave one at that. He could chase these damn Heinies back to Germany all alone."

Then they turned around with these surprised looks on their faces.

"Oh Sergeant, darlin', we didn't know yuh were there. But we mean it."

"Indeed, indeed, sure and we do!"

Now, what could you say about men like these? I knew they were putting one over on me. But what the hell could I do? I threw them the cigarettes.

Well, I wanted to tell you that so you'd have some kind of an idea what the 69th was like. I think all of New York's Irish were proud of it. As for myself, I was nineteen when the rumors started about the regiment going down to the Mexican border. It sounded great to me, so I joined up. It was May 22, 1916. And do you know it was exactly three years later to the day—May 22, 1919—that I was mustered out. And what a three years they were!

You see, our regiment was a little different. Most of the National Guard outfits had some time off between the border and the World War. Not the 69th. We stayed in right through.

In March of '17 we went to Washington, D.C., to be in Wilson's Inaugural Parade. By then it seemed quite obvious that Uncle Sam was going to go to war with Germany, so I guess the government felt what the hell, there's no sense in discharging these men now. We went back to New York to guard reservoirs and what have you. I think we even had some men guarding Grand Central Station. Washington was afraid that with all the German Americans we had in this country, there was bound to be some trouble. I can't remember that there was, though.

The border itself was a huge letdown. We ended up spending all those months hiking up and down the Rio Grande. We got in great shape, all right, but if anyone was killed, it was by boredom. The poor newspapermen were just as badly off as we were. They're getting all this pressure from back in New York to get some battle stories.

Then they got a big break. Some nut on the other side of the river took a potshot at one of our patrols. Oh this was great! Our men could shoot back, anything for a little excitement. But it was all over in a few minutes, with no one getting hit. Well, Jeez, one of the papers, I think it was the *Journal,* broke out these huge headlines, "69th in Big Battle with the Mexicans." You can imagine what concern this caused back home. What a mess! Even the governor was upset. It took a long time to straighten that out.

There was one other incident to relieve our boredom. I can't remember the name of the Mexican town this happened in, but it was directly across the river from us. I had binoculars, so I really had a front-row seat.

Well, this band of rebels attacked the town. It wasn't much of a battle—a lot of firing, then the rebels rode away, leaving one of their group stretched out on the ground. Then I'll be damned if every one in the town didn't come out and take a shot at the poor guy. He must have looked like a piece of Swiss cheese; it was sickening.

All in all, though, you have to call the whole border thing a farce except for one thing: It gave the National Guard outfits a military feeling that helped a great deal when Congress did declare war on Germany. Remember, four of the six divisions to be in France by the first of March 1918 were Guard outfits.

Ours was the 42nd, soon to be called the Rainbow. And we owed that name to none other than Douglas MacArthur. What an officer he was, a peach! He commanded the Rainbow, you know, at the very end. But back at the beginning he was chief of staff for the division.

Now, the government wanted to get a division, made up of men from states throughout the country, to France as soon as possible. At that time we had the old square divisions with four infantry regiments, three artillery ones, three machine-gun battalions, and all these other units such as MPs, medical groups, etc.—there were a total of twenty-six different organizations in each division.

Well, according to what we heard, MacArthur and Newton Baker [the Secretary of War] were deciding on how they would set the division up when Mac came up with the name.

"Mr. Secretary," he said, "the 42nd will have National Guard outfits from all these states; it will cross the country like a rainbow. Why not call it 'the Rainbow Division'?—a rainbow across the land." And that was it.

We were to be one of the infantry regiments, along with the 4th Ohio, 3rd Iowa, and 4th Alabama. And we all got along fine. I know that movie *The Fighting 69th* shows us having some trouble with the Alabama boys. Maybe so, but I don't remember it. And that movie was the biggest phony that ever came down the pike anyway! None of the old 69th people gave a damn about it.

We were now the 165th U. S. Infantry. Along with the 166th (the Ohioans) we made up the 83rd Brigade—that's the way we did it then, two regiments to a brigade. Hell, we had over seven thousand men in our brigade—it was almost as big as some of the French and British divisions all by itself.

Our gathering place was Camp Mills, Long Island. It was here that they started to turn us into a division. And it was here that I got to know our battalion commander, Major William Joseph Donovan. Now, let me point out that my son is named William Donovan O'Neill; that should tell you what I thought about him. But he surely worked us that summer at Mills. But I ask you, was there any other way to get us ready for what was coming? And it came fast enough. We started our trip for France in September 1917, finally landing at Le Havre on November 1. There'll always be a big controversy over which National Guard division landed first, ours or the 26th. They always told us we were the first complete one there. But what difference does it make? Both the Rainbow and the Yankee were there with plenty of time for the war. And that 26th was a good outfit also.

After we landed they shipped us over to Alsace-Lorraine, and it was here that our troubles really began. The hell of it was the foulup in clothing. Here we were in the Vosges Mountain area, with what was to be one of the worst winters in French history be-

ginning, and half the men didn't have their overcoats. Can you
imagine that? Hardly any of them had winter brogans—many were
walking around in those light shoes you'd wear in a dress parade
during the summer. Why, the next thing you knew a lot of the boys
had rags on their feet. And the blankets—we had lightweight summer ones until the first of the year.

I can't say the food supplies were much better. Here, look, this is
a diary I kept that winter:

"December 7: hiked 10 kilometers. Food—coffee like water, luke-
warm—a few strips of bacon—all we had that day. December 10:
hiked ten kilometers—many of the men without shoes—weather
freezing. One meal, some kind of stew."

Now, it wasn't that we didn't have equipment in France. They
just had trouble getting it to us, that's all. But how the boys did
suffer! Nothing was worse than Christmas. We went to Mass in a
cathedral Christmas Eve and the next day had one tiny meal, that
rotten coffee again, and some kind of meat, and a small portion at
that.

At about this time I was sent to a place called Mission. My job
was to set up barns and sheds for the enlisted men, and houses, if
possible, for the officers. I don't know how far it was but because of
the weather, it took me ten days. Most of the time I had to walk,
even though I did hitch a ride or two on farmers' wagons. Once I
even jumped up on a French caisson for a few miles. All in all, that
trip had to be one of the low points of the war for me. At least
when we were doing all that marching down at the border, we
didn't have to worry about frozen feet.

Well, I set things up as best I could, even recruiting many of the
French women to help with the food until the rolling kitchen arrived. A while later the first battalion arrived. There was a little im-
provement in the weather and we did get a chance for some real
training. We needed it.

Then in March we moved into a place called Luneville for our
first spell in the trenches. We were to spend our next four months
here and over at Baccarat going in and out of the trenches.

I can't say this was pleasant, but the real brutal stuff, for D Company anyway, was still a while away. One of our companies took a
real pasting at a place called Rouge Bouquet, where they lost
twenty-four men in a cave-in, but all in all, the worst thing about it

was the living conditions—the mud, the cooties, the rats—just lousy living, that's all.

One of the few good things about our trench tours was the opportunity it allowed me to really establish a friendship with Major Donovan. It was a friendship that would last through two World Wars until 1959, when Bill died.

You know, they always called him "Wild Bill," but not because he was irrational. There had been a manager of the New York Highlanders [later the Yankees] named "Wild Bill" Donovan—that's where Bill got the nickname. In reality, he was anything but. Actually, he was the calmest man under fire I ever saw. Oh you'd think he was standing at the corner of Broadway and Forty-second Street, not in the middle of a barrage.

And he was always in the middle of everything—Bill was no dugout officer. That's why he was such a great leader. Once the men realized that the major was going to keep calm no matter what happened, they began to count on him to do the right thing.

I'll never forget a conversation we had later on when I had to take over command of the company.

"O'Neill," he said to me, "these are great soldiers; they'll take hell with bayonets if they're properly led." And with Donovan leading us, we might have done just that.

Well, after our time in the trenches, we moved into the Champagne sector, where we really got to fight the war. First, we played our part in stopping the last German drive, then we attacked in an area around the Ourcq River. From then on, the Germans were on the defensive until the Armistice.

First came the Champagne defense. Here we were part of Gouraud's Fourth French Army, holding the center of the line. Gouraud was a real old campaigner, with an empty sleeve and a stiff leg from wounds. I think he lost the arm at Gallipoli.

Now, the way we heard it was that MacArthur gave the French the idea for the defense. We knew the Germans were going to attack, so Mac told the French to leave just a few men in the front-line trenches, but to beef up the second line. The Rainbow was right in the middle, with French on either side. None of our battalion was actually in the first trench line; our job was to wait and see what happened. And that waiting was bad business, particularly when the shelling started.

While we had no way of knowing it, this was to be the end of Ludendorff's final offensive. If we could stop them here, at the road to Chalons-sur-Marne, we could start the counterattack that Foch had planned.

Well, I think it was about seven o'clock the morning of July 15 that the Germans came over. Naturally, they had no trouble at first. Most of our men got out of the first-line trenches in a hurry as planned. And were those Germans happy! They thought they'd won a big battle, you see. We could hear them laughing, cheering, singing—it was really a little sad.

Then our concentrated barrage opened up. Oh my Christ, did it ever shock those Heinies! Our artillery had a field day. They'd measured the exact position of the trenches and knew just where those Germans had stopped. It was like ducks in a shooting gallery.

But these were the Prussian Guards. They weren't quite stopped yet. What was left of them kept coming at us. It varied up and down the line depending on the amount of troops. In several areas they reached the second-line trenches, where it turned into a real vicious hand-to-hand affair.

I think it was our second battalion that took it the worst in the 69th. They had some real rough stuff. And they had a couple of great stories to tell.

In one of them four Germans, each with this huge red cross on his arm, were toting a stretcher up to the lines. When they got close enough to us, they threw this blanket off the stretcher and opened up with a machine gun. You can bet those four never saw ze father in ze Fatherland again. Still another group tried to infiltrate our lines dressed in French uniforms. They were also shot down. All in all, I think the Rainbow held its own that day.

Of course, I've been just talking about our regiment because a front-line soldier rarely gets involved with anything larger. And that's pretty high up at that—usually your thinking doesn't go any higher than your battalion.

My point is that there were probably over two hundred thousand Germans attacking along a line of several miles. In some areas I heard they'd made small breakthroughs, but were shortly driven back. From then on until November 11 the Boche were headed the other way. Let me add one more thing before I go into our move to the Ourcq River—I really should tell you this, as it was just about the most incredible thing I saw in France. I can't tell you the day and the hour, but it did happen while we were there in the Champagne sector.

Now, I'll bet you very few Americans realize that we fought alongside of Polish troops in 1918. Well, we did. They were called the Paderewski Brigade because he had raised them. I guess they figured they could have an independent country of their own if they ended up on the winning side. It did turn out that way, but very few of the Polish soldiers that we saw lived to see it—not if what they did at Champagne was any indication of their officers, anyway.

I was standing in a trench when I heard a sound of marching men. I looked over and saw these Polish soldiers moving up the Chalons road. My God, you'd think they were strutting down Fifth Avenue on the seventeenth of March—why, they were actually in close formation in broad daylight. How in the hell they ever thought they'd get away with it I'll never know.

The Germans spotted them, of course, probably from a balloon or a plane. Then they opened up with their artillery. It was plain suicide—I doubt like hell if more than 10 per cent of them weren't hit. And the saddest part was they accomplished absolutely nothing. What a waste!

Well, as I've said, our next stop was over near the Ourcq. Oh we had a few days to recuperate, but the first thing we knew they loaded us on those 40 and 8's for a short ride down near Château-Thierry. They'd been fighting like hell here just a few days before, and we had a first-hand view of the destruction. The area looked as if a cyclone had hit it.

I can't remember where they let us off, but wherever it was they piled us onto these camions for our jaunt to where the Germans were. These camions seemed to be a cross between a bus and a truck. They were driven by Vietnamese. Naturally, we called them Chinks—I doubt if any of the boys had even heard of Vietnamese then.

Now, the Ourcq itself was what we'd call a creek back home. I can particularly remember one of our boys taking one look at it with disgust.

"If this is a river," he croaked, "the Hudson must be an ocean."

River or not, the Germans thought enough of it to have some

very tough *hombres,* including the 4th Imperial Prussian Foot-guard, trying to hold it. Between working our way up to it and finally crossing the damn thing, the 69th experienced just about as tough a fight as it ever had. It was attack, face their counterattack, and attack again. It may be almost sixty years ago, but there are many little things that still stick in my mind about that last week in July of '18.

One of them concerns this grand old Irish sergeant, Tom O'Malley. It happened at Dead Man's Curve just as we were ready to hit the Germans, not far from Meurcy Farm. We were taking a little rest when a couple of officers came by and asked Tom for Company D's commanding officer.

"Sure and there're no officers here," O'Malley told them. "Oh we'd see them all the time back at the camp; Christ, you'd be tripping over 'em! But here, none atall."

"Then we'd better give you a temporary commission, O'Malley. These men can't go against the Germans without an officer."

"What, Tom O'Malley an officer, the devil you say? No Sam Browne belt for me! Now, take that nice young man Dick O'Neill—we'll make Dick the acting captain. I'll see the boys do what he says."

And that's how I was given temporary command of Company D. I was twenty years of age. Hell, O'Malley knew much more about soldiering than I did—I wanted him to have command myself. But we all got a kick out of his crack, "No Sam Browne belt for me!"

Of course, it's the events of the thirtieth of July that have stayed with me the longest, even though my actual fight with the twenty-five Germans is a little hazy. Then again, it always was. When you keep getting hit with bullets and you're fighting as hard as you can to stay alive, you're reacting by instinct.

Strangely enough, one of the things that stands out in my mind is what a beautiful morning it was and how nice it would have been to take a walk through that French countryside. What a contrast between the scenic beauty and the shelling! I said to myself, "Dick, this is a hell of a morning to pick to get killed!"

My pessimism was due to the job Donovan had given us. We knew there were machine guns up ahead but not how many or where. We were to find out where they had them so our artillery could zero in. It was, however, the major's final words that stuck in my mind.

"Dick," he said, "it would be a lot better if your boys could knock out those guns. We could move faster."

Well, we found their machine guns soon enough and went after them; I had thirty-two men with me.

It didn't take the Germans long to open up on us. Christ, there were bullets flying all around. One of them knocked the rifle out of my hand, but being a sergeant, I still had my pistol. I didn't realize it at the time, but I was running so fast that I was way out in front of the men I was leading.

The first thing I knew I climbed this ridge and almost fell into this large gravel pit. Then I got the shock of my life. The hole was filled with about twenty-five Germans and several machine guns. The only thing that saved me was the fact that they were as surprised as I was. I threw a grenade or two and started firing my pistol—of course, they started firing at the same time. They hit me with four or five shots, maybe six, but they weren't bad enough to knock me over; amazingly enough, they were all flesh wounds.

I knew I'd been doing better against them because I could see these gray-clad figures falling over. They later told me there were five dead Germans in the gravel pit—two of them being noncoms. I guess this panicked the rest because they all started to surrender.

Oh, it all sounds great, all right, but put yourself in my place. Here I am with twenty or so Heinie prisoners smack on top of the German lines. They're all jabbering away a mile a minute while I'm pointing a pistol at them that probably didn't have any rounds left in it. I was the one in a hell of a spot, but I guess these Krauts didn't know it.

Anyway, I figured the only thing to do was hike them back to our lines. It seemed like a good idea at the time, but Jeez, we'd no sooner started when whack, a couple of other German machine gunners over on my left opened up on us. They knocked the bejesus out of me, but they also chopped down their own men like cordwood.

Hell, I'd already been hit in one of my legs in the gravel pit—now they really punctured the other one. I couldn't walk, couldn't even crawl. But I could roll—so over and over I barreled down the ridge with their machine-gun fire bouncing all around me. And two more of those damn German bullets didn't miss!

I finally reached the cover of some woods, where some of our men grabbed me. One of my Irish buddies, named Pat, took one look at me and sighed.

"Jee-sus, Dick me boy, you're leaking all over the place! I should carry yuh back on me back."

Well, I knew he wanted to get out of the fighting. Then another Irishman came over.

"And where the hell do yuh think you're going?"

"Oh I want to take care of the sergeant."

"And not yourself, Pat—get back over there. Someone will get the sergeant."

So poor Pat went back over where he belonged, and wouldn't you know it, Pat was killed within the hour.

A short time later two men rolled me in a blanket and headed for a dressing station. Oh I wanted to get patched up, all right, but not before I told Major Donovan precisely where those German machine guns were. The 2nd Battalion was going to attack in that area, and I figured they wouldn't spot them until they'd lost a lot of men. The boys carrying me in the blanket started to argue with me about it.

"I'm not going anywhere," I told them, "until I tell the major where those machine guns are." So they took me to Donovan. I gave him a report, and then I think I collapsed.

My next step landed me in a damn good hospital run by a Jewish group from back home. I think it was connected with New York Hospital. And what a great job they did on me! I was lucky in one respect: None of the bullets had really injured a vital spot. I was also young and healthy, which greatly aided my recovery. The first thing I knew I reached a point where I was really itching to get back with the 69th. When the word came back on how rough things were up in the Argonne, I couldn't take it any longer, so I cornered my doctor.

"Look," I told him, "I could go ten rounds with Jess Willard; I want to get back with my outfit."

"Oh for Christ's sake, O'Neill," he answered, "you looked like a pincushion when they brought you in. You've had your war!"

Well, it went on like this for a few days until I wore him down; then he finally gave up.

"All right, all right," he said, "you're driving us all nuts. If you want to kill yourself, go ahead, but I won't be responsible for you." I moved out as quickly as I could and headed for the 69th.[1]

I joined the boys sometime in October, right in the middle of that donneybrook called the Meuse-Argonne. I was shocked to find so few of the old-timers left. And with that nasty grinding-out stuff, it was fewer every day. The Germans even badly wounded my old friend Sergeant Tom O'Malley. There he was, lying there calmly smoking his pipe.

"Don't worry none about me, boys," he said, "I'll be foine, just foine." And he did make it back home.

It was beginning to get to me also. I took some shrapnel wounds up there, but compared to what happened at the Ourcq, I always figured they didn't count. I did start to occasionally get dizzy spells, but I was determined to stick it out.

Then, on November 8, when we were all tangled up in that mess to see who was going to take Sedan, I collapsed and was out cold for days. When I finally woke up, I was in a hospital bed with clean white sheets, looking out a window right into a beautifully bright dawning. When I turned my head, I saw this smiling nurse with a sparkling starched white uniform.

"Well, holy Christ," I said to myself, "I'm finally dead, and here's an angel. Thank God I'm in heaven and not the other place!" Then the angel started to talk.

"Good morning, Sergeant, I know you'll be glad to know it's all over."

"What's over?"

"Why, the war, of course."

"It is not. Why . . ." Then I began to realize where I was.

---

[1] One report says that the sergeant went AWOL to get back to the 69th. Dick did not say this, only that they did not want him to go back.

"Down on the Border"

You guys think this is bad—hell, you should have been 'down on the border.'

—PROBABLY SAID, WITH SARCASM,
A MILLION TIMES IN 1918 FRANCE

When most people hear of the Mexican border campaign in 1916, they normally shrug it off.

"Oh yeah," they'll say, "that *bandito*, Pancho Villa—you know, the one Wallace Beery played in the movies—he raided some American town,[1] so Wilson sent Pershing into Mexico. But the whole thing never amounted to much." Actually, there was a great deal more to it than that.

Starting roughly in 1910 and going into the 1920s, Mexico was in a constant state of turbulence—revolution followed revolution, and government followed government, in what appeared to be an endless bloodletting. The multinational aspects of the United States were in their primitive stages at that time, but based on 1977 currency, America's Mexican investments in 1916 ran into many millions of dollars. It was thus only natural that American citizens were constantly being caught in the middle, south of the border, and frequently paid for this mistake with their lives. In one case

[1] Columbia, New Mexico, March 9, 1916. In reality, Villa's raid proved quite a disaster for the old rascal. He lost over a hundred men and grabbed very little plunder. The Mexican casualties were about five times that of the Americans.

some revolutionaries stopped a train and took all twenty American passengers off. The Mexicans then lined their captives up and summarily executed nineteen of them—one escaped by feigning death. Mexico during the first part of this century was not a healthy place for the *gringos*.

The U.S. media played each incident to the hilt, and not a one lost anything in the telling. By March of 1916, when Pershing actually crossed into Mexico, a great many Americans expected war between the two countries. One of these was a man named Walter (Kiddy) Karr. I visited with Mr. Karr at the 94th Aerosquadron Restaurant in San Diego. While most of our conversation dwelled on his days as a 1918 naval pilot in France, he also talked freely about his days on the border.

"I joined the Army in 1916 at age eighteen because I felt sure we'd be fighting Mexico." Then he told me what a farce the whole thing was for those regulars who stayed on the border.

"We'd be doing guard duty on one side of the Rio Grande and there'd be Mexicans on the other side, glaring at us. We never knew if they were bandits or regular soldiers, but whatever they were, they'd frequently take shots at us. They never hit anyone, but it surely was a pain in the neck. We weren't allowed to carry any bullets when we went on duty, so we couldn't shoot back.

"Well, after a few weeks of this nonsense, I said the hell with this; I wrote a friend of mine back home and asked him to send us some .30-caliber ammunition. He sent it, all right, and did we ever surprise those clowns across the river when we started shooting back. I caught the 'old Harry' for doing it, but it ended their damn sniping at us."

As frustrating as the border campaign was for the regulars, it was twice as disappointing for the National Guard—those 125,000 civilian-soldiers who were called up by President Wilson. It was a particularly devastating letdown for such outfits as Hartford, Connecticut's B Troop, New Jersey's Essex Troop, and New York City's A Squadron. These National Guard units, and many like them, were really a combination of military and social clubs who immensely enjoyed horseback riding on the weekends. The thought of going down to Mexico and chasing bandits sounded great to a generation who'd been exposed to countless silent motion pictures showing men like William S. Hart riding off into the sunset.[2]

Twelve of the men I interviewed were among those Guardsmen who had been called up. To a man they all complained of two things: heat and boredom. To one of them, Walter Guild, it started out great.

"I was in a mounted troop,"[3] Mr. Guild told me, "and we could at least go on long patrols. But even that became boring after a while. I hope you realize that Wilson didn't call us back home until after the election of '16; he wouldn't have received a single vote from my outfit.

"I'll tell you one thing," continued Walter, and at this he chuckled, "I can clearly remember, and that's how they handled the VD problem. A few of our men came down with it, which infuriated our colonel. He arranged for us all to visit a VD ward at a hospital in San Antonio. Remember, this was before penicillin, and oh what a mess most of those patients were. When I was a colonel in World War II, we had all those training films showing the effects of VD, but nothing ever struck me the same as seeing those poor slobs in that San Antonio VD ward." Mr. Guild also added that he felt the large majority of his troop who had been down on the border ended up going overseas in 1917.

This raises a question that can never be answered: "Was the calling up of the Guard necessary, or was it just done to prepare some military-minded civilians for France?" Each Guardsman I talked to is sure the latter is true, even though President Wilson always denied it. Anyway, the first six U.S. divisions to go to France were loaded with "border men." They never forgot it, and they never let anyone else forget it, either.

[2] One of the Hartford men I talked to gave me a quote from Mrs. Hepburn, the mother of Katharine, the actress. It seems that when she heard that B Troop had been called up, she exclaimed, "Ye gods, don't tell me those Sunday cowboys are actually going to war!"

[3] C Troop, 1st Massachusetts Cavalry.

The Guest of the Kaiser

Michael Shallin

THE YALE CLUB, NEW YORK CITY, MARCH 1976
When Mr. Shallin and I enjoyed a drink together in New York City
he was eighty-two years of age and in excellent health. He talked
of his days spent in the housing development industry and of his
family. He seemed to take great pleasure in describing the various
aspects of his son's musical career.

"But when my son's time came to go into the service for World
War II," Mr. Shallin told me, "I said to him, 'Go into the Navy; I
did all the sleeping in the rain for this family.'"

Most of all, Mike enjoyed talking about his old outfit, the 308th
Infantry of the 77th Division.

"We still hold our meetings at the Williams Club," he said, "not
because we went to Williams but because of Whittlesey—he was a
Williams man. They have a great deal of his stuff there. Isn't that
something! The major's been dead for fifty-odd years, and we still
meet there!"

Corporal Mike Shallin
L Company, 308th Infantry, 77th Division

Good-bye, Broadway, hello, France,
We're ten million strong.
Good-bye, mothers, sisters, brothers,
We won't be gone long.

Don't you worry while we're gone;
It's you we're fighting for.
Good-bye, Broadway, hello, France,
We're here to see you win that war.

When my turn to be drafted came, it didn't bother me at all. As a matter of fact, if I hadn't been drafted, I think I would have gone anyway. Both my parents had been Jewish immigrants from Europe, and this country had been good to our family. Besides, I had been born in Brooklyn, so I was as much an American as anybody.

My group was sent to Camp Upton out at Yaphank, Long Island—you know, that's the place Irving Berlin named his show *Yip, Yip, Yaphank* after. We were to make up one of the first national Army divisions, the 77th. At that time they had three types: the regulars, the National Guard, and the new national Army divisions. But hell, that all went out the window during the summer of '18 in France. Everyone coming over then was a draftee, so they just called us what they should have, U. S. Army divisions.

I became part of the 308th U. S. Infantry Regiment, almost all of the original members coming from New York City.

Well, let me tell you, that winter of '17 and '18 was no bargain at Upton. I think it was one of the coldest on record. We had one day when it reached 13 below zero, and that's cold. I froze my nose, and here I am eighty-two and the damn thing still bothers me.

Now, believe it or not, most of us were itching to go to the other side. All that drilling in the winter was beginning to drive us nuts. The same daily routine was a pain in the ass. If we were there to fight Germans, let's go fight them. That's the way my group, L Company, felt, anyway.

To make matters worse, we had this sergeant who was a regular. He didn't make himself very popular by complaining about what lousy soldiers we were.

"How the hell can we win the war with stuff like you?" he'd carp. "You're going to run the minute you smell a German."

So you know what? The minute we ran into a little shelling around Lorraine, who do you think is useless? The brave sergeant, that's who; they had to send him home to train troops. The poor guy was back in the States for only a month or two before he died of the flu. It just went to prove what we were all saying at the time: "If your number's up, you're going to get it, and that's it."

Well, when spring came, we all boarded a British ship called the *Justian,* and we were on our merry way. It was hardly a joy ride. It seems all they kept feeding us was rabbit stew, and, I swear, it still had the fur on it.

Then there was this limey sailor who would walk throughout the ship at about 5:00 A.M. yelling, "Arise, arise, ye sons of the King." You can imagine how this went over with a bunch of boys from New York City. Someone would always yell back, "Lie down, lie down, ye son-of-a-bitch."

We took the normal zigzag course, landing at Liverpool about thirteen days later. Then they hustled us over to Dover, where we were to embark for France.

The one thing I can remember about our short stay in England was how tired the people looked, really exhausted. This one old lady in particular who came over to greet us when we were standing on the train platform asked, "Did ye come over to die?"

"Well, lady, I hope not, not if I can help it," I answered.

By this time all the boys were laughing like hell, which seemed to puzzle the old lady.

"No, no," she emphasized, "what I mean is, did ye just arrive?"

You see, what she had been saying was, "Did ye come over today?" It was one of our early experiences with the cockney language, but it was just the beginning.

The reason we had stopped in England was so we could take a Channel boat across to Calais. This was in April of '18, and the plan then was to brigade us with the English on the northern end of the line.

Then our real training started. The first thing we had to do was change our Remington rifles for their Enfields. What we really wanted were Springfields; they were the best rifles in the war. But, do you know, we didn't have nearly enough to go around. It seems to me that most of the AEF had either Remingtons or Enfields.

The next step was to learn how to handle our new rifles, so they sent us to musketry school, as the English called it.

Here we saw something that really gave us a chill, made us wonder why we had left old Broadway to come over and try to help these people. As we were marching by we saw this Tommy standing on a stump talking to a large crowd of British soldiers.

"Look at yah," he snarled, "all praying each day for a 'blighty.' Yah'd probably trade an arm or a leg to get back home. To hell with 'em all. Why don't we just walk away, like they done in Russia?"

Of course, they all didn't buy this horseshit—there were plenty of both boos and cheers to be heard.

"Hell, matey,' one of them yelled, "yah sound like yah want to lose the bloody war."

"To hell with the war," came the speaker's retort. "It don't put any shillings in my pocket."

"Oh that's nice," yells this other Tommy, "what about our King and Queen?"

"Fuck the King and fuck the Queen," was the answer.

Of course, we're all in a kinda shock. We'd been hearing all this talk about the gallant Tommies defending poor little Belgium. Then we hear this.

And the speaker wasn't through; I can remember exactly what he said next:

"Mates," he pleaded, "all I want is a bloody piece of bread. I don't give a damn if it's from a King or a Kaiser."

What had happened was simple. As I said earlier, the English were exhausted. Remember, they'd been bled white for almost four years. The Bolsheviks knew this, and they'd planted radicals in all the armies, Allied and German. I don't think they tried hard in ours, though. After all, we were still new and eager.

After we'd learned all about the Enfield, the British started on their favorite weapon, the bayonet.

"In the crotch, in the crotch," this sergeant would yell at us. "If you come at 'im from underneath, you'll stop 'im for sure. And I'll tell yah bloody Yanks another thing," he'd say. "If the Boche comes out with 'is 'ands up yelling '*Komerad*,' give 'im the bayonet in 'is bloody balls. Sure as 'ell 'e's got a potato masher in one of those 'ands."

In the meantime, after we'd tried to learn all about soldiering with the British, the order came down that we were to head South and join the rest of the Americans. Then came the biggest surprise of all: They gave us back our Remingtons. Can you beat that? All that Enfield training for nothing.

The next thing they do is to load us in those 40 and 8's for our trip South to Lorraine. It took all of two days and two nights because of the stop-and-go patterns. It also gave us a chance to learn something of the French farmers. Whenever we'd stop for a while, we'd hang out the window, asking them to fill our canteens. Oh they'd fill them all right—*for a price*. And there was plenty of water in France.

As my mother was Alsatian, I could speak both French and German. I finally asked one French peasant woman how they could do this to brave men who'd come all the way across the ocean to help them. She smiled at me.

"*Les Américains*," she sighed, "*beaucoup d'argent*."

We realized that the French had been through a hell of a lot, but, you know, I think they really hurt the feelings of many of our men. After all, we were New Yorkers—we knew that all these jerkwater towns would up their prices when we'd pass through. There's nothing a New Yorker hates any more than having a rube take him for a ride.

At Lorraine we went through the standard support—reserve—

front-line pattern. It really wasn't bad, particularly when you were in support. Then you'd usually live in a barn, get hot food, and get a chance to bathe in a stream.

That brings up a good one. We all went into this little river one time to wash away the grime. Naturally, we were in the buff. The first thing we knew all the women in the village were pointing at us and giggling away *en français*. Of course, I knew what they were saying. They were playing a little game trying to pick out which of us had the longest one. The poor things; remember, almost all their men were either dead or at the front.

It was here in Lorraine that we relieved the Rainbow Division. I'll never forget the night we passed them—they were going out, and we were coming in.

Someone yelled out, "Hey, is that the 69th New York over there?"

And this guy yells back, "Yeah, you the 308th?"

Well, I'll tell you—all these guys are yelling back and forth, looking for friends and cousins. They tell me an Irish lad in our outfit even talked to his brother. Then it happened. I don't know if it started from them or us, but this voice opened up with:

> East Side, West Side,
> All around the town
> The tots sing, "Ring Around Rosie,"
> "London Bridge Is Falling Down."

The first thing you know, we're all singing it, and so are they. It was great, but I was more homesick than any other time in France. I don't know if the Heinies could hear us or not, but if they could, they must have thought we were crazy. Anyway, the next day this German balloon had a sign, "Good-bye, 42nd. Hello, 77th."

Then, I think it was August, the ball opened in earnest for us when we moved into the Vesle River area. You might say we moved into hell. The shelling, the night patrols into no-man's-land, and those damn raids the Germans would make into our lines were all brutal. Our company lost two lieutenants on the same night while we were there. I can also remember when we were trying to move the Germans out of these caves seeing the captain's orderly actually decapitated. The man who was standing next to him fell down in a heap—he was shell-shocked to such an extent that he was paralyzed. They had to literally carry him out; I don't know if he ever regained his senses or not.

We finally crossed the Vesle River, but not in a very glamorous way. The engineers had found a narrow spot and merely laid a couple of planks across the Vesle, and the first thing we knew we were on the other side. I can remember one of the boys saying "big deal" as we went across.

So here we are, trying to push the Germans back constantly. The only problem was they didn't want to go. And that's how I ended up in the soup.

It all happened on September 5, a few weeks before my outfit moved into the Meuse-Argonne mess. I was in charge of my squad, a rifle grenadier one. You know, those are the ones that shoot out those small bombs like a grenade. The only problem was we didn't have any bombs, so we weren't any stronger with firepower than the rest of our group.

Well, we're moving up through this tough terrain when we spotted some men in the distance who appeared to be running toward us. We had been told to be very careful who we shot at, as the area was loaded with our patrols. These men kept getting closer, and our lead man kept watching them.

"Don't shoot at those guys," he instructed us. "I think they're our scouts." But now we're all looking at them and getting concerned.

"The hell they are," I warned. "I think they're Germans."

Just then they opened up on us with everything they had, tearing us into pieces. It was horrible. I'm not as sensitive as I used to be about it, but I can still hear this badly wounded buddy of mine yelling for his mother in Yiddish.

Well, we're naturally looking around trying to find someplace where we can set up a defense, but the first thing we knew they were on top of us. My sergeant and several of us had jumped into this old trench where we could see that the Germans were all around us, with one of them yelling, *Komerouse, Komerouse.* We didn't have a prayer, so they nabbed all thirty-two of us.

After we surrendered, as we were crawling out of the trench, one of our men takes a shot at a German sergeant, badly wounding him. Christ, all hell broke loose. We were lucky they didn't machine-gun all of us. As the German was lying on the ground, he's cursing the devil out of us, then he bawls out in German, "If you're not going to tell me who fired, I'll do away with all of you."

Fortunately for us, a German officer came over at this time, wanting to know what's going on. Now we can hear all the Heinies crowing in German a mile a minute, and we're scared to death. As for myself, I actually didn't know who fired, so there's not a darn thing I can say.

Finally, the officer tells the wounded man that he can pick out the one who fired; he can shoot him—no one else. Believe it or not, the sergeant points at our medic, the only one of our men who didn't carry a weapon. Then our sergeant gets into the act:

"Wait a minute," he pleads, "that man couldn't have done it—he didn't even have a gun."

At this point the German officer has had enough:

"Take them all back to the rear," he orders, "and don't shoot anyone." I've been thanking God for that officer ever since.

Then they started to march us toward their lines. Remember, the Germans had been there four years or so—they had developed real little communities back there. After we reached a certain point, they stuck us on a single-gauge railroad train that was something similar to what we used to have at Luna Park on Coney Island. We rode this "Toonerville Trolley" until we reached the prison camp. We stayed there for close to a month, and, let me tell you, this was the hellhole of the world. Our barracks had one door with a little window for the guards to look in—nothing more. The ventilation was dreadful, particularly as our only place to relieve ourselves was this big wooden bucket near the door. You can imagine what the smell was like.

We had to sleep on the floor, which knocked the hell out of our kidneys and bowels. The result was that all night long the men were going over to the bucket to take a leak or crap. Naturally, the damn bucket would frequently overflow—you can imagine what that was like. Then there were the fleas; they were everywhere. And the flies were just as bad. You'd spend all night relieving yourself, smelling, scratching, and swatting—with very little sleep.

And the food—God, it was awful. We had no utensils. They took us over to their dump so we could pick up some tin cans to eat with. Every evening they'd give each fifth man a loaf of bread to share with the other four. Naturally, the splitting of the bread was quite an occasion. Anyone who'd try to take more than his share was really in dutch. In the morning we'd get some coffee made out of barley, while the afternoon meal was supposed to be our real feast. This would be a ration of soup made from horseflesh and some kind of a turnip, the same type they fed to the pigs.

Sometime around the first of October they decided to move us into southern Germany, where our treatment changed completely. Everything was much better there—especially the food. I can honestly say that we were constantly allowed to receive the Red Cross food that was sent over for us. We wouldn't even eat the regular rations the Germans gave us; we didn't need them. We used to sneak them over to some French and Russian prisoners, who were practically starving to death. You see, the Germans always gave the best treatment possible to the Americans. As bad as things were at the first camp, the other prisoners always had it worse.

It was while they were taking us through southern Germany that we began to realize how sick the Germans were of the war. And how much they didn't want to fight the Americans. We stopped at one station where they let us off to stretch our legs. I spotted this German civilian with some cigarettes. Now, I hadn't had one since we were captured, and the smell of his tobacco was driving me nuts. I could speak German, so I walked over to him with this pleading look in my eye.

"Could I have one?" I asked.

He looked at me kinda funny and asked, "Are you an American prisoner of war?"

"Yes," I replied.

Do you know, he then gave me two. I still had a little bit of money left—that's another thing, the Germans had taken all our equipment, but not our money—so I offered him some.

"Nix," he said, *"nein, nein,* I have cousins in America, in Milwaukee; we should not fight you."

It was the same way with the guards at the camp. Hell, they were always talking about their relatives in America, hoping they weren't in the war. One guy told us he had once been a doorman in New York. He said to us one day:

"Vhen zis gotdam war is done, I go back to New York—Kaiser is Kaput."

As it became more and more obvious to the Germans that they were in trouble, they became even friendlier, allowing us all types of liberties. One of these concerned women. The guard would tell his officer that such-and-such a prisoner had a bad toothache. As there weren't any dentists at the prison, this meant a trip into town for the American and the guard. Here he could just about have his pick of the *Frauleins* for a bar of soap. You see, we were getting a regular supply from the Red Cross, while the Germans had practically none. The ironic part of the whole thing was that in most ways we were much better off than the German civilians.

Around the first part of November the rumors started to fly about an armistice. When it did come, the Germans actually celebrated. I don't think they gave a damn who won; it was over—that's all they cared about. Hell, you'd think we'd been allies. They'd come into the camp crowing, "Comrade, Comrade." A short while later, Red Cross trains started coming in from Switzerland to take us out. We were on our way home.

Looking back over six decades, there is one more unusual thing I can remember. I am Jewish; so were a lot of the other prisoners. I can't remember seeing one case of anti-Semitism on the part of the German soldiers or civilians. It took Hitler and his gangsters to develop that.

The Lost Battalion

FIRST DOUGHBOY: "Hey, I lost my watch!"

SECOND DOUGHBOY: "What are you harping about? A major over
                    in the 77th has lost a whole battalion!"

When writing a book about the AEF, one immediately thinks about the "Lost Battalion," truly one of the most famous military units in American history. It was right at the top of my list, and one of the first things I did was call the headquarters of the 77th Division, hoping they could help me locate a member of this heroic body of men. I was given the name of a Sam Leavitt in Brooklyn. I immediately called Mr. Leavitt on the telephone; Mrs. Leavitt answered. I had some trouble explaining to Mrs. Leavitt, who couldn't quite understand why her husband would want to buy a book on World War I, what my project was all about. After I did succeed, I received some news from this fine lady that I wasn't prepared for:

"I'm sitting *shiva*,"[1] said Mrs. Leavitt.

"I beg your pardon," I answered.

"Are you Jewish?"

"No."

"Well, I buried Sam yesterday."

I apologized profusely for bothering her at such a time. Then we chatted for a short while, after which I bid her *adieu*. Her last words were, "Oh how Sam loved the Lost Battalion!"

My next move was to once again call the 77th Division. They gave me four more names, and I went back to work. I could only locate one of these men, a Mike Shallin of the Bronx. Mr. Shallin said he certainly would see me, but as he'd been captured near the Vesle River on September 5, 1918, he'd missed the Lost Battalion's fight. Mike turned out to be a delightful fellow and a great interview, but I still did not have my Lost Battalion man.

But I hadn't realized what a nice guy Mike Shallin really is. About a year later I received a phone call from this veteran of the 308th. He had obtained the address of a Jack Herschowitz, one of Major Charles W. Whittlesey's (commander of the Lost Battalion) runners. Once again I was hot on the trail of a member of the famous besieged heroes of the Argonne Forest.

I called Mr. Herschowitz, but the old warrior seemed a bit wary; he finally asked me to write him a letter to explain what I was doing, and he'd think about it. Jack received my letter and called Doubleday to tell me that we could indeed get together. The only problem was he called the Doubleday Advertising Company, not

---

[1] A week's mourning period practiced by the widow, according to Orthodox custom.

the publishing company, where he ended up talking to a young lady named Ella Berry.

Then fate took a hand in my venture. Purely through a coincidence, I do know Ella Berry, even though we're not related. Ella told Mr. Herschowitz that she would relate the message to me. A week later I walked into Mr. Herschowitz's apartment in Great Neck, Long Island—my search for a Lost Battalion member had finally borne fruit.

Mr. Herschowitz's greeting was quite cordial. We sat down at a table where he, adorned in his Orthodox *yarmulke*, quickly showed his hospitality.

"A little scotch, maybe."

I agreed heartily.

"And a cigar."

Once again my answer was in the affirmative, which turned into one of my better decisions of the week. It was a tremendous smoke.

Then Mr. Herschowitz went back to his birth in Romania some eighty-seven years ago and began his story. His family had come to New York City at the turn of the century. Jack had taken quickly to the hurried, wide-open life of the melting pot. By the time 1917 rolled around, he and his brother had built up a healthy dried-food business. When Jack's turn to be drafted came, he wasn't very happy over it.

"I didn't feel like going—who wants to get killed?—so I first tried to get out of it—but vonce I was in there, I did it right. I remember vonce when I was carrying a message in Alsace-Lorraine, the German bullets started coming after me, but I knew I had to get through, so I grabbed a branch and used it like an umbrella. Look, I was a walking tree, but I delivered the message.

"Now, let me tell you, the shelling, oh you could get killed anytime. There was vonce when I was taking a message and I saw my good friend, Father Halligan, the Catholic chaplain.

"'Herschowitz,' he said, 'let's stop and talk.'

"'No, not now,' I said, 'I've got to get this message through.'

"So we both keep moving and bang, this big shell comes, right where we would have been standing. That Halligan, he was a very nice man.

"Oh I had lots of Catholic friends, but vone time they played a trick on me. I was staying in this nice home and these two Irish guys go to the lady who owns the house and they say, 'Look, how can a lady like you let Herschowitz stay at your home when he is a Catholic and doesn't go to Mass?' Oh does she get mad at me, she tells me to get out, *toute de suite*. I have to swear to her that I am a Jewish fellow, not a Catholic who does not go to church."

Mr. Herschowitz kept talking about his regiment while I was eagerly awaiting his memories of the Argonne. When he did reach September 26 in his narrative, it was obvious that his memory was excellent, especially about Major Charles W. Whittlesey.

"Oh he was a great guy, he was from Massachusetts, and what a tall guy and a fair officer—he liked his men. Poor fellow, he jumped overboard from a ship because he thought so much about the men killed over there."

Then Jack recalled the beginning of the Argonne battle on September 26.

"We go into the woods, with Whittlesey in front; he's got this big pistol pointed toward the Germans. Whittlesey, he was always in front, what a good officer, and me, I'm next to him, because I'm his runner. The Germans, they're shooting at us, some of them are even in the trees. We went forward for three days, but we went too far, see. Then Whittlesey finds out we can't go forward or backward, oh these Germans are everywhere!"

What I hadn't realized until visiting with Mr. Herschowitz was that Whittlesey's command was really cut off twice. The first time is what Jack is talking about. On September 29, the major, realizing that he was surrounded, designated Lieutenant Arthur McKeon, Joseph Monson, and Jack Herschowitz to make their way through the German lines and report the battalion's position to regimental headquarters. Jack always has felt that he was not one of McKeon's favorites.

"He called me a buttonhole maker," Jack told me, "but I wasn't one—that means a tailor—I wasn't a tailor. Well, when we started back toward the regiment, I was already sick, that flu, it was bad, and most of the time it was raining. We were trying to make our way back when we spotted this German. I pulled out my revolver and shot him. Then McKeon grabbed me.

"'Herschowitz, go over and see if he's dead.'

"'Oh I don't want to go over there, there might be more Germans,' and I didn't want to look at the guy I shot, but McKeon made me do it—the German was dead, all right.

"After that we stumbled into a German camp. Oh God, we were right in the middle of them! We tried to stay quiet, but finally they saw us and we started to run in different directions. All night long I tried to get back to our regiment—I had nothing to eat but a piece of bread I had in my gas mask.

"Finally, I could see these men in blue uniforms. Thank God, they were Frenchmen. They helped me to get to the headquarters of the 308th, where I delivered my message. Oh was I lucky already!"[2]

(Mr. Herschowitz's Distinguished Service Cross citation is not quite as modest as Jack. It reads: "For extraordinary heroism in action near Vinarville, France, September 29–30, 1918. In order to obtain ammunition and rations, Private Herschowitz with another soldier accompanied an officer in an effort to establish communications between battalion and regimental headquarters. They were attacked by a small party of Germans but drove them off, killing one. When night came, they crawled unknowingly into the center of a German camp, where they lay for three hours undetected. Finally discovered, they made a dash to escape. In order to protect the other two, Private Herschowitz deliberately drew the enemy fire to himself, greatly aiding the others to escape. Private Herschowitz succeeded in delivering his message the next morning.")

After Jack gave the message to the headquarters of the 308th on the morning of September 30, he collapsed from the flu—he had a temperature of 105 at the time. It was the end of the war for Jack,

[2] Munson and McKeon both also made it back, but Jack arrived first.

but not for Whittlesey. The 308th went forward and joined up with Whittlesey's command, but on October 2 the major moved out again. This time his command became so deeply engulfed by the forest and the Germans, it took six days before the rest of the division could reach them. During most of this time they were under constant pressure from the enemy, who were on all sides. Food and ammunition ran out, as did their water. They were belted with rifle and machine-gun fire, gas, mortars, and heavy artillery.[3] They were called upon to surrender but refused. The newspapers stated that Whittlesey told the Germans to go to hell, but the major always claimed it was nothing as colorful as all that—he simply refused to capitulate in what seemed to be a hopeless situation.

Whatever it was that he actually said, the heroic stand of his command captured the imagination of America. It earned Whittlesey the Congressional Medal of Honor but also an early grave. He did commit suicide, probably due to the doubts he had concerning his own decisions. But he had only been obeying orders when he moved forward into what has become known as "the pocket." If his flanks had been protected, he would have never been cut off. The casualties that had been suffered—194 men walked out of "the pocket" that 554 had entered—were in no way the fault of Whittlesey, but apparently their memory haunted him to the extreme.

As for my friend Jack Herschowitz, he came precariously close to dying from his case of the flu, but today he's hale and hearty at age eighty-seven and still very active in the dried-food business. Nature will, of course, eventually achieve what German bullets and the flu couldn't in 1918, but it just might be many years away. Mr. Herschowitz, *mazel tov!*

[3] It appears that they were also shelled by American artillery, but this has never been firmly established.

From Hamilton College to the Argonne

Louis Brockway

THE WEE BURN COUNTRY CLUB, DARIEN, CONNECTICUT, JULY 1976
Lou Brockway was another of the college seniors who headed for
the Army very shortly after they heard that war had been declared.
As a twenty-year-old college man he quickly earned a commission.
Then he was assigned to the 78th, one of the brand-new national
Army divisions being put together in this country.

"We couldn't understand the delay in getting us overseas," remembered Brock. "Then when we got into the middle of things, we
wished it had been a little longer."

After a postwar tour of duty in the Rhineland, Lou returned to
the States and the world of advertising in New York City.

The large majority of his business career was spent with the
highly respected agency of Young & Rubicam (or Y & R, as it is
known in New York City). Before he was through he had risen to
the post of executive vice president.

Brock is remembered not only as one of America's leading professionals in his field but also as having one of the greatest senses of
humor that ever showed up on Madison Avenue. He may no longer
worry about new product campaigns, but his great wit is still completely intact.

First Lieutenant Louis Brockway
Headquarters Company, 310th Infantry, 78th Division

It was up in the Argonne one night, and it was raining cats and dogs. We knew the Germans were up to something. I saw this man crawling toward my hole. Once I heard him whispering, "Brock, Brock," I knew it was my friend Eddie O'Connor.

"Brock," Eddie continued, "do you know what?"

Naturally I felt O'Connor had something important to tell me.

"What is it?" I answered.

"A pig's ass is pork."

Can you beat that!

—LOU BROCKWAY

Delta Kappa Epsilon and the Great War will always have a special connection for me because of my two DKE buddies, Sub Donaghue and Gus Donahue—that's right, the same name but a different spelling. We used to call Sub the elegant Donaghue because he had the g in his name; he'd always claimed that his people, the O'Donaghues, had been the ancient Kings of Ireland.

The three of us had been great pals at the DKE house over at Hamilton College in Clinton, New York. We'd been together on the basketball team and also in the dramatic club. When the war came, we'd joined up as a threesome and gone to Fort Dix, New Jersey.

There we went into the new 310th Infantry, which was to be part of the 78th Division. Then, in May of '18, we'd left for France. You might say we were the DKE's Three Musketeers of the AEF.

It's our last meeting above all that I'll never forget. It happened at the tail end of the Argonne around the end of October in '18.

Now, remember, the Germans had been in the area we were pushing them from for four years. Many of the facilities they had built up were tremendous; one was this huge delousing bath. We were all lousy at this point; you were always scratching those damn cooties, and we looked at this as a godsend. So I rounded up Sub, and the two of us went over to take a bath, and who should turn up there but Gus—he was still in the 310th, but now in a different battalion. You can't imagine how great it was to have the three of us together and to get rid of all that mud and slime we'd been living in.

Well, it was a beautiful autumn day. They didn't have enough frost to make the trees as beautiful as back home, but it was still superb. After we'd put on some clean duds, we sat down by the road to take in the scenery. The first thing you knew, Gus started to muse about Hamilton.

"You know," he reminisced, "I'll bet it's beautiful back in Clinton. Can you remember all those great fall weekends the DKEs had. What I'd give to be back there now!"

We kept talking that way for quite a while, with our thoughts a long way from the AEF. Then Gus came up with an idea.

"We surely have the Heinies on the run now," he pointed out. "Perhaps we can end this thing the first part of next year. If we get home in time, we can all go to commencement—we had to miss our own." It was a great thought.

A few mornings later, our beloved Gus—Walter Emmett Donahue—took a machine-gun burst in his stomach. That same afternoon the Germans started to really pull back; we had practically no casualties at all after that. Gus lingered for a few days, but he never made it back for commencement. God, how we missed him!

You know, as I look back on it, it's an amazing thing what people like Gus and the rest of us were able to accomplish. In the spring of '17 we knew nothing about soldiering; a few months later thousands of us are down at Camp Dix trying to become a division.

I know it's a little vulgar, but I can show you a good case of how unmilitary we really were. When we arrived at Dix, they hadn't finished building the place. Thousands of civilian workers and Army engineers were busy trying to set us up right. They had no water system as yet, so, of course, they had put up outhouses. One of the problems was that the Chic Sales would frequently require a long walk; naturally the men were reluctant to undertake an excursion when nature called. You may not believe this, but they had an official U. S. Army sign, with a U. S. Government stamp on the bottom, that read as follows:

> Please Do Not Shit in Fence Corners.
> It has not the odor of violets,
> And besides, it is hard on shoe leather.

How I wished I had pinched one of those signs!

Well, as I was a second lieutenant by this time, they had put me in charge of a platoon; most of the men in it were Italians from the Utica, New York, area. They spotted me quickly as a shavetail. When I'd try and give out a work detail, they'd come up with:

"No speaka da English, no speaka da English."

I let them get away with this for a few days, then I called this man named Ceilua over to me; he could speak both English and Italian and had been acting as my interpreter.

"Listen," I told Ceilua, "I think these clucks are putting one over on me. What do you think?"

"I know they are," grinned Ceilua. "I wondered when you were going to catch on."

The next day I called the platoon together to straighten them out.

"All right, you men," I warned, "the games are over. The next bird who doesn't understand English goes to the guardhouse." There was no more "No speaka da English."

My, but we really worked our division that summer and fall of '17. By late November we all felt our outfit had been honed to a cutting edge. Then they started the old Army game, transferring our men to help form new divisions—it was twenty-five men here, fifty men there. It was playing the devil with our units. Of course, we always tried to get rid of the yard birds, but most of the time it didn't work out that way.

You know, that brings up an old Army trick on how you could get rid of a lousy officer without raising a big fuss. The CO would have the dental officer make out a form saying that Lieutenant Foulup needed a lot of work on his teeth. Many of the men needed this anyway, so it was a sure way to get rid of your weak links.

Well anyway, every time they'd take our men away, we'd have to start all over again. Finally, after we'd been working hard as hell for about nine months, the word came through: The 78th was to ship out.

That's one scene I'll never forget, our leaving Fort Dix early one foggy morning about the middle of May. I must confess the whole thing made us feel like soldiers. There was no secrecy about it; everyone knew where we were headed. The band was blaring, the colors flying, the horses prancing; it was something out of another age, like those pictures we used to see about the Civil War. Come to think of it, we're about as old now as the Civil War veterans were then.

They marched us down to the railroad station and started to load us aboard. It was the only express train I saw during the war. They had us on the good ship *Beltana* in no time whatsoever.

What a ship! It smelled just like a cattle boat, which was mainly due to the fact that it was a cattle boat. It had just come from taking a load of meat from Australia to Gallipoli. You could see scraps of meat everywhere. We had to scrape all the mess tables off with glass before anyone could eat off them.

It was bad enough for the officers, but it was really hard on the men. If you had put about one thousand aboard, it would have been crowded; we had twenty-five hundred on her. You should have seen it when we had boat drill. The men could barely turn around. God, did they bitch!

We landed at Southampton, then we were off on a beautiful train ride to a place called Folkestone; here we spent the five nicest days I had in Europe. This British doctor and his wife more or less opened their home for several of our officers. Their daughter and many of her friends would show up at tea time, which was a great relief from the daily routine. Each of the girls had a husband who was an officer in France—God, they were lonely! The daughter really gave me a shock, though, when I asked her what her husband did in France.

"He's a *leftenant* in the infantry," she answered.

"How long has he been there?"

"Two years," she sighed, "and that's a very, very long time to last as a *leftenant* in the infantry."

As you can imagine, this wasn't exactly morale-boosting for me, especially when I looked at the casualty report in the London *Times* the next day. Under "officers" it stated, *"leftenants* unless otherwise noted . . ."* One hell of a lot of them had nothing noted after their name.

Then on June 8 we crossed the Channel to France. After being a soldier for more than a year, I was actually where it was all going on. On the other hand, many of our new men had been in the service less than two months.

First they sent us up near Belgium where the British lines were. We spent the next ten weeks or so training with the English. Did you ever eat rabbit five days a week? Don't! We were given all British equipment, even uniforms in some cases. They had one gun, an automatic rifle, called the Lewis Gun, which we thought was great. You know, there was one thing I could never figure out: Back in the United States they had the Browning Automatic Rifle, which was outstanding, and the English had the Lewis. But when we went into real action, we ended up with that Chauchat, the French gun—you couldn't hit anything with that. It did work, however. If it jammed, you'd just bang it against a tree and it would start shooting again—but I still don't know why we didn't have the Lewis or the Browning.

One of the things I vividly remember about our tour with the King's own was the day General Haig came riding over to look us over. His dress was impeccable, and with his entourage and their lances and guidons, he looked like something out of the Middle Ages. He said a few words about how glad he was to have us, what a fine body of men we were, and he was off. He surely looked like a soldier, though!

Then there was the spell I spent with the Royal Welsh Fusiliers in the Forêt de Nieppe. The policy was to send three or four officers and noncoms into the trenches for a few days so we'd know what it was going to be like when we took our own men in. There it all was, the shelling, machine-gun fire, mud; I didn't realize how tame this was until I got into the heavy stuff a little later.

How naïve we all were at this point. I remember hearing these Tommies talking about how nice it would be to get a little "blighty" so they could get the hell out of there. We all felt this was awful; how were they going to win the war that way? What we didn't think about was how long the British had been bleeding. It didn't take us very long to understand their feeling.

In the meantime, we didn't realize all the political ramifications that were going on. Haig wanted to keep us for his coming offensive, the French wanted us to booster their worn-out troops, and Pershing was trying desperately to set up his own army. Finally Black Jack won out, and we headed South to become part of the First United States Army! And to move on Saint Mihiel.

Of course, they then gave us back all our American equipment, including rifles—I think we ended up with our original American-made Enfields. These were somewhat different from the English ones we had trained with. You know, crazy as it sounds, our men had four different kinds of rifles over the period of one year.

When we first arrived at Camp Dix, we were shown several cartons of these old rifles and told to clean them up. After wiping all the grime off, we saw the name Krag-Jorgensen. This was the standard weapon of the Spanish-American War. After we trained with these for several weeks, they gave us Springfields—then, just before we left, American Enfields were issued; these were replaced with British Enfields when we reached France. You might say our men were a little confused.

The trip from the northern end of the line down to join the U.S. forces was great as long as we were on the trains; when we started to march, it became hell. Most of the hiking was done at night, normally with rainfall and tremendous mud. I remember waking up during the daylight— we'd just grab a few hours of sleep whenever we could—and measuring the mud we had been going through: It was eighteen inches deep. Try that sometime!

Our objective was to be in the line for the drive on the Saint Mihiel salient. This was to be the first huge American-directed offensive of the war. How well I can remember the morning of September 12 when it started. We had been up to our usual practice of nighttime marching, all of us wondering if we were getting anywhere at all, when CRASH, the big barrage started. It sounded like Pershing had every cannon in France aimed at the Germans in that salient. I think every Doughboy for miles around could hear it.

We didn't actually move into the rough stuff here for two or three days, just at the end of the drive. Our job was to hold the newly gained ground, near a place called Thiacourt. When we moved in, Thiacourt had hardly been touched at all; when we left, the place was in ruins. The Germans kept shelling and shelling; it seemed they'd never stop!

We spent about three weeks here, mainly just holding our position and going on patrols. We seemed to be at just about the most advanced part of the American lines and were feeling the brunt of the German guns. It appeared that way to us, anyway. I do know our men were getting hit every day. (From September until the Armistice the 78th suffered over seven thousand casualties.)

One of our casualties was a German lad from St. Louis, and therein lies a tale for you. A few days before we were to move in, my platoon sergeant had come to me with this confused look on his face.

"Lieutenant," he pleaded, "what am I going to do with Private Zimmerman? He says he can't go into the lines because he doesn't want to shoot his cousins."

"Oh no!" I answered. "This is a hell of a time for him to spring this on us! Why didn't he tell us this back at Dix? He'd probably still be back there."

I didn't know what to do, so I went to Laurence Mead, our captain. He was in the same boat, so we decided to try Colonel Babcock. He was flabbergasted but firm.

"Put him under arrest," admonished the colonel. "Tell him we're going to try him for cowardliness in the face of the enemy, and if he's guilty, he'll be shot by his own buddies."

Naturally I followed his orders, but damn it, this meant the guy couldn't carry his rifle—not if he was under arrest.

By this time we're just a few hours from moving in, and I have this man without a weapon. I went back to Babcock.

"Colonel," I reasoned, "what am I going to do with Zimmerman? I can't send him in without his rifle. I think he's just scared, which means he has nothing on me."

"Or me either," answered Babcock. "I'll tell you what you do:

Tell him we won't shoot him, and that we'll give him back his rifle if he'll move up with us."

Well, poor Zimmerman, he's still scared to death, but this sounded better than a firing squad, so he agreed.

That first night the Boche really let us have it. You know, there is nothing more terrifying than staying put, down in a hole, when a real barrage comes at you. We were in a wooded area, and you could hear these shells whistling through the trees; every time one would land, the ground would reverberate like an earthquake. And every now and then one would hit one of our men—you could hear the poor guy groaning unless it was a direct hit—then there was nothing.

I had put Zimmerman over on my left not only to keep an eye on him but also because I was now beginning to feel sorry for him. The guy was shaking so much he could hardly hold his rifle. Then, sure enough, a "whizz-bang" landed right on top of him—no more Zimmerman. Hell, I don't think we even tried to bury what was left.

A month or so later I received a letter from his mother. She wrote that her son had mentioned me in his letters and could I give her any details.

"Mrs. Zimmerman," I answered, "he died gallantly charging the enemy. You should be very proud of your son, as are all of us who served with him." After all, what kind of a guy would have written her the truth? She probably kept that letter until she died. The poor devil, I've never forgotten how petrified he was.

I had my own closest call of the war here early one morning. Along with two other officers and a sergeant, I had moved out trying to stalk German machine-gun positions. We had climbed this little hill when their artillery zeroed in, first on one side, then the other, and finally in the middle. One of the officers was killed, the other hit in the side, and the sergeant took one in the leg. I wasn't scratched, although the dead officer was only two or three yards away from me when he was hit. That's the way World War I shelling was. If you were there long enough, you were sure to either get hit or have a real close call.

When they finally moved us out, it was to go into the Meuse-Argonne. Of course, this meant back to that nighttime marching. Like most of the men I was suffering from what you could call the "Kaiser's Quick Step." Can you imagine trying to march a platoon at night through a wooded area with half of your men suffering from the same thing? Besides, we were moving a million or so men around that area; the traffic jams were horrendous. Hell, men were bumping into each other.

Well, as we came into the lines, Babcock called me over.

"Brock," he said, "we need a new man to take over the signal platoon."

"Colonel," I protested, "the only thing I know about a telephone is you put one end at your ear, the other at your mouth, and you talk."

"Brock," he repeated, "you're the man." And that was it: I was the man!

Now, these men in this platoon were pretty professional. There was no sense in trying to bluff them. I called them all together to give them the word.

"Men," I explained, "I don't know a damn thing about telephones or about laying telephone wire. I'll get the orders, tell you where to go, and go out with you; you'll have to do the work." And tough work it was! Not only did we have to line it through those woods, but we also had to go back through and tape it when it broke. All this was frequently done under fire, both day and night.

There was just no place there in the Argonne that was safe. General Hershey, our brigadier general who later commanded the 4th Division, had picked this French captain as his aide and liaison with the French Army. The poor guy really thought he had it made. After all the tough battles he'd been through, he finally ends up with a soft berth at brigade headquarters. I'll be darned if the headquarters doesn't take a direct hit, killing the poor Frenchie. You just didn't have a haven in the Argonne.

The terrain was some of the toughest to fight in you could find. Remember, the Germans had been fortifying this area for four years—no one had been able to drive them from it. Our job was to hit them at an area around Bois des Loges on the Hindenburg Line. The place was loaded with gorges, and on top of them would be wooded areas loaded with German machine guns. It was murder.

One foggy night the colonel called me in to tell me that the wire to the 3rd Battalion had broken down. Our job was to fix it.

"But where the hell's the 3rd Battalion?" I asked.

"You find it," replied Babcock.

So we started out. As there was no moon, everyone kept bumping into each other. And you'd never know when you'd run into a German patrol. Then it started to rain. What a night! It was one I'll never forget.

Toward morning the fog started to lift just as we located our men. They'd also been lost and were settled down in this ravine. What they didn't know was that less than a half mile away were all these German guns. We could see the Heinies, but the men in the 3rd Battalion couldn't. We told them to get the hell out of there or they'd be cut to ribbons. Thank God the Germans never did get to zero in on them.

That rain seemed to be always with you. I had a buddy named Eddie O'Connor, a great guy whom we lost there in the Argonne. One night when we were trying to sleep during a downpour on that wet, soggy ground, Eddie called me over.

"Brock," he groaned, "when I get back home, the first guy who asks me to go on a camping trip is going to get a poke in the nose." Come to think of it, I don't think I ever went camping again after the war.

Well, during all this time our job is, of course, to crack the Hindenburg Line. And in this mess you'd count your gains a yard at a time. The type of officers you had were so important, the colonel in particular. I always felt we had a good one. He'd been a classmate of Pershing's, so he'd had about thirty years in the service.

I'll never forget an incident that occurred just before we went into combat. A bunch of us younger officers were part curious and part scared. I decided to ask Babcock what it was all about.

"Colonel," I inquired, "what is it really like when you get under fire?"

"How the hell do I know?" the feisty Babcock snapped. "The only hostile shot I've ever heard was in a saloon in Nome, Alaska, in '02!"

Can you imagine that? Thirty years in the Army and he'd never been in battle. Before the war started, he'd never had over five hundred men under his command, and all of them had been regulars. Then bang, he has three thousand men, almost all civilian-soldiers.

Everything was by the book as far as he was concerned, but there was one night in the Argonne when we found out what kind of a man he was. Before that night we felt he was fair and brave enough but not very human—all Army, in other words.

This one evening it all changed. We were sitting in this headquarters dugout, or I should say, lying—I was really beat. The rest of the regiment was the same. We were just plain played out. Then the colonel received his new orders from divisional staff. He read them over slowly; I later found out they were for us to attack in a very bad sector.

"My God, My God," moaned Babcock, "they're back there, they don't know what that terrain is like. These men are worn to a frazzle. I can't ask them, I can't ask them!" He buried his head in his hands and began to shake. Then he picked up his head and squared his shoulders.

"Gentlemen," he intoned, "we have orders from headquarters: The 310th will follow them." It sounds a little melodramatic now, but it sure as hell wasn't back then. Remember, this was the man we all thought had a book of Army regulations for a brain; a man who had actually sent an order out back at Fort Dix when we had a shortage of toilet paper that read, "Use four sheets only: one to scrape, two to wipe, and one to polish."

My fondest memory of him, though, occurred on November 11. We'd been pulled back from the lines a few days earlier to rest up and receive replacements. When we heard the news, we were stunned; we just couldn't believe it—we didn't have to go back in. To me it was relief more than joy. I'd just heard that my dear friend Gus Donahue had died, which took most of the joy out of the whole thing. Then the colonel's aide came by and told all the officers to report immediately to his quarters with their canteen cups.

Well sir, Sub Donaghue was there and, along with the others, we went over to this house where the colonel was billeted. Now, keep in mind, Babcock was a good officer, but he was not by any means a jovial man. However, there he was, Colonel Walter Babcock, USA—his blouse unbuttoned, his chair tipped back against the wall, and his feet resting next to this roaring fireplace.

"Gentlemen," he bellowed, "your colonel is plastered, but I can do business anyway." Then we knew for sure it was over!

The Colleges Go to War

"In 1917 I was in my senior year at Harvard Law School," recalled Paul Smart.[1] "Shortly after our declaration of war, Dean Pounds came into one of my classes to address our group.

"'Gentlemen,' he said, 'this is a professional school of law. Your course does not end until June. Anyone who leaves before that time to go into the Army will have to repeat the entire year after the war.'

"Well sir, I want you to know that immediately after he made that pronouncement, the entire class walked out on him. Harvard's President Lowell later overruled the dean, and we all got our degrees. But what a stupid thing for Pounds to say. We were all aching to go."

The reaction of that group of aspiring counselors pretty much sums up the feeling at the colleges and universities across the country: Just about everyone was eager to join something.

Another example was the case of the twenty-six seniors at the University of Minnesota who joined the Marine Corps in April of 1917. One of these young men was George Brown. I visited with George in Laguna, California, in 1976 and asked him if the Marines' "First to Fight" slogan had anything to do with such a body joining the Corps en masse.

"I don't think so," mused this octogenarian. "We had heard that if you joined the Marines, you'd be sent to Mare Island, California,

[1] First Lieutenant Paul Smart served in the 101st Field Artillery of the 26th Division. He received the DSC.

for training. That sounds pretty good when you're in Minnesota during April."[2]

The same eagerness occurred at Princeton, according to Perry Hall, who in later life was to be managing partner of Morgan Stanley.

"I was a member of the Campus Club," Mr. Hall told me at his beautiful home at Woods Hole, Massachusetts. "Not only did every member of that club in the Class of 1917 go into the service, but we all went to France. Come to think of it," continued Perry, "I can't remember any of my friends who were seniors at other colleges who didn't go into something. One of them is now living farther down on the Cape in Chatham. He went into the Navy, and every time I take him fishing, he gets seasick."

There had been attempts to set up military units at the colleges before April of 1917, but the students never took it very seriously. Joseph Cummings of Fall River, Massachusetts, told me it was hardly what you'd call military.

"The men who were to show us how to be soldiers at Harvard were primarily our regular professors. I can remember one of these well-meaning but totally inept, newly made military instructors giving us an incorrect order during a color detail and how flustered he became.

"'Oh goodness, gentlemen,' he whimpered, 'I do beg your pardon.' Of course, we all guffawed.

"It did change after April 6, though," added Cummings. "We immediately received some wounded French officers, who were sent to Cambridge to really give us the word. But by then we were all marking time until they had room for us at Plattsburg."[3]

[2] Mr. Brown's decision to join the Marines was costly. He had spent the summer of 1916 pitching baseball in the Texas League. He had hoped to make it a career. A nasty wound in his throwing arm while serving with the 6th Marines ended that dream. He still has the blouse he was wearing at the time, and the slug that went into his arm. The pocket of his blouse contains a pack of Bull Durham he was using in '18. He advised me not to try and smoke any of it.

[3] Cummings' turn came in July of '17. By April of '18 he was in the trenches with the 1st Division near Cantigny.

In reality, this waiting one's turn for the officers' training camp did present a problem. The desire for the college men to go into the service far exceeded the immediate facilities to train them. Devereux Josephs, who had graduated from Harvard in 1915, found himself back in Cambridge in 1917 awaiting his placement at an officers' training center.

"For some reason that I've never been able to really figure out, they had me taking a course in English," a puzzled Mr. Josephs told me. "But," he bragged, "I had a higher grade in the English-language course there than a Princeton graduate who was in my class. His name was F. Scott Fitzgerald."

All the college men didn't want commissions, however. Harold Bailey left Yale to go into the ranks.

"I wanted to find out what life was all about," recalled Harold, "and I did, shortly after I arrived at Camp Devens, Massachusetts.

"I was on KP one Sunday when the mess sergeant called me over.

"'Bailey,' he said, 'my fiancée and her aunt are going to visit me this afternoon, but it shouldn't bother your work.'

"Haw, haw, some fiancée; it didn't take long for me to figure out that he had a couple of frisky ladies in there. Men were going in and out all afternoon. He was making a bundle. At about 5:00 P.M. he thanked me for keeping my mouth shut and offered me a free one. I was savagely tempted, but I did turn him down. I must admit I used to think about that later on when I was in all that hell around the Marne.[4] It gave me a chuckle when I needed one."

Officers or enlisted men, one thing is a certainty: The college men went to war in huge numbers. There is a plaque at Delta Kappa Epsilon's (a college fraternity) national headquarters in New York City. It lists the names of all DKEs who were killed during World War I. There are 189 names on it. That is a lot from one fraternity.

---

[4] Bailey was with the 59th Infantry of the 4th Division in July and August 1918. He did see hell.

The Kansas Newspaperman

John C. Madden

"Oh you are doing a book on World War I, are you?" said Hugh Donlon, an executive with the Edwin Bird Wilson Advertising Agency. "Well, then get in touch with Jack Madden—he used to run our shop, and he remembers everything about France in 1918."

Mr. Donlon was quite close to being correct. Jack had left his family's Kansas newspaper to go over with the 89th Division, one of the best of the original national Army divisions. It was the unit trained by Leonard Wood, one of Pershing's rivals for the job as commander of the AEF shortly after war was declared. Wood was removed from command of his 89th Division just before it sailed for France.

"We never really could forgive either Woodrow Wilson or General Pershing for doing that to us," recalled Mr. Madden when I visited with him. It was what you'd politically call a "dirty trick" today.

After the war Jack switched his base of operations from Kansas to New York City, where he worked in both the newspaper and advertising businesses. He is now retired and lives in a beautiful home in rustic Carmel, New York. He and his wife have recently donated most of their substantial acreage to a school for exceptional children.

"It will all go to the school after we're both gone," said Jack. "We never had any children of our own, so we'd especially like to do something for some youngsters."

First Lieutenant John C. Madden
G Company, 355th Infantry, 89th Division

Give me a hand grenade
Give me a Boche
And leave the rest up to me.

—SUNG BY ELSIE JANIS TO THE
TUNE OF "GIVE ME THE MOONLIGHT"

Remember the war? Of course I do. Sometimes I can't remember every detail, but they usually come back. Then there're so many other things, real little ones, I can recall as if it were only yesterday. I guess your mind works that way when you're eighty-three.

Now, take that cold day in training at Camp Funston—must have been December of '17. Our division had just been organized by Leonard Wood. Being mainly from Kansas and Nebraska, mostly farmboys, we felt it was really great having a man like General Wood in charge. He'd been a Spanish War hero—a real national figure.

Well, here we were trying to teach these rookies how to drill, when we heard that General Wood himself was riding around the area. Our company commander got all excited and drew us into line.

"Attention!" he yelled out, and we all tried to look as military as we could.

Now get this, he kept us at attention for two hours there in the freezing weather. Wood had undoubtedly left the area—hell, he was probably back in his tent. The point is that our captain was so green he just didn't know what to do. Can you imagine that?

Poor Wood. He wanted so badly to take us to France, had worked so hard putting us together as a division. He'd even been sent over to Europe for a few weeks to see firsthand what it was like so he'd be ready to move us in correctly when our time came.

Then, one day just before we were to leave for France, my platoon sergeant came running into my tent.

"Lieutenant, Lieutenant," he bellowed, "they've stolen our general from us!" And sure enough, they had.

President Wilson wasn't going to let Wood become a war hero again. With all his idealism and his making the world safe for democracy, old Woodrow was quite a politician, something he'd really shown in 1916. That was the year he'd run against Charles Evans Hughes and squeaked through on his "He kept us out of war" platform.

I was editor in chief of my family's newspaper in Mound City, Kansas, at the time. Dad was dead, and as soon as I'd come out of the University of Kansas I had to take over the running of the paper. And please note that Mound City was strong Republican territory.

Haw! Haw! Well, everyone was sure Hughes had the election in the bag. After all, Wilson had only won in '12 because Roosevelt and Taft had split the Republican Party. Then the results started to pour in. Remember, we didn't have any radios or TV then; most of the news came over the telegraph wires and the phone. Anyhow, there seemed to be no doubt about it: Hughes had won it. So I put the paper to bed at ten o'clock and hit the hay myself with my headlines announcing a smashing victory for Hughes. You might say it was just like Truman and Dewey. I really ended up with egg on my face, like Kaltenborn in '48.

Well, back to the war. You must understand that there was a great deal of antiwar sentiment in this country before we went in; this was particularly true out in the plains states of Kansas and Nebraska. While it was also true that a good many of our midwestern farmers were of German descent, you shouldn't think they were pro-Kaiser, however; far from it. Most of their parents had left Europe because of the Prussian militarists—they just didn't want any part of war, that's all.

But it wasn't just the German Americans, it was a lot of people. There was even a song in those days that was quite popular. It went like this:

> I didn't raise my boy to be a soldier,
> I raised him up to be my pride and joy.
> Who dares to put a musket on a shoulder
> To shoot some other mother's pride and joy?

My position was a little different. My dad—he was over fifty when I was born—had fought with the 12th Illinois during the Civil War—Shiloh and Vicksburg and all those places. I'd been brought up listening to his tales of the Union Army. I sure as hell didn't want war, but I felt if that was the only way we could stop those Germans from sinking our ships, well, we had to do something, that's all there was to it.

Shortly after we did declare war, I enlisted. There's one more thing I'd like to add here. After we were actually committed to defeating the Kaiser, every single German American family I knew supported our government; our division was loaded with them, and they were great soldiers.

As a college graduate I became what we called a ninety-day wonder when I was commissioned a second lieutenant by an act of Congress. Well, it could have been by an act of God, but I was still no great military man after only ninety days. I had an expression in those days, "The Star-Spangled Mess;" it referred to just about everything we were doing. What most of us didn't seem to realize was the incredible job our country was trying to do. Looking back on it, with all our blunders, I guess we did all right.

Anyway, they sent me down to Camp Deming, New Mexico, to join the 3rd Minnesota Infantry. These Gophers loved having a Kansas man come in as one of their officers—just like poison they did.

Well hell, National Guard or not, they weren't any more military than the rest of the men going into the Army then. Their colonel decided this was a problem he could cure by developing a snappy martial air as the regiment's song. He figured the best way to do it was to let the men themselves pick their favorite. So, true to the American militia tradition of democracy, they held a vote. The winning song was to be announced by the band as they marched on their Saturday review. You should have seen the colonel's face when they broke into, "It Takes a Long, Lean, Lanky Gal to Make the Preacher Lay His Bible Down." Second place was just as bad, or good, depending on where your taste lies—it was "The Old Gray Mare."

Another thing I remember about Deming was my infantry speech. The colonel had set up a program where each officer had to give a lecture. Well, these guys didn't want lectures, they wanted to fight—that's something I can really say about the First World War, everyone wanted to get over to France as soon as possible. Now, keeping this in mind, I figured I'd tell them how important the infantry really would be when they did get in action. I entitled my talk "The Glory of the Infantry." It was a damn good speech at that.

Then the next day new orders came through. The whole outfit was to be turned into artillery. Can you imagine that? I get them all fired up on the infantry and wham, they're artillery—it was a "Star-Spangled Mess," all right!

Actually, I wasn't really affected by the change, as I was soon transferred out, but I've often wondered what happened to those men. I'm sure a great many of them just didn't have the mathematical aptitude to catch on with the artillery.

My own situation, though, became ideal: I ended up in the 89th Division at Camp Funston, Kansas. While my own new regiment (355th) was mainly Nebraska men, the 353rd was loaded with Kansans. We also had a lot of men from Missouri and the Dakotas—it was a plains division, no doubt about that. I was back home, and I'd stay with them as we journeyed to England, France, Germany, and back to Kansas, almost two years later.

I'm sure other men have told you how tough it was to turn a group of civilians like this into a military unit, so I won't go into all that. Let it suffice to say that most of the lieutenants were ninety-day wonders, so I guess you could say it was the blind leading the blind. But we sure ended up with one great outfit just the same.

There is one thing special that still makes me chuckle. Each evening we'd received a printed order sheet from headquarters on what our training would be the next day. Someone got the bright idea to add news flashes and a weather report to the sheet. So the next night we received our orders with the personal touch added. It ended with, "The weather will be fair and warmer tomorrow—by order of Brigadier General Frank L. Winn." I understand even the general got a kick out of being given the prerogative of the Almighty.

We worked the outfit all winter, with special emphasis on the rifle—Wood was a great believer in the old adage that an infantryman's best friend is his rifle. Then when spring came, we were shipped to Camp Mills, Long Island. This was to be our jumping-off spot for Europe.

It was there that we lost General Wood and one hell of a lot of our trained men. General Winn replaced Wood, but the new men we received were brand-new draftees. Most of them had never even fired a rifle. This truly irritated General Winn—oh he was fit to be tied.

"No one is getting on that ship in my division," he roared, "who hasn't fired a minimum of ten rounds on the range."

So we had to get our new men out to the range as quickly as possible—after all, we were on a daily alert for embarkation. It was really one hell of a job.

One of the recruits in our company—I think he'd been a preacher—knew absolutely nothing about weapons. He loaded up, pointed his piece at the target, and pulled the trigger. Now, get this, he hadn't even taken the Cosmoline out of the barrel, so the darn thing exploded on him. He turned this powder-loaded face toward me, showing a crazy grin.

"Did I hit the target?" he asked. The poor fool thought that was what happened every time you fired.

A few days later we received the word: this was the big day, I think it was early May of '18. As we were packing to move out, one of our medics came over with another problem.

"Christ, Lieutenant," he lamented, "I've got some bad news for you. One of your men [one of the new ones] has the clap."

"Oh no." I sobbed. "What am I going to do?"

"You have two choices," the medic informed me. "Either take him aboard or sail one man short."

"The hell with it," I sighed. "He goes, VD and all!" It seems to me he turned out to be one of our better men.

I can't remember exactly how long the voyage lasted, but we landed in Liverpool sometime in June. There had been a lot of rumors about submarines, but I never saw any.[1]

One of the first things we received in England was a printed greeting from King George. Most of us thought it was a nice touch, but not everyone. We had one Irish lad who told them what they could do with their bloody King. I later heard that he used the greeting the same way the farmers would use a Sears, Roebuck catalogue, if you know what I mean.

While we were in England they put us on English rations. This meant more cheese than you could find in mouse heaven—my God, how those English could eat cheese! I vividly remember one of our mess sergeants coming back from their commissary shaking his head in utter disbelief.

"Christ," he was muttering to himself, "those limeys have enough cheese to constipate the whole AEF!"

The boys got a huge laugh out of it. They'd go around mimicking an American Indian, grunting out:

"Ugh, too much cheese choke 'em asshole."

Then, toward the middle of June, we crossed the Channel. After landing at Le Havre we moved to Brechainville, where training started in earnest. Our trip by rail to the training area should have taken about twelve hours. It took two days. I think the damn train stopped at every farm.

Our camp was about sixty kilometers from the front, so you can bet the boys took our work seriously. I was still a second lieutenant, with my friend Mack Traynor a first lieutenant. Company G's commander was Captain Neville Fisher from Paris, Kentucky, down in the bluegrass country. Fisher was a great officer, all right, and a great guy, but he did like his Bourbon. When we arrived in France, he changed to cognac.

Most of the time the captain kept his drinking habits to himself,

[1] Just about every Doughboy talked about submarines, but as only one Europe-bound transport was sunk (the *Tuscania,* a British ship), it was probably all scuttlebutt.

but there was one hike that I'm sure the boys never forgot; I know
I never did. It was hot as hell, with that French sun beating down
like a furnace. We're all taking nips on our canteen, including
Fisher, the only difference being the captain's canteen was filled to
the brim with cognac. It finally got to him around two o'clock. He
had half the company going in one direction and the rest going in
another. He's giving his right faces, left faces, to the rear march,
this, that, and the other thing. Then he started to laugh.

"The hell with it, boys," he moaned, "let's go home—route
march."

All in all, the training wasn't bad, even though we did have constant irritations. One of them was the lack of mail; we hadn't received any since we left Camp Mills. Then, after we'd been in
France about a month, we received a small pouchful; three of the
letters were for me. You know, I can still remember what they
were: One was a letter from my draft board—what a laugh we had
over that; another was a request from a friend of mine about to go
into the Army—he wanted me to send him a drill manual; the third
was from a man named Morgan, who wanted me to endorse him in
a political election. What a letdown!

By this time most of our new men had rounded into pretty good
shape, but not all of them. Then someone came down with the
chicken pox. What a break—now we could get rid of the foulups.
One by one we called them in.

"Ever had smallpox?"

"No."

"OK, you have to go into quarantine."

When it was all over, we felt we had the best damn company in
the AEF. Chicken pox, smallpox—what's the difference?

Well, all that skullduggery and it didn't work; just before we
went into the trenches, they all came back to us. In the meantime,
we'd received a new second lieutenant named Pat Shea, from Waterbury, Connecticut. Someone came up with the bright idea of giving them to Shea.

Well, it didn't take Pat long to realize we'd hung one on him.

"To hell with you guys," he said. "I'm going to turn this bunch of
clowns into the best damn platoon we have." And you know something, that's just about what he did.

It's a funny thing, here it's almost sixty years since the war, and I can't think about Pat without a lump in my throat. What a great guy he was, and what a shame we lost him. And it all seemed so unnecessary.

He took a nasty leg wound later on in the Argonne. We knew it was bad, all right, but nothing like what it turned into. Shortly after the war ended they took part of his leg off and sent him back to a hospital on Long Island. A lot of us stopped off to see him on our way to the Midwest. He seemed all right, but the damn thing wouldn't heal.

A year or so later I came to New York to go into newspaper work. There was poor Pat, still in the hospital. They kept taking more and more of his leg off but still couldn't properly cauterize the wound.

In 1921 we had our first reunion, back in Kansas City. How Pat wanted to go, but it was impossible. I had all the men I could find from G Company sign a scroll that I brought back to him. I can still remember how happy he was when I showed up with it. A few months later he was dead. It's a long way from the Argonne to Waterbury, Connecticut, but that's where he ended up.[2]

Well, I'm getting off the track, but it's hard for me to think about the war and not think about Shea.

In early August we moved into the trenches. First they marched us into this railhead where a real "Toonerville Trolley" was waiting. We had this railroad man in our company named Bill McQuiston. He took one look at our coming transportation and spit.

"Christ," he carped, "is that what they call a train over here? No wonder they can't win the war!"

Then we received very strict orders—NO SMOKING—once the train started. They were afraid we'd start a fire in the countryside, or alert the Boche, or what have you. It didn't bother me; I guess I was the only guy in the AEF who didn't smoke. But you should have heard the others—they wanted those Luckies and Camels. Then the engine started. Well, goddamn, if every man on the train was smoking two cigarettes at the same time, you wouldn't have

[2] Almost every man I visited with remembered a wounded buddy who died a few years after he returned home. This was particularly true of the gas cases. A classic example, of course, was the immortal "Big Six" of John McGraw's Giants, Christy Mathewson.

half the sparks that came from the engine. Oh well, as the French would say, *c'est la guerre.*

They took us as close to Seicheprey as they could, and we had to walk the rest of the way. We had to get in there fast because the Germans had hit our first group the day before with a fierce gas attack, killing about fifty men from the 354th and wounding another five hundred. This meant a daylight relief, very rare, and a two-mile or so march with our gas masks on. This was really tough. We weren't used to hiking with the masks on; the slobbering could drive you nuts. Those masks were bad enough when you were standing still—but a long hike, Jeezes, they were bad!

Seicheprey was what they called a "quiet sector." Those Yankees from New England (26th Division) had the hell knocked out of them there in April, and the 1st Division lost plenty of men there before that.

They weren't about to let us off the hook either. We were no sooner settled in when it started—all kinds of shells. We all put on our gas masks except this little private named Valepando, who was jumping all over the place.

"Hey, you damn fool," I yelled, "put on your gas mask."

"I can't," he yelled back, "I'm too busy ducking."

I laughed so hard I had to take my mask off. There was no gas then, but it came later.

It wasn't all fun and games, though. When it was over, I saw one of the most horrifying sights I saw in France. Poor Henry Osness had taken a direct hit. He'd been decapitated and looked like a bundle of rags.

We spent the next two weeks or so holding the lines. Then we went into reserve for about a week and came right back in. That trench routine was really unpleasant. We were supposed to be in a quiet sector, but among our patrols, their patrols, and the shelling, we were constantly taking casualties.[3] The boys used to have a good laugh out of the term "artillery duel"—artillery duel, baloney, that's when their artillery would knock the hell out of our infantry, and our artillery would do the same to their infantry.

Another thing I can remember about our time in the trenches

[3] In the "quiet sector" from August 7 until the Saint Mihiel show on September 12, the 89th Division suffered 933 casualties.

was some orders that came down about our feet. First we were told to change our socks every day. Now, how were we going to do that? We only had one or two pairs. As one lad put it, "I guess they want us to change them from one foot to the other." The very next day the order came through not to remove clothing at any time in the trenches. I ask you, how in the hell could you obey both those orders—a Star-Spangled Mess, all right!

While we were in the trenches around Seicheprey, we were part of the Eighth French Army. Then, just before the Saint Mihiel drive, we were moved into Pershing's new First U. S. Army; they finally had most of the Yanks under our own command.

Now, as I remember it, our jumping-off place for the drive was quite parallel to where we were, but we had to march seven miles to reach it.

And that, my friend, produced my most dramatic memory from France. We knew we were really going in—"over the top," as we used to say. It was raining and thundering. As we marched along, the lightning would give us a quick glimpse of the shell-marked area we were crossing. I think most of us were alone with our thoughts of what was ahead when at about 1:00 A.M., CRASH—Holy Christ, the heavens opened up. None of us had seen anything like it. Half our men jumped into shellholes. We had to explain to them that it was our artillery. And what artillery! Really, it's hard to describe, but believe me, it was incredible.

We reached our designated area on time. There was the chalk line to show us our spot. At precisely 5:00 A.M. we moved in.

Now, you probably realize that Saint Mihiel was a rather well-executed movement. Everything seemed to run smoothly—for us, anyway. For our first mile or so we faced some artillery and had to knock out a Maxim, but after that it was mainly pushing forward and taking prisoners. And how many of those Boche gave up. We had one sergeant who captured thirty by just walking into a dugout armed only with a pistol. Most of the Germans would walk out holding their hands high in the air and shouting "Kinder." This meant they had children at home. Naturally, we didn't want to shoot them under those circumstances. We kept moving for the next four or five days, liberating three villages. We finally stopped north of a town called Birney. The Germans had set up a defensive line and resistances. One of the big questions of the war has always been: Should we have stopped or tried to keep going? Who knows?

Anyway, we did halt and went back to that holding-the-line stint. We stayed there until we moved into the Meuse-Argonne. I checked the casualty figures after the war, and our division suffered close to fifteen hundred casualties holding the line there, almost half again as many as we'd had during Saint Mihiel.

There was one patrol we had there that I'll never forget, mainly because it was so mismanaged. This major picked about forty of us from different companies to feel out the German strength. Of course, the mission was to be done at night, but on a real moonlit one.

We started out in good form, but after we'd been moving for about an hour, I said to myself, "This guy's in trouble." And he was: He didn't know where the hell we were. To make matters worse, we kept going, but probably in the wrong direction.

Now for the worst part: He has us strung out Indian style, walking across this ridge. Of course, we're silhouetted against that moonlight like ducks in a shooting gallery. If this wasn't bad enough, he picks that time to break out his map to try and figure out where the hell we are. At the same time he takes out his flashlight to study with. Goddamn, you'd think he was casually walking down Bourbon Street in New Orleans!

Well, the Boche know where we are, and they open up on us. All hell is breaking loose when the major calls me over.

"Madden," he sputters, "the party is over. Tell each man to get back on his own." Oh he wasn't a bad guy, but I never had any respect for him after that.

In the meantime, the big drive in the Meuse-Argonne had started. It seems to me that just about every division we had figured in that one. Our turn came on October 19, when we were sent toward the Bantheville Woods. I say "we" but I mean the division. I had been sent back to rifle and grenade school for ten days and missed the beginning of our show here. And you know, that shows how fate can take a hand. The fighting on October 21 was the worst one day my company had. There were forty casualties, including Pat Shea.

When I did return, the boys of my platoon seemed glad as hell to see me. That's what I figured, anyway, but I kept wondering what all the sly smiles and chuckles were about. I finally asked the sergeant what was going on.

"Oh the boys are glad to see you, all right," he chuckled, "but they're glad as hell you went to that school."

"Why?"

"Well, you see, not having our officer with us, we were more or less in reserve for the big show. Hell, our company alone took ten machine guns; it was no picnic." There was plenty left for me, though, more than enough.

By this time Captain Fisher had left the company, and my buddy First Lieutenant Mack Traynor was in command. I was also a first lieutenant by then, but Mack was my senior.

We started our last push on Halloween and didn't stop until the Armistice. We moved so fast the rolling kitchen couldn't keep up with us; none of us had a hot meal from October 31 until November 11.

On the night of November 6, I was discussing the next day's movements with Mack Traynor when a German shell landed close to one hundred yards away from us. Do you know, a piece of shrapnel came all the way over to the pup tent we were sitting in, tore through the canvas, and hit Traynor in the head. It wasn't fatal, but it meant the end of the war for Mack. I was now in command of Company G.

The next day we took the town of Luzy. Mr. "Heinie" didn't try to defend it, but the French told us they had left a mere fifteen minutes before we arrived. We were pushing toward the Meuse as fast as we could.

At Luzy we saw some of the most heartrending sights of the war when fifty or so of the French inhabitants came out to greet us. God, how happy they were! There was one elderly *monsieur* with some kind of a military hat on, probably from the Franco-Prussian War, saluting us, with the tears streaming down his cheeks trying to sing "La Marseillaise"; hysterical women, many in black mourning, crying, praying, and cheering; children with wondrous eyes, following us and yelling, *"Vive! Vive!"* We were the saviors from across the sea, the knights in shining armor. Somehow it made the whole thing worthwhile.

We had one more nasty show left for us after we reached the Meuse. The Germans were on the other side of the river, but we didn't know how strong they were. And none of us could believe an Armistice was as close as it turned out to be. We only knew that while they were retreating, they seemed to have plenty of firepower left.

On the night of November 9 they called for volunteers to swim across the river and come back with a rundown on just what the hell was over there. As we were soon to find out there was plenty. It seems to me that about twenty men tried it, maybe five or six from Company G.

Well, the Boche picked up their movements right off the top of the barrel, catching the men in midstream, throwing machine-gun and mortar fire at them all over the place. Several of the men were hit and many more driven back. Five or six did reach the other shore, but, as we found out later, were taken prisoner.

One of those who did go whole hog on the stunt was Jimmy Ponder of Company G. We didn't know what had happened to him until the middle of January, when he turned up at our bivouac in Germany. I can picture him now with that silly grin on his face.

"We didn't have much of a chance," he related. "As soon as we crawled out of the Meuse, they were on us like locusts. The very next day the Heinies started moving us North as fast as they could. Then, a day or so afterward, the word came through that the war was over.

"Naturally, the Germans guarding us didn't want any part of going back to the lines," continued Jim, "so they shrugged their shoulders and told us we were on our own. My only problem was I didn't know where the hell I was. I started off as quickly as I could but well might have been going in circles for all I knew. Of course, I started to really get hungry, but all I could find was some turnips and cabbages, which I ate raw. I finally ran into some of our boys from the 91st Division. You know, they had been sent up to Belgium with that Ohio National Guard outfit [37th] the last few weeks of the war. That's what I said, Belgium. I was way up on the other side of the line. I was pretty done in, so they gave me a long stay in the hospital, and here I am."

Naturally, we were glad as hell to see Jimmy, but there I go again getting ahead of my story. And there is one thing more about the war I want to relate: the end of it.

You see, we didn't think it was over. As a matter of fact, when we first heard the news, a guy in Company G said, "Yea, it's over, all right. Over there on the other side of the river, don't you remember what they gave us the other night?"

Now for the strange part. When we did realize there was an armistice, our men just gave a sigh. They lay down, some went to sleep, others started writing letters, a few were obviously praying; no cheering or anything like that.

But the Germans were another story. They were cheering, laughing, singing, just going crazy. Somehow they got ahold of a band and started to play all these German songs—you know, dee-boom-boom, dee-boom-boom, all that brass they use. We were beginning to wonder who the hell had won the thing. Then they wanted to swim across the river, but we wanted none of that. We didn't quite trust old Fritzie that much.

The next day our Episcopal chaplain held a service for all denominations. Just about everybody went. It was quite impressive. Remember, we'd lost those six men just a few nights before, and all those lads at Seicheprey, Saint Mihiel, and the final push in the Argonne. It was hard to believe it was really over.

But it was, and we all wanted to go home. Pershing, however, had other plans for the 89th. We were to be one of the few divisions that was actually to go into Germany. We started off around Thanksgiving, moving through parts of Belgium and Luxembourg, finally crossing into Germany about the sixth of December.

If we were expecting any big event, we were sure disappointed. The Germans, you see, were accustomed to strong discipline. As far as they were concerned, we were now the boss. Some of the families had sent their young boys farther into Germany, thinking we would turn them into slave labor, or even send them back to America. This made me realize what it was all about. This is what they would have done. Once they realized we weren't that way, everything was fine.

Of course, they had been completely innocent as far as the war was concerned—it was all the fault of those damn Prussians, or so they said. Some of them even thanked us for liberating them from the Prussians. But every now and then some of the old ones would give us funny looks; you knew they were thinking of all their young men who weren't coming back. I suppose you couldn't blame them.

There was a strict law against fraternization that we did try and enforce, but it was hard. You did have a bunch of young men away from home and a whole generation of *Frauleins* who had basically missed male companionship for over four years. And there is always the fact that if somebody is nice to you, you're normally nice to them.

Take that big fat cook we had at one of the houses we were billeted in. She was always smiling, being pleasant all the time. We weren't supposed to buy food from the Germans, so we would go over to our commissary and pick it up there. Most of the time things were hunky-dory—that *Frau* could really set a table—until we brought back some oatmeal. The only problem was that Mrs. Boche had never seen oatmeal before. She fixed it up all right, served the finest oatmeal soup you've ever tasted. Christ, it was horrible! We ate it, or drank it, if you will, every drop. And there was our corpulent cook, smiling and nodding through each spoonful.

There was one great postwar triumph for the 89th, one I don't think any of our boys will ever forget. We won the football championship of the whole AEF. You just can't believe how important it was then—the team that wins the Rose Bowl this year won't have any more loyal rooters.

First we beat the other national Army division in Germany, the 90th, 6–0. Then it was the Third Army's headquarters team, 30–0. Our third game was played on February 27, 1919, at Coblenz, against the 4th Division of regulars. This was it—the winner was to represent the Army of Occupation at Paris for the playoff.

Now, you know how college teams have their bands march out on the playing field. Well, we lined up every bugler in both divisions—hell, there must have been a couple of hundred, and at a designated signal they broke out with the soldiers' favorite, pay call. You should have heard the boys cheer that. Actually, they could have well played "Fair Harvard," as our captain, Paul Withington, and the leader of the 4th Division, Hamilton Fish, had both been stars at Cambridge, Massachusetts.

It was a great game, won by us, 14–0. I couldn't help thinking as I sat there that here were two real fighting divisions who just a few months before were trying to gain yards in that tangled mess known as the Argonne. And there were no first downs or penalties back there; it was for keeps. Yet I think our boys were just as interested in whipping the 4th Division as they had been in beating the Boche. Oh well, I guess that's the American way.

I didn't get a chance to see the games in Paris, but I know we came from behind each time. Eddie Mahan, another Harvard great, who was on the first team we beat in France, was so impressed with our boys that he decided to help coach us. The other finalist in the championship was the 36th Division, a National Guard outfit from Texas. As I remember it, we beat them 14–6 in the mud. Oh it was great to be the champs, all right, especially as back in the teens, it was the eastern school teams that got all the publicity. I guess we showed them that a bunch of Midwesterners could play that game.

And I'll tell you something else. We'd just started to set up a baseball league when we got the word we were going home. We had a guy in one of the division's artillery regiments who had pitched for the Cubs. I think he was from Nebraska. Ever hear of him? His name was Grover Cleveland Alexander. Hell, we would have won that championship also; there wasn't anyone going to hit Old Pete. But home we went. I can't remember anyone crying about the baseball league.

Oh there is one more thing. Remember that convention in Kansas City I talked about earlier? Now, knowing the veterans would be a little messy, they had set up these GI cans all over town. Well, I was standing on a street corner talking to one of the boys when all of a sudden we heard this God-awful racket. Someone was obviously throwing some cans down this hill, singing "Hinky Dinky, *Parlez-vous?*" at the top of his lungs. And can you guess who it was? None other than Captain Neville Fisher. He was back where he could get that great Kentucky Bourbon.

More Memories of France

Lieutenant Paul Smart of the 101st Field Artillery was one of the many artillerymen who spoke in awesome tones of watching the snorting horses pulling the guns into position under fire. It seems that this was one sight that was never forgotten by the men who witnessed it. He also told me of an incident from the second battle of the Marne.

"We had been going for about two days at Château-Thierry," related Smart, "when we moved into this beautiful peach orchard. It seemed an ideal spot for the battery to take a greatly needed rest. To make things even better, the Frenchman who owned the place appeared out of nowhere with this whole slew of stewed tomatoes—I can see them now—my God, they looked great!

"I filled up my mess kit to the brim and was just about to dig in when wham, this German 77 crashed into the ground over on my right, knocking me down and smearing the tomatoes all over my face.

"One of my men came running over, crying out, 'Mother of Christ, they've blown Smart's face off!'

"I jumped up, shouting, 'The hell they have! Now let's get *the* hell out of here!'

"We all thought it was pretty funny until an hour or two later, when the Germans zeroed in on us again. This time they killed four of our boys; there was nothing funny about that."

Walter Guild was a very serious student of French at the Boston Latin School. When his outfit, the 102nd Machine Gun Battalion, reached France, he found his services constantly in demand from the rest of the boys.

"A bunch of us went into this place that looked like a nice restaurant in Saint Nazaire. The boys wanted me along because I could speak French. As we sat down, we noticed that most of the waitresses were pretty good-looking. I did all the ordering, and I must say the food was pretty good. Then, after we had finished our meal, one of the waitresses came over to us and calmly lifted up her skirt—she didn't have a darn thing on underneath that skirt. Why, the place was really a high-class whorehouse. Now, I came from a proper Boston family; I was in a state of shock. But not some of my buddies. They started to hoot and whistle. They didn't need an interpreter any longer, so I moved on."

"I just got quite sick of being called the youngest-looking officer in the Army in 1917," chuckled Perry Hall. "I knew I'd have to do something about it.

"Then, one morning, I called my group to attention. One wag from the rear yelled out, 'And a little child shall lead them.' The rest of the men all guffawed.

"I dismissed the men and went to work trying to find a pure white horse. I was finally able to borrow a real big one for the next day.

"The next morning my unit was surprised to see me show up mounted on this giant.

"'All right, men,' I stated, 'we're going to start this day off with a twenty-five-mile hike with full marching gear.' And that's how we spent that day. I didn't hear any more cracks about my youthful countenance for a long while. The news on what I'd done spread throughout the Army, but I didn't realize how far it had spread until after I'd reached France. By then I was a captain and we were being reviewed by none other than John J. Pershing. The commanding general looked me over carefully and smiled.

"'Son,' he said, 'you must be the youngest captain in the AEF. What's your name?'

"'Perry Hall, sir.'

"'Oh God,' laughed the general, 'the man on the white horse.'"

The cootie problem was constant. No matter what efforts were made, if you were on the lines, you were a prime prospect for them.

One of my veterans was still a little squeamish about admitting that he indeed did suffer from the little fellows, so his name will not be used here. His story will.

"I was on our artillery battery's telephone switchboard one night," he said. "When my relief came, I started to look for a bunk but didn't have any luck. Then it dawned on me that our captain wouldn't be back for several hours, so I decided to sneak into his sack for a few hours. Our battery had set its headquarters up in this manor house about three miles behind the lines, and naturally he had taken the master bedroom.

"Oh what a setup! There was all this beautiful tapestry and a great big feather bed—I hadn't seen anything like it since before I went into the Army. It looked like heaven. I had about six beautiful hours of sleep. Boy, did I feel like a new man!

"Then you know what? About three hours later I started to itch— the goddamn captain was lousy. I never had any use for him after that."

Every army that has ever fought has experienced gastric troubles. In combat the bowels seem to always be either loose or tight. Another old artilleryman, Bill Peterson, told me a tale about the Meuse-Argonne.

"I'd been tied up for two days," recalled Bill, "when I decided I had to do something about it. I moved into this wooded area just before dawn with one thought in mind: Let go or die trying.

"Now, unbeknownst to me, a French battery had moved in on our left the night before. Jesus, I think all sixteen guns let go at the same time. Well, I wasn't tied up again until I got back to New York some eight months later."

Hart and the DH-4

Percival Hart

HIS SON'S HOME, NEW YORK CITY, JULY 1976
Percy Hart is now eighty-two years of age. After a post-World War I career that saw him spend several years with the Hughes Aircraft Company, a return to the service for World War II, and work in the real-estate field, Mr. Hart is now enjoying a healthy retirement.

He is a serious student of the Civil War and America's participation in World War I. In this latter area his speciality is the words to the songs that were sung in France.

In the main these songs were either French, British, or parodies on ones being sung back in the United States. In addition to an excellent recounting of his service in 1918 France, he also furnished me with a tape of these songs. This tape will eventually find its way to a museum. There are probably very few men left other than Mr. Hart who can remember those songs. Here are three of them:

> (To the tune of "Where Do We Go from Here, Boys? Where Do We Go from Here?")
>
> Oh Mother, take in your service flag,
> Your boy's in the SOS.
> He's SOL, but what the hell,
> He couldn't suffer less.
> He's weak and pale
> From too much tail,

Unless I miss my guess.
So Mother, pull in your service flag,
Your boy's in the SOS.

("I Want to Go Home"—British)

I want to go home, I want to go home,
The D-Hs they whistle, the Sampsons they roar,
I don't want to ride in a Bréquet no more.
Take me over the sea,
Where Allemandes can't get at me.
Oh my, I'm too young to die, I want to go home.

(The British Observer's Song)

Beside a Belgium water tank
One cold and wintry day
Beneath his battered biplane
A young observer lay.
His pilot hung from a telegraph pole,
But not entirely dead,
And he listened to the words
This young observer said.

"Oh I'm going to a better land
Where everything is bright,
Where handouts grow on bushes
And they stay out late at night.
You do not have to work at all
Or even change your socks,
And little drops of whisky
Come trickling from the rocks."

The pilot breathed his last few gasps
Before he passed away.
I'll tell you how it happened.
A flipper fell away.
The motor wouldn't work at all,
The other flipper too,
A bullet hit the gas tank
And the gas came leaking through.

And, oh yes, he was the only man I met who could sing the great French song "Madelon."

Second Lieutenant Percival Hart—AS, SC
Escadrille Sampson 40—French Army (attached)
135th Aero Squadron, USA

> Oh we don't have to fight like the infantry,
> Ride like the cavalry, shoot like artillery,
> We don't have to fly over Germany,
> WE ARE THE KIWI BIRDS.
>
> —SUNG BY PERCY HART TO THE TUNE
> OF "THE OLD GRAY MARE"

Now, the Kiwi birds were the air service officers who didn't fly. While we loved each individual, as a group we held them in contempt. I suppose it will always be like that: Those who are shot at just seem to gather an aversion for those who don't have to put it all on the line. Oh it was all pretty silly—after all, we had to have them—but you didn't think about that after you'd spent a few hours up with the Boche.

Anyway, I had one of my biggest shocks as far as the Kiwis were concerned when we were first ordered to the front. We were naturally all excited. Then I looked at the duty roster and the name of one of my best friends was not listed. I quickly buttonholed him.

"Bill," I said, "for Christ's sake, what's happened to you?"

"Oh," he answered, "I've put in for radio officer."

"Are you crazy? Radio officer? Why?"

"Well, I've been thinking it over: If anything ever happened to me, it would kill my mother."

Can you imagine that? Didn't he think the rest of us had mothers? I can honestly say, though, that he was in a very small minority. If you were a flier, either observer or pilot, it was because you wanted to fly against the Germans. And most of us did.

Now, to start, let's go back to the spring of 1917. I was a senior at Yale College. As I look back, I cannot believe that most of us were as apathetic about the war in Europe as we were. Here was the greatest conflict in the history of the world going on, and we were more concerned about who was in which fraternity than who was going to win the war.

Then, April 6, and it all changed overnight—Yale turned into an armed camp. Everybody joined something. I can say parenthetically that at least 95 per cent of the undergraduates eventually saw service. In my case it was, at first, the artillery. They had an ROTC unit at New Haven. If you decided to enlist in it, you could drop two courses. At the time I had two real dogs—the only things worse than these courses were the professors giving them, perfectly dreadful. So I killed two birds with one stone by going into the ROTC.

In the meantime, there was a strong movement underfoot for all of us to go down to Fort Sill's School of Fire as one big Yale unit. But this was squashed by the government, and it's a good thing it was, because it would have been catastrophic. You see, in 1917 Yale was quite a cliquey school. You had the "ins" and the "outs" among the students. If we'd all gone together, it would have been merely an extension of Yale, which would have been a hell of a lousy way to fight a war.

Well, instead of going as one big unhappy Yale family, we were told to apply to an OCS training camp near our hometown. I was brought up in Chicago, so the place for me to apply was Fort Sheridan, Illinois. I was accepted so quickly that it was announced in the Chicago *Tribune* before I'd received my card in the mail. You can bet your bottom dollar I was packed as quickly as possible and on my way.

The school was a ninety-day-wonder camp, and you know all the jokes they have about those places; well, not a one was true about Sheridan. They literally worked our asses off. Out of those accepted —almost all college men, incidentally—only 50 per cent or so earned commissions. I honestly feel this was the cream of the crop.

Our high spot of the graduation was the march down Michigan Avenue in Chicago. They may have had parades before the birth of Christ, and I'm sure they'll have them right up to the destruction of the world, but they'll never have a better one than ours. It was the most perfect marching you could ever imagine. We were proud as peacocks. We'd been drilling for three months, and we knew our business. We hadn't lost our sense of humor, though. We had the band play "I Didn't Raise My Boy to Be a Soldier" as we marched along. The bystanders loved it.

After graduation I joined the 86th Division at Camp Grant in Rockland, Illinois. It was a national Army outfit, with most of the men from Illinois and Wisconsin. The day after I arrived, the drafted men started coming into my regiment—the 331st Field Artillery—and we put them to work at once. Christ, did we train, day, and night, but they didn't seem to be in any rush to get us over to France. I figured I wasn't going to see any of the war if I stayed with the 86th.[1]

Then I had a streak of luck. I was walking by the colonel's office when I saw this sign:

"Wanted—Volunteers to become Aerial Observers."

I asked for permission to look into it. The colonel was delighted.

"It's really exciting duty, Mr. Hart," he told me, "and it'll probably mean a quick trip to France. Your job will be to fly over the enemy lines and observe where they have their artillery, ammunition dumps, troop positions, and so forth. You won't be a pilot; you'll be in the second seat, directly behind the man at the controls, but you'll see plenty of the Boche. And you'll relay this back to the American batteries, who in turn will open up on the Germans." It sounded great to me, so I put in my name. It didn't take them long to accept me and to get me down to the aerial observers' school at Fort Sill. I think our training here lasted about two months. After it

[1] Mr. Hart was probably correct. The 86th Division didn't arrive in France until September 21. It never went into action as a division.

was over, they officially transferred us to the Artillery Section of the Signal Corps—the ASSC. We were now fliers—not pilots, fliers. We wore half wings on our blouses, whereas the pilots had the full ones.

From then on things moved very fast. Our group was put aboard a troop train and quickly sent to Garden City, Long Island, to await room on a transport. The ship that we ended up going abroad on was the *Mount Vernon*. Our voyage was rather uneventful, but the ship's return trip to the United States wasn't; she was torpedoed and almost sunk.

By now it was the end of February 1918. I was actually in France, and I didn't have to worry about missing out on the war—there was plenty left for everybody.

The first thing they did was to send us to observers' school at Tours. Here we found out that we would be following the French system of observing. You see, they had two methods: the British one and the French one. In the British system, the pilot did everything—pilot the ship, observe, take the pictures; the only thing the second man did was fire the Lewis gun. Not so the French. In their system it was the other way around. The pilot's only job was to handle the plane; the observer did everything else.

Our next stop was the gunnery school at Cajaux. We spent two weeks here learning the whys and wherefores of the Lewis gun. They started us off shooting .22-caliber rifles at targets out on this lake. While doing this we'd be speeding along on motor launches. This was to accustom us to hitting a target while we were moving. The final stage was shooting from a plane at a sleeve being towed by another plane. This was almost disastrous, however. Some of our boys put some bullets into the plane towing the sleeve. No one was hurt, but you should have heard those Frogs yelling about it.

When those two weeks were over, most of us knew if we were going to be good shots or not. There was one of us about whom there was no question; his name was Gus Lindstrum. Being Americans, we'd always make a bet if it was at all possible to see who was doing the best shooting. You just couldn't beat Gus. He left Cajaux with enough money to last the rest of the war.

The real important thing was learning all about those Lewis guns. As observers we always had two of those gas-operated beauties. You'd pull the trigger of one and then there was a bolt and wire control on the other one that would come down to a pistol grip that you grabbed when firing that second gun. The guns were aimed so the fire would converge at about two hundred feet. Each gun had a drum of ninety-seven bullets. We also had special aerial sights that tried to compensate for our speed and that of the enemy planes. It was all a little complicated, but we did our best to master the details; after all, those guns could save your life.

Well, after the firing school we were ready. At this time, it was the spring of 1918, the Americans were pouring out the observers faster than they were pilots. So the Americans made a deal with the French to farm out our observers as active members of the Fourth French Army. I was sent to Escadrille Sampson 40 on the Rheims Front. This was around the middle of May. I can't tell you the absolute exhilaration I experienced the night that I joined them. And those French—they treated the Americans like brothers. The captain of the Escadrille took me up on my first mission. After that, I went into the regular rotation. I adjusted artillery; I flew reconnaissances; I made out reports. It was all terribly exciting. Then, in July, with all that fighting around the Marne, it turned into a real barn-burner. It was here that we ran into the new Fokker 7 for the first time.

CHRIST, what a plane that was! Remember, my squadron was made up of mainly real seasoned fliers, both pilots and observers. But those Fokkers began to shoot us down like flies. Our captain was killed; our chief observer was killed; oh I think we lost six or seven planes from our squadron alone there. Each time you went up, you didn't know if your plane would come back. Of course, the men weren't always killed if the plane went down, but it was pretty nerve-chilling.

I particularly remember that Champagne-Marne affair on July 15. I was flying over the area, relaying positions on a wireless back to our artillery. We saw Gouraud's Fourth Army stop those Germans cold. Three days later the French Tenth Army started the offensive that turned the tide of the war.

Shortly after our real tough flying around the Marne, I received a telegram from the U. S. Air Service of the AEF. I can remember it word for word:

"Second Lieutenant Percival Hart will report to commanding officer of the 135th U. S. Aero Squadron at Amonte." I didn't know it at the time, but this wire meant that I was to end up flying in the first patrol ever flown in combat that featured American-made planes, the DH-4s with the Liberty motors. I was also to be the observer in the first one to be shot down. Now, I realize that those planes, nicknamed "the flaming coffins," have taken a hell of a lot of umbrage, but damn it, they weren't that bad. I'd definitely put them on a par with the Sampsons.

Before I leave the French, however, I want to make sure I've made myself clear on how marvelous they were to me. There were two Americans here, myself and a man named Jefferson Hays-Davis —he was the grandson of the President of the Confederacy. Well sir, those French couldn't have treated the two of us any better than they did. Their life-style was much more formal than it was with the U.S. fliers, but we soon adjusted to it. Every night we'd sit down to a formal dinner. None of the other officers could be seated until the captain arrived. The food itself was usually quite good, and it was served in the grand manner. We had to be in perfectly correct uniforms before we could even enter the mess. Everything was done in style.

Now, when I say "correct uniforms," I mean that Davis and I were in U.S. uniforms, not French ones. There was one time, though, when I did appear for dinner in the uniform of a French officer. It came a little later in my story, but I'll tell you about it now. At the time this happened I was acting as a liaison officer between the French and the Americans.

Well, one of the wealthy French fliers decided to celebrate his birthday in a very unique way—he took over a whole bordello for the evening. The party was held in a town called Bar-le-Duc, definitely off-limits for the Americans. So *mes amis* dressed me up as a French officer. Christ, I breezed right by the Yank MPs—they even saluted me. That party, what an affair! The birthday man had the whole thing catered from one of those very chic Parisienne restaurants. The wines were all vintage. And the girls, they were all dressed up in fancy gowns. They even developed high-tone accents and mannerisms for the evening. The whole thing was so typically French—they're a great people![2]

[2] Mr. Hart in no way led me to believe that his activities extended past the banquet, even though he said it apparently did with some of the French fliers.

Well, after receiving my telegram I left my French friends and reported to the 135th. By this time I'd had over fifty hours of flying over the German lines—in other words, I was considered a real veteran. The 135th was a brand-new squadron, so new that I was the first man to report in. Shortly after I arrived, the rest of the observers and pilots began to check in. A lot of us had known each other from one place or another, so it was pretty easy for us to pair off. This was really quite important. It made things a lot easier if the pilot and observer got along well. Our commanding officer was a man named Blair Thaw, a brother of William Thaw, who had been the guiding light of the Escadrille Lafayette.

Next to come were our planes, the new American DH-4s. Most of us had already logged combat hours, so the minute the airships arrived, we were ready. The actual date was August 9, 1918, when the new planes first went on patrol. We were over at a field near Nancy at the time.

Naturally, the newspapers made a big thing out of it. You know, "Steely-eyed Yanks take up first American planes." A couple of our pilots had really tied one on the night before—they could have said "red-eyed" Yanks. But whatever, that first flight was a dud. It was a hell of a cloudy day, so all we did was go up to where we thought the lines were and buzz around a bit—couldn't see a damn thing—then headed for home. From then on, though, we started to fly regular missions. And our trip of a week later was quite a little different than that first jaunt.

It was August 15, 1918, to be precise, and quite an event in my life, all right. My pilot was a man named Donald Cole. He's still alive and a great guy, owns a Cadillac agency in Columbus, Ohio. Well, we were to go up on a photographic mission. On this type of a flight we'd always be accompanied by a Spad, because it was impossible for the observer to man the Lewis guns when he was taking the pictures. He'd have to be down in this area at the bottom of the cockpit we called "the office," setting up the plates and picking out the sites to be photographed.

So on this morning we had reached our objective, and I was down in "the office" getting ready to take the pictures when all of a sudden I heard this rat-a-tat-tat. I immediately jumped up and grabbed for my guns and looked around. Oh Christ Almighty, there's this Boche Albatros coming right at us with its guns blazing.

You could actually see the goddamn bullets coming at our plane.

"Aw-oh," I said to myself, "this is going to be bad. This bastard has us."

Then, quick as a wink, our nose went down. I was thrown around like a rubber ball. If I hadn't had my safety belt fastened, I wouldn't be here now. We'd been hit, all right—you could even smell some gasoline. I expected the plane to go up any minute. Our Spad had taken off after that Albatros, so we were all alone in the sky. Cole is yelling like mad, but I couldn't understand a word he was saying. It was obvious though that he was trying to glide us down for a crash-landing behind our lines. I never could figure out how long the whole thing took—sometimes it seemed like an eternity, and others like a flash—but somehow we made it with a huge thud. I jumped out of that plane as fast as I could and checked out Don.

"Get me out of this goddamn plane," he yelled. "I've been hit."

"Oh Christ," I said as I tried to help him out. "Where?"

"In my thigh, in my thigh."

I got him out, and we surmised what had happened. Two bullets had gone through his thigh, one slug above the bone and the other below it. One of them had cut a piece out of the plane's gasoline lead line from the tank to the carburetor. How in heaven's name he'd been able to glide us in, I'll never know. It must have been providential—there is no other explanation.

Well, after I got Cole out of the plane, we spotted these Doughboys coming at us. Hell, most of them didn't know one plane from another, so we started to yell, "Americans, Americans, DON'T SHOOT! Thank God they heard us. They were Midwesterners from the 89th Division. They helped us get out of there in a hurry. The Germans, you see, had spotted our plane, and their artillery opened up on it. We moved out of their fire in the nick of time. I stayed with Cole until he was taken to Evacuation Hospital No. 1. Then I returned to our squadron, where I was met with some bad news.

It seemed that our captain, Blair Thaw, had been taking a plane back to a depot when he'd flown smack into a telephone wire. He was killed in the ensuing crash, and the observer, Cord Meyer, had ended up with a badly broken leg. The whole thing was so ironic. Thaw had spent so many hours flying in combat and he ended up getting killed like that. His brother, William Thaw, came to the funeral, as did his mother. She'd been living in France. Most of our funerals weren't family affairs, but this one was. It was all quite sad.

Shortly after Thaw's death I made a mistake. We had a saying in World War I, "Never volunteer,"[3] and how sage a premise that is. Well, one day our group was asked if any of us could speak French. I was standing next to a guy named Howard Maguire, who had studied *en français* with me at Hyde Park High School in Chicago. We thought it would be a lark to put our hands up. The two of us were then immediately ordered to a place called Rumont. We managed to take the long route, which allowed us to spend a night in Nancy. Let's just say it was a great evening and let it go with that.

When we arrived at Rumont, we were assigned to separate Bréquet Escadrilles under the French. It was during this period, incidentally, that I went to the birthday party at Bar-le-Duc.

It was great to be with the French again until I found out what I was there for. The plans were underfoot, you see, for the battle of Saint Mihiel. I was to be a liaison officer between the Americans and the French during that fight. Well, baloney with that! A big show coming up and I'd been slated to be in liaison—I wanted to be on the lines. You know, all the time I was in France I was eager to be on patrol, but when I'd get up there, I'd say to myself, "Perc, what the hell are you *doing* here?" Anyway, I immediately started to make phone calls to everyone I knew to get back to the 135th. The answer was always the same.

"Hart, you're not running the U. S. Army. Stay where you are."

I'd just about given up hope when late on the afternoon of September 10 my old friend Bill Lynn, the chief observer of the 135th, showed up at Rumont.

"Hello, Perc," he said. "Pack your duds. You're coming back where you belong. We're about to have a big show, and I want my top men up in the sky."

Oh what a great surprise! If ever a man picked up his toothbrush in a hurry, it was yours, truly. I jumped in his car and we headed back to the 135th. What a ride! Everywhere we looked we saw soldiers moving into position, and they were all Americans. I had never seen as many Yanks in one place in France before. The

---

[3] Also a prevalent expression in World War II, and probably the same in the Revolutionary War.

night was pitch dark, and as I remember it, raining most of the time, but I could see enough to know one thing: A big one was coming up.

I spent the next day (September 11) trying to line up a pilot. Then I began to panic. Hell, I couldn't find anyone who didn't already have an observer; it was beginning to look as if I might miss it after all. The next morning I was up about an hour or so before dawn. I was "Johnny at the rat hole," all right, checking everywhere to see if there was an opening. Then I had a stroke of luck. A French captain named Rodival had flown over to the 135th in a Bréquet to make sure our new men knew what to expect when the battle began. He figured that seeing he was there, he might as well go up with the squadron. He didn't have an observer—until I cornered him, that is.

Our job that morning was to fly infantry combat patrol, starting at dawn, or *reconnaissance au point du jour*, as the French called it. Oh they have a beautiful language!

Well, we flew over the lines, checking the position of our troops and those of the Germans. We were told to place special emphasis on the Boche artillery and to quickly report any troop withdrawals. This meant that we'd have to fly very low, which presented a problem—the trajectory of the artillery. The big guns wouldn't necessarily be aiming at us, but we could easily fly right into one of those shells. One of our planes had the bejesus knocked out of it, just blown to pieces, by an American curtain of fire that way.

Now, as we'd be flying along, I'd notice everything I could and write it down, making two carbons of these notes. When I had enough material, I'd put the original and the two copies into three different tin tubes that had these red streamers attached to them. When everything was set, we'd fly over our three headquarters— Army, corps, and divisional [Hart was flying in support of the 89th Division]—and drop one of the tubes over each one. It sounds primitive today, but it did the job.

After we had finished our mission, we flew back to our base expecting a rest, but it wasn't to be—not for me, anyway. I was quickly called into the headquarters of the 135th.

"Perc," one of the officers pleaded, "we have a rookie pilot and a brand-new DH-4. The guy's never flown in combat before, but we need that plane in the air. I don't want to send a green observer up with him. How about it?"

Oh what the hell could I say? So back I went. By this time the battle was at full pitch. We had a lot of close calls, but fortunately came through all right. It was pretty rough on a brand-new man, though. I can still remember the look on his face as he came over to me after we'd landed.

"Holy Christ," he sputtered out, "are they all like that?"

It was now early afternoon, and I figured I was through for the day. I grabbed some food and was all ready to dig in when I got the call again.

"Enjoy your meal, Hart," I was told, "but don't get too comfortable. You're going back up at four on a special mission, this time with Curtin."

I knew Curtin very well; he was a great pilot and a swell guy, but hell, I was beat. Nevertheless, there I was, at 4:00 P.M., back up again. This trip turned out to be a dream come true. I was presented with a perfect shot, and I received official confirmation for a victory. The observers never had anywhere near the opportunities for a victory that the pursuit pilots did; even one was considered something special.

Here's what happened: I had just finished taking some pictures when I looked up and saw this German coming right into the sights of my Lewis guns. He was moving in over our tail, just *not* the way to come at an observer. You see, if they came at you from underneath, it was hard to get a shot—or from the front, where you'd have to shoot through your own wings, that was bad also. But when they came down from behind, bull's-eye. And I shot him down. This time when we returned to the squadron, I just collapsed. I'd been at it from dawn to dusk, and I was utterly beat.

The next day was even tougher—the roughest scrap I was ever in. Curtin and myself went up twice, and on the second mission we ended up right smack in the middle of three American pursuit planes that had been hopped by seven Fokkers. Oh Christ, it was brutal! I kept trying to hold the Boche off, and Curtin was trying to keep the plane beneath the Germans so they couldn't come at us from underneath. The sky was literally filled with planes—God, what a shootout! Then, like it did on so many occasions in 1918, the fight just seemed to break off. Perhaps the Germans were running out of fuel, I don't know, but it was all over. I can thank my lucky stars that we ended up in one piece. Incidentally, I was later told that I had been in the air longer than any other American during that Saint Mihiel battle.[4]

After the battle we spent some time in a rest area, where we picked up some replacements. Two of these men, Ray Krout, he was from New Jersey, and Hunter McDonald, turned into one of the best teams on the Western Front. You can imagine the fun we had with Krout's name; everyone kept telling him he was on the wrong side. But he was a great guy; he could take a kidding.

When we were ready for combat again, the Meuse-Argonne offensive was starting. But our squadron didn't see much of that one. Most of our missions were just on the fringe of the Argonne. In the meantime, Bill Lynn had been made chief operations officer of the 135th, so he made me the chief observer. This didn't change my flying status at all, but it gave me the job of matching up the pilots and the observers in the various planes. It also meant that I could fly with whomever I chose.

Then, toward the end of October, we were assigned to General Bullard's newly created Second Army. We were supposed to get all cranked up for a big show around the middle of November. But during the first week of November I'd gone on a special mission twenty or thirty miles behind the German lines. Hell, I could see there wasn't going to be much more of the war. The Germans could still be formidable when facing the Americans, but behind their lines they were a mess; the Armistice was no shock to me. I came home in February of 1919, which meant I'd spent just about one year in France. Oh but what a year it was!

Well, I'm eighty-one years old now. I have a fine family with lots of grandchildren. But every now and then I can sit back and close my eyes and there it all is. It's France, 1918, not Los Angeles, 1976. I don't dwell much on the bad parts. I think mostly of my buddies and those early-morning flights. Oh they were so beautiful; the only

---

[4] Hart received the Distinguished Service Cross for his work at Saint Mihiel. Part of the citation reads: "On September 13 his steady fire drove off a large patrol of enemy planes that had attacked three Allied planes."

sound was the motor. The dawning was just beginning. On a clear day you could see for miles, the whole French countryside. Remember, we had those open cockpits. The setting was so celestial. Hell, the war seemed hundreds of miles away. Oh it was something, I'll tell you that!

"Hello, Central, Give Me No-man's-land. My Daddy's Over There."

Good-bye, Ma, good-bye, Pa,
Good-bye, mule, with yer old hee-haw!

—WORLD WAR I SONG

One of the main differences between the Doughboy and his GI son was the music, both in the United States and overseas. By and large the World War I American Army did sing, while the force that fought against the Axis powers did not. Colonel Enos Curtin, one of the many retreads from the war against the Kaiser who returned to the service for World War II, was given a 1943 assignment to try to find out why there was a musical difference between the generations. Mr. Curtin told me the results of his findings while we were having a drink in New York City.

"After what this country found out about modern war in 1918," he explained, "the kids of 1943 could find nothing to sing about."

So be it. They did sing, however, in 1918, even though there was usually considerable difference between what they sang Stateside and what they sang overseas. Tin Pan Alley in New York City dictated the music for the United States, while the general conditions of the soldiers in France were responsible for the ditties of the AEF.

It all started with the British songs. "Pack 'Up Your Troubles" and "Tipperary" were smash hits in America long before April 6, 1917, as were many other English and Canadian numbers. Here the language similarity between the United States and Great Britain played a strong psychological part in determining what side the Yanks would eventually be on in the war. Music is a central theme in a country's culture. It was quite unlikely that the guttural songs of the Germans would be sung at the Palace Theater in New York City, and they weren't. But the English ones were. The home fires were kept burning for a lad in Toronto or London, not Berlin; this was a key factor in American thinking.

Once the United States did enter the war, the country was flooded with a new brand of war songs, a huge amount of which had something to say about the Kaiser. Wilhelm had become fair game. "We're All Going Calling on the Kaiser" and "I'd Like to See the Kaiser with a Lily in His Hand" were two that used his name in their titles. "Where Do We Go from Here, Boys?" contained a line that stated, "We'll slip a pill to Kaiser Bill and knock him on his ear" (usually followed by "and when we get Von Hindenburg, we'll ram him in the rear"), and the immensely popular "Good-bye, Broadway, Hello, France" had a version that boasted, "We're going to kick the Kaiser in the pants and it isn't going to take us long." The most outrageous of the lot was the one that went like this:

> We don't want the bacon,
> We don't want the bacon,
> All we want is a slice of the Rhine.
>
> We'll crown Bill the Kaiser
> With a bottle of Budweiser;
> We'll have a wonderful time.

> Old Wilhelm the Gross
> Will shout "*Vas ist los?*"
> When we hit that Hindenburg Line—fine.

All the songs didn't talk about the Kaiser, though. George M. Cohan managed to write one called "Over There" that placed its emphasis on a lad named Johnny who was to get his gun and show the world what the Yanks could do. It was probably the last truly great war song of its kind that will ever be written. Based on the simple strains of a bugle call, it swept the country. One of the veterans I interviewed had originally been deferred from the draft. He explained what "Over There" really could accomplish: "I was standing on the sidewalk in Indianapolis, Indiana, watching a group of soldiers board a troop train. There were a bunch of old-timers in their GAR uniforms saluting these men. Then as the train pulled out, a band started to play 'Over There.' It was too much for me. The hell with the deferment—I went down to the post office and enlisted."

Many of the other songs were either semicomical or just plain absurd. They seemed to be trying to show America that the whole thing was a barrel of laughs. One piece of Americana that will live forever (or will it?) went like this:

> If he can fight like he can love,
> Oh what a soldier boy he'll be.
> I've never seen him in a real good scrap,
> But you're a goner when you're on his lap.
> Then Mr. Hun, you'd better run
> And climb a great big linden tree.
> If he can fight like he can love,
> Then it's good night, Germany!

Even Sergeant Irving Berlin's great army show *Yip, Yip, Yaphank* was full of light tunes such as "Oh How I Hate to Get Up in the Morning," which ended up with "And then I'll get the other pup, the one who wakes the bugler up, and then spend the rest of my life in bed." I suppose these songs played their part on the home front, but they quickly faded when the men went on the lines; they were just too far from the realities of loneliness and death that the men lived with.

A good example of the difference between the Stateside songs and those of France can be found in the ballad "The Rose of No-man's-land." In the United States it ended up:

> 'neath the war's dread curse
> Stands a Red Cross nurse,
> She's the Rose of no-man's-land.

One veteran told me that in France the ending was:

> 'neath the war's dread curse
> There's a big black hearse,
> It's the last ride from no-man's-land.

When you constantly live with death, it eases your mind if you laugh at it—or else you make friends with it. "My Buddy" was one of the few sentimental songs that made it with the Doughboys. Another was "There's a Long, Long Trail Awinding," which some of the men felt meant eternity, while others thought it meant just plain happiness. The sentimental song that was the most popular— and this one definitely held out hope for a bright tomorrow, a time when the clouds would roll by and the soldier could return to his sweetheart—was "Till We Meet Again."

These, however, were the exceptions in France. Most of the Doughboys' songs either laughed at themselves or at something they were supposed to respect, or, of course, they talked about sex. In this latter area there was one tune that stood head and shoulders above anything else. I say tune rather than song because that's what it was, a tune. It appears that it was first a ribald British song about an aging hag called the *mademoiselle* from Armentières, but when the Yanks grabbed it, the only thing that remained was the

"Hinky Dinky, *parlez-vous?*" The lady in question became:

> The *mademoiselle* from Bar-le-Duc, *parlez-vous?*
>
> . . . .
>
> She'll f— you in a chicken coop,
> Hinky Dinky, *parlez-vous?*
>
> The *mademoiselle* from Is-sur-Tille, *parlez-vous?*
>
> . . . .
>
> She can zig-zig-zig like a spinning wheel,
> Hinky Dinky, *parlez-vous?*
>
> The *mademoiselle* from gay Paree, *parlez-vous?*
>
> . . . .
>
> She had the clap and give it to me,
> Hinky Dinky, *parlez-vous?*

And sometimes the *mademoiselle* would disappear entirely. It might be:

> The French they had a custom rare, *parlez-vous?*
>
> . . . .
>
> They shit and piss in the local square,
> Hinky Dinky, *parlez-vous?*

or:

> The 2nd Division is on the Rhine, *parlez-vous?*
>
> . . . .
>
> F—— their women and drinking their wine,
> Hinky Dinky, *parlez-vous?*

Whatever the verse was, it was always ribald. If the men I talked to were any indication, the "Hinky Dinky" tune was sung by more American soldiers than any other tune in the history of the Republic.

It only had one rival among the Doughboys. This was also a simple little ditty, which has been sung by soldiers in one form or another since the beginning of time.

In World War I it went like this:

> Home, boys, home
> That's where I want to be.
> Home, boys, home
> In the land of liberty.
> We'll hang Old Glory
> To the top of a pole,
> And we'll all re-enlist
> In a pig's asshole.

And that pretty well sums up how the Doughboys felt about things.

The Congressman Who Went to War

Hamilton Fish

Ham Fish was one of the first veterans of World War I to be elected to the United States Congress. This was the beginning of a political career that found him serving in Washington, D.C., until 1945. During twelve of these years his Hudson River Valley neighbor, Franklin Roosevelt, was the nation's President. To put it mildly, these two men did not always get along.

The very fact that some sixty years after he had first taken military training in Plattsburg, New York, still found him going to an office daily speaks for the remarkable physical condition of the man. As I sat in his office and discussed his AEF service with him, it was utterly impossible to imagine that this Harvard College football immortal was close to eighty-nine years of age. Many of the men I visited with looked younger than they actually were, but the No. 1 prize goes to Mr. Fish.

The man's stamina is incredible. He couldn't see me the first time I called him on the phone because he was going to make a speech the next day. Then there was a problem concerning a new book he was working on—or was it two new books he was currently authoring?

Then, about six months after our meeting, I noticed a piece in the paper about Hamilton Fish's coming marriage. I naturally felt that this article meant his son, the current Congressman Fish. But no, it was the Hamilton Fish who had helped raise and train the 15th New York (Colored) in 1916 and '17 because he felt the black American was as entitled to fight for the United States as any other American. The 15th New York became the 369th U. S. Infantry, and fight it did. Its record was one of the best in the AEF.

Captain Hamilton Fish
K Company, 369th (15th N.Y.) U. S. Infantry
3rd Battalion

Be it enacted . . . that the American Battle Monuments Commission is hereby authorized and directed to erect near Sechault, France, a suitable monument to commemorate the valiant services of the 369th, 371st, and 372nd American infantry regiments, attached to the French Fourth Army, at a cost not to exceed thirty thousand dollars, from appropriations heretofore or hereafter appropriated by Congress.

—CONGRESSMAN FISH'S ATTEMPT
TO OBTAIN A MONUMENT TO THE
BLACK TROOPS IN FRANCE

You must forgive me if I seem a little down in the dumps today. A dear friend of mine for many, many years, Jim Farley, passed on yesterday and I'm feeling rather low. We were on opposite sides of the fence, but Jim was an honorable man, and I respected him a great deal.

Well, you want to know about the war and my service with the 15th New York. First we'll have to go back to 1915 and '16, when I went to Plattsburg. I was serving in the New York State legislative body in Albany at the time, having first been elected in 1912 as a member of Teddy Roosevelt's Bull Moose Party.

At this time President Wilson was trying to follow a very strict policy of neutrality. However, when the Germans sank the *Lusitania* in February of 1915, a lot of Americans began to feel that at least we should learn some of the aspects of being a soldier.

General Leonard Wood was one of these men; I guess he was really the instigator of the Plattsburg camp. The idea behind this movement was to allow men of officer material to spend several weeks in the summer training so that if we did go to war, we'd have some men who could immediately step into the service with commissions.

I was twenty-seven years of age then and in great physical condition. I'd played a great deal of football at Harvard, you know, and I seemed to take easily to that type of life. After the end of my second summer I figured I should be in a position to acquire my captaincy in the reserves. That's where I ran into a snag.

Many of the officers who were training us, you see, were old-line regulars. And the one I was dealing with had spent all his life in the Army.

"Be a captain and you're only twenty-seven!" he exploded. "Why, look at all the years I've had, and I'm only a major!"

"Yes, I understand, Major," I replied, "but I graduated Harvard with honors, and I've spent two summers here; I think I can pass the captain's examination."

"Not the one I'll give you! Do you think you can answer questions about cooking details?"

"But I don't want to be a cook; I want to be a captain."

"Bah," he snorted, "you should have many years of hard service before you become a captain."

So that was the end of that. But you know, shortly after war was declared we had twenty-one-year-old men becoming captains. I don't know what happened to the old major, but I assume he was too antiquated to go to France.

When I returned to the city the day after my put-down by the major, I ran into Bill Hayward, a prominent attorney whom I'd known for years. I told him my problem, but he just laughed.

"Ham," he said, "if you want to be a captain, I'll make you one on the spot. We're putting together a Negro National Guard outfit, the 15th New York. I'm the colonel. If war does come, I want to be able to take a colored outfit to France right off the bat."

Well, this appealed to me. I'd heard that Governor Whitman had wanted a colored National Guard unit, and so had Theodore Roosevelt. The former President had seen how well they had done in Cuba. I know he was anxious to be involved.

Poor Teddy, that great American, all the time he spent trying to get Wilson to prepare the country, and then when war did come, the President put him on the shelf. I know that Teddy would have loved to have gone to France with our 15th New York.

Well, I accepted Colonel Hayward's offer, and we set out to put together a regiment. Of course, we didn't have an armory like the 7th or 69th New York, so we did our recruiting right on the streets of Harlem. Haw, haw, I remember we even had a cigar store and a dance hall that we used. We did have one thing special: We were offering the black man a chance to be part of a combat outfit that would go to France if our country entered the war. Of course, we didn't use the word "black" in those days, we called them colored or Negro, but whatever they were known as, we picked up some splendid recruits.

And we did just as well with the officers. I'd say about 90 per cent of our men with commissions were white, and the other 10 per cent were black. The whites were almost all graduated from the leading eastern colleges at that time, and all eager to serve in the 15th. Of the black officers we did have one or two lemons, but the rest were outstanding. Before we were through, as far as I'm concerned, we had one of the best National Guard outfits in the country.

There was one thing special we did develop, and here we had the best: That was our band. First we got Jimmy Europe, one of the leading musical figures of the day, as our bandleader. We immediately made him a lieutenant and tried to get as many star performers as we could. Then Jimmy explained the situation to us.

"Look, gentlemen," he said, "you're talking about a twenty-eight-piece band. I can't do anything with that. We've got to get sixty.

And you'll have to pay a little extra to the top ones—I can't get people like Frank de Broit [Europe's great trumpet player] to come here for peanuts."

Well, after all, Europe was the leader and arranger for Vernon and Irene Castle. We figured he knew what he was talking about, so we went to work. We raised a special fund, many thousands of dollars, from a few very wealthy New York families.

Then we discovered another problem: The American blacks were great on trumpets, drums, that type of thing, but they weren't much good on things like flutes. So we sent someone down to Puerto Rico to recruit some blacks who could play reed instruments.

But I suppose Jimmy's greatest coup was getting Noble Sissle as his drum major. I think Europe and Sissle were just about as well known as any black musicians in America in 1917.

And what a band we ended up with! Why, do you know, later on, during our first two or three months in France, our band went all over the country playing for soldiers and civilians alike. They won all the prizes available. Of course, they were a tremendous tonic for our troops, great morale-boosters.

Well, after war was declared, they sent us down to Camp Wadsworth in Spartanburg, South Carolina. What a mistake that was! Those people in that area just weren't ready for a black infantry regiment. Gangs of toughs would push our men off the sidewalks, call them dirty niggers, just abuse them in every way. We had a black captain named Marshall. Why, the man was a New York City attorney, and he was still thrown off a streetcar.

It only took Washington about two weeks to realize they'd better get us out of there before we had an explosion. And I'll tell you something: Our officers, white and black, were just as outraged as the enlisted men. Remember, this was sixty years ago; we knew we'd run into all kinds of difficulties, but we didn't think it would be as bad as it was. Another thing I'd like to tell you is that the 7th New York was also at Spartanburg at that time, and they were as furious as we were. When we were shipped North to Camp Mills, they lined the company streets singing George M. Cohan's new song, "Over There." Our boys waved back at them.

Well, when they got us up to Mills, things weren't much better simply because they bivouaced us right next to an Alabama infantry regiment of the Rainbow Division. Then the trouble started all over again, only this could have been a hell of a lot worse. Rumors started to fly around that the southern boys were actually going to attack us—and we didn't have any ammunition. Oh it would have been horrendous.

Now, the 69th New York was also there, and I knew several of their officers, as did a lot of our leaders. So we went over and told them we were going to do everything we could to stop this, but they better give us some ammunition so our men could defend themselves if they had to. And they did.

Then the trouble started in the middle of the next night when our buglers started blowing "to arms." We had told our men, you see, that if we were attacked to fight it out and not to give an inch of ground. It would mean casualties, but what else could we do, run?

So, I lined my company up and went out into the darkness to seek out some of the Alabamian officers. It didn't take me long to find three or four of them.

"Listen," I said, "this will be utter disaster to start a war here. We've given our men orders to fight back, and a lot of people will get hurt—and, I may add, probably all the officers."

It was pitch dark, and I guess they couldn't see that I had my revolver drawn and was holding it behind my back. I'd just gotten it and wasn't exactly sure how to use it. But I knew if it went off accidentally, there would be hell to pay so I had my thumb between the hammer and the cylinder.

Well, I'm happy to say these fine young officers were as anxious to stop this as I was.

"Don't y'all worry, Captain," they said to me, "we're trying to round up our ringleaders now. Y'all have to appreciate that our boys aren't used to seeing colored as soldiers, especially as they're living next door. But we'll handle it."

And they did. I understand also that they punished the worst offenders.

But that's the way it was. I guess the government started to realize the best thing to do was just send us abroad.

It wasn't as easy as it sounds, though. First, they had to get us a ship—remember, we were not a part of any division, just one black regiment. They finally got us our vessel, and we started out. Well, we'd no sooner got off Sandy Hook when we were rammed by some other ship—one of ours, not a German. So they had to patch that up before we could proceed; you couldn't cross the Atlantic with a hole in your bow.

We ended up in a small convoy but with no destroyers at all. So we had to be particularly careful not to show any lights, and I mean *no* lights. From five o'clock in the evening until 6:00 A.M. that ship was pitch dark.

Then, when we did land at Saint-Nazaire,[1] we had another shock waiting for us: They had no place to put the regiment. They weren't going to put us in a white division, not in 1917, anyway; so our troops were temporarily sent into the SOS as laborers to lay railroad tracks. This naturally upset our men tremendously.

"Ah thought we'se here to fight de Germans," they carped. "Hell, we'se kin do dis back home."

And they were right. This type of thing was in complete contrast to what we'd told them.

Then what seemed to be a perfect solution came up. The French were crying for U.S. regiments to go into the French Army. So I guess Pershing figured he could kill two birds with one stone—solve the problem on what to do with us and give something to Foch. From then on we spent our entire service in the French Army. Oh officially we were still the 369th U. S. Infantry, but to all intent and purposes we were *français*.

Our assignment was to be with General Gouraud. This one-armed French officer had spent many years with French colonial troops—he was more interested in the caliber of our men than in the color of their skin, and I feel this was basically the feeling of the French people in general.

Take the situation with the French women. As you might assume, a great many Americans were concerned about the mingling of the sexes between white and black. Well, I don't think there was more than one man convicted of rape in our regiment. The truth of the matter was the French women liked our men. While efforts were made to keep the two apart, it wasn't always successful. I'm sure there are many people in France today who are the offshoots of the 369th's service in France. Frankly, I feel the concern of many white

[1] December 31, 1917. It was also at this time that the 15th New York became the 369th U. S. Infantry. They were the only National Guard unit to leave the United States as a state regiment.

Americans on this subject was directed more toward the time when these men would return home than concern for the French women.

Well, we moved up near the front for some training, now equipped with everything French except our actual uniforms. The biggest disappointment was with their rifles; their Lebels were nowhere near as good as our Springfields. The French, you see, were great believers in the hand grenade—their rifles seemed more or less something to put a bayonet on. Then there was somewhat of a food situation. The French loved these thick soups, while our boys were accustomed to something more substantial.

Our biggest problem, however, was the wine. The Poilu gets a canteen full of red wine every day, never water; but he's accustomed to it. He'd been sipping wine all his life, so he'd usually have it last all day. Not our men—they'd drink the whole darn thing in about fifteen minutes. Naturally, they'd all get tight. We had to put a stop to that in a hurry; I think we got them all an extra share of sugar instead.

Now, by this time I'd had a chance to get to know my men—and remember, this was the American black man of sixty years ago, not today. Well, there was one thing they wanted above all from a white officer, and that was fair treatment. You see, even in New York City they really didn't get a square deal most of the time. But if they felt you were on the level with them, they'd go all out for you. And they seemed to have a sixth sense in realizing just how you felt. I sincerely wanted to lead them as real soldiers, and they knew it; oh they knew it, all right.

Now, if they were loyal to you, and mine were, you could say things to them that they might resent from other officers.

For instance, take the time I took my company out on a long hike right after they'd been issued new shoes. Well, as I'm sure you know, things don't always fit well in the Army, and it can be tough as the devil if your shoes don't. Oh I'd say everything went all right up until the last two miles or so of our jaunt. Then many of the men just sat right down to examine their feet.

"Cain't go no more, Cap'n," one of them said. "My feet is killing me!"

"Oh come now, men," I said, "this is war; you're going to have much worse things at the front than sore feet. Now let's go." I'm afraid I wasn't getting through, but I couldn't quit.

"Let me ask you one thing," I added. "If we had fifty brown-skinned, beautiful young ladies from Lenox Avenue waiting for you, do you think you could make it?"

"Yessir, Cap'n, yessir," they all answered. "Lawdie, we sure could!" And they all started to hoot and holler. Then they got up, and we were on our way.

Now, I think that if some officers had said that, they might have resented it. But they trusted me and, my God, they were loyal.

Well, I think it was April when they moved us into the trenches, putting each company right in with a French one. It was up in the Givry-en-Argonne area, and the Boche were a mere fifty yards away.

While I knew it wasn't supposed to be a very active sector, I had no idea the trenches would be as deep and as elaborate as they were. The French captain had a dugout that I think was fifty or so feet down, with stairs leading to it. Inside it looked like an apartment.

And the meals! He invited me to lunch the first day we were in, and it was incredible. He had a chef who'd come from Paris. It was like going into a plush French restaurant. But that first day, after we'd finished this scrumptious meal, one of our men came running down to report this tragic accident.

And what a mess it was! One of the Poilu had been walking through a trench wearing one of those long *horizon bleu* overcoats of theirs. Well, this bulky coat had upset a box of French grenades, bouncing them down a set of stairs into a dugout where four or five of my men were resting. Of course, they exploded and did a perfectly horrible job on the men. Strangely enough, I don't think any were killed, but they were dreadfully mangled.

I rushed down to see how they were, and that first sight of what war was all about was one I'll never forget. Naturally, the place was full of smoke, but you could see these poor fellows with blood coming out from every part of their bodies.

If that wasn't enough to baptize us, the next night was worse. The French decided it would be a good time to show us how to operate a prisoner-nabbing raid. So five or six of them started crawling the fifty yards toward the German trenches.

Well, the Boche discovered them early and opened up. Naturally, the French headed back to our lines immediately. Then the opposite artillery opened up, showing how tremendously effective they could be. Both the French and the Germans, you see, had a perfect gauge on where the other lines were. And no sooner had this raiding party returned but a piece of shrapnel hit a mousette bag that one of the Poilu had filled with grenades. Oh it just blew those poor fellows in every direction. After those two days were over, I think all my men knew we were at war.

Now, while the 369th was the only American outfit in the area, it wasn't the only black one. There was quite a group of Moroccans alongside of us. Oh they were very brave fighters, but cruel, very cruel. They used to kill their prisoners, then cut off their ears and wear them on a string. I've actually seen this. The only prisoners who had a chance to live were the young ones; those they'd take back to their trenches and use as boyfriends. There were certainly a lot of shenanigans going on over there that we didn't want to know about.

The Germans hated them worst of all, and when they found out how petrified the Moroccans were of being blown up, they used to throw those *Mieniewaffers* at them all night long. It wasn't that the Africans were afraid of dying; they weren't. What they dreaded was losing their limbs. You see, they believed that if they were blown up, they couldn't go to paradise. And those Germans knew which troops were where. It was tough as the devil on us as far as getting sleep was concerned, but it was murder for the Moroccans.

Speaking of sleep, this could cause some nasty scenes. Sometimes you'd end up putting a young fellow on guard duty who hadn't had any rest for a night or two. Then if we had a quiet spell, the lad was very apt to doze off. This, as you know, is a very serious offense, particularly when you're in the front lines. We had this happen a few times, but I didn't feel I should report the soldier to battalion headquarters. What was the sense in that? Maybe just ruin a good soldier. So I worked out my own scheme of punishment. I had this big paper sign made out that read as follows: "I fell asleep on post last night, endangering the lives of my buddies. For the next thirty days I'll do anything that is asked of me."

Well, everyone thought that was very fair. And they'd make the fellow run all types of errands for them all month. But it was a lot better than giving him a general court-martial. I'll tell you something else: It never happened to the same man twice.

There is one more thing I should mention about our tour in the trenches, and that concerns a former redcap from the Albany depot named Henry Johnson. He wasn't in my battalion, I think he was in the 2nd, but he was the regiment's first hero. And he showed the rest of the men what they could do to the Germans. Here's what happened. Johnson and another man were cut off by the Germans in a prisoner raid. They were both wounded, but Johnson refused to be captured—he just refused, that's all. He had used up the clip from his Lebel rifle and started using it as a club. Then he pulled out his bolo knife and really went to work on the Germans. I think he killed four or five and drove the rest of them off with grenades.[2]

Well, around the first of June we were moved down around the Marne to help stop the German drive; then around the middle of July we pitched in on the counteroffensive. But we were always with the French, even later on in the Meuse-Argonne. Oh we would sometimes be near some American troops. For instance, in the Champagne sector, where the Rainbow was, some of our men were in the front-line outposts with orders to shoot off rockets when the Germans started their charge. But we were never part of the American units.

Our first attack was shortly after that Champagne fight toward a place called Butte de Mesnil. From then on it was just attack, attack. I really can't remember all the towns and villages we went through, but I can remember many details.

Take my orderly, a lad named Howard from Chester in Orange County. This poor fellow had two problems. First, he was probably the worst shot in the regiment, perfectly dreadful. The other was this very high-pitched voice of his; he sounded just like a woman. Both these drawbacks were things the other men would notice, and they gave him an awful riding about them. I really felt sorry for the young fellow, and remember, Chester was in my district back home, so I called him over one day.

"Howard," I said, "how would you like to be my orderly?"

"Oh that would be fine, Captain," he answered in that shrill voice of his. "I'm a good soldier, you wait and see."

[2] In his book *The Doughboy*, Laurence Stallings tells of a white officer asking Johnson where he learned to use the bolo so well. Had he ever been in a razor fight back home? Johnson had to put his face in his pillow to smother his laughter.

Well, in one of our advances a group of us were bogged down by a German machine gun on the other side of this creek. So Howard works his way downstream and circles around behind them. Then he crawls up close enough so he can't miss and shoots the two Germans.

You see, what he lacked in ability, he made up in splendid moral character. He was as honest as the day is long, just a tremendously fine man. Died just a few years ago; I went to his funeral—a fine American!

There were lots of things that happened like that in our outfit, and lots of things that made you realize what a thin line there was between a hero and a coward, if there is such a thing.

I recall one town we went into along with another one of our companies. The other captain, his name was Cobb, was killed there. He was a very close friend of mine, so I went over to see what happened. There was Cobb's body, and one of his lieutenants, standing there with a blank stare in his eyes. I tried to talk to him, but he just kept looking into nowhere.

"Lieutenant," I finally said, "they'll come for Captain Cobb; you'd better head for the rear."

"No," he snapped, "I'll stay with my captain."

"I don't think that'll do; you'd better go back, and that's an order," I answered.

Still there was no change in his expression. Then, all of a sudden, he pulled his revolver. Well, I don't mind telling you, I was scared to death. I could tell he was out of his head. And the next minute he just fell to the ground, out like a light.

You see, what had happened, that poor fellow had given everything he had. There was just nothing left. Isn't that a hero!

Another thing that sticks in my mind is the constant feeling of anxiety. The threat of death was always with you, particularly from the shelling. It seemed that everyone was either getting wounded or gassed.

The shells, you see, could come at any time. I remember once when we started to move in, we had tied thirty of our horses behind this hill. One single shell came over, from God knows where, and killed all thirty at one clip. Then, later on, I was standing not more than fifteen feet from four stretcher bearers taking this wounded man to the rear. It seemed to me this shell landed right on top of them. It killed the wounded man and three of the bearers—didn't scratch the fourth. Can you imagine that? Luck, that's what it was, pure luck! And you needed it to come through!

Well, toward the end of October the 369th was moved to a quiet sector in the Vosges Mountains, and that's where it was when the war ended. I can't remember how many were left, but there were very few from the original outfit.[3]

I hope I haven't gone overboard about these black soldiers, but remember, they spent 191 days on the line—and I think that's the record for the AEF. And they weren't all angels; far from it. One of the stereotyped things that people said about them, their gambling, was true. They were at it every chance they could get, and it caused problems. I know a couple of them were actually killed over a gambling fight, but that happens everywhere.

But taking everything into consideration, I think they did a great job. I often wondered if any of the men who were pushed off the sidewalk in Spartanburg ended up being buried in France.

Well, after the war, I was elected to the United States Congress. And I stayed there for twenty-five years. Due to my wartime experiences, and as I thoroughly believe in our Constitution, I was a leader in the fight for civil rights long before it was fashionable.

When the war clouds once again gathered, I did everything I could to keep us out. I didn't want to see another generation of Americans go through it all over again. But I stayed in the Army Reserve, and by December 8, 1941, I was a colonel. I publicly requested the command of a colored infantry regiment, but F.D.R. would have none of it. We didn't always see eye to eye, you know.

---

[3] After the taking of Sechault in the Meuse-Argonne, for which the entire 369th received the Croix, the third battalion was down to 7 officers and 137 men.

The Blacks in the AEF

Two members of the 369th (15th New York) Infantry (Colored) were walking by the red-light district in Gay Paree. As they just had enough money for one of the two to patronize the ladies of the evening, they decided to flip a coin to see which one should experience the fruits of Babylon. The winner of the toss was gone for about a half hour; then he returned to his buddy.

"Well, well," eagerly chirped the unlucky one, "what it like?"

"My boy," intoned the now experienced Doughboy, "I just say, 'Sex in Harlem is in its infancy!'"

World War I was the first time that large numbers of blacks participated in a massive American involvement. The war was also a tremendous shot in the arm for the southern black's exodus to America's northern cities. A twenty-two-year-old sharecropper just wasn't going to be happy with his dream of "forty acres and a mule" after he'd been to France. It was to the blacks above all that the popular song "How're You Gonna Keep 'Em Down on the Farm After They've Seen Paree?" really meant something.

In actual numbers, some two hundred thousand American Negroes were part of the AEF, but 1917–18 was the Neanderthal age concerning the black struggle for equality. As ironic as it may seem in 1978, the white establishment of World War I did not want the Negro to fight for his country; it was bound to present postwar problems. There were only two divisions—the 92nd (Colored) and the 93rd (Colored)—that were composed of black troops. One of these, the 93rd, was never a complete division, merely four National Guard infantry regiments, with the large majority of its officers being white men. The rest of the black members of the AEF did mainly what they did in the United States, tote the white man's burden, and they did it incredibly well.

Of all the black achievements in France, probably the stevedoring was the mightiest. Crowds of French citizens would stare in amazement as American Negroes would employ their massive muscles, developed through generations of toil on southern plantations, in unloading ship after ship in record-breaking time. To his everlasting credit, Major General James Harbord tried to establish a form of recognition for the mightiest of the laborers, but his efforts were abortive.

One of the most enlightening of my interviews was with a ninety-two-year-old black veteran named Duke Darling. The heart of our chat was, however, not about this former sergeant's days in France; it dwelled upon his earlier days soldiering in the Philippines. This Kentucky-born professional belonged to one of the prewar colored regiments.

"We was all sure surprised when they told us our regiment wasn't going overseas," remembered the sergeant. "Then they done told us we could go and help train some of the new boys and go over with 'em."

Duke then helped form the 813th Pioneers and did go to France with this unit. Perhaps this pioneer outfit, like so many of the other colored ones, was used mainly to rebury the American dead. The blacks were told this was a great honor, but most of them realized that it was also a job that their white comrades did not find appealing.

As for the two combat divisions, it is very difficult to properly evaluate them; this at least applies to the 92nd. The big difference between the two divisions was the fact that the 92nd had mainly black officers, a fact that the majority of the AEF generals were not ready to accept in 1918.

I visited with one of the white officers of the 92nd, "Cap" Hill of South Dartmouth, Massachusetts. As the personal adjutant of the 365th (Colored) Infantry Regiment, he was very familiar with the type of men who made up the regiment.

"All the staff officers were white," stated Mr. Hill, "while all the line officers were colored. I can't really tell you it worked perfectly, because it didn't. You have to remember, though, that these men had never seen other black men in places of real authority. It was quite an experiment. All that type of thing has changed now, but back in 1917 it was really revolutionary."

Then "Cap" started to laugh.

"I'll tell you one thing though, and this is true—believe me, I saw it—and that is that these men did love to shoot craps—God Almighty, how they loved to roll dice! I was the pay officer, you see, and I remember when we were up in the Vosges Mountains, when I'd arrive at the trenches, they'd be waiting for me with the dice in their hands. They were all set to 'roll dem bones.'

"You know," continued Mr. Hill, "there is one other thing I do want to say, and that is how proud these black men were to be in a combat regiment. And the officers, they realized they were on trial, and they sure as hell did the best they could. All in all, I think the experiment can be called a very good beginning, even though you couldn't call it a rousing success."

And a beginning it was. As Captain Hill points out, it has all changed now, but it was rugged then. To the white Doughboy these "buffalo" soldiers were also something different. One white veteran even told me of going to a black free-for-all.

"Jeez," he said, "there were six niggers in a ring with boxing gloves on. They'd go to it, and the last one standing would get first prize."

What the white soldier (and he wasn't a bad fellow at all; his use of the word "nigger" was very common in 1918) didn't realize was that he was being conned. The six blacks would divide up the money among themselves after the fight was over, and during the fight they'd make sure no one would get hurt.

That same white Doughboy probably told many of the colored jokes that flooded the AEF, such as:

This colored soldier couldn't stand the shelling any longer, so he broke and ran. And he ran and ran until he couldn't run any longer, then he sat by the side of the road to rest a spell. Along came a white officer.

"What'sa matter, boy, don't you salute an officer?"

"What you?"

"I'm a colonel."

"Lordie, is I *dat* far from the front?"

The above was one of scores of colored stories I was told by the veterans. Once again, you can't condemn the men who said them; that's the way things were in 1918.

Then there was the very well-meaning newspaper editor who, when complimenting the fighting ability of the American blacks, added:

"Isn't there some way a grateful government can get a boatload of watermelons to these men?"

Perhaps that editor had heard the Doughboys' song:

> The Colored Marines went over the top, *parlez-vous?*
>
> . . . .
>
> They thought they heard a watermelon drop,
> Hinky Dinky, *parlez-vous?*

The Ambulance Driver Who Bombed the Germans

Robert Lowell Moore

HIS SON'S HOME, WESTPORT, CONNECTICUT, MARCH 1976
Bob Moore is, like Ted Curtis, Harold Baldwin, and Charlie Kinsolving, one of the many men who first went to France as an ambulance driver and then ended up as a flier. When I asked Bob why this was a course followed by so many Americans, he said it was due to the ability of these men to drive a motorcar.

"Remember," he informed me, "it was only a small percentage of the population who could drive any type of a motor vehicle in 1917; I guess they figured if you could drive something as big as an ambulance that you'd have a leg up on becoming a flier. So be it."

After the war Mr. Moore went into the hotel business in partnership with a man named Henderson. They prospered. Several years ago they sold their company, then called Sheraton Hotels, to ITT. It goes without saying that they do not have to pass hats for Mr. Moore.

While Bob lives today, in retirement, outside of Boston, we visited at his son's home in Westport, Connecticut.

His son, Robin Moore, spent some time with us during the interview. The author of *The Green Berets* and several other books took a keen interest in my project.

"You're absolutely right," he said. "The country has underrated the job done by these World War I old-timers."

He is right.

First Lieutenant Robert Lowell Moore
AS, USA, Escadrille Br. 29, GB 9

A pilot of great bravery, possessing equally splendid enthusiasm and remarkable presence of mind. On the fourteenth of June 1918, in the course of a combat above the enemy lines, his observer was killed, and he was forced to descend from an altitude of five thousand meters, pursued almost to the ground by two enemy planes, firing at him incessantly. Although he was wounded by three bullets and had his machine seriously damaged, he succeeded, thanks to his dexterity and courage, in reaching the ground.

—GENERAL HENRI PHILIPPE PÉTAIN

In January of 1916 I decided to take a leave of absence from Harvard for a term so I could go to France with the Norton-Harjes ambulance group. It was really quite simple: You signed up, paid for your own transportation, and zip, just like that you were at the front.

The area my group went to was near Verdun. As you know, there was a hell of a lot of real rough stuff going on there at that time. Our job was to pick up the wounded Poilu and deliver them to Bar-le-Duc, a town about thirty miles from where that slaughterhouse of Verdun was raging.

The event that I remember most occurred sometime in March during a comparative lull in the battle. I had dropped off two wounded Poilu at the hospital. Knowing it wasn't exactly a busy time right then, I decided to take a detour on the way back; in short, I decided to visit the city of Verdun.

Now, Verdun is up on a bluff with the River Meuse running around in front of it. On the opposite side of the river you have a row of hills surrounding it. The Germans were coming up at the back of those hills, and the French were on the Verdun side of the river behind their hills. Neither side was actually in Verdun. The Germans would sit back popping away with their 77's, while the French 75's would do the same at the Boche. Incidentally, the French will tell you the Allies won the war because the 75 was superior to the 77, and I guess they're right.

Well, it was a beautiful, crisp day, and I just had to see Verdun. Of course, it was all partitioned off, so I had to take a circuitous route around the French side of the river to get there. There was no traffic at all, so I drove right into the town. It was absolutely dead, not even a rat moving—it looked just like a ghost town. There in the main square I saw just one thing: a Michelin tire sign. I thought this would make a great souvenir, particularly as it was loaded with shrapnel holes. But do you know the damn thing was too firmly anchored to come down; it might be still there, for all I know.

So then I decided to drive up to the top of the highest hill I could see to have a look around. My God, what a panorama! I could see both lines with the men scurrying about: their artillery lined up, their balloons ready to go aloft, the fortification lines, everything. It was just like a huge painting or a massive array of toy soldiers that some boy had arranged.

The thing turned me quite philosophical. I was musing about it, alternating my thoughts between the beauty and the horrifying reality that what they were doing was actually preparing to kill each other. My mind was really in the clouds.

Then, WHAM! A big geyser of earth came out of the ground about fifty yards to my right, hole high. I tailed ass into my ambulance and got out of there as fast as I could. What had happened was simple: One of the German balloons had spotted me and relayed my position to his guns on the ground.

I don't know if this triggered anything off or not, but the next day the battle started in earnest again. We were working around the clock shifts, not even stopping to take our boots off if we could grab a few minutes' sleep. The poor devils—we'd just load them in the ambulance and head for the hospital, over and over again. Some would be dead when we got there, and I'm sure others died later. Of course, we did save many, which was great, but after a while the smell of the blood in the ambulance became intolerable; no matter how hard we tried, we couldn't scrub it off.

This went on for weeks until one day I just collapsed with utter exhaustion. The ironic part was that they took me to the hospital in my own ambulance. The entire following week was a blank—that's how long it took me to get my senses back.

When I did come around, they sent me to a quiet sector, where I finished off my tour of duty. Then I bid *la belle France adieu* and returned to fair Harvard to finish my education. As far as I was concerned, *la guerre—finit*.

It turned out to be just a respite from the bloody thing, but a great one. Harvard had a strong football team that year, even though they lost a heartbreaker to Yale. And the Red Sox—why, they had Babe Ruth pitching for them! I still can vividly remember watching him play—they won the World Series that year, you know. And what a treat to see some American girls again. You see, most of the people around Harvard had some kind of a romantic illusion about the war. As I had been there, I was kind of a king of the walk. Of course, I'd seen all that death and destruction. I knew better.

Then came April of '17; naturally I joined up, this time in the U. S. Air Service of the Signal Corps. My group was sent to MIT for ground school for six weeks, leaving there around the first of July to start our trip to France. I've always gotten a kick out of the fact that here I was, on my way to France to fly against the renowned German Air Force, and I'd never even been up in a plane.

Remember, this was July of '17; we weren't sending many troops over at that time. We had to spend three days at Bedloe's Island [now Liberty Island], where the Statue of Liberty is, waiting for transportation to Halifax. Then it was another two weeks at Nova

Scotia gathering a convoy. There were plenty of German submarines around then, and Uncle Sam didn't want to lose the first bunch of pilots-to-be that America was sending over. We finally left there, and just in time. Shortly afterward, a munitions ship in the harbor blew sky high, killing everything in sight.[1]

There was one thing about the trip over that always gives me a chuckle. Of the seventy men on the ship from the Air Service, there were ten who'd already done their basic flying. These men were first lieutenants; the other sixty of us were sergeants. This meant that the ten lieutenants were topside in cabins, while the rest of us were down in steerage. As I remember, Quentin Roosevelt was one of the officers, Cord Meyer was another. Well, hell, we all had known each other, and you can bet we gave those birds the raspberries about their soft living—but none of them offered to change places.

We arrived in France in September of '17, being immediately sent to the splendid French aviation school at Tours. Here we were given primary flying training with those beautiful little ships called Coltron G-3s. It was such a fun plane to fly; hell, I don't think it could go over forty miles an hour. You had to land it with skids, and, of course, on soft turf. But it was ideal for learning the real basics of flying.

Then we went to the French school at Avord to learn to fly the Nieuports. By the time we finished this training, we all felt we were pilots but still hadn't received our commissions. Things were so confused in France during that fall of '17 I guess we just figured the government had forgotten us.

We found out differently in November, when we were sent to open the new American flying school at Issoudun. It was here that we became first lieutenants and were given flying numbers. I can still remember mine, and when I tell it to you, you'll know why: it was No. 13. Can you imagine being No. 13 with the planes we flew in 1917?

My number wasn't the worst thing about Issoudun, though, for it was just about the most all-around godforsaken place you could

[1] On September 15, 1917, a French munitions ship blew up mysteriously in Halifax Harbor. Over sixteen hundred people were killed. Americans who stopped at Halifax on their way to France always mentioned this.

imagine. A guy named Laydon Brewer—Laddie Brewer, we used to call him—wrote a wonderful epic poem where he mentions Issoudun. I'm sure it's long out of print, but I can still remember the part that went:

> Issoudun—God's mudhole, where God said,
> "Let there be mud"; and there was mud. Such mud
> As Noah might have gazed on when the Ark
> Was stranded at the top of Ararat.

And was there mud, my God, but there was mud everywhere. Why, the barracks weren't even finished! We had very few planes, which was a good thing, as the field wasn't finished either. The first two weeks we were there were spent picking up rocks from the field. Here we worked right alongside these German POWs who were also at Issoudun. We didn't mind working with them, but their quarters did get our goat. The POWs' barracks were finished, while ours weren't—they had better living conditions than we did. We were beginning to wonder which side we were on.

Then, finally enough Nieuports arrived for us to do some flying—I think they were fifteen- and twenty-three-meter planes. This made things a lot better, unless you happened to land in one of the muddy areas. Then you were bound to get stuck.

Of course, by now we're beginning to think we're really pilots, so they sent us to the French gunnery school at Cozaux. We had these older Nieuports here with a single Vickers gun that we'd shoot through the propeller. One plane would haul this old balloon along and we'd try to pepper it. I think the best shot we had at this time was a wonderful guy named Hobie Baker; boy, what a peach he was! He'd been a great hockey player at Princeton, you know; I still think they feel he was the best that ever played there.

Eddie Rickenbacker was with us here also—and he was another great shot, maybe as good as Baker. And that brings up a good one. You see, we were all college men, with the exception of Rick, but he'd been so famous as a racing driver that we all knew of him. When Rick arrived, we sent one of our group over to size him up; unfortunately, we sent a snob. After our friend returned, we all crowded him, and one of us said, "Well, what's he like?"

"Oh he's all right," came a condescending reply, "but he's really quite common."

Rickenbacker, common? We soon found out he was anything but. For all-around performances I'd have to rank Rick and Baker as the best two we had. Poor Baker; he was killed in an accident later on, shortly before he was to go home.[2]

After Cozaux my bubble burst. They were starting to make up the American pursuit groups when I and about six others were sent to the Hythe gunnery school in England. We all wanted to get into the air and go against the Germans, so you can see how envious we were of those who stayed for the pursuit groups.

At Hythe they'd turned this golf course into a target area where we could learn to use the Lewis gun. The Vickers was for the pursuit pilot, while the Lewis was for the second man in an observer or bombing plane.

I must say the conditions here were tremendous. The English couldn't have been nicer to us. Each afternoon around four the war would end for us. We would change into our slacks and sit around drinking tea. It was a great life, all right, but if we wanted that, we could have stayed at home. And remember, we weren't pilots. Our job was to sit in the second seat and fire the Lewis gun.

Then there was the horrifying experience I witnessed the first day we were there. I had a buddy named Frank Montgomery from Spartanburg, South Carolina, a great fellow. As we went up alphabetically, I was waiting for Monty to take his turn before I could go up. His English pilot—remember, Monty was in the second seat—started to do these loop-de-loops—showing off, I guess. Anyway, the first thing you knew, we all saw this yellow bundle falling from the plane. It was the British pilot. Poor Monty, up there in a pilotless plane. His only chance is to crawl into the vacant cockpit where he can take the controls. We're all watching this and praying. He almost made it before the crash. He was killed instantly. The tragedy certainly took the heart out of my stay in England.

Then from there I was sent back to France to act as aerial gunnery instructor at the 7th Aviation Instruction Center at Clermont-Ferrand. My duty here was to work with the Bréquet bombing squadrons that were being formed here. Naturally, I was very un-

[2] The hockey rink at Princeton is named in honor of his memory.

happy about that. With all the schooling and training I'd had, I still hadn't seen one minute of combat flying. I kept pestering the commander for combat duty, without any luck. Finally, I cornered him with a new angle:

"Look," I pleaded, "how can I be a good instructor about combat if I haven't seen any?"

"Oh all right, Moore," he answered, "we'll put you with a French bombing group for a while."

You can imagine how delighted I was when they sent me to the Groupe de Bombardement 9, French Army, outside of Paris. This was a Bréquet bombing group, each plane carrying several five hundred-pound bombs in a series under each lower wing. They were triggered by the observer, who would pull a handle to release them. You might say our methods were a little primitive compared to World War II, but we did manage to do some damage to the German supply trains.

Well, as you know, the Germans made their last push to take Paris in June of '18. Like everyone else, we were trying to do everything we could to stop them. On June 14 we centered on the railheads near Soissons, maybe twenty miles behind their lines. On the way back we were attacked by a squadron of Fokkers. As I was the last plane in the formation, they hit me first. This fellow made a swipe at our plane, killing my observer, Lieutenant Giquel of the French Air Force, with his first burst. To make matters worse, Giquel's body was wedged on some of the controls in the second cockpit, making it very difficult for me to maneuver.

By this time we're getting close to our lines and I'm going full speed trying to shake not only the first German but also a second one, who had joined him. I had no gun myself, so once Giquel was gone, my only hope was flight.

Each time one of those birds would get close enough they'd let a blast go. Naturally, they're riddling my plane but somehow not hitting any vital spots; the same held true for yours, truly. I picked up these slugs in my arm and then another in my side.

I've been asked on several occasions, "Bob, how did you keep going?"

My answer is simple: "Consider the alternative!"

Anyway, with a shot-up plane and a dead gunner in the rear, I somehow managed to land behind our lines. I was at once sent to the hospital at Guilly and later evacuated to Paris. About two or three months later I returned to instructing at Clermont-Ferrand. Only this time I could tell the lads exactly what it was like.

Now I'll tell you an interesting story about what happened after the war—oh I'd say it was about ten years later. I met this chap in New York City who was a real history buff on the air war of '14 to '18. I told him my story, and he said he could get me all the facts and the name of the German who wounded me. Well, a few months later I found out that my vanquisher was a German aristocrat named Bolle, one of the Kaiser's crack pilots. My historian friend even sent me this picture of the fellow—my God, doesn't he look like a real Prussian? I was lucky to escape with my life!

The Last Shot

"Early on the morning of November 11," Walter Guild related, "our outfit [the 102nd Machine Gun Battalion] was on the southern end of the line at a place called the Heights of the Meuse; it was a little east of Verdun. Around dawn we had started an advance—hell, we'd been advancing for days and always receiving German fire.

"Well, I can't remember exactly what time it was, sometime that morning I'd had a little chat with one of my good friends, Bill Klingman. He was also from the Boston area and had been down on the Mexican border with me in 1916. Shortly after our visit he moved over to where our captain was trying to direct us forward.

"In the meantime, we're all moving ahead, trying not to draw any fire, when all of a sudden a German machine gun opened up on us. Poor Klingman was killed instantly. I've never forgotten that. After all we'd been through, and then he catches it right at the end; it was dreadful.

"An hour or so later, we received orders to find a hole and stay in it until hearing future orders. We were not to fire unless the Germans attacked us. Our outfit just collapsed where we were; we were beat to our skins. They didn't have to tell us twice.

"You know," continued Guild, "I stayed in the Army after World War I and served all through the Second World War, finally retiring as a colonel. That situation with Klingman still remains the saddest memory I have of all my years in the Army."

So it was up and down the line: The Americans knew they had the Germans really moving back, but in most places every advance was still costing infantrymen their lives.

It wasn't much different with the artillery, although most of them did receive orders at least an hour or so before the time of the designated cease-fire not to send any more shells over after 11:00 A.M.

According to Sergeant Howard Fisher of the 306th Field Artillery, 77th Division, the artillery was as worn out as the infantry.

"We were not in very good shape," he recalled. "We'd seen a great deal of action since the beginning of August—the fight around the Vesle River and, of course, the Argonne. We were near exhaustion. Our biggest problem was the horses. The few we had left looked like scarecrows. If the war had gone on much longer, we would have been pulling those 75's by hand."

Another artilleryman, Harry Croft of the 76th Field Artillery, was on an escarpment overlooking the Woeree River.

"We received the order not to fire our 75's after 11:00 A.M.—the war was all over. Oh man, everyone in my outfit [D Battery] wanted to fire that last shot. We decided each of us would put a hand on the lanyard and pull at the same time. And that's just what we did, at 10:59 A.M., November 11, 1918.

"What a racket: All up and down the line guns were firing from both sides.

"As I look back on it, I realize how stupid it was. Americans and

Germans must have been killed by that last barrage. But that's what happened."

A day or two after the war ended, Shipley Thomas was talking with a German officer. They really didn't have much to say to each other, but Thomas remembered the last words the German uttered.

"He shook my hand," Shipley said, "and kind of smiled."

"'At least *ve* vill be home for Christmas,' he told me. Then he saluted and headed North.

"Well," Thomas continued, "the big difference was that I would eventually be going back to America, while the Boche was going back to a snarled-up Germany."

"In September of 1917," my Uncle Ed once told me, "I was about to go into the Army. I still had a few days left, so your father and I decided to go down to New York City to see some ball games and a show or two. We were walking over to Keene's Chop House on West Thirty-sixth Street when we ran into Charley Coughlin from Hartford. Charley was in the 102nd at the time.

"'Hello, Charley,' I said, 'I thought you guys had already left for France.'

"'Well, we did,' answered Charley, 'but when we got a little ways outside of the harbor, they thought they saw a German submarine, so we came back. We'll be going again in a few days.'

"The three of us had dinner together," continued my uncle, "then your father and I wished Charley luck and went back to our hotel.

"Jeez, poor Charley, he was killed on November 7, 1918, just before the damn thing ended."

After the war the city of Hartford planted trees in Colts Park in memory of the local men who had been killed. In 1938 Hartford was struck by a hurricane. Coughlin's tree was knocked down. One of these days I'm going to drive to Hartford to see if they've ever replanted his tree. I'll bet they have not.

"The Days Grow Short"

In the late summer of 1975 I was playing golf at the Hartford Golf Club. The game was not an earth-shaking one—it was a standard foursome Nassau match. In this type of a golf game each man has a partner and the best ball of each twosome is matched against the other twosome's best ball on each hole. My partner was my then eighty-one-year-old Uncle Ed. We were one down as we approached the seventeenth hole. This is a 157-yard par-three hole; it is also, as they say in golf, well trapped. As our team had won the sixteenth hole, we had the honors, allowing us to drive first.

In such a match each twosome has a captain, who always leads off. Uncle Ed was our captain. He reached for his five wood with his usual comment, "Jeez, I remember when I could put a six-iron on that baby!" Then, as he started to tee up, he broke wind—when you are in your eighties, such things rarely embarrass you. He chuckled and turned toward the rest of us with that great smile of his:

"Well, boys," he said, "excuse me, just a little kiss for the Kaiser."

The other two players, who had never heard that expression before, started to laugh, but not for long. Their glee quickly terminated when Ed placed his shot in the center of the green.

My uncle had the low ball on that hole and also on the eighteenth. We won the match one up; it was often said at Hartford that beating Ed Berry in a Nassau match was as difficult as eating spaghetti with a knife.

Six months later, my uncle was bowling when he complained of chest pains. A friend drove him to the hospital, but it was all over in a day or so.

There were the usual expressions of sympathy, such as, "Wasn't it wonderful that he was so remarkably active up to the end?" Of course this was true, but among his large coterie of friends he has still been missed sorely.

Each day the obituary columns in the newspapers carry the death report of a man who, like my uncle, was "late of the AEF." Naturally, as I was putting this book together, I took a great deal of interest in these notices. There were some well-known names, such as movie producer William Wellman and educator Robert Hutchins, but by and large they were men who represented a cross section of their generation. Sometimes the notice would give some mention of their service in France, but usually there'd be obvious errors in the details, such as incorrect unit numbers (the 107th Infantry of the 27th Division frequently becomes the 127th Infantry, for instance), battle locations, dates, and so forth. The actual details of the AEF still remain an enigma to most people.

This is not so, however, as far as the veterans themselves are concerned. Most of them are well aware of the part they played in world history, and they are a little put out that even their own country seems to have forgotten it so soon. They may be at an age where the shadows are rapidly closing in on them physically, but mentally they remain quite keen, particularly when it concerns their service in France. As they struggle with two of the less appealing aspects of old age—rejection and loneliness—this lack of recognition of what one veteran called "America's forgotten involvement" does disturb most of them.

"Hell," one of them said, "if we hadn't gone over there, God knows what would have happened to the world!"

But they did go, and some of the more hearty ones still show up and march in the Memorial Day parades to remind people of this fact. They won't be marching much longer, though. Many of them have already reached the stage where they are driven in limousines, and soon what is left of them who care to participate in such events will be all riding in cars at the front of the parade. However, if what one of the veterans told me represents the general line of thought, there will not be many of them who will care to go through the limousine stage.

"I tried it last year," the veteran told me, "but all I could think about was those old Civil War fogies they used to drag out for those parades in the twenties and thirties—the hell with it!"

They do like to talk about '17 and '18, though; when tomorrow does not seem to offer a great deal, yesterday can become very attractive. While the ranks of these old Doughboys are thinning out each day, there will be thousands of them left throughout the United States for some time to come. If anyone is interested in spending an hour or two with one of them, I suggest the following formula:

Call him on the phone and tell him that you are keenly interested in America's participation in World War I and could the two of you set up a meeting and discuss his memories of it. The veteran might well hesitate a bit at first, perhaps telling you such statements as, "Oh that's all so long ago, I don't really know what I can remember about it," or "Gee, nobody cares about that anymore."

If he does this, tell him you realize this, but that you'd really be interested in anything he can remember about the war. The chances are pretty good that he will see you, which he probably wants to do anyway.

Now, most of these gentlemen still do enjoy a drink or two. The WCTU may hate me for saying that, but it's true. If the veteran is in the majority here, have a drink with him and let him get started on the war. He'll open up in a rather formal manner, but the first thing you know you'll hear something like:

"Well, there was this time, it was 'up in the Argonne' "—from then on you'll have smooth sailing. If your meeting ends up anything like every one of mine did, you'll have a tremendously fine time. And so will the old Doughboy. If he's like the ones I visited with, you'll find that he's "to the mustard."

Index

Murtaugh, Joe, xviii–xix, 154–55
Music, 7, 392–94, 406–11, 415–16
Mustard gas, 5, 34, 53, 195, 198–99
"My Buddy," 409

Nancy, 168–69, 239–40, 400, 402
National Guard, 11–12, 97, 184–85, 205, 328, 329, 340–41. *See also* specific units
Naval Air Corps, xxi, 224–25
Navy, 291
Nebraska, 274–75. *See also* 89th Division
Nelson (Goldsmith's buddy), 278–79, 281–82
Neufchâteau, xvi, 74–75, 185
New Haven, Conn., 190. *See also* Yale
Newsmen, 115, 230–31
New York, 127–28, 205. *See also* 42nd Division; 69th N.Y. Irish; 107th Infantry; specific cities
New York City, i, 13, 25, 48–49, 62, 70, 84–85, 106, 118, 171, 190, 191, 219, 224, 227, 228, 307, 319, 328, 329, 340, 342, 353, 357, 372, 380, 392, 406, 407, 412, 437, 439 (*See also* 69th N.Y. Irish; 308th Infantry); baseball, 309; Bedloe's Island, 432; blacks (*See* Blacks); DKE national headquarters, 371; Harlem, 415; Russian immigrants, 322–23; Yorkville, 323
Nicholas II, Czar, 1
Nieppe Forest, 362–63
Nieuports, xv, 229, 245, 246, 252, 259 ff., 433, 434
9th Infantry, 82, 108
9th Massachusetts, 184
90th Division, 46
91st Division, 8, 46, 385
92nd Division, 426–27
93rd Division, 19, 22, 426
94th Aero Squadron, 13, 241, 242–54, 261, 340
95th Aero Squadron, 20, 247, 258–65
96th Bombing Group, 263–64
Nivelle, Robert, 51
Nolan, Dennis, 10
Nolan, Joe, 202
Nordhoff, Charles B., 224, 248 n
Normandy, 18

North Africa, 158, 169
Northumberlands, 125
Norton-Harjes, 266, 268, 430–32

O'Brien, John (Jack—12th Artillery), 99–113, 304–5
O'Brien, John (110th Infantry), 153–54
Observers, xxi, 50–52, 110–11; aerial, 396–406
O'Connor, Eddie, 358, 367
O'Daniel, Iron Mike, 162, 163
Ohio. *See* 37th Division; 42nd Division; 166th Infantry
"Oh How I Hate to Get Up . . . ," 408–9
Okinawa, 66
Oklahoma. *See* 36th Division
Olympic (ship), 106–7
O'Malley, Tom, 335, 338
101st Ambulance Company, 45
101st Artillery, 45, 369 n, 389
101st Engineers, 45
101st Field Hospital, 45
101st Field Signal Battalion, 45
101st Infantry, 45, 185, 186
101st Machine Gun Battalion, xv, xvii, xix, 46, 176–83
101st Supply Train, 45
101st Train Headquarters and Military Police, 46
102nd Ambulance Company, 46
102nd Artillery, 45
102nd Field Hospital, 46
102nd Infantry, xvii, xviii, xix, 45, 155, 165 n, 177, 195, 200, 202
102nd Machine Gun Battalion, 39 n, 45, 201, 389–90, 437
103rd Ambulance Company, 45
103rd Field Hospital, 45
103rd Infantry, 45, 188–200, 325
103rd Machine Gun Battalion, 46
104th Ambulance Company, 46
104th Field Hospital, 45
104th Infantry, 46
107th Infantry (7th New York), i, 84, 203, 204–19, 309, 416
110th Infantry, 153–54
111th Engineers, 292–303
127th Infantry, 282
128th Infantry, 273–85
129th Artillery, 220